SBI Bank PO Mains MOCK Test Papers

SBI Bank PO Mains MOCK Test Papers

duenorth Academics (An IIM Alumni Body)

B L O O M S B U R Y
NEW DELHI • LONDON • OXFORD • NEW YORK • SYDNEY

First published in India 2017

ISBN 978 93 86432 33 9
2 4 6 8 10 9 7 5 3 1

Bloomsbury Publishing India Pvt. Ltd
Second Floor, LSC Building No.4
DDA Complex, Pocket C – 6 & 7, Vasant Kunj
New Delhi 110070
www.bloomsbury.com

Typeset by Manipal Digital Systems

Printed and bound in India by Rajkamal Electric Press, Kundli

Contents

SBI PO Mains MOCK Test Paper 1

Structure of this MOCK Test

S. No.	Name of section	No. of Questions	Total marks	Allotted Time
1	Reasoning and Computer Aptitude	45	60	60 minutes
2	Data Analysis and Interpretation	35	60	45 minutes
3	General/ Economy/ Banking Awareness	40	40	35 minutes
4	English Language	35	40	40 minutes
Total		155	200	3 hours

- There is 1/4th Negative marking for every wrong answer.
- If a question is left blank, i.e. no answer is marked by the candidate, there will be no penalty for that question.

Section 1: Reasoning and Computer Aptitude

Directions (1–5): In each question given below four statements are followed by two conclusions numbered I and II. You have to take the four statements to be true even if they seem to be at variance from the commonly known facts. Read the conclusions and decide which logically follows from the given statements disregarding commonly known facts:

Answer:

1. If only conclusion I follows.
2. If only conclusion II follows.
3. If either conclusion I or II follows.
4. If neither conclusion I nor II follows.
5. If both conclusions I and II follow.

1. **Statements:–** Some blades arc knifes. All swords are knifes.Only blades are sharps. Some blades are pencils.

Conclusions:-

I. Some swords are blades.

II. No blades is swords.

2. **Statements:-** Some blades are knifes. All swords are knifes. Only blades are sharps. Some blades are pencils.
Conclusions:-
I. All sharps being swords is a possibility.
II. No swords being sharps is a possibility.

3. **Statements:-** Some fruits are tasty. All mangoes are tasty. Some mangoes are apples. No mangoes is grapes.
Conclusions:-
I. Some tasty are not grapes.
II. Some apples not being grapes is a possibility.

4. **Statements:-** Some fruits are tasty. All mangoes are tasty. Some mangoes are apples. No mangoes is grapes.
Conclusions:-
I. At least some fruits are grapes.
II. All apples being fruits is a possibility.

5. **Statements:-** Some mangoes are grapes. All blacks are grapes. Some blackberry are black. No grapes is tasty.
Conclusions:-
I. Some mangoes being tasty is a possibility.
II. Some blackberry not being tasty is a possibility.

6. If M > R and M > Q is definitely true, what should replace the question mark (?) in the given expression?
L > M = N ? O = P > Q > R
1. = 2. > 3. < 4. > 5. Either 1.or 4.

7. Which of the following expressions shows that either R > O or O > R ?
1. L > M = N > O, O > P > M = R 2. L > M = N > O, R > M < P > Q
3. L > M = N > O, R < M < P > Q 4. O < N = M < L, Q < P > M < R
5. None of these

8. If W > S and X > R are definitely true, what should replace the question mark (?) in the given expression?
R < T < U ? V < W, X > Y > U ? Z > S
1. <, > 2. <, > 3. >, < 4. = ,> 5. None of these

9. Which among the following expressions shows that E > M and I > J, both are definitely false?
1. M < L < G = K > J, E > F = G > H = I 2. E < F = G < H = I, M< L < G = K > J
3. E < F = G > H = I, M < L < G = K > J 4. E < F = G > H = I, M > L = G < K < J
5. None of these

10. Which among the following expressions shows that L > M is definitely true and O > I is definitely false?
1. I < J = K < L, N = K > M > O 2. I > J = K < L, N = K > M > O
3. I > J = K < L, N =K > M > O 4. I < J = K < L, N = K > M > O
5. None of these

11. The questions given below contain two statements giving certain data. You have to decide whether the data given in the statements are sufficient for answering the question.
How many sons does P have?
I. B and A are the only sister of R
II. P is mother of R

Mark answer:-
1. If statement I alone is sufficient but statement II alone is not sufficient.
2. If statement II alone is sufficient but statement I alone is not sufficient.
3. If each statement alone (either I or II) is sufficient.
4. If statement I and II together are not sufficient.
5. If both statement together are sufficient, but neither statement alone is sufficient.

12. The questions given below contain two statements giving certain data. You have to decide whether the data given in the statements are sufficient for answering the question.
What is the P's position from the left end of a row of thirty children?
I. Q is tenth from the right end of the row and there are five children between Q and P.
II. There are nine children between P and M.

Mark answer:-
1. If statement I alone is sufficient but statement II alone is not sufficient.
2. If statement II alone is sufficient but statement I alone is not sufficient.
3. If each statement alone (either I or II) is sufficient.
4. If statement I and II together are not sufficient.
5. If both statement together are sufficient, but neither statement alone is sufficient.

13. The questions given below contain two statements giving certain data. You have to decide whether the data given in the statements are sufficient for answering the question?
Among P,Q,R,S and T each having a different height, who is the shortest?
I. Q and R are taller than P and T.
II. S is shorter than P but taller than T.

Mark answer:-
1. If statement I alone is sufficient but statement II alone is not sufficient.
2. If statement II alone is sufficient but statement I alone is not sufficient.
3. If each statement alone (either I or II) is sufficient.
4. If statement I and II together are not sufficient.
5. If both statement together are sufficient, but neither statement alone is sufficient.

14. The questions given below contain two statements giving certain data. You have to decide whether the data given in the statements are sufficient for answering the question.
How is 'Ever' written in a code language?
I. 'Ever do this' is written as 'Pa da na' in that code language and 'do this again' is written as 'naka da' in that code language.
II. 'Always do this' is written as 'ma pa ja' in that code language.

Mark answer:-
1. If statement I alone is sufficient but statement II alone is not sufficient.

2. If statement II alone is sufficient but statement I alone is not sufficient.
3. If each statement alone (either I or II) is sufficient.
4. If statement I and II together are not sufficient.
5. If both statement together are sufficient, but neither statement alone is sufficient.

15. The questions given below contain two statements giving certain data. You have to decide whether the data given in the statements are sufficient for answering the question.
Four person P,Q,T,U sit around a circular table, in which direction they are facing (Either towards centre or opposite the centre)?
I. T is opposite to U, and T is first to the right of Q. **II.** P is first to the left of U and second to the left of Q.

Mark answer:-

1. If statement I alone is sufficient but statement II alone is not sufficient.
2. If statement II alone is sufficient but statement I alone is not sufficient.
3. If each statement alone (either I or II) is sufficient.
4. If statement I and II together are not sufficient.
5. If both statement together are sufficient, but neither statement alone is sufficient.

Directions for questions 16–20: Study the following information carefully and answer the questions given below:-

Following are the alternative eligibility criteria for short-listing candidates for interview for entry level job in a bank: **(I)** The candidate should have passed SSC with atleast 80% marks. **(II)** The candidate should have passed HSC with atleast 75% marks. **(III)** The candidates should be a/an Arts/Science/Commerce graduate with atleast 60% marks. **(IV)** The candidate should be an engineer with atleast 55% marks. **(V)** The candidate should be a post-graduate in any discipline with atleast 50% marks.

Any candidate can be eligible under any one or more of the above criteria depending upon their academic pursuits. In each of the following questions, details of one candidate is given. You have to find out under which of the above condition(s) the candidate is eligible and mark your answer accordingly based on the alternatives provided after each question. You are not to assume anything other than the information provided in each of above questions.

16. Sunil has secured 75% marks in SSC. He has completed his B.com with 65% marks after completing his higher secondary in commerce. He has now enrolled in the master's degree of commerce.
   1. Eligible under (I) only
   2. Eligible under (II) only
   3. Eligible under (III) only
   4. Eligible under (I) and (III) only
   5. None of these

17. Usha has completed M.A. with 50% marks after passing B.A. exam with 60% marks. She had secured 75% marks in SSC and 80% marks in HSC.
   1. Eligible under (I), (II),(III) and (IV) only
   2. Eligible under (I), (II) and (IV) only
   3. Eligible under (II), (III) and (IV) only
   4. Eligible under (III) and (IV) only
   5. None of these

18. Mohan is a Mechanical Engineer. He has secured 60% marks in his final degree exam. He has secured 65% marks in HSC. He has secured 55% marks in his post-graduation in Mechanical Engineering.
   1. Eligible under (II), (IV) and (V) only
   2. Eligible under (IV) and (V) only
   3. Eligible under (III), (IV) and (V) only
   4. Eligible under (I), (IV) and (V) only
   5. None of these

19. Subhas has secured 85% marks in graduation in Science. He has also secured 65% and 75% marks in HSC and post-graduation respectively. He is presently pursuing his second post-graduation degree.
   1. Eligible under (II), (III) and (IV) only
   2. Eligible under (IV) and (V) only
   3. Eligible under (II), (IV) and (V) only
   4. Eligible under (III) and (V) only
   5. None of these

20. Aruna Basak is a post-graduate in Physics. She has secured 80% marks in SSC. She has also secured 70% marks both in HSC and graduation.
   1. Eligible under (I), (II) and (III) only
   2. Eligible under (II) and (III) only
   3. Eligible under (I) and (III) only
   4. Eligible under (III) only
   5. None of these

Directions for questions 21: Read the following information carefully and answer the question:
Statements:- The center government has asked state government to compulsorily buy 4% of their purchasing from units run by Dalits as well as scheduled cast and scheduled tribe entrepreneurs.

21. Which of the following can be inferred from the given information? (An inference is something that is not directly stated but can be inferred from given information)
   1. State is purchasing all its goods from centre government only.
   2. The products available at stores run by SC, ST and Dalits are of good quality.
   3. It is the step taken by centre goverment to improve the condition of Dalits in country.
   4. It is the step taken by state government to improve the condition of SME's.
   5. None of these

Passage:
These questions are based on the information given below & sentences labeled **(A)**, **(B)**, **(C)**, **(D)** and **(E)**.
Statements:- A state in Western India has declared war on poaching by sanctioning its forest guards to short hunters on sight. **(A)** Government has taken this step as an effort to curb rampant attacks against wildlife. **(B)** This action against poachers is a significant step to reduce the number of criminals. **(C)** Wildlife species is reducing day by day and now they are at the threat of extinction. **(D)** The illegal hunting, killing or capturing of animals is a punishable offence. **(E)** The poachers have lost all fear and they just go in and poach what they want.

22. Which of the statements numbered (A), (B), (C), (D) and (E) can be assumed from the facts given in the statements?
   1. A   2. B   3. C   4. D   5. E

23. Which of the statements numbered (A), (B), (C), (D) and (E) can be the advantage for wildlife from the facts given in the statements?
1. A 2. B 3. C 4. D 5. E

24. Which of the statements numbered (A), (B), (C), (D) and (E) define poaching?
1. A 2. B 3. C 4. D 5. E

25. Which of the statements numbered (A), (B), (C), (D) and (E) is incorrect in context of the facts given in the statements?
1. A 2. B 3. C 4. D 5. E

26. What should come in the place of question mark (?) in the series given below?
2 F 3 L 4 T (?) D 6 P 7 D 8
1. 4 2. 6 3. 3 4. 5 5. None of these

Passage:
Read the following information carefully and answer the questions given below-(A) 1#2 means 1 is the son of 2. (B) 1$2 means 1 is the daughter of 2.(C) 1@2 means 2 is the father of 1. (D) 1%2 means 2 is the mother of 1.(E) 1*2 means 1 is the wife of 2.(F) 1&2 means 2 is the husband of 1.

27. Which of the following expressions shows that P is the grand-daughter of K?
1. P$O*M#E%K 2. P$O*M%E%K 3. P$O%M$E&K
4. P$O*M#E&K 5. None of these

28. Which of the following expressions shows that Seema is the grand mother-in-law of Rani?
1. Ravi$Rani@Vimal#Ramesh%Seema
2. Ravi#Rani*Vimal#Ramesh@Seema
3. Ravi#Rani*Vimal#Ramesh%Seema
4. Ravi#Rani*Vimal#Ramesh#Seema
5. None of these

29. In the expression Vinod#Komal*Vivek#Premlata@Simran, how will Premlata be related to Vinod?
1. Father 2. Mother 3. Grand-father 4. Grand-mother
5. Can't be determined

30. In the expression 1#2*3#4%5, how will 3 be related to 5?
1. Daughter 2. Son 3. Grand-daughter
4. Grand-son 5. None of these

31. The activity of getting one's password over Email or phone is known as-
1. Spoofing 2. Phishing 3. Spamming 4. Bugging 5. None of these

32. In computer science, a self-contained step by step set of operations to be performed is known as?
1. Suite 2. Algorithm 3. Database 4. Software 5 Processor

33. Ctrl, shift and alt are called ____________ keys.
1. adjustment 2. function 3. modifier 4. alphanumeric 5. None of these

34. The system unit
    1. Coordinates input and output devices
    2. is the container that houses electronic components
    3. is a combination of hardware and software
    4. controls and manipulates data
    5. does the arithmetic operations

35. Which of the following is an example of first generation computer?
    1. ENIVAC 2. IBM 7094 3. UNIVAC 9000
    4. EMICAV 5. Machintosh

36. Which of the following functions does input unit performs?
    1. Accepts the list of instructions
    2. converts the instructions in computer acceptable format
    3. Supplies converted instructions to the computer system
    4. All of these
    5. None of these

37. ____________ is not an output device?
    1. Monitor 2. Printer 3. Digitizer 4. Speaker 5. Projector

38. The physical components of a computer system is/are.
    1. Software 2. Hardware 3. CPU
    4. All of these 5. None of these

39. The command to access the memory of the I/O device is carried by.
    1. Control bus 2. System bus 3. Data bus
    4. Expansion bus 5. Internal bus

40. __________ is not a classification of memory?
    1. Cache Memory 2. Primary Memory
    3. secondary Memory 4. Data memory 5. None of these

41. Optical storage method is used in.
    1. Floppy Disk 2. Hard Disk 3. CD-ROM 4. Pen drive 5. Magnetic Tape

42. The storage element for a static RAM is the __________.
    1. diode 2. Resistor 3. Capacitor 4. flip-flop 5. None of these

43. NTFS is introduced by ____________.
    1. Microsoft 2. IBM 3. Apple 4. Intel 5. Xerox

44. __________ takes basic computer instructions and converts them into pattern of bits that computer can understand.
    1. Assembler 2. Driver 3. Operating system
    4. Server 5. GUI

45. Data (information) is stored in computers as __________.
    1. files 2. directories 3. floppies 4. matter 5. None of these

Section 2: Data Analysis & Interpretation

Passage:

Read the following pie-chart and table carefully and answer the questions given below.

Percentage distribution of total mobile phone connection users

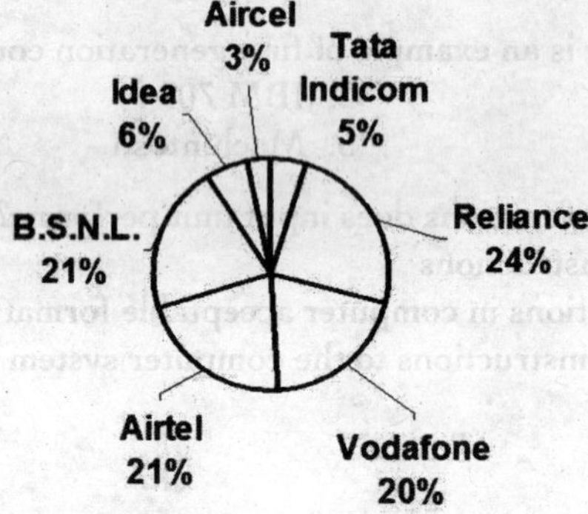

Ratio of male and female among these connections:

Company	Male	:	Female
Reliance	5	:	3
Vodafone	9	:	5
Airtel	2	:	1
B.S.N.L	2	:	5
Idea	5	:	7
Aircel	3	:	4
Tata Indicom	5	:	9

Total users = 14 crore

46. The number of female users of Airtel is approximately what percent of total number of users of Airtel?
    1. 24 2. 33 3. 29 4. 21 5. 36

47. What is the respective ratio between the number of male users of Reliance and female users of Aircel?
    1. 35 : 4 2. 12 : 1 3. 19 : 5 4. 17 : 8 5. None of these

48. What is the difference between female users of Vodafone and male users of Airtel?
    1. 66 lakhs 2. 6.6 lakhs 3. 66 thousands 4. 6 lakhs 5. None of these

49. What is the number of total female users?
    1. 7.21 crore 2. 6.25 crore 3. 7.36 crore 4. 7.45 crore 5. None of these

50. The number of female users of Reliance is what percent less than the female users of B.S.N.L.?
    1. 40 2. 50 3. 56 4. 60 5. None of these

Passage:

Read the following table carefully and answer the questions given below.

Average marks of boys and girls in five schools A, B, C, D and E, maximum marks in each subject is 100 and number shows the number of students in respective category.

	A		B		C		D		E	
	Boys	Girls	Boys	Girls	Boys	Girls	Boys	Girls	Boys	Girls
Number	60	40	70	30	80	20	75	25	60	35
Economics	70	75	72	70	80	85	73	68	75	70
Computer	80	70	82	80	82	85	85	82	80	76
English	72	60	65	60	60	55	50	40	65	65
Maths	57	65	65	62	57	57	60	50	57	58
Science	65	62	67	58	62	62	60	50	63	60

51. What is the difference between the total marks of boys and girls in school C?
1. 4088 2. 802 3. 97440 4. 20440 5. None of these

52. In which subject in school D students got minimum marks?
1. English 2. Science 3. Maths 4. Economics 5. None of these

53. What is the difference between the total percentage marks in Computer and Economics in school B and C?
1. 4.26% 2. 8.45% 3. 5.4% 4. 3.25% 5. None of these

54. What is the difference between the average marks got by girls in all the subjects in school D and E?
1. 7.2 2. 8 3. 8.2 4. 12 5. None of these

55. How much total marks did girls get in all subjects in school A?
1. 12830 2. 13280 3. 14620 4. 11280 5. None of these

Passage:

Read the following graph carefully and answer the questions given below.

Percentage of students in three disciplines (B.Tech., M.Tech. and MBA) in an institute from 2005 to 2010

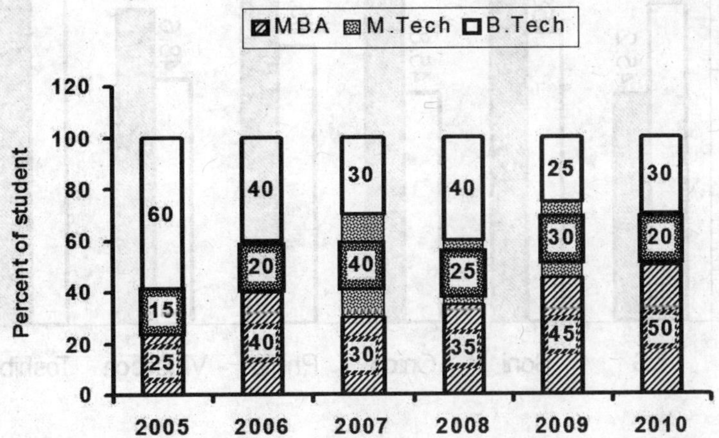

56. If in 2008 and 2010 the number of students in M.Tech are 280 and 550 respectively, the number of students in B.Tech in 2008 is what percent of the number of students in MBA in 2010? (approx)
1. 47 2. 43 3. 56 4. 33 5. 51

57. If the number of B.Tech students in the year 2007 and 2010 is equal to 480 each, what is the ratio of M.Tech students in 2007 and 2010 respectively?
1. 3 : 2 2. 2 : 1 3. 3 : 5 4. 2 : 5 5. None of these

58. What is the maximum difference between the number of students in MBA for the given period for any two years?
1. 45 2. 40 3. 35 4. Can not be determined
5. None of these

59. If the number of B.Tech students in 2005 and 2007 is equal to 360 each, then the number of M.Tech students in 2005 is what percent of the M.Tech students in 2007?
1. 18.75 2. 20 3. 18.5 4. 24 5. None of these

60. If the number of MBA students in 2008 is 490 and the number of B.Tech students in 2006 is 600, what is the difference between the total number of students in 2008 and the total number of students in 2006?
1. 125 2. 80 3. 100 4. 150 5. None of these

Passage:

Read the following pie chart carefully and answer the questions given below. Production of computer and A.C. (in thousands) and percentage of exported computer and A.C. by different companies in 2012.

Production of computer and A.C. (In thousands)

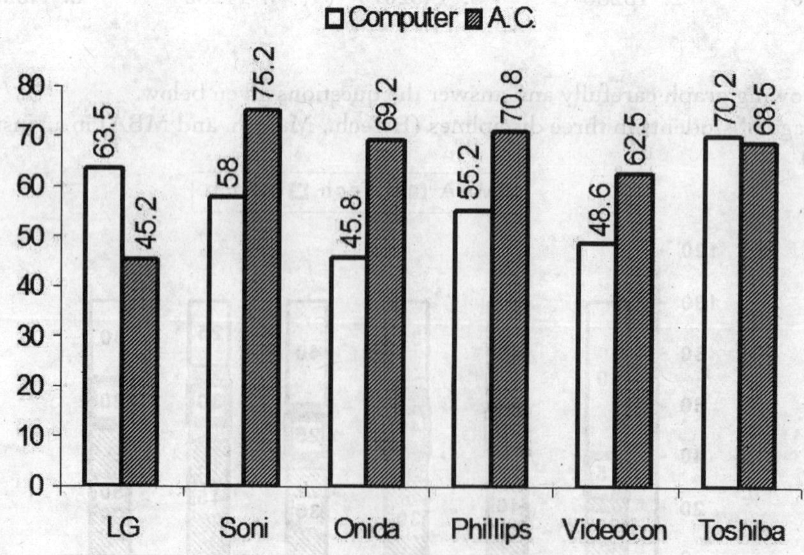

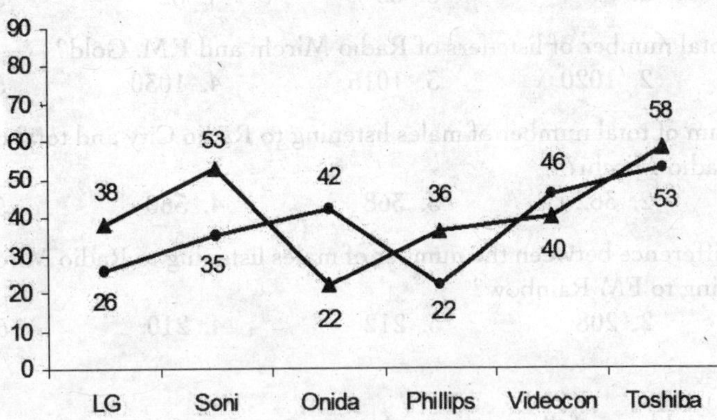

61. The number of exported A.C. by Toshiba is **approximately** what percent of the number of A.C. produced by Onida?
   1. 57 2. 60 3. 53 4. 65 5. 68

62. What is the total number of computers exported by all companies?
   1. 135228 2. 118295 3. 146115 4. 127752 5. None of these

63. What is the approximate average number of total A.C. produced by all the companies?
   1. 62620 2. 64840 3. 68180 4. 61610 5. 65230

64. What is the difference between the number of exported computer and A.C. by Onida?
   1. 3846 2. 4012 3. 4580 4. 4240 5. None of these

65. What is the total number of A.C. exported by Philips and Videocon?
   1. 48280 2. 52390 3. 50488 4. 55610 5. None of these

Passage:

Read the following information carefully and answer the questions given below.

There are total 1800 listeners of different radio channels in a city who listen to Radio Mirchi. Radio City, Red FM, FM Gold and FM Rainbow. The ratio of number of males and female is 7 : 5 respectively. 20% of the total number of female listen to Radio Mirchi and 26% of the total number of female listen to F.M. Rainbow. Total number of listeners of Radio City is 280. The number of listeners of Red F.M. is160. The ratio of number of males and females listen to F.M. Rainbow is 2 : 3. 20% of the total number of males listen to Radio City. The ratio between the number of males and females listen to Rad F.M. is 2 : 3. The number of males and females listen to FM Gold is equal. The number of listeners of Radio Mirchi is 557.

66. To which channels the number of female listeners is maximum and number of male listeners is minimum?
   1. Radio City and Red F.M. 2. F.M. Gold and Red F.M.
   3. F.M. Rainbow and F.M. Gold 4. Red F.M. and Radio Mirchi
   5. None of these

67. The number of females listening to Red FM is approximately what percent of the number of males listening to F.M. Rainbow?
1. 71 2. 79 3. 65 4. 62 5. 74

68. What is the total number of listeners of Radio Mirchi and F.M. Gold?
1. 1035 2. 1020 3. 1015 4. 1030 5. None of these

69. What is the sum of total number of males listening to Radio City and total number of females listening to Radio Mirchi?
1. 364 2. 362 3. 368 4. 360 5. None of these

70. What is the difference between the number of males listening to Radio Mirchi and number of females listening to FM Rainbow?
1. 205 2. 208 3. 212 4. 210 5. None of these

Passage:
Study the following table carefully to answer the questions that follow-

The amount of money invested (in rupees crore) in core infrastructure areas of two districts

District (1)			District (II)		
Core Area	2010	2011	Core Area	2010	2011
Electricity	1225.4	1420.2	Electricity	2840.4	3260.2
Chemical	972.5	1024.2	Chemical	1640.2	1848.4
Thermal	868.2	920.4	Thermal	1820.5	2050.2
Solar	895.4	940.2	Solar	1720.8	2120.8
Nuclear	842.8	910.2	Nuclear	1648.4	2240.2

71. The investment in thermal & Solar in 2010 in these two districts formed approximately what % of the total investment made in that year?
1. 42% 2. 40% 3. 36% 4. 46% 5. 30%

72. What was the approximate percent the total investment in the districts (II) more in 2011 as compared to that in 2010?
1. 19% 2. 32% 3. 27% 4. 15% 5. 40%

73. What is the difference between total investment in 2011 in both the districts?
1. 6104.2 2. 6304.6 3. 6402.4 4. 5842.4 5. None of these

74. In district (II) which area has minimum investment during the years 2010 & 2011?
1. Electricity 2. Chemical 3. Thermal 4. Solar 5. Nuclear

75. What is the average investment in nuclear area in both the districts?
1. 1250.2 2. 16110.40 3. 1840.2 4. 1410.4 5. None of these

Passage:
Read the following graph and table carefully and answer the questions given below.

Number of candidates appearing in SSC and Railway examination from different cities (in thousands)

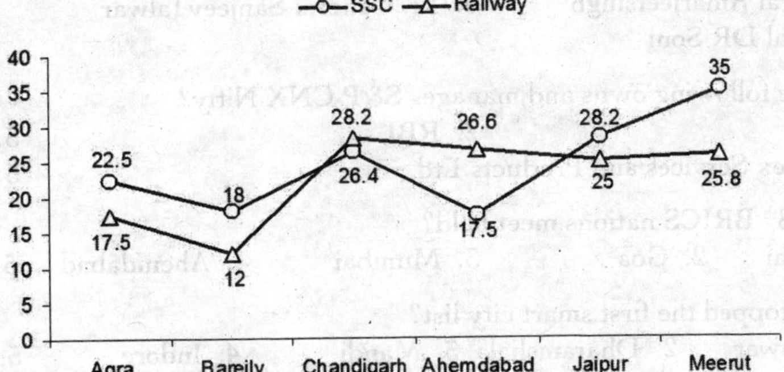

Percentage of selected candidates in SSC and Railway

City	% of selected student in SSC	% of selected student in Railway
Agra	36	19
Bareily	27	42
Chandigarh	31	28
Ahemadabad	46	38
Jaipur	23	17
Meerut	18	23

76. What is the respective ratio between the number of selected candidates in SSC from Meerut and number of selected candidates in Railway from Bareilly?
1. 1 : 3 2. 1 : 4 3. 5 : 4 4. 3 : 2 5. None of these

77. What is the difference between the number of selected candidates in Railway from Chandigarh and Jaipur?
1. 3646 2. 3280 3. 3510 4. 3352 5. None of these

78. The number of candidates selected in SSC from Bareilly is **approximately** what percent of the number of selected candidates in Railway from Ahemedabad?
1. 42 2. 53 3. 37 4. 55 5. 48

79. What is the sum of number of selected candidates in SSC from Jaipur and Meerut?
1. 14246 2. 12786 3. 13825 4. 14910 5. None of these

80. The number of selected candidates in Railway from Ahemadabad is **approximately** what percent more than the number of selected candidates in SSC from Meerut?
1. 60 2. 74 3. 70 4. 67 5. 56

Section 3: General/Economy/ banking Awareness

81. Name the DGMO(Director General of Military Operations) who led the Surgical operations along the line of Control in September 2016.
1. Lt. General Ranbir Singh 2. Lt. General RK Sharma

3. Lt. General Amarjeetsingh 4. Lt. General SanjeevTalwar
5 Lt. General DR Soni

82. Which of the following owns and manages S&P CNX Nifty?
1. SEBI 2. RBI 3. AMFI
4. India Index Services and Products Ltd. 5. SIDBI

83. Where was 8th BRICS nations meet held?
1. New Delhi 2. Goa 3. Mumbai 4. Ahemdabad 5. Jaipur

84. Which City topped the first smart city list?
1. Bhubneshwar 2. Dharamshala 3. Mandi 4. Indore 5. Sirsa

85. Who is the Indian envoy to Pakistan?
1. Abdul Basit 2. GautamBambawale 3. Rajeev Rishi
4. Deepak Gupta 5. Syed Akbaruddin

86. How many nations are there in Commonwealth?
1. 46 2. 48 3. 52 4. 57 5. 60

87. Which of the following banks is not a part of Scheduled Commercial Banks in India?
1. Public sector Banks 2. Private Sector Banks
3. Co-operative Banks 4. Foreign Banks
5. Regional Rural Banks

88. According to Fortune 500, which is the biggest company in India in terms of Revenue?
1. Reliance Industries 2. Wipro
3. Indian Oil Corporation 4. Tata Motors 5. ONGC

89. Man Booker Prize 2016 was give to-
1. Marlon James 2. Stephen King 3. Paul Beatty 4. John Grisham 5. Roger Priddy

90. What is India's rank in overall Global Competitive Index 2016-17?
1. 25th 2. 39th 3. 34th 4. 45th 5. 56th

91. From which year Paris Pact will become operational?
1. 2024 2. 2018 3. 2020 4. 2022 5. 2026

92. What was Goa Declaration adopted by BRICS?
1. To Fight Black Money 2. To Fight Terrorism
3. To Fight Global Recession 4. To Fight Natural Calamities
5. To Fight Money Laundering

93. How many schemes on Black money have been launched in India since 1950?
1. 16 2. 24 3. 8 4. 12 5. 18

94. Kisan Divas is celebrated on
1. 7 December 2. 10 December 3. 18 December 4. 23 December 5. None of these

95. How much Black money was declared under Income Declaration Scheme 2016?
1. Rs. 40560 cr 2. Rs. 65250cr 3. Rs. 50380 cr 4. Rs. 54760 cr 5. Rs. 56230 cr

96. How many alphanumeric codes does IFS Code (Indian Financial System Code consist of?
1. 10 2. 12 3. 11 4. 14 5. 16

97. SARFAESI Act 2002 related to ________.
1. Recovery of Bad Loans 2. Transferring Money abroad
3. Financial Inclusion 4. ECGC
5. Limited Liability Partnership

98. What is the ranking of India in 2016 Global Hunger Index?
1. 97th 2. 84th 3. 69th 4. 78th 5. 86th

99. In which state in India, is World's largest Solar Power Plant opened?
1. Tamil Nadu 2. Kerala 3. Karnataka 4. Rajasthan 5. Gujarat

100. In MICR code, first 3 digits represent the ________.
1. City 2. Bank 3. State 4. Branch 5. None of these

101. What does 'R' stands in CRD?
1. Reserve 2. Restructuring 3. Ratio 4. Rate 5. Regulation

102. What is the theme of the 2016 World Population Day?
1. Investing in teenage girls
2. Investing in teenage boys
3. Investing in vulnerable populations
4. Investing in uneducated population
5. None of these

103. Which country topped the ranking of global competitiveness index 2016-2017?
1. France 2. Italy 3. Turkey 4. China 5. Switzerland

104. According to Fortune 500, which is the biggest companies in the World in terms of Revenue?
1. Reliance 2. Toyota 3. Exxon mobile 4. Walmart 5. Volkswagen

105. The Bihu dance is a folk dance of which of the following state?
1. Assam 2. Meghalaya 3. Bihar 4. Tripura 5. West Bengal

106. Which is the most economically competitive state in India as per Asian competitive Institute?
1. Maharashtra 2. Gujarat 3. Rajasthan 4. Punjab 5. Kerala

107. Where was 11th G-20 meet held?
1. Melbourne 2. Hangzhou 3. Moscow 4. Mexico 5. Paris

108. How many customers were affected by Debit Cards fraudulent withdrawal in India in 2016?
1. 39 lac people 2. 48 lac people 3. 32 lac people 4. 64 lac people 5. 26 lac people

109. The term "bank money" is used to denote?
1. Loans and advances granted by the bank. 2. demand deposits used as money.
3. Time deposits of the bank 4. Loans granted by RBI
5. None of these

110. India is the ________ largest producer of coal in the world.
1. 1st 2. 2nd 3. 3rd 4. 4th 5. 5th

111. Where was 2016 World Cup Kabaddi played?
1. Kochi 2. Ahmedabad 3. Goa 4. Mumbai 5 New Delhi

112. Which company was ranked as the top employer in IT industry in India by NASSCOM?
1. Infosys 2. TCS 3. Tech Mahindra 4. HCL 5. MindTree

113. Which online website was launched by RBI to help curb Ponzi scheme?
1. Amazon.com 2. Gmail website
3. Wikipedia website 4. Sachet Website 5. learnvest.com

114. Who is the most followed Indian on Twitter?
1. NarendraModi 2. Sachintendulkar
3. Amitabh Bachchan 4. ArvindKejriwal 5. ViratKohli

115. Which company to launch first REIT(Real Estate Investment Trust) in India?
1. Blackstone 2. DLF 3. Phoenix Mills 4. Omaxe 5. Parsvnath

116. Who has recently become CMD of Power Finance Corporation?
1. Shikha Sharma 2. VinodRai 3. Rajeev Sharma
4. Urjit Patel 5. Deepak Gupta

117. Insolvency and Bankruptcy Board of India was constituted under the chairmanship of __________.
1. NachiketMor 2. MS Sahoo 3. UshaTharot 4. Urjit Patel 5. VinodRai

118. Rupee coins are legal tender in India under the provisions of
1. Reserve Bank of India Act 1934 2. Negotiable instruments Act 1881
3. Banking Regulation Act 1949 4. Indian coinage Act 1906
5. None of these

119. World Investment report is released by
1. IMF 2. UNCTAD 3. World Bank 4.Unesco 5. None of these

120. Which of the following banks does not have its head office in Mumbai?
1. State Bank of India 2. Central Bank of India 3. Canara bank
4. Bank of India 5. None of these

Section 4: English Language

Directions (Qs 121–125): Read each sentence to find out whether there is any error in it. The error if any, will be in one part of the sentence, the name of the part is the answer. If there is no error, the answer is (5).

121. Demonetization may be grabbing 1./all the eyeballs, 2./ but another crack-down 3./ is happening quietly elsewhere. 4./ No error 5

122. Like in all of walks1./ of life, intent 2./ is a massive commodity 3./ in cricket too 4.. / No error 5

123. As he have seems 1./ to have decided 2./ to be a complete iconoclast 3./ and even dispense with the mandatory additions to his job. 4./ No error 5

124. The policy aims to 1./ promote creation of a sustainable 2./ software product industry, 3./ which is largely being driven by the startup sector. 4./ No error 5

125. The basic requirement 1./ to knowing God 2./ is to nurture the urge 3./ to know in the seeker's mind.4./ No error5

Directions (Qs 126–130): In each of the following sentences, there are two blank spaces. Below each sentence there are five pair of words denoted by numbers 1., 2., 3., 4., 5. Find out which pair of words can be filled up in the blanks in the sentences in the same sequence to make the sentence grammatically correct.

126. Many teachers ________ the lack of professional freedom as the ________ for leaving the job.
 1. cited, reason 2. explained, force 3. claimed, understanding
 4. argued, culprit 5. believe, ground

127. Unpredictable ________ of the child could not lead the consultants to any ________.
 1. performance, setting 2. belief, judgment
 3. operation, purpose 4. behavior, conclusion 5. react, decision

128. Few professions can ________ the sheer variety and constant ________ of being a doctor.
 1. like, struggle 2. share, enthusiast 3. match, challenge
 4. draw, work-load 5. justify, exception

129. Narendra's ________ in athletics yielded rich ________ as he got a scholarship.
 1. performance, money 2. defeat, results 3. behavior, appreciation
 4. excellence, dividends 5. failure, disappointment

130. The leaders were ________ needed by those to ________ they addressed.
 1. angrily, who 2. readily, which 3. scarcely, whom
 4. rarely, where 5. joyfully, when

Directions (Qs 131–140): Read the following information and answer the questions that follow:

India's colleges and universities, with just a few exceptions, have become large, under-funded, ungovernable institutions. At many of them, politics has intruded into campus life, influencing academic appointments and decisions across levels. Under-investment in libraries, information technology, laboratories, and classrooms makes it very difficult to provide top-quality instruction or engage in cutting-edge research.

The rises in the number of part-time teachers and the freeze on new full-time appointments in many places have affected morale in the academic profession. The lack of accountability means that teaching and research performance is seldom measured. The system provides few incentives to perform. Bureaucratic inertia hampers change. Student unrest and occasional faculty agitation disrupt operations. Nevertheless, with a semblance of normality, faculty administrators are able to provide teaching, coordinate examinations, and award degrees.

Even the small top tier of higher education faces serious problems. Many IIT graduates, well trained in technology, have chosen not to contribute their skills to the burgeoning technology sector in India. Perhaps half leave the country immediately upon graduation to pursue advanced study abroad — and most do not return. A stunning 86 per cent of students in science and technology fields from India who obtain degrees in the United States do not return home immediately following their study. Another significant group, of about 30 per cent, decides to earn MBAs in India because local salaries are higher — and are lost to science and technology. A corps of dedicated and able teachers work at the IITs and IIMs, but the lure of jobs abroad and in the private sector make it increasingly difficult to lure the best and brightest to the academic profession.

Few in India are thinking creatively about higher education. There is no field of higher education research. Those in government as well as academic leaders seem content to do the "same old thing." Academic institutions and systems have become large and complex. They need good data, careful analysis, and creative ideas. In China, more than two-dozen higher education research centers, and several government agencies are involved in higher education policy.

India has survived with an increasingly mediocre higher education system for decades. Now as India strives to compete in a globalised economy in areas that require highly trained professionals, the quality of higher education becomes increasingly important. So far, India's large educated population base and its reservoir of at least moderately well-trained university graduates have permitted the country to move ahead. But the competition is fierce. China in particular is heavily investing in improving its best universities with the aim of making a small group of them world class in the coming decade, and making a larger number internationally competitive research universities. Other Asian countries are also upgrading higher education with the aim of building world class-universities.

To compete successfully in the knowledge-based economy of the 21st century, India needs enough universities that not only produce bright graduates for export but can also support sophisticated research in a number of scientific and scholarly fields and produce at least some of the knowledge and technology needed for an expanding economy. How can India build a higher education system that will permit it to join developed economies? The newly emerging private sector in higher education cannot spearhead academic growth. Several of the well-endowed and effectively managed private institutions maintain reasonably high standards, although it is not clear that these institutions will be able to sustain themselves in the long run. They can help produce well-qualified graduates in such fields as management, but they cannot form the basis for comprehensive research universities. This sector lacks the resources to build the facilities required for quality instruction and research in the sciences. Nor can enough money be earned by providing instruction in the mainstream arts and sciences disciplines. Most of the private institutions do not focus on advanced training in the sciences.

Only public universities have the potential to be truly world class institutions. Institutions and programs of national prominence have already been identified by the Government. But these institutions have not been adequately or consistently supported. The top institutions require sustained funding from public sources. Academic salaries must be high enough to attract excellent scientists and scholars. Fellowships and other grants should be available for bright students. An academic culture that is based on merit-based norms and competition for advancement and research funds is a necessary component, as is a judicious mix of autonomy to do creative research and accountability to ensure productivity. World class universities require world class professors and students — and a culture to sustain and stimulate them.

131. What according to the author, is the shortfall of our government officials as well as academicians when it comes to higher education?
   1. They are of the opinion that India has the best system of higher education in the World.
   2. They believe that it is the responsibility of private institutions to bring about a change in higher education.
   3. They are unaware of the new developments in the field of higher education.
   4. They are unwilling to invest money in higher education despite getting sufficient grants for the purpose.
   5 They don not think innovatively in the direction of bringing about a change in higher education and are struck in a rut.

132. Which of the following is/ are the problem/a faced by Indian colleges and universities?
(A) political interference in decision making.
(B) Lack of funding necessary for improvement in classrooms, libraries, etc.
(C) Hiring a teachers on a part time basis only.
1. Only (A) 2. Only (B) 3. Only (B) and (C)
4. Only (C) 5 All (A), (B) and (C)

133. Which of the following is possibly the most appropriate title for the passage?
1. Literacy in India. 2. State of higher education in India.
3. Top universities in India. 4. Educational institutes in India.
5. Comparatively study of higher education in India and China.

134. Which of the following problems do top institutes in India face in terms of contribution to academics?
(A) teachers of these institutes get enticed by the openings in foreign countries.
(B) Many graduates from these institutes find opportunities abroad and never return.
(C) Graduates from these institutes who do not migrate to foreign countries are unfit for teaching in these institutes.
1. Only (A) 2. Only (B) 3. Only (A) and (B)
4. Only (B) and (C) 5 All (A),(b) and (C)

135. How, according to the author, has India progressed despite a mediocre higher education system?
1. borrowing idea as well as technology from the best.
2. By convincing the world that it is more knowledgeable than it actually is.
3. On the basis of its fairly competent graduates and a large number of educated population.
4. Because of its sound and progressive economic policies.
5. On the basis of the goodwill accumulated by it over the years.

Directions (Q.136–137): Choose the word which is most OPPOSITE in meaning of the word printed in bold as used in the passage.

136. FIERCE
1. strong 2. weak 3. tame 4. timid 5. None of these.

137. MEDIOCRE
1. Superlative 2. middle 3. average 4. pleasant 5. None of these.

Directions (Q.138–40): Choose the word, which is most SIMILAR in meaning of the word, printed in bold as used in the passage.

138. JUDICIOUS
1. shrewd 2. difficult 3. legal 4. Thoughtful 5. None of these.

139. CONTENT
1. unhappy 2. matter 3. satisfied 4. substance 5. All of the above.

140. INCENTIVE
1. discouragement 2. motivator 3. prompt 4. cash 5. All of the above

Directions (Qs 141–150): Read the following information and answer the questions that follows:

The role of the agriculture market is to **(141)** agricultural produce from the farmer to the consumer in the most **(142)** way. Agriculture markets are **(143)** in India through the APMC Acts. **(144)** to the **(145)** of the APMC Acts of the state, every APMC(Agriculture Produce Marketing Committee) is **(146)** to collect market fees from the buyers/traders in the **(147)** manner on the sale of agriculture produce. The **(148)** high incidence of commission charges on agriculture produce **(149)**their marketing cost high, which is an **(150)** outcome.

141.
1. deliver 2. make 3. produce 4. gather 5. accumulate

142.
1. delicate 2. exquisite 3. gentle 4. efficient 5. tender

143.
1. improve 2. standardize 3. superintended 4. regulated 5. optimize

144.
1. Way 2. According 3. Allowing 4. Awarding 5. Taking

145.
1. equipment 2. supply 3. provisions 4. methods 5. value

146.
1. regulated 2. authorized 3. discouraged 4. segregated 5. supplied

147.
1. prescribed 2. spontaneous 3. independent 4. autonomous 5. optional

148.
1. estimate 2. price 3. lowly 4. intentional 5. relatively

149.
1. withhold 2. conceal 3. win 4. renders 5. suppress

150.
1. alluring 2. undesirable 3. covetable 4. prudent 5. appropriate

Directions (Q. No. 151–155): Rearrange the following sentences (A), (B), (C), (D), (E) and (F) to make a meaningful paragraph and then answer the questions that follow.

A. I was idly looking around wondering why I was there, and a handful of gulal landed on my chest.

B. This happened five years ago on the day of Anant Chaturdashi, when Ganpati idols are immersed in water after 10 days of festivities.

C. I got up and rushed out into the street.

D. I was trying to complete some work at home so that I could be free by 6:00 pm to watch it.
E. Suddenly I heard a voice from within asking me to come down to the street to have darshan- it was as though a Ganpati idol in the procession was calling me.
F. By 4:00 pm, I could hear the sound of bands playing music in the distance.

151. Which of the following sentences should be the Fourth after rearrangement?
1. C 2. A 3. D 4. E 5. B

152. Which of the following sentences should be the Sixth(Last) after rearrangement?
1. A 2. B 3. C 4. E 5. F

153. Which of the following sentences should be the First after rearrangement?
1. A 2. B 3. D 4. E 5. F

154. Which of the following sentences should be the Second after rearrangement?
1. A 2. B 3. D 4. E 5. F

155. Which of the following sentences should be the Third after rearrangement?
1. A 2.. B 3. D 4. E 5. F

ANSWER KEY

1. 3	2. 5	3. 1	4. 2	5. 1	6. 2	7. 3	8. 4	9. 4	10. 3
11. 4	12. 4	13. 5	14. 1	15. 4	16. 5	17. 5	18. 2	19. 4	20. 1
21. 3	22. 5	23. 1	24. 4	25. 2	26. 4	27. 4	28. 3	29. 5	30. 4
31. 2	32. 2	33. 2	34. 3	35. 1	36. 4	37. 3	38. 2	39. 1	40. 4
41. 3	42. 4	43. 1	44. 1	45. 1	46. 2	47. 1	48. 5	49. 5	50. 1
51. 5	52. 1	53. 3	54. 5	55. 2	56. 4	57. 2	58. 4	59. 1	60. 3
61. 1	62. 4	63. 5	64. 2	65. 3	66. 2	67. 5	68. 1	69. 4	70. 3
71. 3	72. 1	73. 2	74. 2	75. 4	76. 3	77. 1	78. 4	79. 2	80. 1
81. 1	82. 4	83. 2	84. 1	85. 2	86. 3	87. 3	88. 3	89. 3	90. 2
91. 5	92. 2	93. 4	94. 4	95. 2	96. 3	97. 1	98. 1	99. 1	100. 1
101. 2	102. 1	103. 5	104. 4	105. 1	106. 1	107. 2	108. 3	109. 2	110. 3
111. 2	112. 2	113. 4	114. 1	115. 1	116. 3	117. 2	118. 4	119. 2	120. 3
121. 5	122. 1	123. 1	124. 5	125. 2	126. 1	127. 4	128. 3	129. 4	130. 3
131. 5	132. 5	133. 2	134. 3	135. 3	136. 2	137. 1	138. 4	139. 3	140. 2
141. 1	142. 4	143. 4	144. 2	145. 3	146. 2	147. 1	148. 5	149. 4	150. 2
151. 4	152. 1	153. 2	154. 3	155. 5					

Solution and Explanations

1. 3.

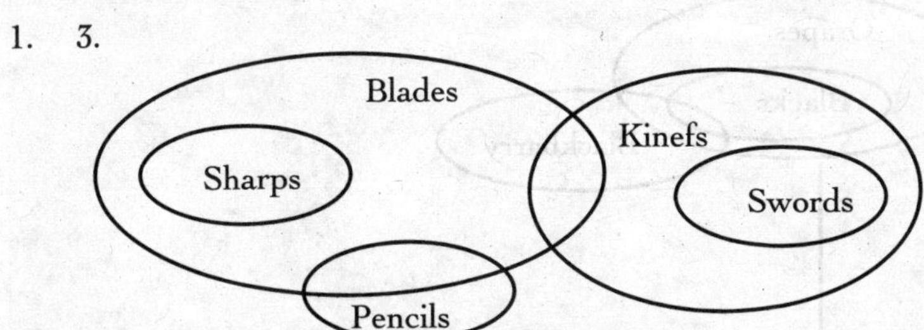

2 5.

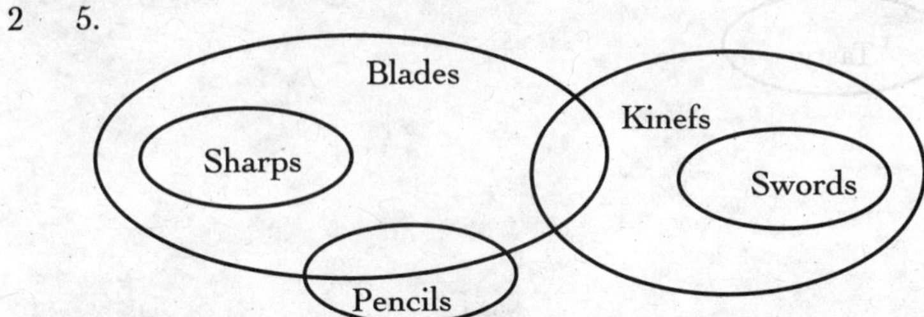

Both conclusions I and II follow

3. 1.

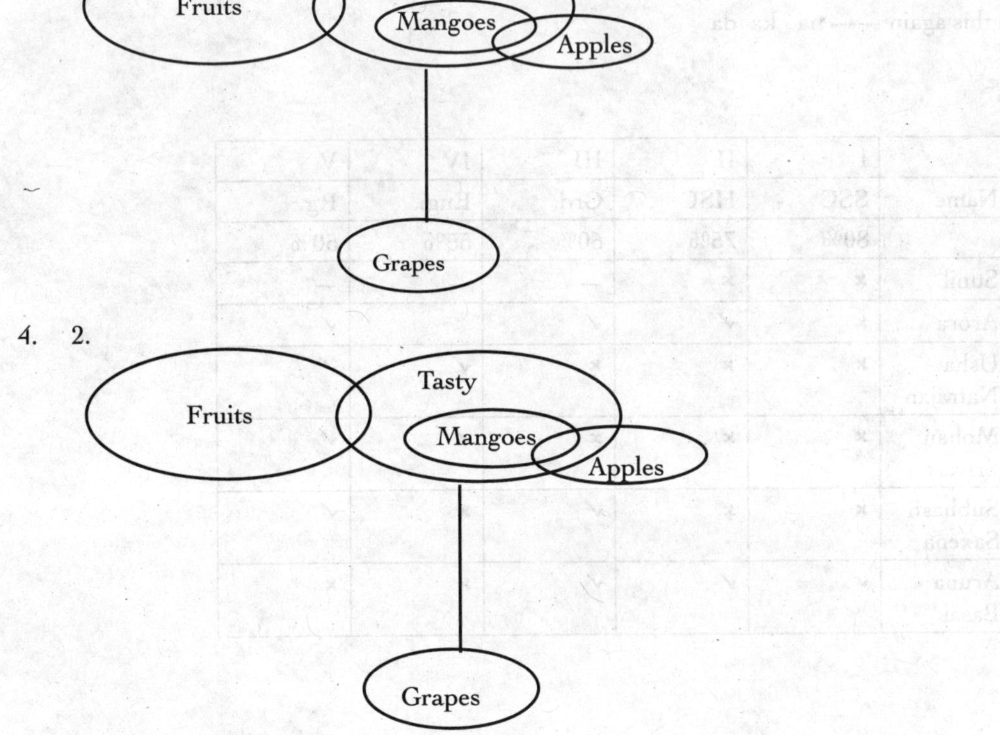

Only conclusion II follows.

5. 1.

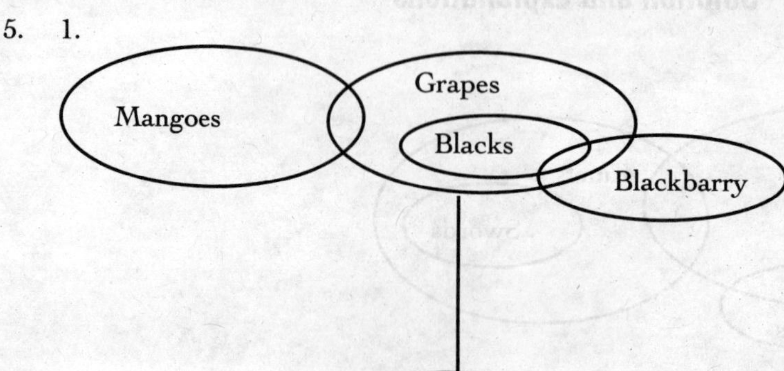

6. 4.

7. 4.

8. 5.

Q, R > P > S > T

9. 1.

Ever - Pa
Ever do this ----- Pa da na
do this again ------ na ka da

10. 4.

11. 5.

	I	II	III	IV	V
Name	SSC	HSC	Grd.	Engi.	P.g.
	80%	75%	60%	55%	50%
Sunil	✗	✗	—	—	—
Arora	✗	✓	✓		✓
Usha Natrajan	✗	✗	✗	✓	✓
Mohan Srivast	✗	✗	✗	✓	✓
Subhash Saxena	✗	✗	✓	✗	✓
Aruna Basak	✓	✓	✓	✗	✗

12. 5.

	I	II	III	IV	V
Name	SSC	HSC	Grd.	Engi.	P.g.
	80%	75%	60%	55%	50%
Sunil	×	×	—	—	—
Arora	×	✓	✓		✓
Usha Natrajan	×	×	×	✓	✓
Mohan Srivast	×	×	×	✓	✓
Subhash Saxena	×	×	✓	×	✓
Aruna Basak	✓	✓	✓	×	×

13. 2.

14. 4.

15. 1.

16. 3.

17. 5.

18. 1.

19. 4.

20. 2.

21. 4.

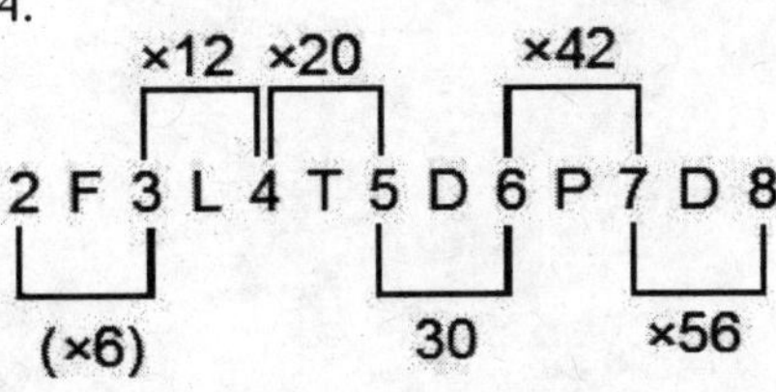

The last letter of the alphabet order are again counted from the beging of letters place value will be taken.

22. 4.

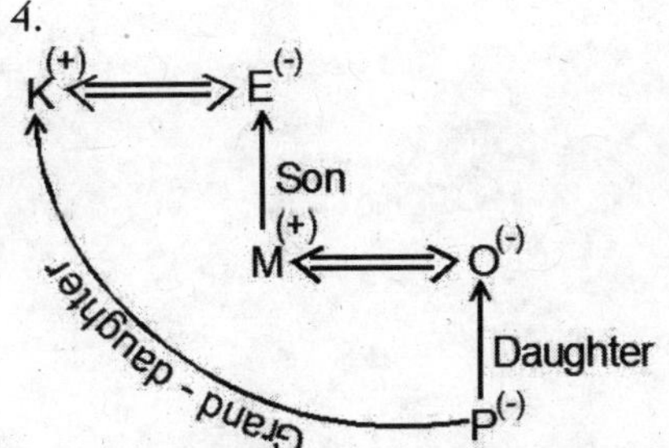

23. 3.

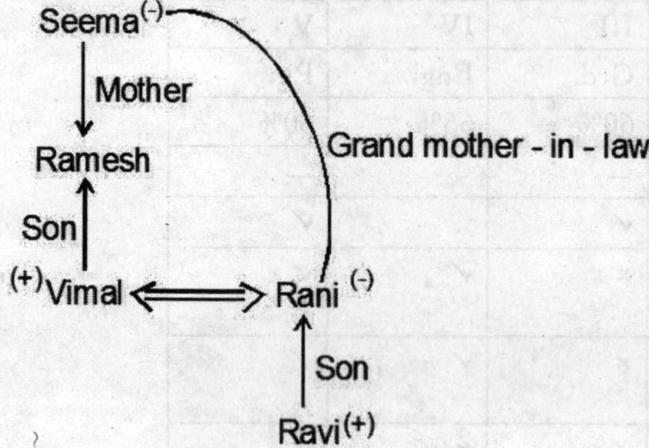

24. 5

We don't have any information about Premlata's gender.

25. 4.

26. 4.

×12 ×20 ×42

2 F 3 L 4 T 5 D 6 P 7 D 8

(×6) 30 ×56

The last letter of the alphabet order are again counted from the beging of letters place value will be taken.

27. 4.

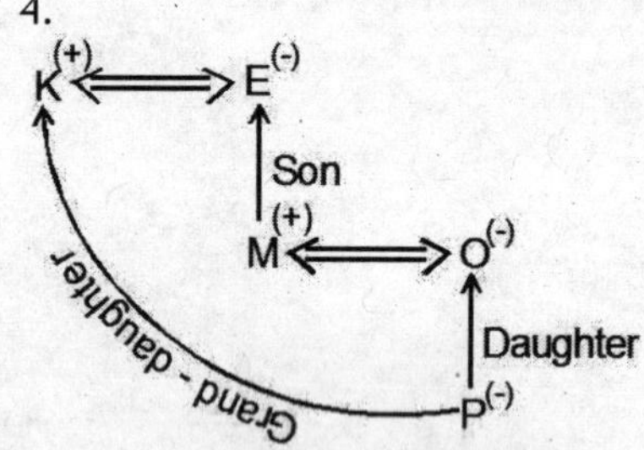

28. 3.

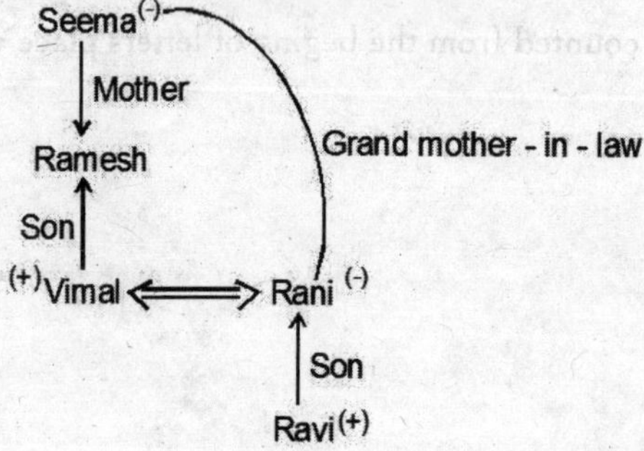

29. 5.
We don't have any information about Premlata's gender.

30. 4.

46. 2.

Required percentage = $\frac{98}{294} \times 100 = 33$ (approx)

47 1.

Ratio = 210 : 24 = 35 : 4

48. 5.

Difference = 196 – 100 = 96 lakh

49. 5.

Total number = 126 + 100 + 98 + 210 + 49 + 24 + 45= 652 lakh = 6.52 crore

50. 1.

Percentage decrease = $\frac{84}{210} \times 100 = 40$

51. 5.
Difference = 80 (80 + 82 + 60 + 57 + 62) – 20(85 +85 +55 + 57 + 62) = 27280 – 6880 = 20400

52. 1.

53. 3.
Difference percent

$= \frac{12960 + 3400}{20000} \times 100 - \frac{10780 + 4500}{20000} \times 100$

= 81.8 – 76.4 = 5.4%

54. ()

Difference = $\frac{329}{5} - \frac{290}{5} = 65.8 - 58$
= 7.8

55. 2.

Total marks = 40 (75 + 70 + 60 + 65 + 62)
= 13280

56. 4.
Req. percent = $\frac{448}{1375} \times 100 = 33\%$ (approx)

57. 2.
Ratio = 640 : 320 = 2 : 1

58. 4.

59. 1.

Req. percent = $\frac{90}{480} \times 100 = 18.75$

60 . 3.
Difference = 1500 – 1400 = 100

61. 1.
Percentage
$= \frac{39730}{69200} \times 100$ (Approx)

62. 4.
Total number = 127752

63. 5.
Average number = $\frac{391400}{6} = 65230$

64. 2.
Difference = 19236 - 15224 = 4012

65. 3.
Total number = 25488 + 25000 = 50488

66. 2.

	Male	Female
Total	1050	750
Radio Mirchi	407	150
Radio City	210	70
Red FM	64	96
FM Gold	239	239
FM Rainbow	130	195

67. 5.

	Male	Female
Total	1050	750
Radio Mirchi	407	150
Radio City	210	70
Red FM	64	96
FM Gold	239	239
FM Rainbow	130	195

Percentage = $\frac{96}{130} \times 100 = 74$ (Approx)

68. 1.

	Male	Female
Total	1050	750
Radio Mirchi	407	150
Radio City	210	70
Red FM	64	96
FM Gold	239	239
FM Rainbow	130	195

total number = 1035

69 4.

	Male	Female
Total	1050	750
Radio Mirchi	407	150
Radio City	210	70
Red FM	64	96
FM Gold	239	239
FM Rainbow	130	195

Total number = 360

70. 3.
Difference = 212

71. 3.
Required percentage = $\frac{5304.9}{14474.6} \times 100$CRS 36%

72. 1.
% increment = $\frac{11519.8 - 9670.3}{9670.3} \times 100$
19%

73. 2.

Reqd. difference = 11519.8 – 5215.2
= 6304.6

74. 2.

75. 4.

76. 3.
Ratio = 6300 : 5040 = 5 : 4

77. 1.
Difference = 7896 – 4250 = 3646

78. 4.

Percentage = $\frac{4860}{10108} \times 100$ = 48 (Approx)

79. 2.
Sum = 6486 + 6300 = 12786

80. 1.
Percentage increase = $\frac{3808}{6300} \times 100$
= 60 (Approx)

81. 1.

82. 4.

83. 2.

84. 1.

SBI PO Mains MOCK Test Paper 2

Structure of this MOCK Test

S.No.	Name of section	No. of Questions	Total marks	Allotted Time
1	Reasoning and Computer Aptitude	45	60	60 minutes
2	Data Analysis and Interpretation	35	60	45 minutes
3	General/ Economy/ Banking Awareness	40	40	35 minutes
4	English Language	35	40	40 minutes
Total		155	200	3 hours

- There is 1/4th Negative marking for every wrong answer.
- If a question is left blank, i.e. no answer is marked by the candidate, there will be no penalty for that question

Section 1: Reasoning & Computer Aptitude

Directions (1–6): Study the following information carefully and answer the questions given below.

Twelve friends P, Q, R, S, T, U, V, W, X, Y, Z and M are sitting in a row facing east. Y sits third to the left of T, who sits sixth to the right of P. V sits fourth to the right of M, who is not an immediate neighbor of R. Q sits fifth from the right end and W sits second to the left of S. T is not an immediate neighbor of X or U, but sits second to the right of Q. There are two friends between R and Z. Z is not an immediate neighbor of Y.

1. What is the position of U with respect to W?
   1. Third to the right
   2. Second to the left
   3. Seventh to the left
   4. Can't be determined
   5. None of these
2. If Z is an immediate neighbor of X, then who among the following is on the immediate right of S?
   1. U
   2. T
   3. M
   4. P
   5. None of these

3. How many persons are there between V and T?
 1. Two 2. Three 3. four 4. five 5. None of these

4. If U is immediate neighbor of M, then who among the following sit on the extreme ends of the line?
 1. ZS 2. MX 3. WU 4. XU 5. None of these

5. Who among the following sits third to the right of the eighth from the right end?
 1. Q 2. W 3. T 4. U 5. None of these

6. Four of the following five are alike in a certain way and hence form a group. Which is the one that does not belong to that group?
 1. RP 2. QR 3. YW 4. TQ 5. ZM

Directions (7–11) : Study the following information carefully and answer the questions given below.

Eight family members A, B, C, D, K, L, M and N are sitting around a circular table facing the centre. There is no grandfather in the family. The husband of N sits second to the right of B, who sits exactly between two males. L sits second to the left of the son of D. L is sister of M, who is sister of C. L is not an immediate neighbor of N's husband. Only one person sits between A and L. A is father of M. D, who is brother of N, sits on the immediate left of his mother. Only one person sits between N's mother and K. Only one person sits between N and M. M is not an immediate neighbor of K. C sits second to the right of D and is not the sister of M. The son of D sits second to the left of B.

7. What is the position of B with respect to K?
 1. Second to the left 2. Immediate left
 3. Third to the right 4. Second to the right 5. None of these

8. How many persons sit between L and her maternal uncle if counted anticlockwise from L?
 1. Three 2. One 3. Four 4. Two 5. None of these

9. Who among the following sits third to the left of A?
 1. D 2. K 3. N 4. Can't be determined
 5. None of these

10. What is the position of M with respect to her sister?
 1. Second to the right 2. Immediate left 3. Third to the left
 4. Immediate right 5. None of these

11. Who among the following sits fourth to the right of A's wife?
 1. M 2. L 3. K 4. C 5. None of these

Directions (12–14) : Study the following information carefully and answer the questions given below.

Six students A, B, C, D, E and F obtained differentmarks in an examination. A obtained more marks than only two students. B obtained more marks than D but not the highest. F obtained more marks than only C. The one who obtained the second highest marks obtained 280. The one who obtained the second lowest marks obtained 190 marks.

12. If the total marks of the examination are 500, then who among the following possibly obtained 60% marks?
 1. D 2. E 3. Either A or C 4. Either D or E 5. None of these

13. If A Obtained 200 marks, then who among the following possibly obtained 245 marks?
1. D 2. B 3. E 4. F 5. None of these

14. Who among the following obtained the lowest marks?
1. F 2. E 3. C 4. B 5. None of these

Directions (15–19) : In these questions, relationship between different elements is shown in the statements. The statements are followed by two conclusions. Study the conclusions based on the given statements and select the appropriate answer

15. **Statements:**
$L = P < W < V < N < R; Q < L ; N = M$
Conclusions:
I. $Q < V$ II. $P > M$
1. Only conclusion I is true 2. Only conclusion II is true
3. Either conclusion I or II is true 4. Both conclusions I and II are true
5. Neither conclusion I or II is true

16. **Statements:**
$T > U = B < S; U < P < X$
Conclusions:
I. $X > B$ II. $T > P$
1. Either conclusion I or II is true 2. Neither conclusion I nor II is true
3. Only conclusion I is true 4. Only conclusion II is true
5. Both conclusions I and II are true

17. **Statements:**
$A > U < P = T < O; A < Z > R$
Conclusions:
I. $R > P$ II. $P < R$
1. Both conclusions I and II are true 2. Either conclusion I or II is true
3. Only conclusion I is true 4. Neither conclusion I nor II is true
5. Only conclusion II is true

18. **Statements:**
$A > U < P = T < O; P < Z > R$
Conclusions:
I. $U < Z$ II. $Z = U$
1. Neither conclusion I nor II is true 2. Both conclusions I and II are true
3. Only conclusion I is true 4. Either conclusion I or II is true
5. Only conclusion II is true

19. **Statements:**
$P > Q < R < T; Q > S = M$
Conclusions:
I. $M > R$ II. $M < T$
1. Only conclusion I is true 2. Both conclusions I and II are true
3. Only conclusion II is true 4. Either conclusion I or II is true
5. Neither conclusion I nor II is true

20. **Statement:**

The government has decided to expand the coverage of its Jan Aushadhi scheme, which offers 439 life-saving medicines, including cancer and cardiovascular drugs, as well as 250 medical devices like stents and implants at 40-50% discounted prices. ***Which of the following statements would strengthen the argument given in the above statement?***

1. **The government is concerned about exorbitantly priced medicines to treat critical diseases like cancer, diabetes and cardiovascular conditions.**
2. **Poor people can now easily afford these medicines.**
3. **Drug making companies have reduced the prices of important drugs.**
4. **Life of people can't be saved with the reduction in the prices of important drugs.**
5. **Only 1. and 2.**

21. **Statement:**

Airlines have sent out a clear message to passengers, 'Behave yourself or face handcuffs'. *Which of the following can be inferred from the above statement?*

1. Passengers should behave themselves while travelling by the airlines.
2. Misbehaving with the air hostess in the flight will lead to punishment.
3. Punishment shall be imposed on the airlines' crew if they misbehave with the airlines' passengers.
4. Behave yourself while travelling by the airlines.
5. None of these

22. **Statement:**

The Railways has decided to limit the number of tickets, of online booking to six from one user ID.

Which of the following will not be an effect of the step taken by the Railways?

1. Tourists will not be able to book bulk online tickets.
2. Regular travellers may face discomfort by the new rules.
3. People will create multiple user ID.
4. There will be longer queues at the railway station ticket counter.
5. None of these

Directions (23–24): Each of the question below consists of a questions and two statements numbered I and II are given below it. You have to decide whether the data provided in the statements are Sufficient to answer the question. Read both the statements and Give answer:

1. The data either in statement I alone or statement II alone are sufficient to answer the question.
2. The data in both statements I and II are necessary to answer the question.
3. The data in statement I alone are sufficient to answer the question while the data in statement II are not sufficient to answer the question.
4. The data in statement II alone are sufficient to answer the question while the data in statement I are not sufficient to answer the question.
5. The data in both statements I and II together are not sufficient to answer the question.

23. How many people are standing in a straight line (Note: All are facing north)?

I. J stands third from the right end of the line. Q stands to the immediate left of J. Only two people stand between Q and T. No person stands to the left of T.

II. R stands third from the left end of the line. Q is one of the immediate neighbors of R. Only two people stand between Q and S.

24. How far is Point X from Point J?
    I. Point Q is 2.5m to the west of Point J. Point P is 2.5m to the south of Point Q. Point X is to the east of Point F such that Point F is the midpoint of a 5m line formed by joining point P and X.
    II. Point R is 5m to the south of Point Q. Point Z is to the east of Point R. Point X is 2.5m to the north of Point Z. Point J is 2.5m to the east of Point Q.

25. Read the given information and answer the question.
'Ever since we started involving our employees in the key decision making process from the last year, the productivity of our employees has been 100%' statement by HR manager of company D.
Which of the following statements can be inferred from the given statement? (An inference is something by which you can logically deduce something to be true based on known premises.)
    1. Employees of Company D will always take correct decisions in all the situations.
    2. Company D completely relies on its employees for all key decisions.
    3. The productivity of employees of Company D has always been satisfactory in the past.
    4. Involving employees in decision making process is an effective method to motivate them.
    5 Employees of company D have now become competent enough to give valuable suggestions.

26. Read the given information and answer the question.
Carmakers Kellbahn's domestic sales have surged as they have reported sales of 12000 cars this December. This number is more than double the number of cars sold by them in the third quarter (October-December) put together last year.
Which of the following can be concluded from the given statement?
    1. If 6000 more cars were sold in the third quarter of last year, the two numbers would have become equal.
    2. Kellbahn definitely sold less than 6000 cars in December last year.
    3. Addition of International sales figures would have made performance of last quarter better.
    4. If 6000 less cars were sold in December this year, the number of cars sold would have been same as that in December last year.
    5. Kellbahn definitely sold less than 12000 cars in November this year.

27. **Study the given information carefully to answer the question given.**
'Kalikaar' is a famous fabric threadwork that originated in city G of a country. 'Kalikaar' was an innovation of 'Hardali' tribe of City G. Though the tribe lost its existence long ago, 'Kalikaar' is still very much in demand. Only the authentic 'Kalikaar' depicts fruits and flowers of a specific tree that was worshipped by 'Hardali' tribe.
Which of the following can be inferred from the given information?
(Note : An inference is something by which you can logically deduce something to be true based on known premises.)
    1. The 'Hardali' tribe did not worship Gods and Goddesses.
    2. Some people not belonging to the tribe have taken the 'Kalikaar' work forward and managed to keep fulfilling its demand.
    3. During the existence of 'Hardali' tribe, 'Kalikaar' was the only means of their income.
    4. No city other than city G sells authentic cloth materials of 'Kalikaar' threadwork.
    5. Since not many people belonged to the 'Hardali' tribe, others came to know about the tribe only through its innovation of 'Kalikaar'.

Directions (28–32): Study the following arrangement carefully and answer the questions given below:

F 4 % D A © I 9 B @ 2 R 5 H 6 E * N $ 1 U W 3 P T 8 9 V # Z Q

28. Which of the following is twelfth to the left of the twenty second from the left end of the above arrangement?
1. R 2. @ 3. 2 4. U 5. None of these

29. Four of the following five are alike in a certain way based on their positions in the above arrangement and so form a group. Which is the one that does not belong to that group?
1. FD4 2. TV8 3. OBI 4. HRE 5. 13U

30. If all the numbers from the above arrangement are dropped, then which of the following will be the sixteenth element from the right end?
1. B 2. @ 3. R 4. U 5. None of these

31. How many such consonants are there in the above arrangement, each of which is immediately preceded by a symbol and immediately followed by a vowel?
1. Four 2. One 3. Two 4. Three 5. None

32. How many such symbols are there in the above arrangement, each of which is immediately preceded a vowel and immediately followed by a letter?
1. One 2. Two 3. Three 4. Four 5. None of these

33. ________ is the interleaving of processes in time to give the appearance of simultaneous execution.
1. Threads 2. Concurrency
3. Synchronization 4. deadlock 5. None of these

34. External fragmentation is avoided using ________ technique.
1. Rounding 2. Paging 3. Scheduling 4. Dispatching 5. None of these

35. Which of the following requires a device driver?
1. Register 2. Cache 3. Main memory 4. Disk 5. None of these

36. Which of the following is not a form of memory?
1. Instruction cache 2. Instruction register
3. Instruction opcode 4. Translation look-a-side-buffer
5. All of these

37. The process of assigning load addresses to the various parts of the program and adjusting the code and date in the program to reflect the assigned address is called.
1. assembly 2. parsing 3. relocation
4. symbol resolution 5. None of these

38. Computers manipulate data in many ways, and this manipulation is called ________.
1. utilizing 2. batching 3. upgrading 4. processing 5. None of these

39. A computer's type, processor and operating system define its-
1. brand 2. size 3. platform 4. speed 5. None of these

40. Where does most data go first within a computer memory hierarchy?
1. RAM 2. ROM 3. BIOS 4. CACHE 5. None of these

41. What is the swap space in the disk used for?
 1. Saving temporary HTML pages 2. Saving process data
 3. Storing the super block 4. Storing device drivers
 5. None of these

42. Increasing the RAM of a computer typically improved performance because-
 1. virtual memory increases 2. larger RAM are faster
 3. fewer page faults occur 4. fewer segmentation faults occur
 5. None of these

43. The signal within the database of a computer are
 1. analog 2. mix of analog and digital 3. binary digital
 4. multi level digital signals 5. None of these

44. Which of the following storage is volatile?
 1. Floppy disk 2. Bubble memory 3. Semiconductor memory
 4. core memory 5. None of these

45. Sorting is useful for-
 1. report generation
 2. minimizing the storage needed
 3. making searching easier and efficient
 4. responding to queries easily

Section 2 : Data Analysis& Interpretation

Directions (46–50) : Study the given chart and table carefully to answer the given questions. The graph shows the production of Rice, Maize, Pulses and Wheat in six different years.

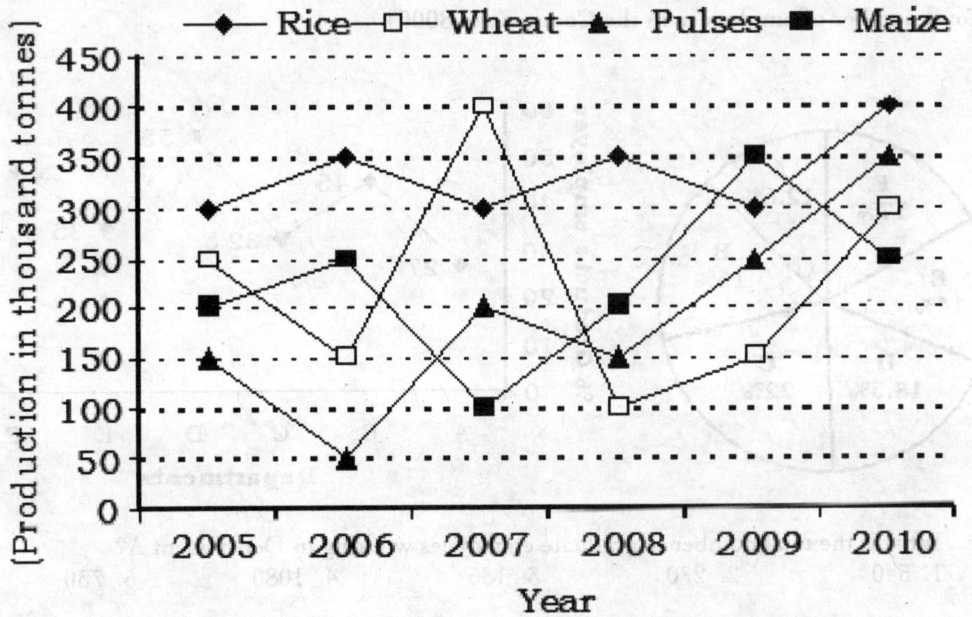

Percentage of the total production used under various heads

Year	Export(%)	PDS Supply(%)	In open market(%)
2005	40%	12%	48%
2006	20%	18%	62%
2007	25%	16%	59%
2008	30%	14%	56%
2009	15%	20%	65%
2010	20%	22%	58%

46. In 2009 what is the difference between the amount of PDS supply and that used in export?
1. 53000 tones 2. 56000 tones 3. 54500 tones 4. 52500 tones 5. 59000 tones

47. What is the ratio of the production of Pulses to that of Wheat over the six years?
1. 25 : 27 2. 23 : 25 3. 23 : 28 4. 23 : 27 5. 22:27

48. In which year is the production the minimum?
1. 2006 and 2008 2. 2009 3. 2010 4. 2007 and 2009 5. 2005

49. In which year is the quantity of export the maximum?
1. 2005 2. 2006 3. 2007 4. 2008 5. 2009

50. In which year is the quantity of PDS supply the minimum?
1. 2005 2. 2006 3. 2010 4. 2009 5. 2008

Directions (51–55): The given pie-chart shows the percentage distribution of employees among different departments of a Company and the line graph shows the percentage of graduate employees among them. Answer the following questions based on these graphs.

(Total number of employees in the Company is 8000)

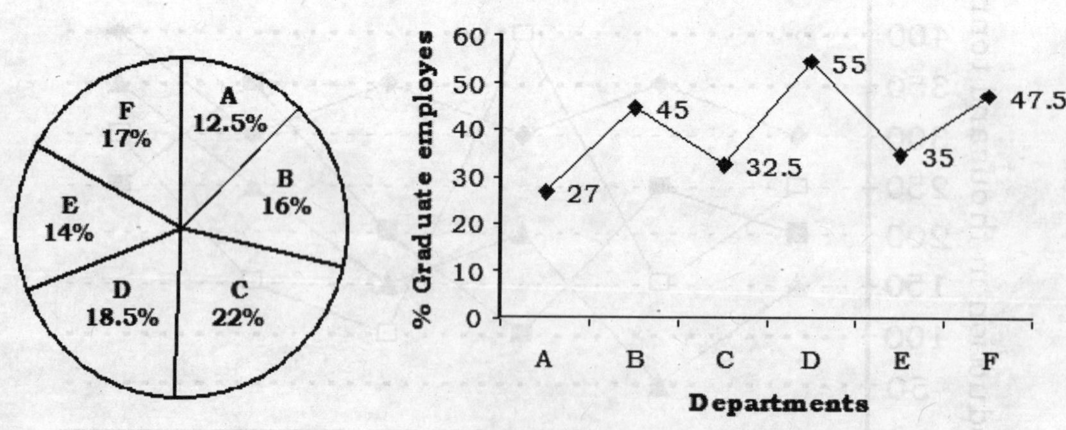

51. What is the total number of graduate employees working in Department A?
1. 540 2. 270 3. 135 4. 1080 5. 730

52. What is the total number of employees working in the Company who are non-graduates?
1. 3780 2. 3940 3. 4360 4. 4730 5. 5730

53. The total number of graduate employees working in Department E is what percent of the total number of employees of the Company?
1. 7.2% 2. 6.4% 3. 4.9% 4. 4.3% 5. None of these,

54. The total number of graduate employees working in Department D is approximately what percent more or less than the total number of non-graduate employees working in that department?
1. 18% more 2. 22% more 3. 24% less 4. 27% less 5. 32% less

55. What is the average number of graduate employees working in the Company in all departments together?
1. 535 2. 545 3. 555 4. 565 5. 575

Directions (56–60): Study the table carefully to answer the questions that follow.
Percentage of Marks Obtained by Different Students in Different Subjects of MB

Student	SUBJECTS (Maximum Marks)					
	Strategic Management (150)	Brand Management (100)	Compensation Management (150)	Consumer Behaviour (125)	Service Marketing (75)	Traning Devekionent (50)
Priti	66	75	88	56	56	90
Lucky	82	76	84	96	92	88
Monika	76	66	78	88	72	70
Ashu	90	88	96	76	84	86
Javed	64	70	68	72	68	74
Saiyad	48	56	50	64	64	58

56. How many marks did Priti get in all the Subjects together?
1. 369 2. 463 3. 558 4. 496 5. None of these

57. Marks obtained by Ashu in Brand Management is what percent of marks obtained by Lucky in the same Subject? (rounded off to two digits after decimal)
1. 86.36% 2. 101.71% 3. 115.79% 4. 133.33% 5. None of these

58. What are the average marks obtained by all students together in Compensation Management?
1. 116 2. 120 3. 123 4. 131 5. None of these

59. Who has scored the highest total marks in all the subjects together?
1. Lucky 2. Javed 3. Saiyad 4. Ashu 5. Monika

60. How many Students have scored the highest marks in more than one Subject?
1. three 2. two 3. one 4. none 5. None of these

Directions (61–65): Read the following table carefully and answer the questions given below. Total number of passed students in a board examination in different schools, ratio of boys and girls and percentage of passed boys and girls in first class

School	Total number	Boys:Girls	Boy% (1st class)	Girls % (1st Class
A	800	5:3	17	24
B	740	1:1	30	20
C	750	8:7	28	22
D	980	4:3	25	30
E	600	2:1	23	27
F	720	7:5	20	28

61. What is the respective ratio between the number of passed boys from school D and F?
1. 2:3 2. 4:3 3. 3:1 4. 5:2 5. None of these

62. What is the difference between the number of boys and girls passed in first class from school E?
1. 34 2. 40 3. 36 4. 30 5. None of these

63. The number of passed girls from school D is approximately what percent more than the number of passed girls from school B?
1. 20 2. 25 3. 28 4. 22 5. None of these

64. What is the average number of passed boys in first class from all schools?
1. 100 2. 110 3. 104 4. 112 5. None of these

65. The number of passed boys in first class from school A is approximately what percent of the number of passed boys in first class from school D?
1. 56 2. 52 3. 48 4. 61 5. 63

Directions (66–70): Following pie-chart shows the percentage distribution of total population of different cities and the distribution of literate males and females among them. Total population of all six cities together is 1.5 crore and the ratio of males to females among them is 8 : 7. Total literate males and females in all cities are 40 and 25 lakh respectively.

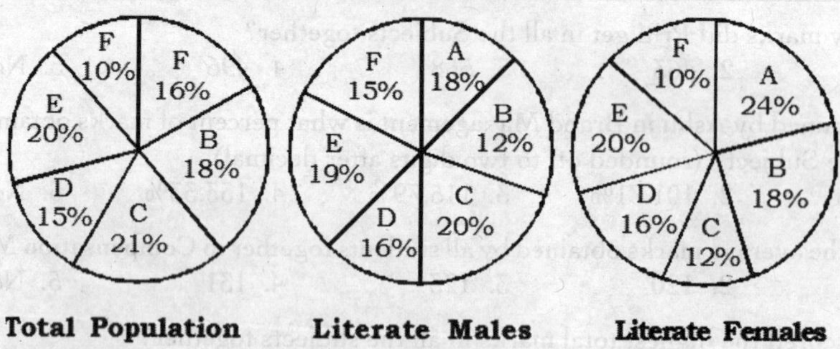

66. What is the total illiterate population of City A?
1. 10.8 lakh 2. 14.2 lakh 3. 16.8 lakh 4. 18 lakh 5. None of these

67. Total literate males of City E are what percentage of total literate females of City F?
1. 32.89% 2. 118% 3. 196% 4. 240% 5. 304%

68. Total literate population of City E is what percentage of its total population?
1. 25.33% 2. 16.66% 3. 26% 4. 42% 5. 64%

69. What is the difference between total illiterate population and total literate population of City C?
1. 8.5 lakh 2. 9.5 lakh 3. 10.5 lakh 4. 11 lakh 5. 20.5 lakh

70. Total number of literate males of City D is what percentage more than the total number of literate female of City D?
1. 60% 2. 38.46% 3. 61.538% 4. 120% 5. 160%

Directions (71–75): Study the following tables carefully to answer the given questions. Number of candidates (in lakhs) appearing in an entrance examination from six different cities and the ratio of candidates pass and fail the same.

City	A	B	C	D	E	F
Number of Candidates	1.25	3.14	1.08	2.27	1.85	2.73

Ratio of candidates passing and failing within the city

City	Pass	Fail
A	7	3
B	5	3
C	4	5
D	1	3

71. What is the ratio of the number of candidates fail in the exam from City D to that of those fail the exam from City A?
1. 289 : 42 2. 42 : 289 3. 227 : 50 4. 50 : 227 5. None of these

72. The number of candidates appearing for the exam from City C is what percent of the number of candidates appearing for the exam from City B? (Rounded off to the nearest integer)
1. 27% 2. 34% 3. 42% 4. 21% 5. 38%

73. The number of candidates passing in the exam from City F is what percent of the total number of candidates appearing from all the cities together? (Rounded off to two digits after the decimal)
1. 12.93% 2. 14.46% 3. 10.84% 4. 11.37% 5. None of these

74. Which city has the highest number of students fail in the entrance exam?
1. F 2. C 3. B 4. D 5. None of these

75. What is the number of candidates passing the exam from City E?
1. 13,000 2. 11,10,000 3. 1,13,000 4. 11,000 5. None of these

Directions (76–80) : In the following pie-chart, the percentage distribution of population of six cities is given. Total population of these six cities is 24 lakh. The given table shows the ratio of males to females and the percentage of adult population in these cities.

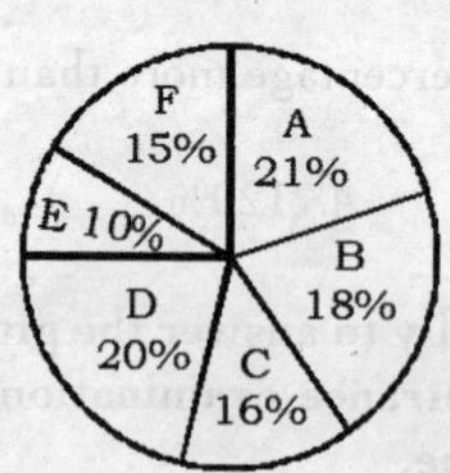

City	Male:Female	% Adult
A	4:3	60%
B	5:4	64%
C	5:3	72%
D	2:3	70%
E	1:1	75%
F	3:2	65%

76. What is the total number of male population in city D?
   1. 1.88 lakh 2. 1.92 lakh 3. 1.96 lakh 4. 2.04 lakh 5. 2.12 lakh
77. What is the number of persons in city C who are not adult?
   1. 107520 2. 108410 3. 109560 4. 110800 5. 121400
78. What is the number of females in city A who are adult?
   1. 74400 2. 74500 3. 75400 4. 75500
   5. Can't be determined
79. What is the difference between the number of males and the number of females in city B?
   1. 42000 2. 44000 3. 45000 4. 48000 5. None of these
80. The number of adults in city E is what percent of the number of males in city D?
   1. 82.5% 2. 87.75% 3. 92.5% 4. 93.75% 5. 95%

Section 3: General / Economy / Banking Awareness

81. Union cabinet has just approved the 7th Pay commission Report. The commission was headed by -
   1. Justice A.K Mathur 2. B.S Chauhan 3. Y.V Reddy
   4. B.N.Srikrishna 5. None of these
82. Recently 'My Speed' App has been launched by which of the following to measure the real time mobile Internet speed?
   1. Airtel 2. Idea 3. Reliance Jio 4. Vodafone 5. None of these
83. Union cabinet has just approved the 7th Pay commission Report. The commission was headed by -
   1. It is an organization that deals with the Maritime disputes all over the world.
   2. It works under the guidance of United Nations.
   3. It is a biennial International Maritime exercise in which many countries takes part.
   4. It is an United Nation Initiative to protect aquatic animals in Pacific Ocean.
   5. None of these.

84. Renowned philanthropist Abdul Sattar Edhi, known as father Teresa, has died at the age of 88. Which one of the following country he belongs to?
1. Iran 2. Saudi Arab 3. Pakistan 4. Afghanistan 5. Indonesia

85. Leonardo Dicaprio grabbed the Oscar Award 2016 for actor in a leading role for the film-
1. The Revenant 2. Room 3. Spotlight 4. Trumbo 5. Brooklyn

86. Andy Murray of Britain has won the Wimbledon 2016 title by defeating Milos Raonic of -
1. Spain 2. Canada 3. Germany 4. France 5. None of these

87. Indian Railways has conducted the first ever trial run for high-speed Talgo trains on the 90-km Bareilly-to-Moradabad route. It is a leading manufacturer of energy-efficient passenger trains, it is based in which one of the following country?
1. France 2. Japan 3. China 4. Russia 5. Spain

88. The construction of the Salma dam has stretched the capacity of Indian diplomacy With Afghanistan, the dam is constructed in the Chishti-Sharif district of Herat on the HerayRud River. The dam is constructed by -
1. WAPCOS 2. Larsen & Toubro Limited
3. Essar group 4. IRCON International Ltd
5. ShapoorjiPallonji& Co Ltd

89. Which one of the following pair is incorrectly matched?
1. World Refugee Day - 25th June 2. World Milk Day - 1st June
3. World Environment Day - 5th June 4. World No Tobacco Day - 31st May
5. World Asthma Day - 3rd May

90. The Copa America cup is an international men's football tournament hosted in the United States this year. Chile won the cup by defeating which of the following country?
1. Uruguay 2. Colombia 3. Paraguay 4. Venezuela 5. None of these

91. Consider the following pairs regarding Rio Olympics 2016. Which one of the following is incorrectly matched?
1. Manish Rawat -Athletics 2. Laxmi Rani Majhi - Shooting
3. DattuBhokanal - Rowing 4. Shiva - Boxing
5. None of these

92. A cess is a tax that is collected by the government to be used for a specific purpose. Arun Jaitley while announcing the Budget 2016 has introduced 'Krishi Kalyan Cess',which is levied at a rate of -
1. 0.25% 2. 0.50% 3. 0.75% 4. 1.25% 5. None of these.

93. BeiDou Navigation System(BNS)is a 2nd generation navigation system of which of the following country which is seen as a rival to the US's Global Positioning System (GPS)?
1. Russia 2. France 3. China 4. North Korea 5. Germany

94. Defexpo Goa, India 2016, is India's biggest ever land, naval and homeland security exhibition. The theme of the expo was-
1. "Rise of Power" 2. "Rise of Futurism"
3. "Unity is our strength" 4. "Way to future Weapons"
5. "stop terrorism"

95. The Union Ministry of Health and Family Welfare launched India's first indigenous rotavirus vaccine named 'Rotavac' to combat-
1. Infant mortality due to diarrhoea. 2. Increasing no. of H.I.V patients.
3. Increasing no. of Tuberculosis patients. 4. Diabetes mellitus.
5. None of these.

96. State Bank of India (SBI) recently had launched which of the following scheme for social media banking platform for Facebook and Twitter users, it will allow SBI's customers to access various banking services via these social platforms?
1. SBI mingle 2. SBI Oracle 3. SBI In touch
4. SBI ConnectU 5. None of these

97. Who has been appointed as Executive Director of RBI? He will replace the NS Vishwanathan who was elevated as Deputy Governor of RBI.
1. Dr. Nachiket Mor 2. Prof Damodar Acharya 3. Dr Urjit Patel,
4. R Gandhi 5. Sudarshan Sen

98. The Union Cabinet has approved merger of country's largest lender State Bank of India (SBI) and its associate banks. Which of the following is not one of them?
1. State Bank of Saurashtra 2. State Bank of Bikaner and Jaipur.
3. State Bank of Hyderabad 4. State Bank of Travancore
5. None of these.

99. A five member committee has been setup to review the working of Fiscal Responsibility and Budget Management Act (FRBM Act) over the last 12 years. Who is the Chairman of this committee?
1. Rathin Roy 2. Sumit Bose 3. Urjit Patel 4. Arvind Subramanian
5. N.K Singh

100. Consider the following pairs:-

Author	Book
1. Han Kang	The Vegetarian
2. ChetanBhagat	Making India Awesome
3. Yashwant Singh	One life is not enough
4. Dalai Lama	Beyond Religion: Ethics for a whole world
5. N. Narayana	A better India: A betterMurthy World

Which one of the above pair is incorrectly matched?

101. The World Economic Forum (WEF) is the International Organization for Public-Private Cooperation, committed to improving the state of the world. Recently the annual meeting of WEF was recently held at -
1. Paris, France 2. Milan, Italy
3. Davos, Switzerland 4. Beijing, China
5. Berlin, Germany

102. Consider the following pairs:-

Capital	Currency
1. Argentina	Peso
2. Maldives	Rufiyaa
3. South Africa	Rand

4. Myanmar Baht
5. Vietnam Dong

Which one of the above pair is incorrectly matched?

103. In order to further strengthen the lenders' ability to deal with stressed assets and to put real assets back on track, the Reserve Bank of India has introduced 'S4A' Scheme. What does S4A stands for?
1. Scheme for Susceptible Structuring of Stressed Assets
2. Scheme for Sensible Structuring of Stressed Assets
3. Scheme for Suitable Structuring of Stressed Assets
4. Scheme for Sustainable Structuring of Stressed Assets
5. None of these

104. SK Roy, who recently resigned, was the chairman of which of the following government-owned corporation?
1. Bharat Sanchar Nigam Limited.
2. Insurance Regulatory and Development Authority.
3. Securities and Exchange Board of India.
4. Telecom Regulatory Authority of India.
5. Life Insurance Corporation of India.

105. Which of the following country observes its Independence Day on 04 July?
1. France 2. Brazil 3. United States of America 4. Sri Lanka
5. Canada

106. Which of the following Indian Bank is related to Small Industries?
1. IDBI 2. NABARD 3. ICICI 4. Gramin Bank 5. None of these

107. Words Bull and Bear is related to which trade area?
1. Foreign Trade 2. Banking 3. Share Market
4. Heavy Industries 5. None of these

108. Which of the following Tax Structures is followed by Indian Economy?
1. Degressive 2. Progressive 3. Proportionate 4. Regressive 5. None of these

109. Recently the president of World Bank Jim Yong Kim visited India. World Bank has decided to lend 1 billion dollar for the development of which of the following sector?
1. Solar projects 2. Make in India
3. Skill development 4. Women empowerment 5. None of these

110. In India during the British Rule the first census (1872) held in tenure of which of the following viceroy?
1. Lord Litton 2. Lord Rippon 3. Lord Mayo 4. Lord Duffrin 5. None of these

111. Which of the following condition shows the state of oligopoly?
1. A few seller, many buyers 2. Many sellers, many buyers
3. A few seller, one buyer 4. A few sellers, a few buyers
5. None of these

112. Consider the following statements regarding India:-
A. It shares the longest International boundary with China.

B. It is the sixth largest country in the world.
C. The nearest country with which India does not share a boundary is Maldives.
Which of the above statements is/are correct?
1. Only A is correct
2. Only B is correct
3. Only C is correct
4. All are correct
5. All are incorrect

113. A five member committee was set up for drafting a new education policy for the country. The committee has submitted its report in June 2016. The committee is headed by –
1. TSR Subramanian
2. P K Sinha
3. Justice RV Easwar
4. Justic MB Shah
5. Srikrishna committee

114. Union cabinet has given approval to the LIGO-India mega science proposal for research on gravitational waves. LIGO stands for:-
1. Laser Interferometer Gravitational wave Observation.
2. Laser Interference Gravitational wave Observation.
3. Laser Interferometer Gravitational wave Observatory.
4. Laser Interfererence Gravitational wavelength operation.
5. None of these

115. Which of the following Bank has won the IBA Banking Technology Award in the category of best Risk and Fraud Management Initiative?
1. Bank of India
2. Bank of Maharashtra
3. Karnataka Bank
4. Andhra Bank
5. Syndicate Bank

116. Which of the following is appointed as a new chairman of GST committee?
1. Amit Mitra 2. Sugata Bose 3. K M Mani 4. Arvind Mayaram
5. None of these

117. Consider the following pairs:-

	Tournament	Host Country
1.	2017 FIFA under-17 World Cup	India
2.	2018 FIFA World Cup	France
3.	2019 Cricket World cup	England and wales
4.	2020 Summer Olympics	Tokyo
5.	2018 Common Wealth Games	Gold Coast

Which of the above is incorrectly matched?

118. What will be the Impact of increase in C.R.R by Reserve Bank of India?
1. Reduction in government debt
2. Increase in bank credit capacity
3. Reduction in liquidity in the economy
4. Increase in the foreign investment
5. Flow of money in the market will increase

119. Which of the following country is not a member of South Asian Association for Regional Cooperation (SAARC)?
1. Afghanistan 2. Maldives 3. Bhutan 4. Bangladesh 5. None of these

120. Which of the following Foreign Bank working in India have the most number of branches?
1. City Bank 2. B.N.P Paribas 3. Standard Chartered Bank
4. H.S. B.C 5. Kukmin Bank

Section 4: ENGLISH LANGUAGE & COMPREHENSION

Directions (121–130) : Read the following passage carefully and answers the questions given below it. Certain words have been printed in bold to help you locate them while answering some of the questions.

It is difficult to imagine the **extraordinary** number of controls on Indian industry before 1991. Entrepreneurs needed permission to invest and could be penalized for exceeding production capacity. Even with the given investment capacity they had, entering certain areas was prohibited as these were reserved for the public sector. If they had to import anything, they required licenses. To get these licenses was tough, they had to persuade a bureaucrat that the item was required but even so permission was unavailable if somebody was already producing it in India. The impact of the reforms was not 'instantaneously and permanently wonderful'. In India's case, it began to show after about a year and a-half. After 1993, there came three years of rapid industrial growth of about 8% or so. But, in the second half of the 90s there was a tapering of industrial growth and investment. After 1997 and the East Asian crisis there was global slowdown which had an impact on the Indian industry. But, the last few years there has been a tremendous upturn. With the rise of investment industrial growth has reached double or close.

However even during the period when industrial growth was not that rapid, there is a lot of evidence that positive results of the reforms were seen. There were companies that didn't look at all internally but instead performed remarkably in the highly competitive global market. For instance, the software sector's performance was outstanding in an almost totally global market. Reliance built a world class refinery. Tats developed an indigenously designed car. The success of the software sector has created much higher expectations from and much high confidence in what Indian industry can do. On the Government's side it's a vindication that liberalization of both domestic and external policies, including the increased inflow of Foreign Direct Investment, has created an environment in which industry can do well, has done well and is preparing to do even better. What they need is not sops, but good quality infrastructure. For the 11th Plan an industrial growth rate of around 12% is **projected.** It will have methods of developing infrastructure, which will close the deficit. This can be done through increased investment in public sector for those infrastructure areas, which cannot **attract** private investment, and through efforts to improve private participation in different ways of public private participation.

In the early stages of reforms, the liberalization of trade policies and a shift to a market determined exchange rate had the effect of removing constraints on agriculture in terms of depressed prices. The removal of protection on industry helped to produce amore level playing field, because the earlier system was extremely unfair to agriculture. The lesson to be learnt from the reforms process is to **persevere** in reforming the strategic parts of the economy, which will lead to even higher growth rate. India has to do better than its current average growth rate of 8% and ensure that benefits from this higher growth go beyond industry and urban areas and extend to agriculture.

121. Which of the following was NOT a restriction on Indian industry prior to 1991?
(A) A private business needed government sanction to invest in any sector
(B) Industrial growth had to be maintained at a certain percentage fixed by the government.
(C) It was difficult to obtain licenses,
1. All A, B and C 2. Only B 3. Only C
4. Both A and C 5. None of these

122. How did software companies deal with slow industrial growth in an open Indian economy?
1. They focused on strengthening their position in the domestic market.
2. They campaigned for infrastructure development.
3. They diversified into different sectors.
4. They entered into partnerships with public sector enterprises in reserved sectors.
5. They targeted global markets.

123. Which of the following is NOT true in the context of the passage?
(A) India experienced a slowdown in growth during the late 1990s because initially the economic growth rate was too rapid.
(B) There were a few stringent regulations on Indian industries which kept economic growth below 12%
(C) Companies did not get import licenses for goods if they were being indigenously produced,
1. Only A 2. Both B and C 3. Both A and B
4. All A, B and C 5. None of these

124. Why was investment by private businesses disallowed in certain sectors?
1. To ensure proper development in these sectors
2. To prevent corruption in key sectors like infrastructure
3. To ensure steady not inconsistent growth in key sectors
4. To protect the interests of the public sector in these sectors
5. None of these

125. What was the impact of the flourishing Indian software sector?
1. Other companies were unable to be competitive in the global market
2. It fuelled expectations of a good performance from the Indian economy.
3. Growth rate rose to 12%.
4. It created cut throat competition among software companies which would hinder the sector in the long run.
5. None of these

126. Which of the following factors was responsible for the fall In India's growth rate in the late 1990s?
1. The implementation of economic reforms was too rapid.
2. It was expected after achieving & high growth rate of 10%.
3. There was a slowdown in the global economy.
4. There were sanctions against East Asian countries by WTO.
5. The software sector grew but the other sectors were neglected.

127. Which of the following can be said about the reforms of 1991?
1. They benefited Indian industry immediately

2. All Indian companies began to focus on indigenous development instead of looking for opportunities abroad.
3. They were targeted only at the software sector.
4. India was among the worst affected countries by the East Asian economic crisis because it had opened up its economy
5. They encouraged foreign direct Investment in India.

128. What does the author recommend to ensure that the industrial sector continues to perform better?
1. Subsidies should be provided in infrastructure development
2. Government should keep control of and monitor all infrastructure projects.
3. Wipe out any infrastructure deficit by transferring responsibility of those projects to the private sector
4. Ensure a combination of public and private sector involvement in developing infrastructure
5. None of these

129. What is the author's opinion about the government's decision to liberalise the economy in 1991?
1. It was beneficial because it created confidence in the Indian economy.
2. The timing was wrong since the economy experienced a slowdown in growth rate,
3. It led to a focus on software and other sectors were neglected
4. Foreign companies took advantage of the new policies and exploited certain sectors
5. None of these

130. How did the economic reforms affect the agriculture sector?
1. A system of market determined exchange rate was introduced.
2. Constraints in agriculture increased.
3. Prices were depressed because there was a removal of protection of the sector.
4. Agriculture growth rate doubled.
5. The agriculture sector was not a part of the reforms process.

Directions (131–135): In each of the following sentences, there are two blank spaces. Below each sentence, there are five pairs of words denoted by letters 1., 2., 3., 4. and 5.. Find out which pair of words can be filled up in the blanks in the sentence in the same sequence to make the sentence meaningfully complete.

131. After having been friends for more than a decade, they had a________last year and have not ______each other ever since.
1. fight; talked
2. argument; met
3. dispute; seen
4. quarrel; admired
5. difference; introduced

132. The workers, several of ________ had complained about their low wages earlier have now_________ to move to the court for the labor rights.
1. who; indicated
2. who; decided
3. which; threatened
4. them; resolved
5. number; warned

133. The hutment dwellers were jubilant when the government __________ an apartment to each of them at __________ rates.
1. demolished; fast
2. announced; less
3. provided; high
4. acquired; low
5. promised; subsidized

134. The organization was deeply __________ by difficulties a decade ago, but the new CEO brought many __________ changes in it and took it to a new high.
1. indebted; necessary
2. plagued; vital
3. coping; more
4. hurt; critical
5. shaken; inevitable

135. The Prime Minister who is __________ in his holiday home at the moment said that he was very __________ by the news of India winning the World Cup.
1. visiting; happy
2. residing; obliged
3. intruding; dejected
4. staying; pleased
5. resting; cheerful

Directions (136–145): In the following passage, there are blanks, each of which has been numbered. Against each, five words are suggested, one of which fits the blank appropriately. Find out the appropriate word in each case.

Visual experience can **(136)** children, teenagers and even adults learn and absorb more due to its highly stimulating and **(137)** engaging impact. It is for this reason that we are seeing an increase in schools across the globe **(138)** content provider programmes into their class curriculum to **(139)** lessons through video. Visual excursions and school collaborations are **(140)** by advances in high-definition video, high-fidelity audio and content sharing, allowing students to experience a richer and more stimulating learning experience.

Schools that have previously transported students to excursions in **(141)**, now face increased transportation costs, higher insurance premiums, attendance costs for the families and strict duty of care policies for students while **(142)** school property. Virtual excursions **(143)** students to improve their presentation, research, learning and speaking skills while they engage in a live learning session. Students also now have the ability to meet peers from many cultures, speak to subject-matter **(144)** like scientists or authors, practise a foreign language with students from another country, and learn about global issues from the **(145)** of their own classrooms.

136.
1. help 2. aiding 3. prescribe 4. feature 5. present

137.
1. plus 2. lonely 3. ably 4. many 5. deeply

138.
1. incorporating 2. pressing 3. following 4. parting 5. leaving

139.
1. make 2. demand 3. impart 4. vision 5. need

140.
1. dissolved 2. enhanced 3. measured 4. failed 5. blasted

141.
1. deed 2. total 3. parent 4. person 5. lieu

142.
1. involving 2. saving 3. away 4. off 5. vacating

143.
1. let 2. enable 3. present 4. pressure 5. collect

144.
1. clauses 2. dictionaries 3. books 4. experts 5. partners

145.
1. vacancy 2. availability 3. safety 4. comfortable 5. gap

Directions (146–150): Rearrange the following six sentences (A), (B), (C), (D) and (E) in the proper sequence to form a meaningful paragraph; then answer the questions given below them.

(A) The central ammunition depot at Pulgaon is one India's biggest ammunition depot.
(B) This has led to an extraordinary number of deaths and injuries to army personnel.
(C) A massive fire broke out at the Central Ammunition Depot (CAD), Pulgaon, in Maharashtra.
(D) It was for the first time in the history of this depot that such fatalities has occurred.
(E) It recently got an award for using solar energy for disposing expired ammunition.

146. Which of the following should be the **LAST** sentence after rearrangement?
1. A 2. B 3. C 4. D 5. E

147. Which of the following should be the **FOURTH** sentence after rearrangement?
1. F 2. A 3. C 4. E 5. D

148. Which of the following should be the **FIRST** sentence after rearrangement?
1. E 2. F 3. A 4. C 5. D

149. Which of the following should be the **THIRD** sentence after rearrangement?
1. B 2. C 3. E 4. A 5. F

150. Which of the following should be the **SECOND** sentence after rearrangement?
1. C 2. B 3. D 4. E 5. A

Direction (151–155): Read each sentence to find out whether there is any grammatical or idiomatic error in it The error, if any, will be in one part of the sentence. The number of that part is the answer. If there is 'No error', the answer is 5.. (Ignore errors of punctuation, if any.)

151. 1. Australia has won / 2. the 2016 Men's Champions Trophy / 3. title of Hockey / 4. defeating India at London. / 5. No error

152. 1. The was second Copa America title / 2. won by Chile after winning / 3. for the first time in 2015 / 4. by defeating Argentina. / 5. No error

153. 1. One of the most respected journalist / 2. of the country, / 3. Malhotra had worked with The Statesman / 4. and The Times of India, New Delhi. / 5. No error

154. 1. Syed Nayeemuddin will be honour with / 2. the MohunBaganRatna 2016 for his / 3. overall contribution / 4. both as a football player and a coach. / 5. No error

155. 1. The PEN Pinter Prize is an annual literary award / 2. given to a British writer / 3. or a writer residence in Britain / 4. of outstanding literary merit. / 5. No error

ANSWER KEY

1. 4	2. 1	3. 3	4. 2	5. 1	6. 3	7. 4	8. 4	9. 1	10. 2
11. 4	12. 2	13. 1	14. 3	15. 1	16. 3	17. 4	18. 4	19. 3	20. 1
21. 1	22. 5	23. 3	24. 3	25. 4	26. 2	27. 5	28. 2	29. 4	30. 1
31. 2	32. 2	33. 2	34. 2	35. 4	36. 3	37. 3	38. 3	39. 4	40. 1
41. 2	42. 3	43. 3	44. 3	45. 3	46. 4	47. 4	48. 1	49. 1	50. 1
51. 2	52. 4	53. 3	54. 2	55. 2	56. 2	57. 3	58. 1	59. 4	60. 2
61. 2	62. 5	63. 1	64. 3	65. 4	66. 1	67. 5	68. 4	69. 2	70. 1
71. 3	72. 2	73. 1	74. 4	75. 5	76. 2	77. 3	78. 2	79. 1	80. 5
81. 1	82. 5	83. 3	84. 3	85. 1	86. 2	87. 5	88. 1	89. 1	90. 5
91. 2	92. 2	93. 3	94. 2	95. 1	96. 1	97. 5	98. 1	99. 5	100. 3
101. 3	102. 4	103. 4	104. 5	105. 3	106. 5	107. 3	108. 1	109. 1	110. 3
111. 1	112. 5	113. 1	114. 3	115. 3	116. 1	117. 2	118. 3	119. 5	120. 3
121. 2	122. 2	123. 1	124. 4	125. 2	126. 3	127. 5	128. 4	129. 1	130. 1
131. 3	132. 4	133. 5	134. 2	135. 4	136. 1	137. 5	138. 1	139. 5	140. 2
141. 4	142. 5	143. 2	144. 4	145. 3	146. 4	147. 4	148. 4	149. 4	150. 2
151. 2	152. 2	153. 1	154. 1	155. 3					

Reasoning and Computer Aptitude

(1–6) :

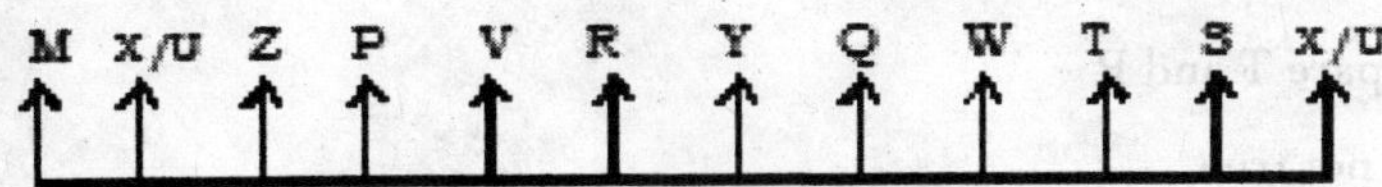

1. (4) 2. (1) 3. (3)

4. (2)

5. (1) Third to the right of eight from the right end = (8 – 3 =) 5th from the right end, ie Q.

6. (3)

(7–11) :

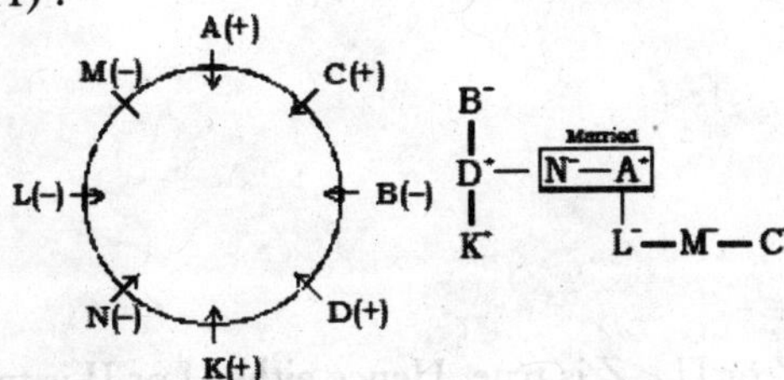

7. (4) 8. (4) 9. (1)

10. (2) 11. (4)

(12–14) :

E > B > D > A > F > C

B ↓ 280, F ↓ 190

12. (2) 60% of 500 = 300

Hence the possible marks 300 was obtained by E.

13. (1) 14. (3)

15. (1) **Given statements:**

$Q < L = P \leq W < V \leq N = M \leq R$

Now, $Q < V$ is true. Hence I is true.

$P \leq Z < V \leq N = M$

Again, $P < M$ is true. Hence II ($P > M$) is not true

16. (3) **Given statements:**

$T \geq U = B < S$ ...(i)

$U \le P < X$ ...(ii)

From (i) and (ii), we get

$T \ge U = B \le P < X$

Thus, we can't compare T and P.

Hence II ($T \ge P$) is not true.

Again, $B < X$ or $X > B$ is true.

Hence I is true

17. (4) **Given statements:**

$R < Z \ge A \ge U \le P = T < O$

Thus, we can't compare R and P. Hence neither I ($R > P$) nor II ($P \le R$) is true.

18. (4) **Given statements:**

$A \ge U \le P = T < O$ ...(i)

$P \le Z > R$ ...(ii)

Combings (i) and (ii), we have

$A \ge U \le P \le Z > R$

Thus, $U \le Z$ is true. It means either $U = Z$ or $U < Z$ is true. Hence either I or II is true.

19. (3) **Given statements:**

$P \ge Q \le R < T$ ...(i)

$Q > S = M$ ...(ii)

Combining (i) and (ii), we get

$T > R \ge Q > S = M$

Thus, $R > M$ is true. Hence I ($M \ge R$) is not true.

Again, $T > M$ or $M < T$ is true. Hence II is true.

20. (1)
21. (1) We can't infer any specifics.
22. (5) All of these will be effects.
23. (3) From statements I,

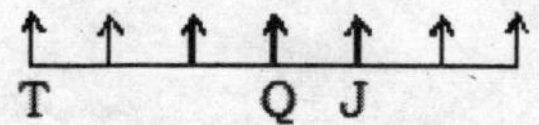

24. (3) From statements I,

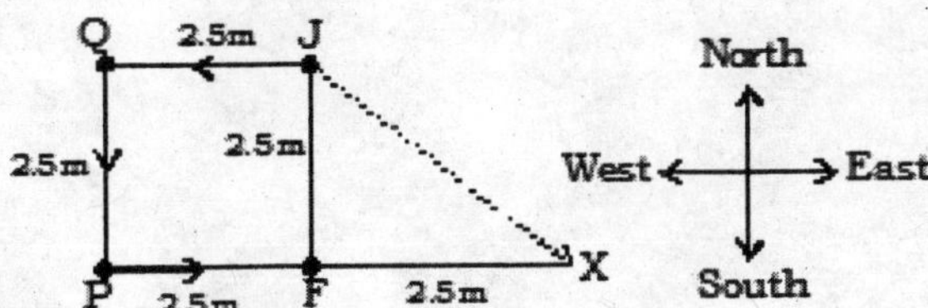

25. (4)

26. (2)

27. (5)

28. (2) Twelfth to the left of the twenty second from the left end is (22–12=) 10th from the left, i.e @.

29. (4)

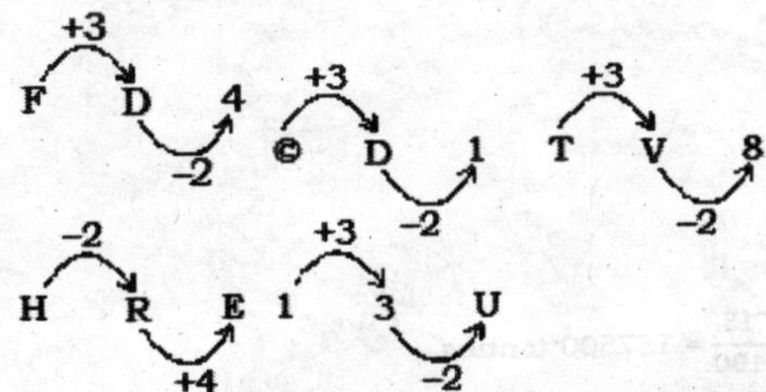

30. (1) New arrangement becomes:

F % D A I B @ R H E * N $ U W P T 9 V # Z Q.

Hence sixteenth from the right end is @.

31. (2) | Symbol | Consonant | Vowel | i.e % DA

32. (2) | Vowel | Symbol | Letter | i.e, AI, E * N,

(33–38):

W Y Z X V T U

↑ ↑ ↑ ↑ ↑ ↑ ↑ Facing north

33. 2

34. 2

35. 4

36. 3

37. 3

38. 3

39. 4

40. 1

41. 2

42. 3

43. 3

44. 3

45. 3

Data Analysis and Interpretation

46. (4) Total production of all products in 2009

$= (150 + 250 + 300 + 350) \times 1000$

$= 1050000$ tonnes

∴ Amount used in PDS supply

$= 1050000 \times \frac{20}{100} = 210000$ tonnes

∴ Amount used in Exports = $1050000 \times \frac{15}{100} = 157500$ tonnes

∴ Reqd difference = $(210000 - 15750)$

$= 52500$ tonnes

47. (4) Production of pulses during six years

$= (150 + 50 + 200 + 150 + 250 + 350) \times$

$1000 = 1150000$ tonnes

Production of Wheat during six years

$= (250 + 150 + 400 + 100 + 150 + 300) \times 1000 = 1350000$ tonnes

∴ Reqd ratio = 1150000 : 1350000

= 115 : 135 = 23 : 27

48. (1) Total production in 2005 = $(150 + 200 + 250 + 300) \times 1000 = 900000$ tonnes

Total production in 2006 = $(50 + 150 + 250 + 350) \times 1000 = 800000$ tonnes

Total production in 2007 = $(100 + 200 + 300 + 400) \times 1000 = 1000000$ tonnes

Total production in 2008 = $(100 + 150 + 200 + 350) \times 1000 = 800000$ tonnes

Total production in 2009 = $(150 + 250 + 300 + 350) \times 1000 = 1050000$ tonnes

Total production in 2010 = $(250 + 300 + 350 + 400) \times 1000 = 1300000$ tonnes

∴ In year 2006 and 2008 the production is the minimum.

49. (1) Quantity of exports in 2005

$= 900000 \times \frac{40}{100} = 360000$ tonnes

Quantity of exports in 2006

$= 800000 \times \frac{20}{100} = 160000$ tonnes

Quantity of exports in 2007

$= 1000000 \times \frac{25}{100} = 250000$ tonnes

Quantity of exports in 2008

$= 800000 \times \frac{30}{100} = 240000$ tonnes

Quantity of exports in 2009

$= 1050000 \times \frac{15}{100} = 157500$ tonnes

Quantity of exports is maximum in the year 2005.

50. (1) Quantity of PDS supply in 2005

$= 900000 \times \frac{12}{100} = 108000$ tonnes

Quantity of PDS supply in 2006

$= 800000 \times \frac{18}{100} = 144000$ tonnes

Quantity of PDS supply in 2008

$= 800000 \times \frac{14}{100} = 112000$ tonnes

Quantity of PDS supply in 2009

$= 1050000 \times \frac{20}{100} = 210000$ tonnes

Quantity of PDS supply in 2010

$= 1300000 \times \frac{22}{100} = 286000$ tonnes

In 2005, the quantity of PDS supply is the minimum.

51. (2) Total number of graduate employees working in Department

$A = 8000 \times \frac{12.5}{100} \times \frac{27}{100} = 270$

52. (4) Total number of non - graduate employees

$= \frac{8000}{100 \times 100}\{12.5 \times 73 + 16 \times 55 + 22 \times 67.5 + 18.5 \times 45 + 14 \times 65 + 17 \times 52.5\}$

$= 0.8\{912.5 + 880 + 1485 + 832.5 + 910 + 892.5\} = 0.8 \times 5912.5 = 4730$

53. (3) Total number of graduate employees working in Department E

$= 8000 \times \frac{14}{100} \times \frac{35}{100} = 392$

Required% $= \frac{392}{8000} \times 100 = 4.9\%$

54. (2) Total number of graduate employees working in Department D

$= 8000 \times \frac{18.5}{100} \times \frac{55}{100} = 814$

Total number of non - graduate employees working in Department D

$= 8000 \times \frac{18.5}{100} \times \frac{45}{100} = 666$

Required % $= \frac{814 - 666}{666} \times 100$

$= \frac{14800}{666} = 22.22\% \approx 22\%$ more

55. (2) Total number of non - graduate employees = 4730 (see explanation no. 52)

Total number of graduate employees

$= 8000 - 4730 = 3270$

Required average $= \frac{3270}{6} = 545$

56. (2) Total marks of Priti

$= \frac{150 \times 66}{100} + 75 + \frac{150 \times 88}{100} + \frac{56 \times 125}{100} + \frac{56 \times 75}{100} + 45$

$= 99 + 75 + 132 + 70 + 42 + 45 = 463$

57. (3) Marks obtained by Ashu in Brand Management = 88% of 100 = 88

Marks obtained by Lucky in Brand Management = 76% of 100 = 76

Required % $= \frac{88}{76} \times 100 = 115.78 \approx 115.79\%$

58. (1) Average marks obtained by all the students together in Compensation Management

$\left(\frac{88 + 84 + 78 + 96 + 68 + 50}{6 \times 100} \times 150\right) \quad \frac{464}{600} \times 150 = 116$

59. (4) Total marks obtained in all the subjects together by

Monika: 76% of 150 + 66% of 100 + 78% of 150 + 88% of 125 + 72% of 75 + 70% of 50

$$= \frac{76 \times 150}{100} + \frac{66 \times 100}{100} + \frac{78 \times 150}{100} + \frac{88 \times 125}{100} + \frac{72 \times 75}{100} + \frac{70 \times 50}{100}$$

= 114 + 66 +117 + 110 + 54 + 35 = 496

Lucky: 82% of 150 + 76% of 100 + 84% of 150 + 96% of 125 + 92% of 75 + 88% of 50

$$\frac{82 \times 150}{100} + \frac{76 \times 100}{100} + \frac{84 \times 150}{100} + \frac{96 \times 125}{100} + + \frac{88 \times 50}{100}$$

= 123 + 76 + 126 + 120 + 69 + 44 = 558

Ashu: 90% of 150 + 88% of 100 + 96% of 150 + 76% of 125 + 84% of 75 + 86% of 50

$$= \frac{90 \times 150}{100} + \frac{88 \times 100}{100} + \frac{96 \times 150}{100} + \frac{76 \times 125}{100} + \frac{84 \times 75}{100} + \frac{86 \times 50}{100}$$

= 135 + 88 + 144 + 95 + 63 + 43 = 568

Javed: 64% of 150 + 70% of 100 + 68% of 150 + 72% of 125 + 68% of 75 + 74% of 50

$$= \frac{64 \times 150}{100} + \frac{70 \times 100}{100} + \frac{68 \times 150}{100} + \frac{72 \times 125}{100} + \frac{68 \times 75}{100} + \frac{74 \times 50}{100}$$

= 96 + 70 + 102 + 90 + 51 + 37 = 446

Saiyad: 48% of 150 + 56% of 100 + 50% of 150 + 64% of 125 + 64% of 75 + 58% of 50

$$= \frac{48 \times 150}{100} + \frac{56 \times 100}{100} + \frac{50 \times 150}{100} + \frac{64 \times 125}{100} + \frac{64 \times 75}{100} + \frac{58 \times 50}{100}$$

= 72 + 56 + 75 + 80 + 48 + 29 = 360

Clearly, Ashu scored the highest total marks in all the subjects together.

60. (2) Lucky (Consumer behaviour and services marketing) and Ashu (Strategic management, brand management and compensation management).

61. Ratio = 560 : 420
= 4:3

62. Difference = 92 – 54 = 38

63. Percent increase $= \frac{70}{350} \times 100$
= 20

64. Average number $= \frac{624}{6} = 104$

65. Percent $= \frac{85}{126} \times 100 = 67$ (approx)

66. (1)

∴ Total illiterate population

= 2400000 – (720000 + 600000) = 1080000

= 10.8 lakh

67. (5)

68. (4) Total population of E

$= 1.5 \times \frac{20}{100} = 0.30$ crore = 30 lakh

Total literate males of E

$= 40 \times \frac{19}{100} = 7.6$ lakh

Total literate females of E

$= 25 \times \frac{20}{100} = 5$ lakh

∴ Total literate of E = 7.6 + 5 = 12.6 lakh

∴ Required % $= \frac{12.6}{30} \times 100 = 42\%$

69. (2) Total population of C $= 1.5 \times \frac{21}{100}$

= 0.315 crore = 31.5 lakh

Literate males of C $= 40 \times \frac{20}{100} = 8$ lakh

Literate females of C $= 25 \times \frac{12}{100} = 3$ lakh

∴ Total literate of C = 8 + 3 = 11 lakh

∴ Total illiterate of C = 31.5 – 11

= 20.5 lakh

∴ Required difference = 20.5 – 11 = 9.5 lakh

70. (1) Literate males of D = $40 \times \frac{16}{100} = 6.4$ lakh

Literate females of D = $25 \times \frac{16}{100} = 4$ lakh

Required % = $\frac{(6.4 - 4)}{4} \times 100 = 60\%$

71. (3) Required ratio = $\frac{3}{4} \times 2.27 : \frac{3}{10} \times 1.25$
= 1.7025 : 0.375 = 227 : 50

72. (2) Required percentage

$= \frac{1.08}{3.14} \times 100 = 34.39\% \approx 34\%$

73. (1) Total number of candidates appearing from all the cities together

= (1.25+3.14+1.08+2.27+1.85+2.73) lakhs

= 12.32 lakhs

Number of candidates pass from City F

$= \frac{7}{12} \times 2.73 = 1.5925$ lakh

Required percentage

$= \frac{1.5925}{12.32} \times 100 = 12.93$

74. (4)

75. (5) Number of passed students from City E

$= \left(\frac{3}{5} \times 1.85\right)$ lakhs = 1,11,000

76. (2) $\text{Total}_D = 2400000 \times \frac{20}{100} = 480000$

$\text{Male}_D = \frac{480000}{5} \times 2 = 192000$

77. (1) $\text{Total}_C = 2400000 \times \frac{16}{100} = 384000$

Non-adults = $384000 \times \frac{28}{100} = 107520$

78. (5)

79. (4) $\text{Total}_B = 2400000 \times \frac{18}{100} = 432000$

$\text{Male}_B = \frac{432000}{9} \times 5 = 240000$

$\text{Female}_B = 432000 - 240000 = 192000$

$\therefore$ Difference = 240000 – 192000 = 48000

80. (4) $\text{Adult}_E = \frac{75}{100} \times \left(2400000 \times \frac{10}{100}\right) = 180000$

$\text{Male}_D = \frac{2}{5} \times \left(2400000 \times \frac{20}{100}\right) = 192000$

$\therefore$ Requrired percentage = $\frac{180000}{192000} \times 100$

= 93.75%

English Language

146. (4)

147. (4)

148. (4)

149. (4)

150. (2)

151. (4) Add 'after' or 'by' before 'defeating'.

152. (2) Add 'it' after 'winning'.

153. (1) Replace 'journalist' by 'Journalists'.

154. (1) Replace 'honour with' by 'honoured with'.

155. (3) Replace 'residence' with 'resident'.

SBI PO Mains MOCK Test Paper 3

Structure of this MOCK Test

S. No.	Name of section	No. of Questions	Total marks	Allotted Time
1	Reasoning and Computer Aptitude	45	60	60 minutes
2	Data Analysis and Interpretation	35	60	45 minutes
3	General/ Economy/ Banking Awareness	40	40	35 minutes
4	English Language	35	40	40 minutes
Total		155	200	3 hours

- There is 1/4th Negative marking for every wrong answer.
- If a question is left blank, i.e. no answer is marked by the candidate, there will be no penalty for that question.

Section 1: Reasoning and Computer Aptitude

Directions (1–5): In these questions relationship between different elements is shown in these statements are followed by two conclusions.

Answer-

1. If only conclusion I is true.
2. If only conclusion II is true.
3. If either conclusion I or II is true.
4. If neither conclusion I nor II is true.
5. If both conclusions I and II are true.

In the following questions the symbols ©, $, %, @ and # are used with the following meaning as illustrated below.
'P @ Q' means 'P is neither greater than nor equal to Q'.
'P $ Q' means 'P is not smaller than Q'.'
P # Q' means 'P is neither smaller than nor greater than Q'.

'P © Q' means 'P is not greater than Q'.
'P % Q' means 'P is neither smaller than nor equal to Q'.

1. **Statements:** J # R, R % K, K @ D
   Conclusions: **(I)** K @ J **(II)** D @ J

2. **Statements:** M © T, K % T, K @ N
   Conclusions: **(I)** N % M **(II)** K % M

3. **Statements:** V $ D, D © R, R % F
   Conclusions: **(I)** R % V **(II)** V @ F

4. **Statements:** B @ E, E # S, S $ Z
   Conclusions: **(I)** Z @ E **(II)**E # Z

5. **Statements:** H % M, N © M, N $ T
   Conclusions: **(I)** H # T **(II)** H % T

Directions (6–10): Study the following information carefully and answer the questions given below.

A word and number arrangement machine when given an input line of words and numbers rearranges them following a particular rule in each step. The following is an illustration of input and various steps of rearrangement.

Input: 26 analytics 45 job104 paper 33 business 54 data

Step I: 104 26 analytics 45 job paper 33 business 54 data

Step II: 104 26 45 analytics job paper 33 business 54 data

Step III: 104 54 26 45 job paper 33 business data analytics

Step IV: 104 54 26 45 job paper 33 data analytics business

Step V: 104 54 45 26 job paper 33 data analytics business

Step VI: 104 54 45 26 job paper 33 analytics business data

Step VII: 104 54 45 33 26 job paper analytics business data

Step VIII: 104 54 45 33 26 paper analytics business data job

Step IX: 104 54 45 33 26 analytics business data job paper

And step IX is the last step of the rearrangement as the desired arrangement is obtained. As per rules followed in the above steps, find out in each of the questions the appropriate step for the given input.

Input for the questions:
Class 16 work 5 race 63 hard 54 join 79 take 21

6. What is the position of 'work' in the Step VII?
   1. Seventh from the left end 2. Eighth from the right end

3. Fifth from the left end
4. Fifth from the right end
5. Sixth from the left end

7. Which of the following is the ninth from the right in step VI?
1. race 2. 16 3. work 4. 54 5. 5

8. What is the position of '5' in the step IX?
1. Seventh from the left end
2. Eighth from the left end
3. Fifth from the right end
4. Seventh from the right end
5. Eighth from the right end

9. How many steps are required to complete this arrangement?
1. 26 2. 12 3. 10 4. 9 5. None of these

10. Which of the following represents the step X?
1. 79 63 54 21 16 work5 race take class hardjoin
2. 79 63 54 21 16 5 class hardjoin race take work
3. 79 63 54 21 16 5 work class hard join race take
4. 79 63 54 21 16 5work take class hardjoin race
5. There is no such step

Passage:

Below in each questions are given two statements **(A)** and **(B)**. These statements may be either independent causes or may be effects of independent causes or a common cause. One of these statements may be the effect of the other statement. Read both the statements and decide which of the following answer choice correctly depicts the relationship between these two statements.

11. A. The Lakme range of lipsticks is very costly, compared to other lipsticks of about the same quality.

B. The Lakme range has not been able to penetrate much of the market.
1. statement (A) is the cause and statement (B) is its effect.
2. statement (B) is the cause and statement (A) is its effect.
3. both the statements (A) and (B) are independent causes.
4. both the statements (A) and (B) are effects of independent causes.
5. both the statements (A) and (B) are effects of some common cause.

12. A. Kalyan Yadav has been expelled from the Bhartiya Kisan Dal.

B. Kalyan Yadav was the founder member of Bhartiya Kisan Dal.
1. statement (A) is the cause and statement (B) is its effect.
2. statement (B) is the cause and statement (A) is its effect.
3. both the statements (A) and (B) are independent causes.
4. both the statements (A) and (B) are effects of independent causes.
5. both the statements (A) and (B) are effects of some common cause.

13. A. Bolt has been awarded the Linkan award for excellence in sports

B. Bolt is a very dedicated player.
1. statement (A) is the cause and statement (B) is its effect.
2. statement (B) is the cause and statement (A) is its effect.

3. both the statements (A) and (B) are independent causes.
4. both the statements (A) and (B) are effects of independent causes.
5. both the statements (A) and (B) are effects of some common cause.

14. A. Ramesh succeeded

B. Ramesh worked hard.
1. Statement (A) is the cause and statement (B) is its effect.
2. Statement (B) is the cause and statement (A) is its effect.
3. both the statements (A) and (B) are independent causes.
4. both the statements (A) and (B) are effects of independent causes.
5. both the statements (A) and (B) are effects of some common cause.

15. A. Madan has failed in annual examination

B. Madan did not buy books of MEPL Publication.
1. statement (A) is the cause and statement (B) is its effect.
2. statement (B) is the cause and statement (A) is its effect.
3. both the statements (A) and (B) are independent causes.
4. both the statements (A) and (B) are effects of independent causes.
5. both the statements (A) and (B) are effects of some common cause.

In each question below is given a statement followed by two assumptions numbered I and II. An Assumption is something supposed or taken for granted. You have to consider statement and the following assumption and decide which of the assumptions is implicit in the statement. Give Answer:-

16. **Statement:** The head of the organization congratulated the entire staff in his speech for their sincere effort to bring down the deficit and urged them to give their best for attaining a more profitable position in future.

Assumptions:

I. The employees may get motivated and maintain and if possible enhance their present level of work.

II. The employees may now relax and slow down in their day-to-day work as there is no immediate threat of huge deficit.
1. If only assumption I is implicit.
2. If only assumption II is implicit.
3. If either assumption I or II is implicit.
4. If neither assumption I nor II is implicit.
5. If both assumption I and II are implicit.

17. **Statement:** The head of the organization has decided to reward those employees who will help reducing expenditure substantially by suggesting innovative techniques.

Assumptions:

I. The employees may be able to come out with innovative ideas.

II. The employees may be encouraged to apply their mind to earn the reward.
1. If only assumption I is implicit. 2. If only assumption II is implicit.

3. If either assumption I or II is implicit.
4. If neither assumption I nor II is implicit.
5. If both assumption I and II are implicit.

18. **Statement:** The regulatory authority has set up a review committee to find out the reasons for unstable stock prices.

Assumptions:

I. The investors may regain confidence in stock market by this decision.

II. The review committee has the expertise to find out the causes for volatility in the stock market.

1. If only assumption I is implicit.
2. If only assumption II is implicit.
3. If either assumption I or II is implicit.
4. If neither assumption I nor II is implicit.
5. If both assumption I and II are implicit.

19. **Statement:** The government has set up a fact-finding mission to look into the possible reasons for the recent violence in the area.

Assumptions:

I. The mission may be able to come up with credible information about the incidents.

II. The people in the area may cooperate with the mission and come forward to give detailed information related to the incidents.

1. If only assumption I is implicit.
2. If only assumption II is implicit.
3. If either assumption I or II is implicit.
4. If neither assumption I nor II is implicit.
5. If both assumption I and II are implicit.

20. **Statement:** Without reforming the entire administrative system, we cannot eradicate corruption and prejudice from the society.

Assumption:

I. The existence of corruption and prejudice is good.

II. There is enough flexibility to change the administrative system.

1. If only assumption I is implicit.
2. If only assumption II is implicit.
3. If either assumption I or II is implicit.
4. If neither assumption I nor II is implicit.
5. If both assumption I and II are implicit.

Read the following information carefully and answer the question s given below-

Six members Daud, Dhawan, Dayal, Damini, Dharemendra and Dhruv of a family are going to Nainital by train. Dayal is the son of Damini but Damini is not mother of Dayal. Dharemendra is the daughter of Dhawan. Dhruv is the brother of Dayal. Dhawan and Damini are a married couple. Daud is the brother of Damini.

21. Which of following is pair of females?
    1. Dayal and Dharemendra
    2. Dhruv and Dharemendra
    3. Dhawan and Dharemendra
    4. Dhawan and Daud
    5. None of these

22. How is Daud related to Dharemendra?
    1. Father
    2. Brother
    3. Uncle
    4. Cousin
    5. None of these

23. Who is the wife of Daud?
    1. Dhawan
    2. Dhruv
    3. Dayal
    4. Data Inadequate
    5. None of these

24. Who represents Lakme and Peter England brands?
    1. Sarah
    2. Megha
    3. Nicole
    4. Bruna
    5. Both 1 and 3

25. Who represents Lakme, Bebe and Peter England brands?
    1. Megha
    2. Nicole
    3. Sayali
    4. Sarah
    5. None of these

26. How many meaningful English words can be made with the letters D, R, A and O using each letter only once in each word?
    1. None
    2. One
    3. Two
    4. Three
    5. More than three

27. The position of how many digits in the number **'9820384167321'** will remain unchanged after the digits are rearranged in ascending order within the number?
    1. None
    2. One
    3. Two
    4. Three
    5. More than three

28. Four of the following five are alike in a certain way and so form a group. Which is the one that does not belong to that group?
    1. Cake
    2. Biscuit
    3. Bread
    4. Pastry
    5. Sweet

29. How many such pairs of letters are there in the word **'INTERNATIONALGOLD'** each of which has as many letters between them in the word as they have between them in the English alphabet?
    1. Six
    2. Seven
    3. Eight
    4. Nine
    5. None of these

30. The position of the first and the sixth digits in the number **'9812736524'** are interchanged, similarly the positions of the second and the seventh digits are inter-changed and so on then which of the following will be the seventh digit from the right end after the rearrangement?
    1. 5
    2. 4
    3. 2
    4. 9
    5. None of these

31. Most of the data base management systems, make use of which of the following:
    1. MS excel
    2. unix
    3. Java
    4. C++
    5. C

32. In a distributed controlled network, the different topologies are-
    1. ring and bus
    2. ring and star
    3. tree and bus
    4. tree and loop
    5. ring and loop

33. When an ATM is not connected to bank's data base, it is called-
    1. online
    2. offline
    3. standalone
    4. networked
    5. None of these

34. Start and stop bits are used in serial communication for
1. error detection
2. error correction
3. synchronization
4. slowing down the communication
5. None of these

35. Bit stuffing refers to
1. inserting a '0' in user data stream to differentiate it with a flag
2. inserting a'0' in flag stream to avoid ambiguity
3. Appending a nibble to the flag sequence
4. Appending a nibble to the user data stream
5. None of these

36. The method of network routing where every possible path between transmitting and receiving DTE is used is called-
1. random routing
2. packet flooding
3. directory routing
4. message switching
5. none of these

37. Which one of the following network uses dynamic or adaptive routing?
1. TYMNET
2. ARPANET
3. SNA (IBM's System Network Architecture)
4. TYMNET
5. None of these

38. Virtual memory is –
1. an extremely large main memory
2. an extremely large secondary memory
3. an illusion of an extremely large memory
4. a type of memory used in super computers
5. none of these

39. Page fault occurs when
1. the page is corrupted by application software
2. the page is in main memory
3. the page is not in main memory
4. one tries to divide a number by 0
5. none of these

40. The page replacement policy that sometimes leads to more page faults when the size of the memory is increased is
1. FIFO
2. LRU
3. LIFO
4. no such policy exists
5. None of these

41. Dijkstra's banking algorithm in an operating system solves the problem of
1. deadlock avoidance
2. deadlock recovery
3. mutual exclusion
4. context switching
5. None of these

42. In paged memory systems, if the page size is increased, then the internal fragmentation generally
    1. becomes less
    2. becomes more
    3. remains constant
    4. sometimes becomes less, sometimes more
    5. None of these

43. Which of the following is not a part of document management system?
    1. Word processing
    2. Desktop Publishing
    3. Spreadsheet
    4. PDA
    5. None of these

44. In field of computers DCL stands for
    1. Data Control Language
    2. Dynamic Control Language
    3. Data Complex Language
    4. Dynamic Complex Language
    5. none of these

45. Firewalls are used to protect against ________
    1. Unauthorized Attacks
    2. Virus Attacks
    3. Data driven Attacks
    4. Fire Attacks
    5. None of these

Section 2: Data Analysis & Interpretation

Directions (46–50): Study the given bar graph carefully to answer the questions. Time taken to travel (in hours) by five vehicles on Monday and Tuesday.

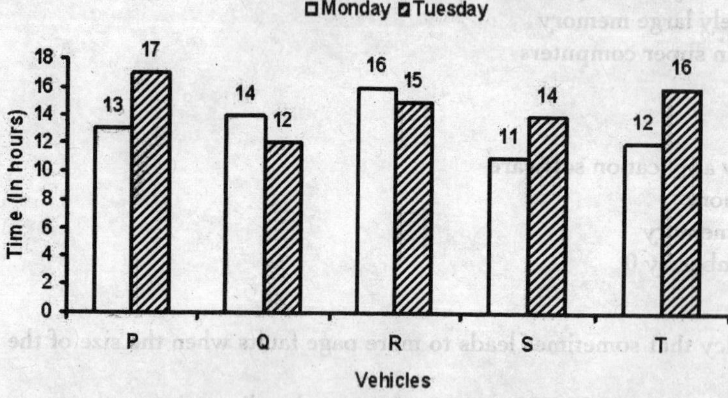

Distance covered (in kilometres) by five vehicles on each day.

Vehicle	Monday	Tuesday
P	624	782
Q	728	672
R	896	870
S	484	840
T	696	832

46. What is the ratio of the speeds of vehicle R and vehicle T on Monday ?
1. 28 : 31 2. 27 : 29 3. 28 : 29 4. 28 : 27 5. None of these

47. Which vehicle has the maximum speed on Tuesday ?
1. Vehicle P 2. Vehicle Q 3. Vehicle R 4. Vehicle S 5. Vehicle T

48. What is the average speed on Monday ?
1. 48 km/hr 2. 72 km/hr 3. 45 km/hr 4. 51.6 km/hr 5. None of these

49. What was the sum of the speed of vehicle S on Tuesday and speed of vehicle Q on the same day?
1. 112 km/hr. 2. 116 km/hr. 3. 124 km/hr. 4. 120 km/hr. 5. None of these

50. If the expenditure on fuel of per kilometer is Rs. 2.50 on Monday and Rs. 3.25 on Tuesday then what is the total expenditure on fuel ?
1. Rs. 19850 2. Rs. 20250 3. Rs. 21557 4. Rs. 21647 5. None of these

Passage:
Study the following graph carefully and answer accordingly. The following pie-chart shows the enrollment of students in different schools for the session of 2004-2005.Total enrollment in session 2004-2005 in school A5 = 6000

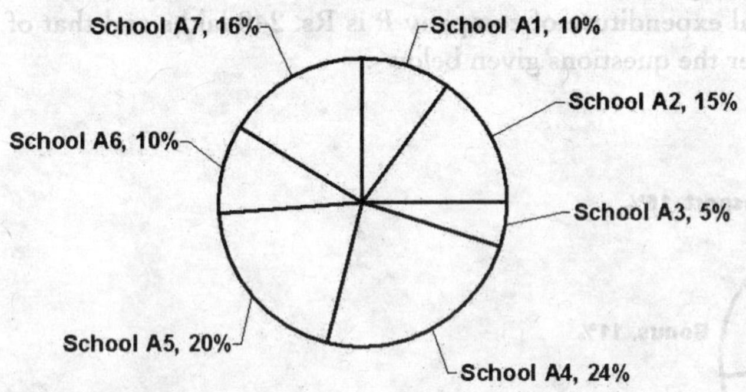

The following graph shows percentage of boys and girls enrollment in different schools for the session of 2004 - 2005

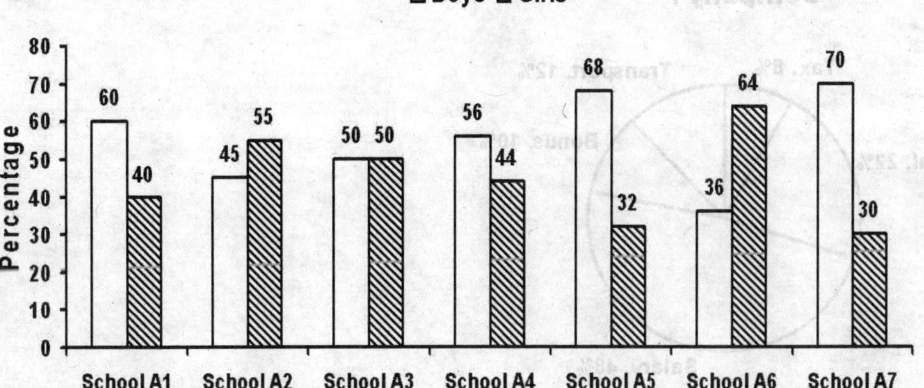

51. Find the difference between the number of boys of school A4 and the number of girls of school A6.
    1. 2212 2. 2412 3. 2240 4. 2112 5. None of these
52. If the fee of each student enrolled in school A3 is Rs. 850, the total collected fees in school A 3 is-
    1. Rs. 14.25 lakhs 2. Rs. 13.75 lakhs
    3. Rs. 12.25 lakhs 4. Rs. 12.75 lakhs
    5. None of these
53. In how many schools are the numberof boys less than that of girls?
    1. 4 2. 3 3. 2 4. None 5. None of these
54. What is the ratio of the number of boys of school A6 to the number of boys of school A3?
    1. 25 : 16 2. 23 : 25 3. 14 : 17 4. 36 : 25 5. None of these
55. The number of boys in school A4 is **approximately** what percent more than the number of girls in school A2?
    1. 48% 2. 52% 3. 50% 4. 63% 5. 75%

Passage:

The following pie-chart shows the percentage distribution of total expenditure of company P and company Q in the year 2011. If the total expenditure of company P is Rs. 240 lakhs and that of company Q is Rs. 400 lakhs, then answer the questions given below-.

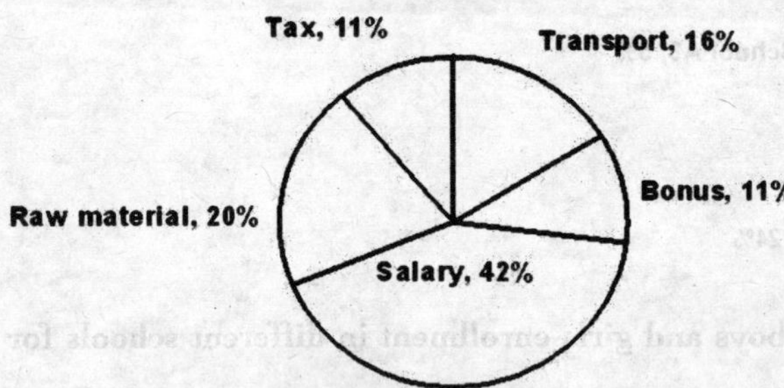

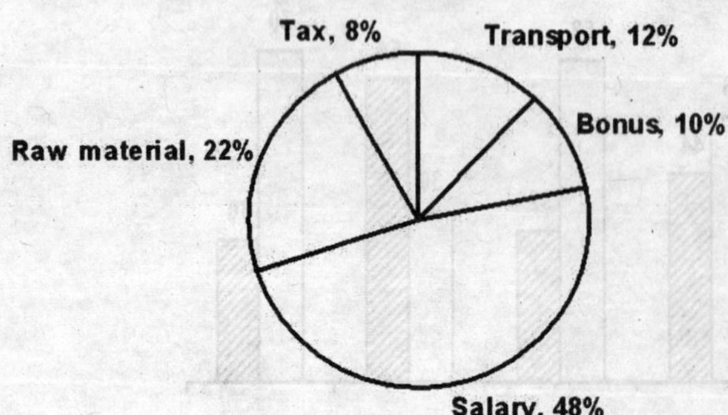

56. What is the sum between money spent on bonus by these two companies?
1. Rs. 72 lakhs 2. Rs. 62 lakhs 3. Rs. 60 lakhs 4. Rs. 65 lakhs 5. None of these

57. For which item the money spent by both companies are minimum?
1. Bonus 2. Transport 3. Tax 4. Raw Material 5. None of these

58. What is the ratio between money spent by company Q on tax and money spent by P on salary?
1. 23 : 121 2. 33 : 144 3. 47 : 144 4. 144 : 157 5. None of these

59. The money spent by company P on transport is **approximately** what percentage of money spent on raw material ?
1. 30% 2. 42% 3. 48% 4. 45% 5. 54%

60. What is the difference between money spent by both companies on tax (in lakh Rs.) ?
1. 26.8 2. 24.4 3. 24.6 4. 23.8 5. None of these

Passage:
Study the following table carefully and answer these questions given below-Number of five types of cars produced (P) and rejected (R) by a company over the years (In thousand)

Car	Type I		Type II		Type III		Type IV		Type V	
Year	P	R	P	R	P	R	P	R	P	R
2003	46	4	50	4	40	0.5	60	4	75	5
2004	56	5	62	2	30	0.75	72	2	78	4
2005	25	0.5	45	1.5	27	0.25	54	3	60	3
2006	35	0.4	48	2.5	28	2.5	64	5	70	1.5
2007	20	1.5	60	2	35	1.5	68	2	80	4
2008	30	1	52	3	24	2	72	6	60	3

61. The number of acceptable type III cars in 2006 was what percent of that in 2004 of the same type of car? (Up to two places of decimal)
1. 82.40 2. 87.50 3. 84.60 4. 88.25 5. None of these

62. What is the difference between the total produced cars in year 2005 and 2008?
1. 28500 2. 26000 3. 27000 4. 27200 5. None of these

63. In the case of type IV cars, in which year was the ratio of rejection to production the lowest among the given years?
1. 2008 2. 2006 3. 2007 4. 2005 5. None of these

64. What is the total number of rejected cars in year 2003 and 2007? (In thousands)
1. 26.5 2. 28.5 3. 27.2 4. 28.8 5. None of these

65. What is the ratio between the produced cars of type-I in year 2005 to produced cars in 2006 of all types of cars?
1. 43 : 5 2. 5 : 49 3. 43 : 7 4. 5 : 7 5. None of these

Passage:
Study the following graph carefully and answer the questions given below?

Destination wise pattern of all India exports

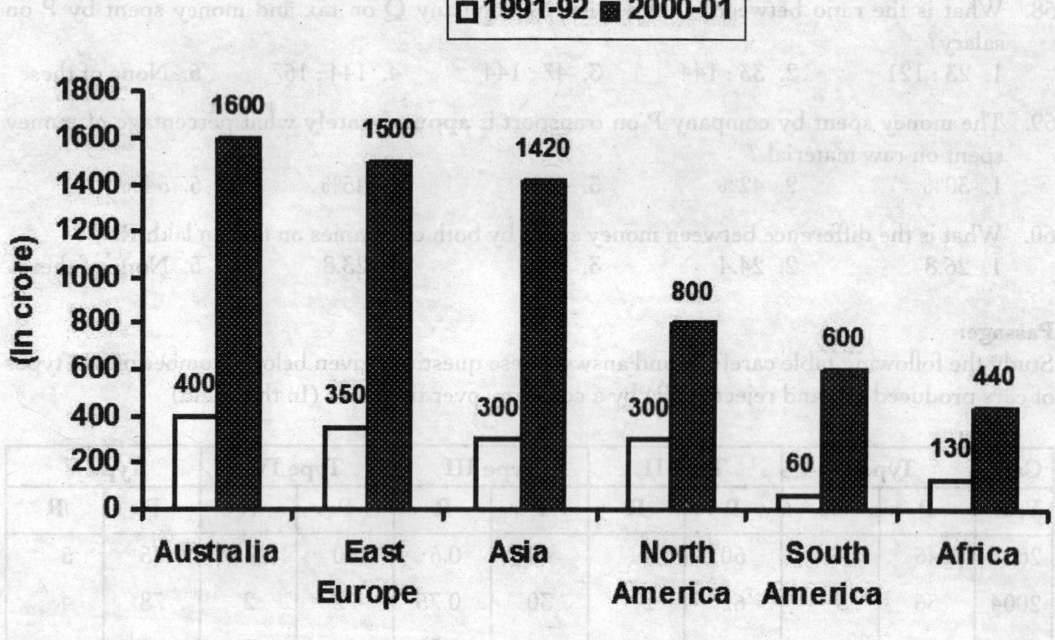

66. In 2000-01 India's exports were **approximately** (In Rs. crore)?
1. 8000 2. 5000 3. 6500 4. 7500 5. 9000

67. What is the **approximately** percentage share of Australia continent in 2000-01 in India's exports?
1. 30 2. 25 3. 28 4. 42 5. 20

68. India's exports to which of the following continent increased most in terms of percentage between 1991-92 and 2000-01?
1. North America 2. East Europe 3. Australia
4. Africa 5. None of these

69. In terms of percentage share, India's exports to which continent have increased the least between 1991-92 and 2000-01 ?
1. North America 2. Australia 3. South America
4. East Europe 5. None of these

70. If India's exports to the various continent were arranged in decreasing order for 1991-92 and 2000-01, then which of the following continent would have deteriorated its ranking?
1. Africa 2. Australia and North America
3. Africa and North America 4. East Europe
5. None of these

Passage:

Read the following graph carefully and answer the questions given below.

Profit percent earned by two companies A and B in different years

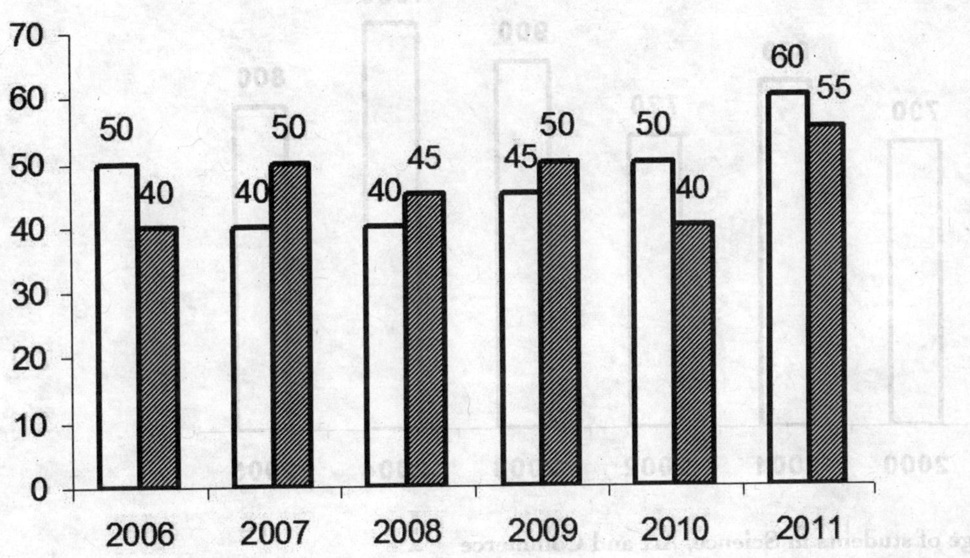

71. If the ratio of income of company B in 2008 and 2009 was 4 : 5, what was the ratio of expenditure of that company in both years?
1. 21 : 17 2. 19 : 13 3. 23 : 29 4. 16 : 29 5. None of these

72. If total expenditure of company A in all the years together is Rs. 148.5 lakhs, what was the total income of that company in all the years together?
1. Rs. 167.5 Lakh 2. Rs. 173 Lakh 3. Rs. 208.5 Lakh
4. Cannot be determined 5. None of these

73. If ratio of expenditure of company A in 2009 and 2010 was 5 : 6, what was the ratio of income of that company in both the same years?
1. 29 : 36 2. 21 : 26 3. 20 : 29 4. 9 : 10 5. None of these

74. If expenditure of company A and B in 2007 was same and total income of both companies was Rs. 116 lakhs, what was total expenditure of both companies in the same year?
1. Rs. 65 Lakh 2. Rs. 80 Lakh 3. Rs. 42 Lakh
4. Can not determined 5. None of these

75. The expenditure of company A in 2010 and 2011 is Rs. 14 lakhs and Rs. 16.5 lakhs. What is the total income of company A in 2010 and 2011?
1. Rs. 41.2 Lakh 2. Rs. 48.5 Lakh 3. Rs. 46.4 Lakh
4. Rs. 46.9 Lakh 5. None of these

Passage:

Read the following graph carefully and answer the questions given below -

Number of students in a college

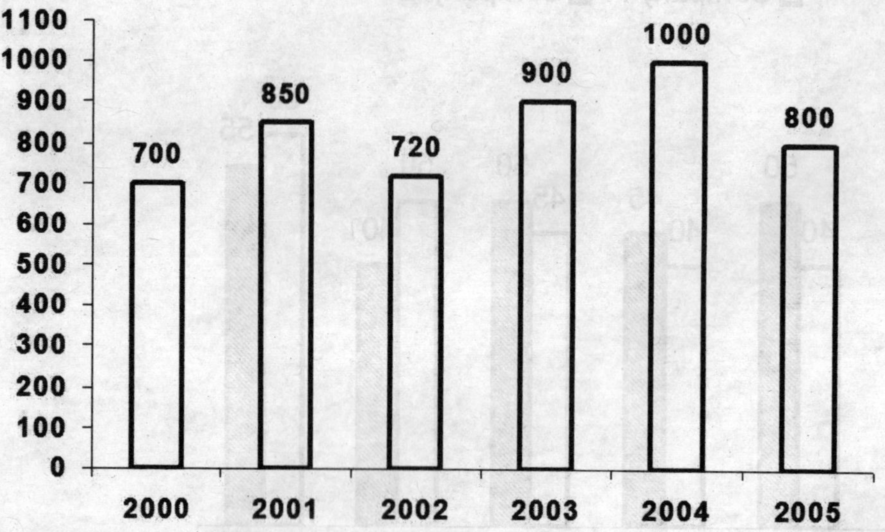

Percentage of students in Science, Art and Commerce

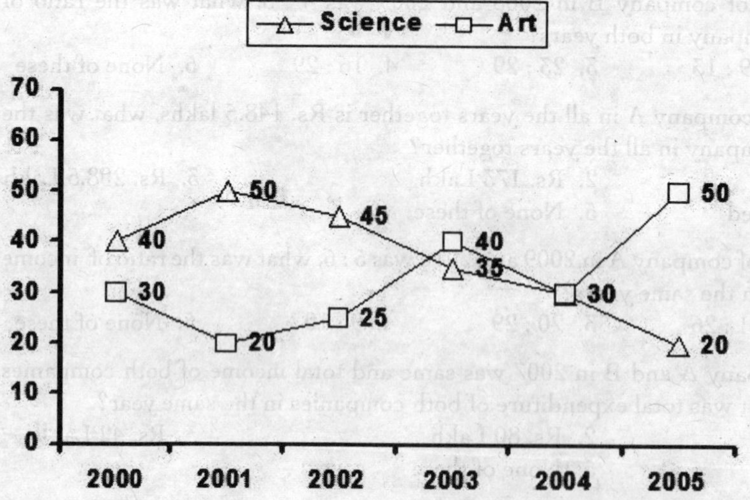

76. What is the total number of students in Commerce in all the years?
   1. 1548
   2. 1550
   3. 1545
   4. 1546
   5. None of these

77. What is the respective ratio of number of students in Science in 2003 and that in Commerce in 2001 ?
   1. 21 : 17
   2. 19 : 13
   3. 18 : 11
   4. 17 : 10
   5. None of these

78. The number of students in Science in 2001 is what percent more than that in Commerce in 2005 ?
1. 72 2. 82 3. 68 4. 64 5. 77

79. The number of students in Art in 2002 is what percent of the total number of students in Art in all the years ?
1. 15 2. 11 3. 20 4. 30 5. 24

80. What is the **approximate** average number of students in Science in all the years ?
1. 315 2. 332 3. 300 4. 335 5. 350

Section 3: General/Economy/ banking Awareness

81. INNOPROM 2016 is the largest annual international industrial trade fair of which country?
1. Russia 2. Germany 3. France
4. United Kingdom 5. South Africa

82. World population day is celebrated on-
1. 15 September 2. 18 June 3. 11 July
4. 27 August 5. 13 May

83. Name the App launched by TRAI for measuring real time mobile Internet speed of consumers.
1. Speed Test 2. MY Speed 3. Mobile Speed
4. Speedo Track 5. Speed Measure

84. ECB's can be raised as:
1. Loans 2. Capital Market instruments 3. FCCB
4. FCEB 5. All of Above

85. NSSF stands for -
1. Net Secured Short term Fund 2. Net Security Saving Fund
3. National Security saving Fund 4. National Small Saving Fund
5. None of these

86. The opening of new branches and shifting of existing branches of banks is governed by the provisions of Section ______ of the Banking Regulation Act, 1949.
1. 20 2. 21 3. 22 4. 23 5. 24

87. India witnessed demonetization in the years
1. 1954, 1986, 2016 2. 1948, 1978, 2016
3. 1946, 1978, 2016 4. 1952, 1976, 2016
5. None of these

88. Tata group was founded in the year
1. 1832 2. 1868 3. 1887 4. 1912 5. 1914

89. _________ founded Tata Steel, Tata Power & Tata chemicals.
1. Jamsetji Tata 2. Dorabji Tata
3. N.B. Saklatwala 4. J.R.D Tata 5. None of these

90. What is the turnover limit for the company for filling GST?
1. 10 lakhs 2. 20 lakhs 3. 30 lakhs 4. 40 lakhs 5. 50 lakhs

91. Foreign Direct Investment permitted in Defence Sector is-
1. 74% through Government approval route
2. 56% through Government approval route
3. 100% through Government approval route
4. 87% through Government approval route
5. 65% through Government approval route

92. The 1st Indian company that has issued the Masala Bond?
1. ICICI 2. HDFC 3. SBI 4. PNB 5. Yes Bank

93. President signed the GST Bill under Article ___________.
1. 110 2. 111 3. 112 4. 113 5. 114

94. Which state is developing Indigenous cow (Desi Cow) for producing A2 type beta casein protein containing milk?
1. Punjab 2. Himachal Pradesh 3. Haryana
4. Uttar Pradesh 5. Gujarat

95. Zika Virus was first found in India in-
1. Mumbai in 1987 2. Pune in 1952
3. Bangalore in 1976 4. Bangalore in 1987 5. Pune in 1976

96. Which party recently became the National Party?
1. Aam Aadmi Party 2. BSP
3. Trinamool Congress 4. JDU 5. None of these

97. Chairman of ISRO is-
1. A S Kiran Kumar 2. K Radhakrishnan
3. G Madhavan Nair 4. Mylswamy Annadurai 5. None of these

98. Who is the chairman of 7th Pay Commission?
1. T S Vijayan 2. Ashok Kumar mathur 3. Upendra Sinha
4. G Madhavan Nair 5. None of these

99. How many soldiers were killed by terrorist attack in Uri?
1. 16 2. 17 3. 18
4. 19 5. 20

100. Which of the following is not a famous work of Bob Dylan?
1. Things have changed 2. Like a rolling stone
3. Playing the Life 4. Blown in the wind 5. None of these

101. Who won the Noble prize in Economics 2016?
1. Olivar Hart and Bengt Holmstrom
2. Andrei Sleifer and Jean Tirole
3. Sanford J Grossman and Jean Tirole
4. Oliver E Williamson
5. None of these

102. In Swachh Survekshan 2016 as per NSSO the cleanest city in India is________.
1. Mandi 2. Chandigarh 3. Sikkim 4. Jharkhand 5. Mysore

103. Which service provider is having highest number of Internet users?
1. Vodafone 2. Bharti Airtel 3. idea Cellular 4. Reliance Jio 5. None of these

104. Which state has started the Mayer House Scheme?
1. Assam 2. West Bengal 3. Nagaland 4. Tripura 5. None of these

105. Most aggressive Bidder in spectrum auction was-
1. Vodafone 2. Bharti Airtel 3. Reliance Jio 4. Idea Cellular 5. Videocon

106. 15th ASEAN will be held in-
1. New Delhi 2. Philippines 3. Geneva 4. New York 5. None of these

107. What will be the new date for presentation of Union Budget?
1. Jan 1, 2017 2. Jan 15, 2017 3. Feb 1, 2017 4. Feb 15, 2017 5. None of these

108. Overall limit of External Commercial Borrowing is-
1. $ 10 bn 2. $ 20 bn 3. $ 30 bn 4. $ 40 bn 5. $ 50 bn

109. One family one bank is the tag line of-
1. Allahabad bank 2. Andhra Bank
3. Bank of Maharashtra 4. Indian Bank
5. Corporation Bank

110. R.D. Birla Award is associated with _______ field.
1. Music 2. Public Service 3. Literature
4. Medical Services 5. Science

111. In India, which of the following agencies is responsible for announcing the foreign Trade Policy?
1. RBI 2. EXIM Bank
3. Foreign Ministry 4. Industry and Commerce Ministry
5. None of these

112. In Rio Olympics which country received maximum number of medals?
1. China 2. Japan 3. USA 4. India 5. Germany

113. India's largest Stock Exchange by volume is-
1. National Stock Exchange 2. Bombay Stock Exchange
3. OTC exchange of India 4. Inter-Connected Stock exchange of India
5. None of these

114. RBI retained the tag "Too Big Too Fail" for two banks-
1. SBI and HDFC 2. SBI and PNB
3. SBI and Yes bank 4. SBI and ICICI
5. None of these

115. For availing short term crop loan interest subsidy, the eligible loan amount is:
1. up to Rs. 3 lac 2. up to Rs. 2 lac 3. up to Rs. 5 lac
4. up to Rs. 1 lac 5. any amount

116. Tax GDP ratio of India in 2014-15 was-
1. 7.53% 2. 9.93% 3. 11.53% 4. 14.63% 5. 17.17%

117. What role do MSME play in a country's economic and industrial development?
(a) They have the capacity to absorb skilled and unskilled labor available in the country.
(b) Such institutions help in distribution of income in a wide spectrum and do not allow it to get concentrated in a few hands or in few areas.
(c) They help in eradication of poverty by providing self employment opportunities.
1. Only a 2. Only b 3. Only c 4. Only a and c 5. All a, b, c

118. Which of the following statements about Agro and allied activities is not correct?
1. Farmers do not get adequate credit for purchase of cattle.
2. There is a need to improve breed and genetic characteristics of the cattle folk.
3. India has huge forest cover and also degraded and marshy land which can be used for productive purposes
4. India is the 10th largest producer of medicinal and aromatic plants. But the products are not of commercial value.
5. Animal husbandry plays an important role in providing sustainability under rain fed conditions.

119. India's foreign policy is based on several principles, one of which is ________.
1. Panchsheel 2. Satyamev Jayate
3. Live and Let Live 4. Vasudhaiv Kutumbkam
5. None of these

120. India's currency rating by S&P is-
1. AAA 2. BBB 3. BB 4. BB+ 5. None of these

Section 4: English Language

Read the following passage carefully and answer the questions given below it. Certain words have been printed in **bold** to help you locate them while answering some of the questions.

Much before organic food and healthy living caught the fancy of Indians, the Bombay Oil Industries launched Saffola, a healthy cooking oil, in the early 1960s. Positioned **explicitly** as being good for the heart, Saffola grabbed consumer attention with its **dramatic** communication. Clarion Advertising launched the brand and the early ads created a rather terrifying scenario of a man being wheeled into a hospital on a stretcher with the **wailing** of ambulance sirens in the background. A distressed wife looking on sought to reinforce the message that food cooked in Saffola could save your life - and your family.

The cooking oil market in the 1960s was largely disorganised, with a very large loose oil segment. It was against this backdrop that Saffola was launched on the platform of being 'Healthy for the Heart'. There was no other brand offering this benefit and hence there was no direct competition from within the category. While this message clearly connected with people who had heart trouble - or those who feared it - it also **alienated** those who were confident they could never have a heart attack. The big challenge was to carve out a niche among the health-conscious. It was a Herculean challenge at that time, but the brand was ready to ride the long haul.

In the 90s when Grey handled the brand, and by which time the consumer products division of Bombay Oil was spun off into Marico, communication for Saffola **transformed**- from being a product for those with heart trouble into a brand that everyone who aims for a healthy lifestyle should adopt. "Heart patients were a shrinking group and there was an obvious need to change this perception," says a senior professional from the agency working on the brand.

More than 50 years since the brand was launched, "Saffola today is not just a brand but a way of life. Today a lot more people are conscious of their health; they make an effort to read information on the back of the pack and general awareness levels have gone up massively," says The Marketing head. He adds that today in any health related conversation Saffola definitely makes an appearance. This positive rub-off has helped the parent brand extend into categories like salt, oats, rice and atta on the health platform.

121. Why was there no competition between the brands dealing with the oil segment and Saffola?
   1. Because the other brands couldn't advertise in the same way as Saffola did.
   2. Because no other brand was launched on the platform of being 'Healthy for the Heart.'
   3. Because the other brands except Saffola, couldn't clearly connect with people who had heart trouble.
   4. Lack of competition was felt because the brand 'Saffola' couldn't meet the challenge of carving out a niche among the health conscious.
   5. The other brands couldn't give Saffola a tough competition because 'Saffola today is not just a brand but a way of life.'

122. How did 'Saffola' succeed in grabbing the attention of the consumers?
   1. The brand succeeded in attracting the consumers as it connected with people suffering from incurable diseases.
   2. Consumers have liked 'Saffola' since 1960 and they have made it a successful brand.
   3. Feeling the essence of the 'Pure quality' and 'cheap rates', the consumers themselves got attracted towards the brand and made it a successful one.
   4. Both 2 and 3
   5. 'Saffola' succeeded in grabbing the attention of the consumers from all over the world because of its heart-touching advertising.

123. When was 'Saffola' launched?
   1. It was launched in the middle of 1960s.
   2. 'Saffola' was launched fifty years ago.
   3. It was launched in the early 1960s.
   4. It was launched in the year 1970s.
   5. Not mentioned in the passage.

124. Why a lot more people are conscious of their health today?
   1. Because a number of people are suffering from heart diseases.
   2. Because in today's world people want to remain fit and healthy.
   3. As, the graph of fatal diseases is increasing day by day similarly, the number of health-conscious people is also increasing.
   4. Not clearly mentioned in the passage.
   5. None of these

125. When did the communication for Saffola transformed from being a product for those with heart trouble into a brand that everyone who aims for a healthy lifestyle should adopt?
   1. If was transformed when Grey handled the brand.
   2. The transformation of the communication took place when consumer products division of Bombay oil was spun off into Marico.

3. The transformation took place in the 90.
4. All 1, 2 and 3
5. Both 2 and 3

126. Why did the wife of the man in the advertisement look distressed?
1. She was shocked to see the condition of her husband.
2. She was worried abouth her children as the condition of her husband was extremely serious.
3. The wife looked distressed on sought to reinforce the message that food cooked in Saffola could save one's life.
4. The female in the advertisement looked distressed because she didn't cook the food for her husband in 'Saffola.'
5. None of these

127. Why is Saffola considered not just a brand but a way of life?
1. Because it has really helped people to stay healthy.
2. Because it has helped the heart -patients to stay healthy and live a happy life.
3. Saffola is not just a brand because it is available at a cheaper rate in the market so even poor people can afford it and this is how their lives have become easy.
4. Both 1 and 3
5. None of these

128. What does the word 'Herculean Challenge' mean in context to the passage?
1. It means a 'manageable challenge'.
2. It means a 'difficult challenge.'
3. It means an 'uncomplicated challenge.'
4. It means an 'easy going challenge.'
5. None of these

129. In which of the following categories, has Saffola still not extended its business?
1. Salt 2. Oats 3. Rice 4. Bajra 5. Atta

130. What does the phrase 'rub-off' means in context to the passage?
1. It means to remove something
2. It means to have an effect through close association
3. It means not to explore in different field
4. It means to diminish
5. None of these

Passage:

Rearrange the following sentences (A), (B), (C), (D) and (E) in the proper sequence to form a meaningful paragraph, then answer the questions given below them.

(A) For an undisclosed amount.(
(B) Animation, gaming and live action.
(C) Entertainment company has sold the(
(D) 3D television series chaplin and co. to Cartoon Network.
(E) Broadcast rights of its.

131. Which of the following should be the **THIRD** sentence after rearrangement?
1. A 2. C 3. D 4. E 5. B

132. Which of the following is the **FIFTH** sentence after rearrangement?
1. C 2. D 3. B 4. A 5. E

133. Which of the following is the **FIRST** sentence after rearrangement?
1. E 2. B 3. A 4. C 5. D

134. Which of the following is the **SECOND** sentence after rearrangement?
1. B 2. C 3. A 4. D 5. E

135. Which of the following is the **FOURTH** sentence after rearrangement?
1. B 2. D 3. E 4. A 5. C

Passage:

In the following passage there are blanks, each of which has been numbered. These numbers are printed below the passage and against each, five words are suggested, one of which fits the blank appropriately. Find out the appropriate word in each case.

(41) remains one of the most challenging issues for businesses today, across the world, **(42)** of the type of organisation, country of operation or industry sector. Indian companies are increasingly looking **(43)** and engaging in acquisitions outside India. This exposes companies to a whole **(44)** of risks including fraud risks. Thus, it becomes extremely important for CFOs to manage fraud risk in a proactive rather than reactive manner. In the best of organisations, managing fraud is a multi **(45)** challenge. Risks like cyber crime are very significant in the IT industry. Technology itself can be misused and enable fraud or can, if properly used, be a significant mitigator of fraud. Asset **(46)** bribery and corruption are other fraud risks **(47)** by organisations.

One of the bigger problems in the growth market **(48)** is how to make organisations scalable. The other **(49)** is building a framework for fraud management. That said, dealing with fraudsters requires a consistent and **(50)** process today.

136. Choose the correct option for (41).
1. robbery 2. theft 3. ditching 4. fraud 5. Issues

137. Choose the correct option for (42).
1. despite 2. regardless 3. instead 4. regarding 5. regards

138. Choose the correct option for (43).
1. outward 2. inward 3. exterior 4. in 5. behind

139. Choose the correct option for (44).
1. risk 2. issues 3. gamut 4. matters 5. story

140. Choose the correct option for (45).
1. discipline 2. disciplinary 3. disciplined 4. disciples 5. talented

141. Choose the correct option for (46).
1. appropriate 2. appropriation
3. misappropriation 4. frauds 5. exactly

142. Choose the correct option for (47).
1. dealt 2. focused 3. managed 4. controlled 5. faced

143. Choose the correct option for (48).
1. yesterday 2. tomorrow 3. today 4. nowaday 5. present day

144. Choose the correct option for (49).
1. aspects 2. expectations 3. matters 4. aspect 5. issues

145. Choose the correct option for (50).
1. weak 2. robust 3. extensive 4. flabby 5. unhealthy

Passage:
In each of the following sentences there is a blank space given. Below each four words have been denoted by numbers (A), (B), (C), (D) and (E). Find out which two words can be filled up in the blank alternatively to make the sentence meaningfully complete.

146. The trap cameras will have motion sensors and night vision to capture the ––––––of any wildlife passing in front of it.
A. Thought B. image C. wonder D. picture
1. A and C 2. A and B 3. B and D 4. C and D 5. A and D

147. Stay on ––––––in case you are getting persistent calls from companies offering you promising jobs and handsome salaries
A. Guard B. curiosity C. alert D. provision
1. A and B 2. A and C 3. C and D 4. B and C 5. B and D

148. Animal rights activists have lamented that the manifestos of all major parties have the pending Animal Welfare Act, which would have helped protect all animals and also give ––––––punishments to offenders.
A. Harsher B. deliberately C. feeble D. severe
1. A and C 2. B and C 3. C and D 4. A and D 5. B and D

149. The industrial town of Marwar region with over 600 textile dyeing units is desperately looking for a candidate who could –––––––their woes and ensure smooth functioning of their industries.
A. End B. address C. shuffle D. modified
1. A and B 2. B and D 3. B and C 4. A and C 5. C and D

Passage:
Rearrange the following sentences **(A), (B), (C), (D) and (E) in** the proper sequence to form a meaningful paragraph, then answer the questions given below them.

A. However, our politicians seem to be confused over what is oratory and what is demagoguery. **B.** Reform should first emanate from within society if any change is to be expected in future. **C.** Many speeches are in bad taste, crossing the boundaries of civility. **D.** Leaders need to break into inspirational speeches to influence the masses. **E.** Civil society should shoulder some of the blame for nurturing and cultivating this kind of political disclosure.

150. Which of the following would be the **LAST** statement after rearrangement?
1. A 2. B 3. C 4. D 5. E

151. Which of the following would be the **SECOND** statement after rearrangement?
1. A 2. B 3. C 4. D 5. E

152. Which of the following would be the **FIRST** statement after rearrangement?
1. A 2. B 3. C 4. D 5. E

153. Which of the following would be the **THIRD** statement after rearrangement?

1. A 2. B 3. C 4. D 5. E

154. Which of the following would be the **FOURTH** statement after rearrangement?

1. A 2. B 3. C 4. D 5. E

155. In each of the following sentences there are two blank spaces. Below each five pairs of words have been denoted by numbers (1), (2), (3), (4) and (5). Find out which pair of words can be filled in the blanks inorder to make a meaningful sentence.

After ______________ the explosive, the bomb squad said the bomb was powerful enough to cause ______________ damage in the locality.

1. Pacifying, protected
2. Alarmed, exclusive
3. Defusing, extensive
4. Restricting, persuasive
5. Fainted, comprehensive

ANSWER KEY

1. 1	2. 5	3. 4	4. 3	5. 2	6. 5	7. 2	8. 4	9. 1	10. 3
11. 1	12. 4	13. 2	14. 2	15. 5	16. 1	17. 5	18. 1	19. 5	20. 4
21. 3	22. 3	23. 4	24. 5	25. 4	26. 2	27. 3	28. 5	29. 4	30. 3
31. 2	32. 1	33. 2	34. 3	35. 1	36. 2	37. 2	38. 2	39. 3	40. 1
41. 1	42. 2	43. 4	44. 1	45. 1	46. 3	47. 4	48. 4	49. 2	50. 3
51. 4	52. 4	53. 3	54. 4	55. 4	56. 5	57. 3	58. 5	59. 5	60. 5
61. 5	62. 3	63. 5	64. 2	65. 2	66. 3	67. 2	68. 2	69. 1	70. 5
71. 5	72. 4	73. 1	74. 2	75. 5	76. 4	77. 1	78. 5	79. 2	80. 3
81. 1	82. 3	83. 2	84. 5	85. 4	86. 4	87. 3	88. 2	89. 2	90. 2
91. 3	92. 2	93. 2	94. 2	95. 2	96. 3	97. 1	98. 2	99. 4	100. 3
101. 1	102. 3	103. 2	104. 4	105. 1	106. 2	107. 3	108. 3	109. 3	110. 4
111. 4	112. 3	113. 1	114. 4	115. 1	116. 2	117. 4	118. 5	119. 1	120. 4
121. 2	122. 5	123. 3	124. 5	125. 4	126. 3	127. 2	128. 2	129. 4	130. 2
131. 4	132. 4	133. 2	134. 2	135. 3	136. 4	137. 2	138. 1	139. 3	140. 2
141. 3	142. 5	143. 3	144. 4	145. 2	146. 3	147. 2	148. 4	149. 1	150. 2
151. 1	152. 4	153. 3	154. 5	155. 3					

Solutions and Explanations

1. **Solution:**

Statement: $J = R, R > K, K < D$
$J = R > K < D$

Conclusions:
(I) $K < J$ (True)
(II) $D < J$ (False)

2. 4.
Solution:
@ means $P < Q$
$ means $P \geq Q$
# means $P = Q$
© means $P \leq Q$
% means $P > Q$

Statement: $M \leq T, K > T, K < N$
$M \leq T < K < N$

Conclusions:
(I) $N > M$ (True)
(II) $K > M$ (True)

3. @ means $P < Q$
$ means $P \geq Q$
# means $P = Q$
© means $P \leq Q$
% means $P > Q$

Statement: $V \geq D, D \leq R, R >$
$V \geq D \leq R > F$

Conclusions:
(I) $R > V$ (False)
(II) $V < F$ (False)

4. @ means $P < Q$
$ means $P \geq Q$
# means $P = Q$
© means $P \leq Q$
% means $P > Q$

Statement: $B < E, E = S, S \geq Z$
$B < E = S \geq Z$

Conclusions:
(I) $Z < E$ either I or II true
(II) $E = Z$

5. @ means P < Q
$ means P ≥ Q
# means P = Q
© means P ≤ Q
% means P > Q

Statement: H > M, N ≤ M, N ≥ T
H > M ≥ N ≥ T

Conclusions:
(I) H = T (False)
(II) H > T (True)

(6–10)

After careful analysis of the given input and various steps of rearrangement it is evident that in the first step the highest number is placed at the extreme left position and in the second step the word which comes first in the alphabetical order is placed at the extreme right position. In the next step the second highest number is placed at the second position from the left. After that step the word which comes second in the alphabetical order is placed at the extreme right position. These two steps are continued alternately till all the numbers get arranged in the descending order from the left and all the words get arranged in alphabetical order after the numbers.

Input: Class 16 work 5 race 63 hard 54 join 79 take 21

Step I: 79 Class 16 work 5 race 63 hard 54 join take 21

Step II: 79 16 work 5 race 63 hard 54 join take 21 class

Step III: 79 63 16 work 5 race hard 54 join take 21 class

Step IV: 79 63 16 work 5 race join take 21 class hard

Step V: 79 63 54 16 work 5 race join take 21 class hard

Step VI: 79 63 54 16 work 5 race take 21 class hard join

Step VII: 79 63 54 21 16 work 5 race take class hard join

Step VIII: 79 63 54 21 16 work 5 take class hard join race

Step IX: 79 63 54 21 16 5 work take class hard join race

Step X: 79 63 54 21 16 5 work class hard join race take

Step XI: 79 63 54 21 16 5 class hard join race take work

And, step XI is the last step.

6. 5.
The word 'work' is sixth from the left end in step VIII.

7. 2.
'16' is the ninth from the right in step VI.

8. 4.
'5' is seventh from the right end in step IX.

9. 1.
Eleven steps were required to complete the arrangement.

10. 3.

11. 1.

12. 4.
The two events have no causative link with each other.

13. 2.
The award is an effect. The cause of this effect is his success in various races. The cause of his success is his talent and her dedication. His dedication is a cause of the award.

14. 2.
Normally we take hard work to be a sufficient cause for success.

15. 5.
There is no link between the two statements. Unless we assure that books of MEPL publication are necessary for success. The two statements are uncorrelated.

16. 1.
To motivate the employees for the enhancement of their work, the head of the organisation congratulated the entire staff in her speech and appreciated their effort.

17. 5.
Why a reward for a good suggestion? Obviously, authorities are assuming that the reward will motivate employees to evolve innovative techniques. Hence, II is implicit. On the other side, seeking help from employees in order to evolve innovative techniques implies that employees may have the required caliber. Hence, I is also implicit.

18. 1.

19. 5.
Here both the assumptions are valid. If it were no so, there would be no benefit fo setting up such a mission.

20. 4.

21. 3.

(+) Brother (+) (–)
Daud ⟶ Damini ⟺ Dhawan
Son Daughter
(+) (+) (–)
Dhruv Brother ⟶ Dayal Dharemendra

22. 3.

(+) Brother (+) (–)
Daud ⟶ Damini ⟺ Dhawan
Son Daughter
(+) (+) (–)
Dhruv Brother ⟶ Dayal Dharemendra

23. 4.

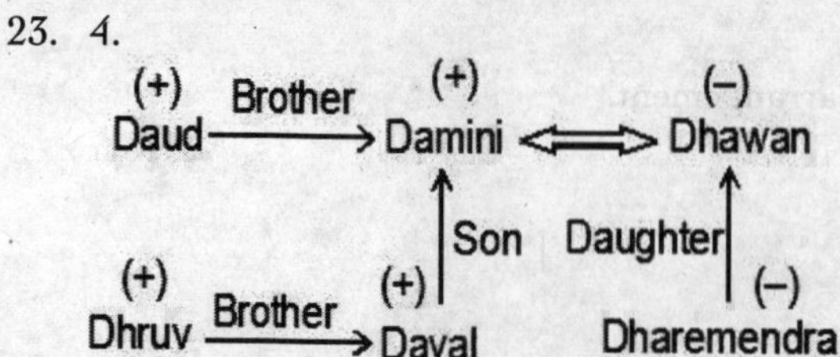

24. 5.

(+) Daud —Brother→ (+) Damini ⟺ (–) Dhawan

Son ↑ Daughter ↑

(+) Dhruv —Brother→ (+) Dayal (–) Dharemendra

25. 4.

(+) Daud —Brother→ (+) Damini ⟺ (–) Dhawan

Son ↑ Daughter ↑

(+) Dhruv —Brother→ (+) Dayal (–) Dharemendra

26. 2.
Road

27. 3.

9 8 2 0 3 8 4 1 6 7 3 2 1
0 1 1 2 2 3 3 4 6 7 8 8 9

28. 5.
Except sweet, all others require baking to prepare them.

29. 4.

I N T E R N A T I O N A L G O L D

46. Required ratio = $\frac{56}{58} \Rightarrow \frac{28}{29}$

47. Speed of vehicle P = $\frac{782}{17} \Rightarrow$ 46 km./hr.

Speed of vehicle Q = $\frac{782}{17} \Rightarrow$ 56 km./hr.

Speed of vehicle R= $\frac{870}{15} \Rightarrow$ 58 km./hr.

Speed of vehicle S = $\frac{840}{14} \Rightarrow$ 60 km./hr.

Speed of vehicle T = $\frac{832}{16} \Rightarrow$ 52 km./hr.

Maximum speed of vehicle S.

48. Average speed = $\frac{(48 + 52 + 56 + 44 + 58)}{5}$ = 51.6 km./hr.

49. Sum of speeds = $\frac{840}{14} + \frac{672}{12}$ = 60 + 56 = 116 km./hr

50. Total expenditure = 3428 × 2.5 + 3996 × 3.25 = 8570 + 12987 = Rs. 21557

51. Required difference = 4032 – 1920 = 2112

52.. Total students = 1500
Total sum collected = 1500 × 850 = 1275000 = Rs. 12.75 lakhs

53. Two

54. Required ratio = $\frac{1080}{750} \Rightarrow \frac{36}{25}$

55. Required percent = $\frac{(4032 - 2475) \times 100}{2475}$

$= \frac{(1557 \times 100)}{2475} \approx 63\%$

56. Required sum = 24 + 44 = Rs. 68 lakhs

57. On tax

58. Required ratio = $\frac{55}{144}$

59. Required percent = $\frac{28.8}{52.8} \times 100$ = 54% (approx)

60. Required difference = 44 –19.2= Rs. 24.8 lakh

61. Required percentage = $\frac{25.5 \times 100}{29.25}$ = 87.17%

62. Required difference = (238 – 211) Thousand = 27 thousand = 27000

63.

Year	Ratio
2003	0.06
2004	0.027
2005	0.05
2006	0.07
2007	0.029
2008	0.083

Minimum ratio in year 2004.

64. Required sum = 17.5 + 11 = 28.5 Thousand

65. Required ratio = $\frac{25}{245} = \frac{5}{49}$

66. 3.

67. Percentage share of Australia

$$= \frac{1600}{6360} \times 100 \approx 25$$

68. 2.

69. North America = 166%

70. In 1991-92, Africa was ahead of South America but in 2000-01, if feel behind South America.

71. Ratio $= 4x \times \frac{100}{145} = 5x \times \frac{100}{150} = 24 : 29$

72. 4.

73. Ratio $= 5x \times \frac{145}{100} = 6x \times \frac{150}{100}$

$\frac{29x}{4} = 9x = 24 : 29$

74. $I = I_1 + I_2$

$= Ex \frac{145}{100} + Ex \frac{150}{100}$

$= E (1.4 + 1.5)$

$116 = E \times 2.9$

E = Rs. 40 Lakh

Total expenditure = 40 × 2 = Rs. 80 Lakh

75. Total income $= 14 \times \frac{150}{100} + 16.5 \times \frac{160}{100}$

= 21 + 26.4 = Rs. 47.4 Lakh

76. Total number of students

= 210 + 255 + 216 + 225 + 400 + 240 = 1546

77. Ratio = 315 : 255 = 21 : 17

78. Percent increase $= \frac{185}{240} \times 100 = 77$

79. Percent $= \frac{180}{1620} \times 100 = 11$

80. Average number $= \frac{1804}{6} \times 100 = 300$ (Approx)

135. 4.

The sequence is BCEDA

Note:- B would be the first sentence as it is highlighting the main topic which is discussed in the entire passage and as 'Animation, gaming and live action' is the name of the company, C sentence would follow it.

136. 3.

Fraud -it is used as a noun and means the crime of getting money by deceiving people.
For other options:-

Ditching- means to get rid of or give up or to end a relationship with (someone) peremptorily.
Eg:- She ditched her husband to marry the cleaner.
Theft- means the action or crime of stealing.
Eg:- He was convicted of theft.

137. 2.
Regardless- (adverb)- means despite the prevailing circumstances.
Regardless of- means without regard or consideration for.
For other options:-
Instead- means as an alternative or substitute.
Eg:- She never married , preferring instead to remain single.
Despite-(preposition)- means without being affected by.
Eg:- He remains a great leader despite age and infirmity.

138. 1.
Outward- means of, on, or from the outside.

139. 3.
Gamut- it is used as a noun and means the complete range or scope of something.

140. 2.
Disciplinary- This word is used as an adjective and means concerning or enforcing discipline.

141. 3.

142. 5.

143. 3.

144. 4.
Aspect- means a particular part or feature of something.

145. 2.
Robust- means able to withstand or over come adverse condition.
For other options:-
Flabby- (of a part of a person's body) soft, loose and fleshy.
Eg:- This exercise help to flatten a flabby stomach.

146. 3.

147. 2.

148. 4.
For other options:
Feeble (adj)- weak

149. 1.

150. 2.

151. 1.

152. 4.

153. 3.

154. 5.

The arrangement is DACEB. The paragraph discusses the nature of political speech delivered by modern leaders and its impact on society.

155. 3.

Defusing, extensive

For other options:

Persuasive (adj)- capable of convincing

Comprehensive (adj)-complete

SBI PO Mains MOCK Test Paper 4

Structure of this MOCK Test

S.No.	Name of section	No. of Questions	Total marks	Allotted Time
1	Reasoning and Computer Aptitude	45	60	60 minutes
2	Data Analysis and Interpretation	35	60	45 minutes
3	General/ Economy/ Banking Awareness	40	40	35 minutes
4	English Language	35	40	40 minutes
Total		155	200	3 hours

- **There is 1/4th Negative marking for every wrong answer.**
- **If a question is left blank, i.e. no answer is marked by the candidate, there will be no penalty for that question**

Section 1: Reasoning and Computer Aptitude

Directions (1–5): Read each statement carefully and answer the following questions:

Input:- "rohan 85 rather busy 40 queen 55 talk 71 tom 28 60"
Step I:- 60 rohan 85 rather 40 queen 55 talk 71 tom 28 busy.
Step II:- 55 60 rohan 85 rather 40 talk 71 tom 28 busy queen.
Step III:- 71 55 60 rohan 85 40 talk tom 28 busy queen rather.
Step IV:- 40 71 55 60 85 talk tom 28 busy queen rather rohan.
Step V:- 85 40 71 59 65 tom 28 busy queen rather rohan talk.
Step VI:- 28 85 40 71 59 65 busy queen rather rohan talk tom.
Step VI is the last step of the above arrangement.
As per the rules followed in the steps given above, find out in each of the following is the appropriate step for the given input.

Input for the question :-
"done 31 39 vault heart 97 john 84 gear 70 sport 65"

1. Which word/number would be at fifth position from right end in step IV?
   a. john b. sport c. 70 d. 65 e. gear

2. Which of the following would be step III?
   a. 84 65 70 31 39 vault 97 john sport done gear heart.
   b. 84 65 31 70 39 vault 97 john sport done gear heart.
   c. 84 65 70 31 39 vault 97 john done sport gear heart.
   d. None of these. e) Cannot be determined

3. Which step number should be the following output?
   "97 39 84 65 70 31 vault done gear heart john sport"
   a. Step IV b. Step V c. Step VI d. Step VII e. Step III

4. Which word/number would be at 7th position from left in Step III ?
   a. 39 b. vault c. 97 d. 31 e. none of these

5. How many steps are required to get the final output?
   a. 6 b. 5 c. 4
   d. 3 e. Cannot be determined

Directions (6-10): Study the information and answer the following questions:
Seven friends namely M,N,O,P,Q,R and S attend different language classes namely French, English, Spanish, Sanskrit, Chinese, German and Japanese not necessarily in the same order, from Monday to Sunday(of the same week).

M attend a class on Friday. Only two people attend classes between M and the one who is learning Sanskrit. R attends a class immediately before P, neither R nor P is learning Sanskrit. Only one person attends a class between R and the one who is learning Spanish. The one who is learning Spanish does not have a class on Monday. N attends a class immediately before the one who is learning French. M is not learning French. Only one person has a class between R and Q. O is learning German. Only two people have classes between O and the one who is learning Chinese. Q is not learning Japanese.

6. Which of the following represent those who have language classes immediately before and immediately after N?
   a. P,M b. Q,M c. Q,R d. Other than those given as option
   e. R,P

7. Which of the following language is Q learning?
   a. Other than those given as option.
   b. Chinese. c. English. d. Spanish. e. Sanskrit.

8. As per the given arrangement Q is related to Chinese and R is related to Japanese in a certain way. To which of the following is P related to in the same way?
   a. Sanskrit. b. Other than those given as option. c. Spanish.
   d. English. e. French.

9. Who amongst the following is learning Japanese?
   a. N b. M c. S d. R
   e. Cannot be determined

10. On which of the following days does P have a class?
    a. Monday. b. Thursday. c. Wednesday. d. Tuesday. e. Sunday.

Directions (11–15): Read each statement carefully and answer the following questions:

11. **Statements:** N≤Q; R>P; P=N; S>T; T≥R

Conclusions:

I. S>N

II. Q=P

III. P<Q

IV. T<P

a) Only I is true

b) Only II is true

c) None is true

d) Either II or III and I are true

e) All are true

12. **Statements:** A=B; C≤D; E>C; B<D

Conclusions:

I. D < B

II. D > E

III. A > E

IV. A > C

a) None is true

b) Only II is true

c) Only I and II are true

d) Only II and III are true

e) Only IV is true

13. **Statements:** T>O; S>R; S≤O; R≤F; U≤F

Conclusions:

I. T>S

II. O>R

III. F≥U

IV. O≤U

a) Only I, II and III are true

b) Only II is true

c) Only I, II and IV are true

d) Neither I nor II is true

e) None is true

14. **Statements:** C<R; R≤N; N=M; M≥F; Q≥M; M<O

Conclusions:

i. R≤F

ii. C<Q

iii. Q≤M

iv. F<O

a) Only I, II and III are true

b) Only II is true

c) Only II and IV are true

d) Neither I nor II is true

e) None is true

15. **Statements:** P ≥ Q; R > M; P ≥ O; Q ≥ R; N = Q

Conclusions:

I. R > O

II. O > Q

III. Q > M

IV. N > P

a. Only I is true b. Only II is true
c. Either I or II true d. Neither I nor II is true
e. Only III is true

Directions (16–20): Read the information carefully and answer the following questions

If A + B means A is the father of B
If A × B means A is the sister of B
If A $ B means A is the wife of B
If A % B means A is the mother of B
If A ÷ B means A is the son of B

16. What should come in place of the question mark, to establish that J is the brother of T in the expression? J ÷ P % H ? T % L
a. × b. ÷ c. $
d. Either ÷ or x e. Either + or ÷ 22.

17. Which among the given expressions indicate that M is the daughter of D?
a. L % R $ D + T × M b. L + R $ D + M × T
c. L % R % D + T ÷ M d. D + L $ R + M × T
e. L $ D ÷ R % M ÷ T

18. Which among the following options is true if the expression 'I + T % J × L ÷K' is definitely true ?
a. L is the daughter of T b. K is the son-in-law of I
c. I is the grandmother of L d. T is the father of J
e. J is the brother of L

19. Which of the following expressions is true if Y is son of X is definitely false?
a. W % L × T × Y ÷ X b. W + L × T × Y ÷ X
c. X + L × T × Y ÷ W d. W $ X + L + Y + T
e. W % X + T × Y ÷ L

20. What should come in place of the question mark, to establish that T is the sister-in-law of Q in the expression R % T × P ? Q + V
a. ÷ b. % c. × d. $ e. Either $ or ×

Directions (21 -25)

These data sufficiency problems consist of a question and two statements, labelled (1) and (2), in which certain data are given. You have to decide whether the data given in the statements are sufficient for answering the question. You must indicate whether -

A. Statement (1) ALONE is sufficient, but statement (2) alone is not sufficient to answer the question asked.
B. Statement (2) ALONE is sufficient, but statement (1) alone is not sufficient to answer the question asked.
C. BOTH statements (1) and (2) TOGETHER are sufficient to answer the question asked, but NEITHER statement ALONE is sufficient to answer the question asked.
D. EACH statement ALONE is sufficient to answer the question asked.
E. Statements (1) and (2) TOGETHER are NOT sufficient to answer the question asked, and additional data specific to the problem are needed.

21. **If m, s are the average and standard deviation of integers a, b, c, and d, is s > 0?**
   a. m > a
   b. a + b + c + d = 0

22. **Is xy positive?**
   a. (x + y)2 < (x - y)2
   b. x = y

23. **How many of the numbers a, b, and c are positive if each of these numbers is less than 10?**
   a. a + b + c = 20
   b. a + b = 14

24. **When a positive integer 'p' is divided by a divisor 'q', the remainder is 24. What is q?**
   a. When 2p is divided by q, the remainder is 23.
   b. When 3p is divided by q, the remainder is 22.

25. **Is a < b?**
   a. ab < ba
   b. $\frac{a}{b} > 1$

Directions (26-30): In each of the questions below are given two/three statements followed by two conclusions numbered I & II. Assuming the statements to be true find the conclusions which follow and mark the correct option.

26. **Statements:** All metals are black.
   Some pots are black. No black is thread.
   Conclusions:
   I. At least some thread are pots.
   II. All thread being pot is a possibility
   III. Some metals are black.
   a. Only I follows
   b. Only II & III follow
   c. All follow
   d. Only I and III follows
   e. None of these

27. **Statements:** Some boys are rude.
   Some rude are human. All human are good.
   Conclusions:
   I. All human being boys is a possibility.
   II. At least some rude are good.
   III. Some good are not boys.
   a. Only I follows
   b. Only II & III follow
   c. All follow
   d. Only I and III follows
   e. None of these

28. **Statements:** Some trains are metro.
No bus is a train. All taxi is a metro.
Conclusions:
I. Some metro is not a bus.
II. At least some taxi is a bus.
III. All bus being metro is a possibility.
a. Only I follows
b. Only II & III follow
c. All follow
d. Only I and III follows
e. None of these

29. **Statements:** All managers are clerk.
Some boss is a clerk. All peons are boss.
Conclusions:
I. All boss is a peon.
II. No manger is boss.
III. All manager being peon is a possibility.
a. Only I follows
b. Only III follows
c. Only II follows
d. None follows
e. Only I & III follow

30. **Statements:** No chain is gold.
Some metal is chain. Some pots are gold.
Conclusions:
I. Some pots are not chain.
II. All metal being gold is a possibility.
III. Some pots are metal.
a. Only I & III follow
b. Only I follow
c. Only II & III follows
d. All follows
e. None follows

Direction (31-45) Choose the correct option of the given questions:

31. Clip Art is
a. text
b. graphics
c. Both '1' and '2'
d. All of these
e. none of these

32. Can text be mingled with graphics?
a. Yes
b. No
c. Both '1' and '2'
d. All of these
e. None of these

33. Word Art is a
a. text
b. graphic
c. independent program
d. All of these
e. None of these

34. You can set margins by using the dialog box
a. font
b. page setup
c. margins
d. All of these
e. None of these

35. Two main orientations are portrait and
 a. landscape b. photo c. lying d. All of these e. None of these

36. Instruction's to computer are given through
 a. input unit b. ALU unit c. keyboard d. pen drive e. None of these

37. Calculations are made in computer with the help of its
 a. memory b. control unit c. ALU d. CPU e. None of these

38. A unit of measure equal to approximately 1 billion bytes is called a
 a. 1 MB b. 2 MB c. 2 GB d. 1 GB e. None of these

39. Which of the following is a unit of measurement used with computer system?
 a. Byte b. Megabyte c. Gigabyte d. All of these e. None of these

40. Which command used to copy files?
 a. Copy b. Disk copy c. Type d. All of these e. None of these

41. To copy the hidden system files of DOS to another disk you can use the command
 a. copy b. Ren c. Sys d. Disk copy e. None of these

42. Disk copy command in DOS is used to
 a. Copy a file
 b. Copy contents of one floppy disk to another
 c. Copy contents of CD-ROM to another
 d. All of the above e. None of these

43. The command used to copy a file named temp.doc from drive C: to drive A: is
 a. copy temp.doc to a: b. copy c: temp.doc a:
 c. copy c: a: d. Copy temp a: c:
 e. None of these

44. External command in DOS are
 a. copy, edit, sys, format b. edit, sys, chkdsk
 c. chkdsk, prompt, date d. sys, ver, vol
 e. None of these

45. Can you shade your text?
 a. Yes b. No
 c. Both '1' and '2' d. None of these
 e. Either A or B

Section 2: Data Analysis and Interpretation

Directions (46–50): Two equations (I) and (II) are given in each question. On the basis of these equations, you have to decide the relation between x and y and give answer.

46. I. $21x^2 - 122x + 165 = 0$
 II. $3y^2 - 2y - 33 = 0$
 a. if $x > y$ b. if $x \geq y$ c. If $x < y$ d. if $x \leq y$
 e. if $x = y$, or no relation can be established between x and y.

47. I. $5x^2 - 29x + 36 = 0$
II. $10y^2 - 3y - 27 = 0$
a. if $x > y$ b. if $x \geq y$ c. If $x < y$ d. if $x \leq y$
e. if $x = y$, or no relation can be established between x and y.

48. I. $7x^2 - 54x + 99 = 0$
II. $4y^2 - 16y + 15 = 0$
a. if $x > y$ b. if $x \geq y$ c. If $x < y$ d. if $x \leq y$
e. if $x = y$, or no relation can be established between x and y.

49. I. $5x^2 - 87x + 378 = 0$
II. $3y^2 - 49y + 200 = 0$
a. if $x > y$ b. if $x \geq y$ c. If $x < y$ d. if $x \leq y$
e. if $x = y$, or no relation can be established between x and y.

50. I. $14x^2 - 37x + 24 = 0$
II. $28y^2 - 53y + 24 = 0$
a. if $x > y$ b. if $x \geq y$ c. If $x < y$ d. if $x \leq y$
e. if $x = y$, or no relation can be established between x and y.

Directions (51-55) Study the following graph and answer the question given below.
Number of car production (in thousands) and percentage of car sold by an automobile company over the years

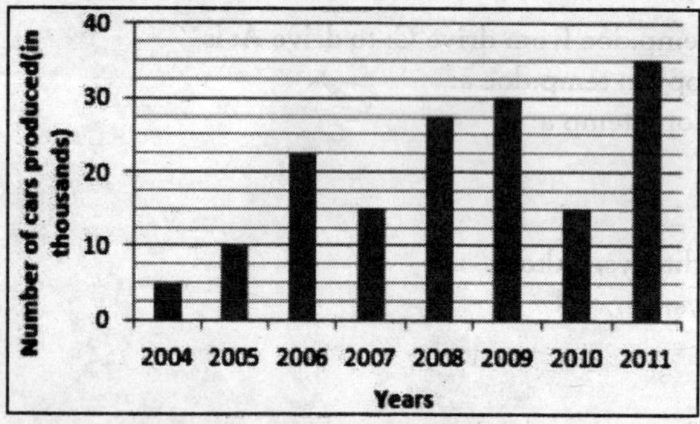

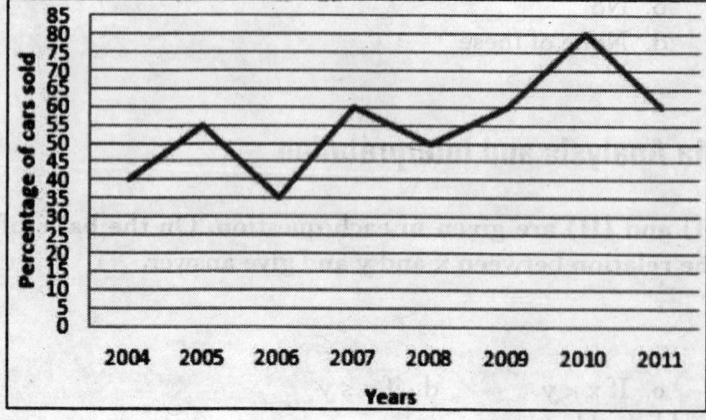

51. What was the ratio between the number of cars produced in 2004 and the number of cars sold in 2011?
a. 21 : 2 b. 2 : 21 c. 5 : 21 d. 21 : 5 e. None of these

52. In which of the following years number of cars sold was highest?
a. 2011 b. 2009 c. 2008 d. 2010 e. None of these

53. What was the percentage drop in the number of cars sold from 2009 to 2010?
a. 50 b. 33(1/3) c. 37.25 d. 62.5 e. None of these

54. The number of cars produced in 2008 was approximately how much percent more than the number of cars that were not sold in 2006?
a. 78% b. 88% c. 84% d. 80% e. 90%

55. The number of cars sold in 2010 was what percent of the cars produced in 2006?
a. 58 b. 33 c. 53(1/3) d. 35 e. None of these

Directions (56-60): Study the following graph and answer the questions given below.
The production of company A and Sales of company B in tonnes from 2007-2011

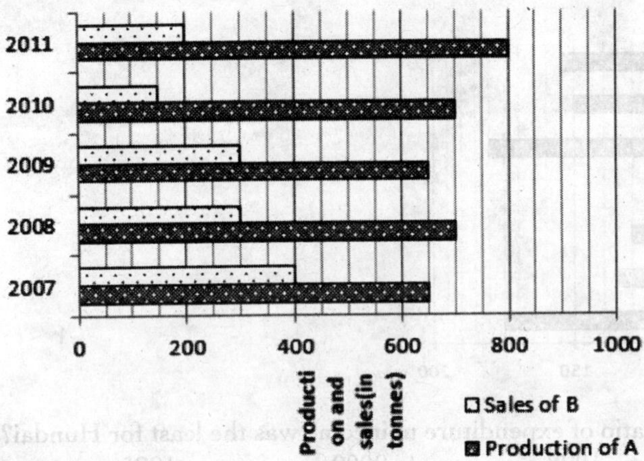

The table given below represents the respective ratio of the production of B and (A+B) and the respective ratio of the sales of A and (A+B)

Year	Production	Sales
2007	4 : 9	3 : 5
2008	4 : 11	2 : 5
2009	3 : 8	4 : 7
2010	2 : 9	5 : 8
2011	3 : 11	3 : 5

56. What is the average production of company B from the year 2007 to the year 2011?
a. 263 b. 362 c. 623 d. 236 e. None of these

57. What is the average sale of company A from the year 2007 to the year 2011?
a. 300 b. 250 c. 350 d. 200 e. None of these

58. The difference between the total sales and the total production of company A is what percent of the total sales of company A from the year 2007 to 2011?
a. 25 b. 75 c. 50 d. 100 e. None of these

59. Sales of company A is approximately what percent of the production of company B from the year 2007 to the year 2011?
a. 67 b. 103 c. 97 d. 83 e. 88

60. What is the difference between the sale of company A and production of company B?
a. 100 tonnes b. 90 tonnes c. 80 tonnes d. 70 tonnes e. None of these

Directions (61-65): Study the following graph carefully and answer accordingly:
The following graph shows the percentage profit of company Renault and Hundai over the years.

61. In which of the following years the ratio of expenditure to income was the least for Hundai?
a. 1996 b. 1999 c. 1998 d. 2000 e. 1995

62. If the total expenditure of company Renault in 1997 was Rs. 150 lakhs, what was the total income?
a. Rs. 240 lakhs
b. Rs. 255 lakhs
c. Rs. 250 lakhs
d. Data inadequate
e. None of these

63. In which of the following years was the total income more than double the total expenditure in that year for Renault?
a. 1996 b. 1999 c. 2001 d. 1998 e. 2000

64. In which of the following given years the percentage of expenditure with respect to the income of company Hyundai was less than fifty per cent?
a. 1999 b. 1997 c. 1995 d. 1998 e. 2000

65. If the total income of Hyundai in 2001 was Rs. 200 lakhs, what was the expenditure of Renault in the same year?

a. Rs. 111.11 lakhs b. Rs. 114.28 lakhs
c. Rs. 110 lakhs d. Can't be determined
e. None of these

Directions (66-70): Study the following graphs carefully and answer the questions given below.

Number of students who appeared (In thousands) and Percentage of girls appeared in an examination over the years

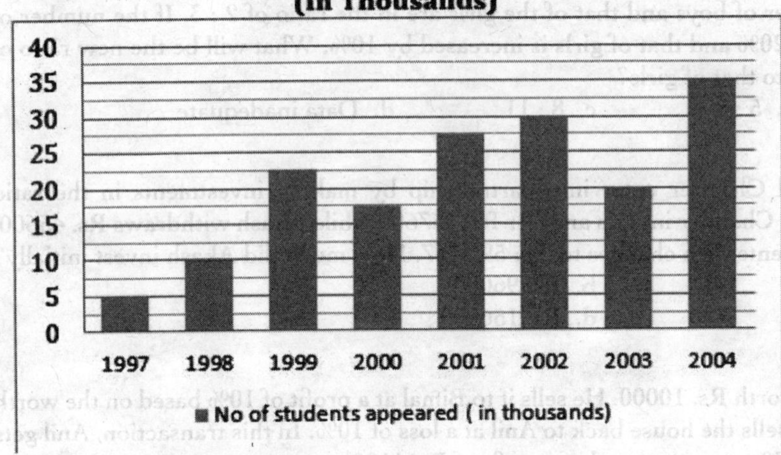

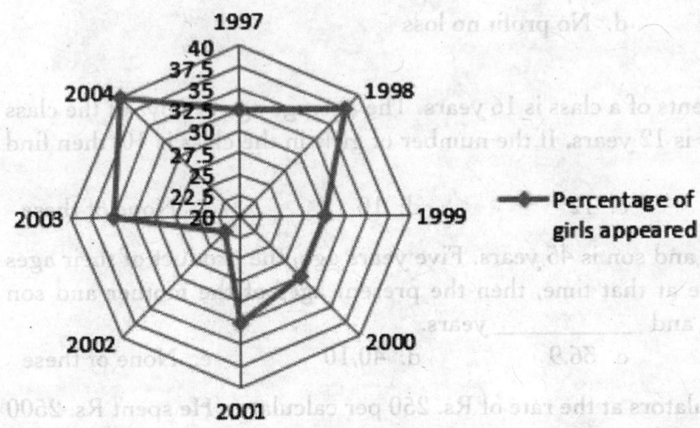

66. What was the ratio between the number of students appeared in 1997 and the number of girls appeared in 2004?
a. 14 : 5 b. 5 : 14 c. 3 : 7 d. Data inadequate
e. None of these

67. In which of the following years was the number of girls appeared the lowest among the given years?
a. 1997 b. 2002 c. 2001 d. 1998 e. None of these

68. What was the percentage drop in the number of students appeared from the year 2002 to 2003?
a. 66 (2/3) b. 30 c. 70 d. 33 e. None of these

69. How many girls appeared in the year 2002?
a. 6750 b. 13500 c. 9900 d. Cannot be determined
e. None of these

70. The number of girls appeared in 1999 was what percentage of the number of students appeared in 1998?
a. 68.5 b. 70 c. 32.5 d. 67.5 e. None of these

71. In a class the number of boys and that of the girls are in the ratio of 2 : 3. If the number of boy is increased by 20% and that of girls is increased by 10%. What will be the new ratio of the number of boys to that of girls?
a. 4 : 5 b. 5 : 8 c. 8 : 11 d. Data inadequate
e. None of these

72. Akash, Bhuvan and Chander enter into partnership by making investments in the ratio 3 : 5 : 7. After a year, Chander invests another Rs. 337600 while Akash withdraws Rs. 45600. The ratio of investments then changes to 24 : 59 : 167. How much did Akash invest initially?
a. Rs. 45600 b. Rs. 96000
c. Rs.141600 d. Rs. 156000
e. None of these

73. Anil owns a house worth Rs. 10000. He sells it to Bimal at a profit of 10% based on the worth of the house. Bimal sells the house back to Anil at a loss of 10%. In this transaction, Anil gets
a. a profit of Rs. 2000 b. a profit of Rs. 1100
c. a profit of Rs. 1000 d. No profit no loss
e. None of these

74. The average age of all the students of a class is 16 years. The average age of boys of the class is 21 years and that of the girls is 12 years. If the number of girls in the class is 10, then find the number of boy in the class.
a. 4 b. 8 c. 12 d. 10 e. None of these

75. The sum of the ages of mother and son is 45 years. Five years ago, the product of their ages was four time the mother's age at that time, then the present ages of the mother and son respectively are __________ and __________ years.
a. 39,6 b. 35,10 c. 36,9 d. 40,10 e. None of these

76. A shopkeeper bought 150 calculators at the rate of Rs. 250 per calculator. He spent Rs. 2500 on transportation and packing. If the marked price of calculator is Rs. 320 per calculator and the shopkeeper gives a discount of 5% on the marked price then what will be the percentage profit gained by the shopkeeper?
a. 20% b. 14% c. 15% d. 16% e. None of these

77. Anshul deposited two parts of a sum of Rs. 25000 in different banks at the rates of 15% per annum and 18% per annum respectively. In one year he got Rs. 4050 as the total interest. What was the amount deposited at the rate of 18% per annum?
a. Rs. 9000 b. Rs. 18000 c. Rs. 15000 d. Rs. 10000 e. None of these

78. The different between the simple and the compound interest compounded every six months at the rate of 10 per cent per annum at the end of two years is Rs. 124.05. What is the sum?
a. Rs. 10000 b. Rs. 60000 c. Rs. 12000 d. Rs. 8000 e. None of these

79. In two alloys, copper and zinc are present in the ratios of 4:1 and 1:3. 10 kg of 1st alloy 16 kg of 2nd alloy and some of pure copper are melted together. An alloy was obtained in which the ratio of copper to zinc was 3:2. Find the weight of the new alloy.
a. 34 kg b. 35 kg c. 36 kg d. 30 kg e. None of these

80. Ramesh can finish a job in 20 days. He worked for 10 days alone and completed the remaining job working with Dinesh, in 2 days. How many days would both Dinesh and Ramesh together take to complete the entire job?
a. 4 b. 5 c. 10 d. 12 e. None of these

Section 3: General and Banking Awareness

81. Who among the following is all set to return as the new Prime Minister of Sri Lanka after the recent Parliamentary elections?
a. Chandrika Kumaratunga
b. Maithripala Sirisena
c. Ranil Wickremesinghe
d. Mahinda Rajapaksa
e. Sarath Fonseka

82. The Reserve Bank of India has given "in-principle" approval to 11 applicants to set up payments banks. Which of the following is NOT among them?
a. Department of Posts
b. Reliance Industries Ltd
c. Tech Mahindra Ltd
d. Vodafone m-pesa Ltd
e. None of these

83. The RBI's "in-principle" approval granted to 11 applicants to set up payment banks will be valid for a period of 18 months. The Payment Banks will NOT be allowed to
a. accept demand deposits
b. remit money
c. provide Internet banking
d. issue ATM/debit cards
e. issue credit cards

84. Name the novelist who has won the annual James Tait Black Award 2015 for his debut novel "In the Light of What We Know".
a. Zia Haider Rahman
b. Imdadul Haq Milon
c. Anisul Hoque
d. Humayun Ahmed
e. Sunil Gangopadhyaya

85. The central govt has decided to declare which of the following cities as 'twin national heritage cities,' the first instance of such a tag being given?
a. Hyderabad-Sikandrabad
b. Haridwar-Rishikesh
c. Ghaziabad-Faridabad
d. Jaipur-Jodhpur
e. None of these

86. The Australian govt has appointed who among the following cricketers as its inaugural ambassador to India on education?

a. Shane Warne b. Glenn McGrath
c. Matthew Hayden d. Adam Gilchrist e. Ricky Ponting

87. Who among the following has been named an advocate for UN's "HeForShe" campaign, the campaign on gender equality?
a. Anil Kapoor b. Salman Khan
c. Anupam Kher d. Amitabh Bachchan
e. Akshay Kumar

88. _______ has been conferred with "Maharashtra Bhushan" award, the state's highest honour.
a. Anant Sadashiv Altekar b. DP Khambete
c. Satish Alekar d. Babasaheb Purandare
e. Gopal Ganesh Agarkar

89. To check black money generation, the govt on 20 Aug approved signing and ratification of the agreement between India and _________ for exchange of information with respect to taxes.
a. Morocco b. Seychelles
c. Algeria d. Mauritania
e. Mauritius

90. Who among the following has been appointed new Chairman and Managing Director of Air India?
a. Rohit Nandan b. Ashwani Lohani
c. Vivek Sahai d. Vinay Mittal
e. Arunendra Kumar

91. Indira Gandhi Centre for Atomic Research, established in 1971, is located at?
a. Indore b. Kolkata
c. Trombay, Maharashtra d. Kalpakkam, Chennai
e. Gujrat

92. In which year did Sir Edmund Hillary reach the summit of Mount Everest?
a. 1952 b. 1953 c. 1954 d. 1955 e. 1956

93. India's first fast breeder neutron reactor was..?
a. Zerlina b. Apsara c. Purnima-I
d. Kamini e. None of the above

94. Human Rights Day is on......
a. 10 December b. 24 February
c. 15 May d. 21 July
e. 19 January

95. India became a member of the United Nations in........
a. 1963 b. 1960 c. 1951 d. 1959 e. 1945

96. India has....
a. largest turmeric production b. largest ginger production
c. largest tea production d. All of the above
e. Only a. and (b)

97. India's first indigenously built submarine was?
a. INS Shalki b. INS Delhi c. INS Vibhuti d. INS Savitri
e. None of the above

98. The largest cantilever bridge of India is....?
a. Howrah Bridge b. Chambal Bridge
c. Mahatama Gandhi Setu d. Coronation Bridge e. Ellis Bridge

99. The language spoken in Lakshadweep island is...?
a. Tamil b. Telegu c. Malayalam d. Kannada e. Oriya

100. The last Hindu king who party succeeded in establishing "Hindu Swaraj" was..?
a. Chhatrapati Shivaji b. Akbar, the Great
c. Chandragupta Maurya d. Bahadurshah Zafar Khan
e. None of the above

101. In which year during World War I, USA declared war on Germany, Britain defeated Turkey and captured Baghdad and Jerusalem?
a. 1917 b. 1918 c. 1919 d. 1920 e. 1914

102. Who is the present Chief Minister of Assam?
a. Sarbananda Sonowal b. Dr. Mukul Sangma
c. Laxmikant Parsekar d. T R Zeliang
e. None of the above

103. The Melghat Tiger reserve is in...?
a. Orissa b. Assam c. Karnataka d. Maharashtra e. Gujrat

104. The state having maximum cities is....?
a. Uttar Pradesh b. West Bengal
c. Madhya Pradesh d. Kerala
e. Maharashtra

105. The national museum is located at...?
a. Pune b. Mumbai c. Lucknow d. New Delhi e. Kolkata

106. Ashok Lavasa has recently been appointed as the new?
a. Chief Economic Adviser b. CEO of NITI Aayog
c. Finance Secretary d. Census Commissioner
e. Chief Information Commissioner

107. Under the Pradhan Mantri Fasal Bima Yojana for all Rabi crops the premium to be paid by farmers is?
a. 5% b. 2% c. 1% d. 1.5% e. 2.5%

108. Which city hosted the first Maritime India Summit in April 2016?
a. Kochi b. Chennai c. Mumbai d. Visakhapatnam
e. Kolkata

109. Who is the present Chairman of National Human Rights Commission?
a. Justice T.S. Thakur b. Justice K.G. Balakrishnan
c. Justice R.M. Lodha d. Justice H.L. Dattu
e. Justice P. Sadashivam

110. What is India's rank in the 2016 World Happiness Index?
a. 118 b. 127 c. 131 d. 115 e. None of these

111. Rhodesia is the old name of which of the following African countries?
a. Botswana b. Zimbabwe c. Mozambique d. Tanzania e. Angola

112. Pradhan Mantri Krishi Sinchai Yojana is related to which of the following?
a. Organic farming
b. Pulses production
c. Irrigation
d. Oilseeds production
e. Minimum support price

113. Which of the following is the largest cash transfer program in the world?
a. Jan Dhan Yojana
b. PAHAL
c. Pradhan Mantri Ujjwala Yojana
d. DISHA
e. None of these

114. Which is the first organic farming State in India?
a. Arunachal Pradesh
b. Telangana
c. Goa
d. Sikkim
e. Meghalaya

115. Apurvi Chandela is associated with which of the following sports?
a. Archery b. Gymnastics c. Cricket d. Hockey e. Shooting

116. Padma Sachdev won the Saraswati Samman for 2015 for her autobiography written in which of the following languages?
a. Dogri b. Punjabi c. Hindi d. Bodo e. Maithili

117. Which of the following is the autobiography of the renowned tennis player Sania Mirza?
a. Playing to Win
b. Playing It My way
c. The Test of My life
d. Out of My Comfort Zone
e. Ace Against Odds

118. Which of the following is a private bank?
a. Dena Bank
b. Allahabad Bank
c. Bank of Maharashtra
d. Karnataka Bank
e. Punjab & Sind Bank

119. The European Union is a politico economic union of how many member States?
a. 27 b. 29 c. 28 d. 26 e. 25

120. Who was crowned Femina Miss India 2016?
a. Natasha Singh
b. Sushruti Krishna
c. Navpreet Kaur
d. Gayatri Reddy
e. Priyadarshini Chatterjee

Section 4: English Language

Directions: Read the following passage carefully and answer the questions given below it. Certain words/ phrases are given in bold to help you locate them while answering some of the questions.

Almost everything has implications for the poor, whether it is education, health, family planning, employment, or the environment, or the environment: they are all fields where current performance hurts the poor in particular. Policies that enhance economic growth, and agriculture growth, will favour reduction of poverty. The lives of poor people are most threatened by potential shortages of water and low water quality, and by air pollution; pressures on common pool resources also bear most heavily on the poor, and on women in particular.

Since half of India's poor are in the persistent category, the country's anti-poverty programmes can at best, have only a limited impact. They are excessively scattered and unrelated to basic processes in the economy. They focus on regions with particular problems, such as drought prone areas; subsidy programmes such as the Targeted Public Distribution System for food; a number of employment-related schemes, and social security measures for the very poor. Most of them have been shown to be inefficient in terms of the proportion of expenditure actually reaching the poor, and in terms of their lasting effects. But greater impacts on poverty could be made by improved performance in the social sectors and the environment generally, concentrating on the states with the greatest backlogs. Better health and nutrition and better education for all, and clean air and water are the best anti-poverty programmes. To these must be added reproductive health services and family planning, again most needed in the poorest states : they too are pro poor measures in themselves for high fertility households.

The majority of the poor remain in rural areas, and measures to redress poverty must concentrate on enhancing both agricultural growth and non-farm employment. Yet India, for all its anti-poverty commitment, has not seen the increases in the key investments--irrigation, rural roads, and agriculture research—that would help to achieve this. Anti-poverty strategies all over the world rightly give an important place to the empowerment of the poor, and their involvement in the design and management of schemes intended for their benefit. India has made considerable strides in these directions : in water, moving to farmer managed watershed development; in a range of activities devolving budgets and management to panchayats and pushing decentralization. Much of this experience has been positive; but much has not. Instead of empowering the poor, it has empowered local-vested interests. Like, markets, devolution and decentralization cannot be guaranteed to help the poor. There is an indispensable role for the state. But frequently public action by state institutions has not delivered either.

Policies to redress poverty require the positive engagement of central and state governments as well as NGOs, local communities, and group of beneficiaries. With greater account ability and transparency India's own resources will be adequate to overcome poverty. Accountability is needed most particularly in public services that affect the poor : health, education and the police perhaps more than any other, as well as the general working of bureaucracy. If resources are not invested or distributed where they are needed, and policies are not framed to benefit the poor or to ensure that the poor receive the benefits meant for them, this projection of slow poverty decline could become a reality. It is ultimately down to politics. If more of India's politicians see electoral promise in genuinely addressing the needs of the poor, poverty can and will decline much faster.

121. Irrigation, rural roads and agriculture research will help to achieve
   a. watershed development by vested interest
   b. empowering state government to plan the budget
   c. reduction of food subsidy   d. agricultural growth   d) None of these

122. In rural areas anti poverty commitments should pay attention to
   A. reproductive health-services and family planning.
   B. good nutrition and education for all.
   C. farm based and non-farm based employment.

   a. Only (C)   b. Only (A) and (B)   c. Only (A)
   d. Only (A) and (C)   e. Only (B)

123. Which of the following programmes provides relief to the poor?
   A. Targeted Public Distribution System
   B. Pro-poverty strategies
   C. Reproductive health-service and family-size management

   a. Only (A)   b. Only (B)   c. Only (C)   d. Both(A) and (B)
   e. None of these

124. What kind of policies will help curtail poverty?
   A. Water conservation and pollution control measures
   B. Economic development and agricultural growth programmes.
   C. Employment schemes and social security.

   a. Only (C)   b. Only(A) and (B)   c. Only (A)
   d. All (A),(B) and (C)   e. Only B)

125. According to the passage what is 'down to politics'?
   a. Social security measures
   b. Considering strides in education
   c. Framing anti-poor policies
   d. Projection of slow poverty decline
   e. None of these

126. Which has to play an important role in promoting decentralisation?
   a. State through the implementation of competent and effective policies
   b. Centre by reserving common pool resources
   c. Politician's promised made during elections
   d. Management by imitating policies of other countries
   e. None of these

127. Why do anti-poverty programmes have only a limited impact?
   A. They are unrelated to basic economic processes.
   B. Their focus is on general problem and broader issues.
   C. They are balanced in terms of expenditure and benefit.
   a. Only (C)   b. Both (B) and (C)   c. Only (A)
   d. Both (A) and (C)   e. None of these

128. According to the passage what should be the fundamental role of the state?
   a. Monitoring working of bureaucracy
   b. Implementation of anti-poverty strategies
   c. Reducing role of panchayats
   d. Empowering local-vested interest
   e. None of these

129. How will India's own resources and systems be helpful to diminish poverty?
   a. Positive engagement of central and state government
   b. With higher accountability and transparency
   c. General working of bureaucracy
   d. Devolving budgets and managements to panchayats
   e. None of these

Directions: Choose the word/phrase which is most nearly the same in meaning as the word printed in bold as used in the passage.

130. Implications
   a. impacts b. advantages c. production d. expenses e. arrangements

131. Current
   a. fresh b. recent c. shock d. hidden e. voltage

132. Prone
   a. affected b. unassailable c. incited d. liable e. vulnerable

Directions: Choose the word/phrase which is most opposite in meaning as the word printed in bold as used in the passage.

133. excessively
   a. closely b. absurdly c. meagrely d. profusely e. moderately

134. lasting
   a. temporary b. first c. final d. timely e. concluding

135. heavily
   a. animated b. thickly c. relaxing d. lightly e. delicately

Directions (136-140) chose the correct option which should replace the underlined in the given statement:

136. With his sub-four minute mile Bannister broke a psychological barrier, <u>inspiring thousands of others to attempt overcoming</u> seemingly insurmountable hurdles.
   a. inspiring thousands of others to attempt overcoming
   b. inspiring thousands of others to attempt to overcome
   c. inspiring thousands of others to overcome
   d. and inspired thousands of others to attempt to overcome
   e. and inspired thousands of others to attempt overcoming

137. Ricks has written extensively <u>on not only major figures in English poetry like Milton and Housman, but also on</u> the lyrics of Bob Dylan.
   a. on not only major figures in English poetry like Milton, but also on
   b. not only on the poetry of such major figures as Milton and Housman, but also on
   c. not only on major figures in English poetry like Milton and Housman, but also on
   d. on major figures in English poetry like Milton and Housman, as well as
   e. on major figures in English poetry such as Milton and Housman, but also on

138. An analysis of sixteenth century probate inventories in the major English towns <u>show that even some artisans and yeomen owned silver spoons, cups or</u> salt cellars.
   a. show that even some artisans and yeomen owned silver spoons, cups or
   b. show that some artisans and yeomen even owned silver spoons, cups or
   c. show that even some artisans and yeomen owned silver spoons, cups and
   d. shows that some artisans and yeomen owned even silver spoons, cups and
   e. shows that even some artisans and yeomen owned silver spoons, cups or

139. Stress-induced amnesia is a rare phenomenon; it strikes the patient apparently without warning and the memory loss can be <u>as complete as that induced by physical trauma</u>.
   a. as complete as that induced by physical trauma
   b. as complete as is induced by physical traumas
   c. as least as complete as physical trauma induces
   d. at least as complete as physical trauma
   e. just as complete as those induced by physical trauma

140. <u>The publishers, unwilling to shoulder the entire risk, insisted that the author should pay half the cost of the initial print run of his controversial new book.</u>
   a. The publishers, unwilling to shoulder the entire risk, insisted that the author should pay half the cost of the initial print run of his controversial new book.
   b. The publishers, unwilling to shoulder the entire risk, insisted that the author should be paying half the cost of the initial print run of the author's controversial new book.
   c. The publishers, unwilling to shoulder the entire risk, insisted that the author pay half the cost of the initial print run of his controversial new book.
   d. Unwilling to shoulder the entire risk, the publishers insisted the author should pay half the cost of the initial print run of his controversial new book.
   e. Unwilling to shoulder the entire risk, the author was required by the publisher to pay half the cost of the initial print run of his controversial new book.

Directions (141-145): Pick out the most effective pair of words from the given pair of words to make the-sentence(s) meaningfully complete.

141. Some people have a ________ need to control all aspects of their lives and to eliminate all ________ of chance. These individuals seldom achieve a sense of fulfilment.
   a. habitual , possessions
   b. dramatic, factors
   c. powerful, nuances
   d. compulsive, elements
   e. drastic, hindrances

142. Leaders interested in achieving performance need an ________ ________ of the relationship between work-related stress and performance.
   a. durable, understanding
   b. optimum, awareness
   c. holistic, utility
   d. powerful, analysing
   e. effective, suggestion

143. Ms. Jayalalithaa __________ Mr. Stalin's greetings to her, by declaring that she looked __________to working with him and his party "for the betterment of the State."

a. said, towards
b. reciprocated, forward
c. saying, at
d. announced, in lieu of
e. congratulate, toward

144. The objectives for which Vayudoot was formed originally are __________. Political, social and economic requirements demand that __________ areas be brought within the **communication links.**

a. creditable, forbidden
b. refutable, disturbed
c. viable, enlarged
d. questionable, formidable
e. laudable, inaccessible

145. Vivekananda remained a devoted pupil and would often __________, with some fondness, his master's guiding hand that __________ him through life and destiny.

a. recount, steered
b. ponder, engaged
c. replenish, advised
d. mentioned, proved
e. narrate, forwarded

Directions (146-155): In the following passage, some of the words have been left out, each of which is indicated by a number. Find the suitable word from the options given against each number and fill up the blanks with appropriate words to make the paragraph meaningfully complete.

Everyone needs quality sleep every single night, but lifestyle ...(1)... and hurdles make sleep disorders more common than good sleep. This poor sleeping pattern has serious ...(2)... on our health, and the first thing we ...(3)... is unhealthy weight gain or weight loss, low concentration, and mood swings. If you have ...(4)... sleeping ...(5)... every day and this lack of sleep is ...(6)... your day to-day routine, then you may be suffering from one of the many (and most common) sleep disorders. You will be surprised to know that there are many more sleep disorders than just insomnia and sleep apnoea. There are ...(7)... sleep disorders and their ...(8)..., You should take proper ...(9)... before they take a ...(10)... on your life.

146. a. cozen b. choices c. abjure d. deter e. rustic

147. a. coerce b. rampage c. repercussions d. rattle e. assent

148. a. covert b. denounce c. bleak d. notice e. point

149. a. mutilate b. trouble c. rear d. dismay e. cozy

150. a. utmost b. in c. for d. at e. almost

151. a. glimmering b. gamut c. fortifying d. affecting e. cascading

152. a. bland b. copious c. various d. alternate e. growing

153. a. warning b. symptoms c. signs d. indicia e. indication

154. a) treatment b) healing c) hubris d) overt e) regimen

155. a) abject b) toll c) barge d) muse e) poised

ANSWER KEY

1. b	2. a	3. b	4. c	5. a	6. c	7. c	8. b	9. c	10. b
11. d	12. a	13. a	14. c	15. e	16. a	17. b	18. b	19. d	20. d
21. a	22. a	23. a	24. a	25. e	26. b	27. e	28. d	29. b	30. a
31. b	32. a	33. c	34. b	35. a	36. a	37. c	38. c	39. d	40. a
41. c	42. b	43. b	44. b	45. a	46. e	47. b	48. a	49. a	50. b
51. c	52. a	53. b	54. b	55. c	56. b	57. c	58. d	59. c	60. e
61. e	62. a	63. b	64. c	65. d	66. b	67. a	68. e	69. a	70. d
71. c	72. d	73. b	74. b	75. c	76. b	77. d	78. d	79. b	80. a
81. c	82. e	83. e	84. a	85. b	86. d	87. c	88. d	89. b	90. b
91. d	92. b	93. d	94. a	95. e	96. e	97. a	98. a	99. c	100. a
101. a	102. a	103. a	104. e	105. a	106. c	107. d	108. c	109. d	110. a
111. b	112. c	113. b	114. d	115. e	116. a	117. e	118. d	119. c	120. e
121. d	122. b	123. e	124. d	125. d	126. e	127. c	128. b	129. b	130. e
131. b	132. a	133. c	134. a	135. d	136. d	137. b	138. e	139. a	140. c
141. d	142. b	143. b	144. e	145. a	146. b	147. c	148. d	149. b	150. e
151. d	152. c	153. b	154. a	155. b					

Explanation

Answer(1-5)

The given input and the last step shows that words are arranged in alphabetical order.

Numbers are arranged alternately in the increasing order and alternatively in decreasing order, i.e least number followed by highest number, second least number followed second highest number and so on.

In the input given for the questions, two elements are moving. Numbers are moving to left end words are moving to right end in a particular order.

Input :-
"done 31 39 vault heart 97 john 84 gear 70 sport 65"
Step I:- 70 31 39 vault heart 97 john 84 gear sport 65 done.
Step II:- 65 70 31 39 vault heart 97 john 84 sport done gear.
Step III:- 84 65 70 31 39 vault 97 john sport done gear heart.
Step IV:- 39 84 65 70 26 vault 97 sport done gear heart john.
Step V:- 97 39 84 65 70 26 vault done gear heart john sport.
Step VI:- 26 97 39 84 65 70 done gear heart john sport vault.

Answer(6-10)

By the given information, day of work, friends name and language are arrange in following table:

Day	Mon	Tue	Wed	Thur	Fri	Sat	Sun
Name	Q	N	R	P	M	S	O
Language	ENGLISH	SANSKRIT	FRENCH	CHINESE	SPANISH	JAPANESE	GERMAN

Answer(26-30)

26.

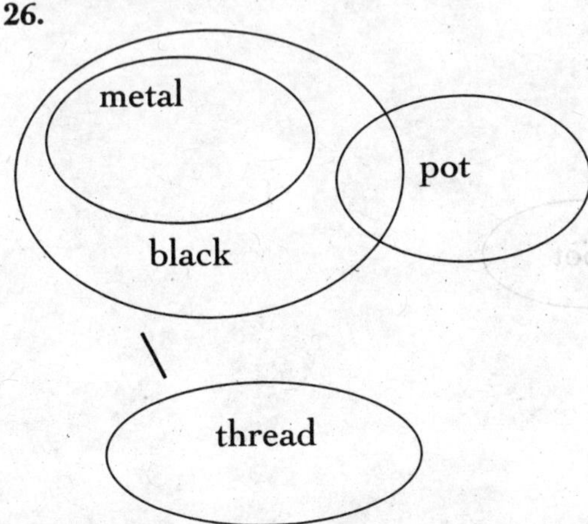

27.

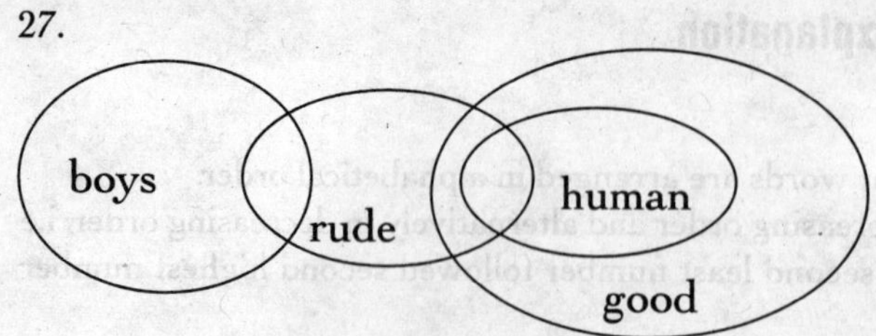
boys
rude
human
good

28.

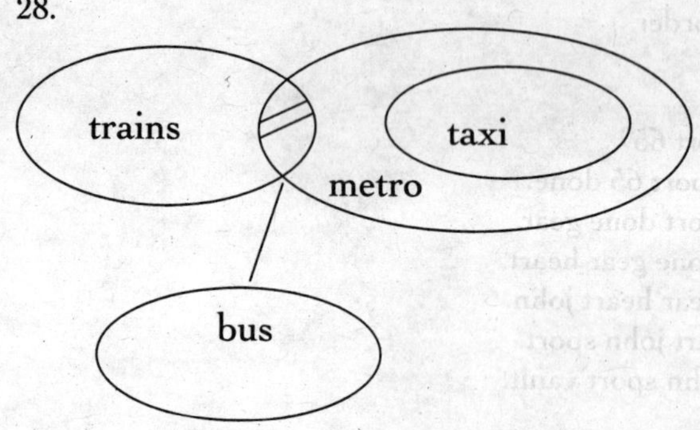
trains
taxi
metro
bus

29.

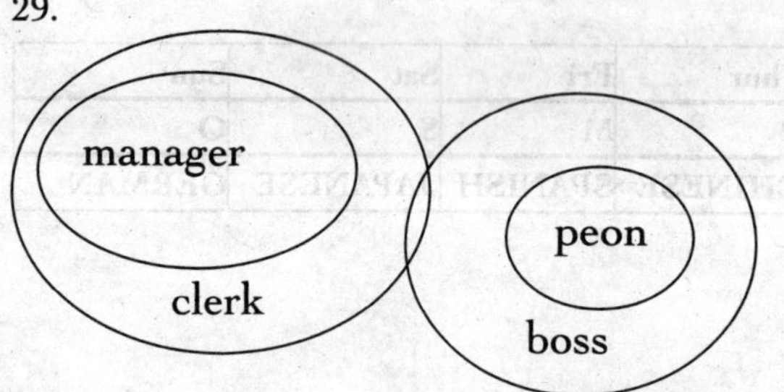
manager
clerk
peon
boss

30.

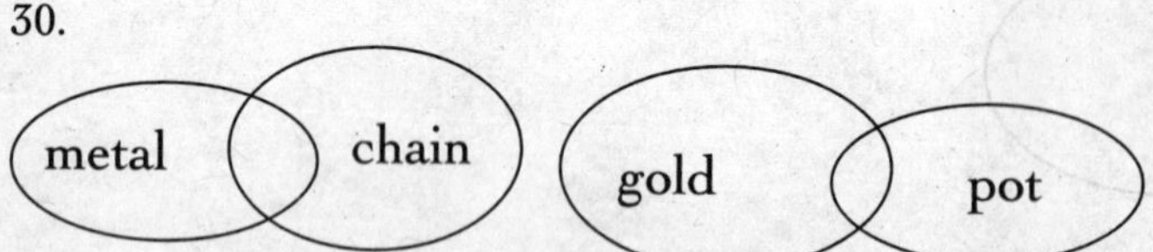
metal
chain
gold
pot

SBI PO Mains MOCK Test Paper 5

Structure of this MOCK Test

S.No.	Name of section	No. of Questions	Total marks	Allotted Time
1	Reasoning and Computer Aptitude	45	60	60 minutes
2	Data Analysis and Interpretation	35	60	45 minutes
3	General/ Economy/ Banking Awareness	40	40	35 minutes
4	English Language	35	40	40 minutes
Total		155	200	3 hours

- There is 1/4th Negative marking for every wrong answer.
- If a question is left blank, i.e. no answer is marked by the candidate, there will be no penalty for that question

Section 1: Reasoning & Computer Aptitude

Directions (1-5): Study the following information carefully to answer the given questions. A word and number arrangement machine when given an input line of words and numbers rearranges them following a particular rule in each step. The following is an illustration of an input and its rearrangement:

Input: must core fight read before married
Step I: before must core fight read married
Step II: before married must core fight read
Step III: before married core must fight read
Step IV: before married core read must fight
Step V: before married core read fight must.

And Step V is the last step of the above input. As per the rules followed in the above steps, find out in each of the following questions the appropriate step for the given input.

Input: follow action engineer family related are

1. How many steps will be required to complete the given input?
   a. Three b. Two c. Five d. More than five
   e. None of these

2. Which of the following will be the third step for the above input?
   a. engineer follow action family related are
   b. engineer action related are follow family
   c. engineer action related follow family are
   d. engineer related follow action family are
   e. None of these

3. What is the position of 'are' in Step IV?
   a. Third from the right end b. Fifth from the left end
   c. First from the right end d. Third from the left end
   e. Fourth from the right end

4. If in the second step of an input is 'bookie mobile nice from see bee' which of the following steps would be the last step of that input?
   a. III b. IV c. V d. VI e. None of these

5. If 'companies element tight answer how seven' is the second step of an input, which of the following will be the input?
   a. eight answer seven companies how element
   b. answer eight seven how element companies
   c. element how seven companies eight answer
   d. Can't be determined
   e. None of these

Directions (6–10): Study the information and answer the following questions:
Eight persons Elesh, Vikram, Vinay, Denny, Ela, Farukh, Gurpreet and Hitesh - are sitting around a circular table facing away from the centre. Each of them likes a novel of a different writer, viz Chetan Bhagat, William Faulkner, Charles Dickens, Leo Tolstoy, Mark Twain, George Eliot, Bob Mayor and Marcel Proust, but not necessarily in the same order.
Elesh, who likes Leo Tolstoy, sits third to the right of Ela. The one who likes Marcel Proust sits second to the left of Denny, who likes the novel of Chetan Bhagat. Vinay, who likes William Faulkner, sits between the persons who like George Eliot and Marcel Proust. Denny sits second to the left of Vikram, who cannot sit adjacent to Ela. Gurpreet likes Bob Mayor and sits second to the right of Hitesh, who likes Charles Dickens.

6. What is the position of Denny with respect to the person who likes the novel of William Faulkner?
   a. Third to the left b. Third to the right
   c. Second to the right d. Fifth to the right
   e. Fourth to the left

7. Which of the following combinations is definitely true?
   a. Elesh - Marcel Proust b. Hitesh - Chetan Bhagat
   c. Ela - Bob Mayor d. Farukh - Leo Tolstoy
   e. Vikram - Mark Twain

8. How many persons are sitting between Ela and the person who likes the novel written by Leo Tolstoy (if counted from Ela in clockwise direction)?
   a. One b. Two c. Three d. None
   e. More than three

9. Who likes the novel of George Eliot?
   a. Vikram b. Denny c. Ela d. Farukh e. Hitesh

10. Denny is related to "Marcel Proust" and Gurpreet is related to Charles Dickens. In the same way, Farukh is related to whom among the following?
   a. Chetan Bhagat b. George Eliot c. Bob Mayor
   d. William Faulkner e. Leo Tolstoy

Directions (11-15): Read each statement carefully and answer the following questions:

In a certain code language-
"attitude is good quality" is written as "kt lt ho gt",
"plain and simple attitude" is written as, "mt ta pt kt",
"quality creates net worth" is written as, "zi lt ne ki",
"attitude creates simple life" is written as "zi mt kt da".

11. What is the code for "attitude" in the given code language?
   a. gt b. ho c. pt d. kt e. da

12. What is the code for "creates" in the given code language?
   a. zi b. mt c. either kt or do d. ne e. lt

13. What is the code for "quality" in the given code language?
   a. lt b. ho c. kt d. zi e. da

14. What is the code for "simple" in the given code language?
   a. kt b. da c. mt d. ga e. zi

15. What is the code for "life" in the given code language?
   a. mt b. zi c. kt d. da
   e. Cannot be determined

Directions (16-20): Read each statement carefully and answer the following questions:

16. Rahul put his timepiece on the table in such a way that at 6 P.M. hour hand points to North. In which direction the minute hand will point at 9.15 P.M. ?
   a. South-West b. South c. North d. West e. None of these

17. Rasik walked 20 m towards north. Then he turned right and walks 30 m. Then he turns right and walks 35 m. Then he turns left and walks 15 m. Finally he turns left and walks 15 m. In which direction and how many metres is he from the starting position?
   a. 15m west b. 30m east c. 30m west d. 45m east e. None of these

18. Two cars start from the opposite places of a main road, 150 km apart. First car runs for 25 km and takes a right turn and then runs 15 km. It then turns left and then runs for another 25 km and then takes the direction back to reach the main road. In the mean time, due to minor break down the other car has run only 35 km along the main road. What would be the distance between two cars at this point?
   a. 65km b. 75km c. 80km d. 85km e. None of these

19. Starting from the point X, Jayant walked 15 m towards west. He turned left and walked 20 m. He then turned left and walked 15 m. After this he turned to his right and walked 12 m. How far and in which directions is now Jayant from X?
a. 32m, south b. 47m, east c. 42m, north d. 27m, south e. None of these

20. One evening before sunset Rekha and Hema were talking to each other face to face. If Hema's shadow was exactly to the right of Hema, which direction was Rekha facing?
a. North b. South c. East d. Data inadequate
e. None of these

21. A boy rode his bicycle Northward, then turned left and rode 1 km and again turned left and rode 2 km. He found himself 1 km west of his starting point. How far did he ride northward initially?
a. 1 KM b. 2 KM c. 3 KM d. 5 KM e. None of these

Directions (22-26) : Study the information and answer the following questions:
L, N, P, R, M, Q, T and Y are the members of a committee sitting around a circular table but not facing the centre. Each member has a different zodiac sign, viz Leo, Virgo, Libra, Cancer, Aries, Gemini, Pisces and Scorpio, but not necessarily in the same order. T is third to the right of P. The one whose sun-sign Leo is second to the left of the one whose sun-sign is Libra.
Y's sun-sign is Libra and is sitting exactly between P and L. The one whose sun-sign is Pisces sits second to the right of N. The one whose sun-sign is Aries is second to the right of the person whose sun-sign is Gemini. P sits third to the left of the person whose sun-sign is Virgo. Neither Q nor L is the immediate neighbour of N. Q is fourth to the left of L. N's sun-sign is neither Cancer nor Ariel. The person whose sun-sign is Leo is sitting second to the right of the person whose sign is Cancer. R's sun-sign is Leo and is not an immediate neighbour of N.

22. Which of the following is N's sun-sign?
a. Pisces b. Scorpio c. Gemini d. Can't be determined
e. None of these

23. Who sits third to the right of L?
a. P b. Y c. R d. Q e. None of these

24. What is Y's position with respect to Q?
a. Third to the left b. Fourth to the left
c. Second to the right d. Third to the right
e. 2nd to the left

25. How many persons are there between P and N?
a. None b. Two c. Three d. Four e. None of these

26. What is the sun-sign of P?
a. Gemini b. Libra c. Leo d. Can't be determined
e. None of these

Directions (27-30)
These data sufficiency problems consist of a question and two statements, labelled (1) and (2), in which certain data are given. You have to decide whether the data given in the statements are sufficient for answering the question. Choose the correct option which follow.

27. IN a general body election 3 candidates p, q and r were representing for a membership of the board. How many votes did each receive?

I. p received 17 votes more than q and 103 votes more than r.

II. Total votes cast were 1703.

a. If the data in statement I alone is sufficient to answer the question, while the data in statement II alone is not sufficient to answer the question.

b. If data in statement II alone is sufficient to answer the question, while the data in statement I alone is not sufficient to answer the question.

c. If the data either in statement I or in statement II alone is sufficient to answer the question

d. If the data even in both statements I and II together are not sufficient to answer the question.

e. If data in both statements I and II together are necessary to answer the question.

28. What is the distance between P and Q?

I.P and Q are two points on the semicircle with centre at the point O.

II. The angle POQ is 30 degrees

a. If the data in statement I alone is sufficient to answer the question, while the data in statement II alone is not sufficient to answer the question.

b. If data in statement II alone is sufficient to answer the question, while the data in statement .I alone is not sufficient to answer the question.

c. If the data either in statement I or in statement II alone is sufficient to answer the question.

d. If the data even in both statements I and II together are not sufficient to answer the question.

e. If data in both statements I and II together are necessary to answer the question.

29. If C1 and C2 are the circumferences of the outer and inner circles respectively, what is C1:C2?

I. The two circles are concentric

II. The area of the ring is 2/3 the area of greater circle

a. If the data in statement I alone is sufficient to answer the question, while the data in statement II alone is not sufficient to answer the question.

b. If data in statement II alone is sufficient to answer the question, while the data in statement I alone is not sufficient to answer the question.

c. If the data either in statement I or in statement II alone is sufficient to answer the question.

d. If the data even in both statements I and II together are not sufficient to answer the question.

e. If data in both statements I and II together are necessary to answer the question.

30. What is the height of the triangle ABC?

I. BC is the base and the sum of the sides is 15 cm.

II. The ratio of the sides BC, CA and AB is respectively 2:2:1

a. If the data in statement I alone is sufficient to answer the question, while the data in statement II alone is not sufficient to answer the question.

b. If data in statement II alone is sufficient to answer the question, while the data in statement I alone is not sufficient to answer the question.

c. If the data either in statement I or in statement II alone is sufficient to answer the question.

d. If the data even in both statements I and II together are not sufficient to answer the question.

e. If data in both statements I and II together are necessary to answer the question.

31. **Which among the following option does DBMS helps to achieve?**
    a. Data independence
    b. More redundancy
    c. Centralised manner to control of data
    d. Both (a) and (c)
    e. None of the above

32. **Which among the following is a Super computer series developed by Indian scientists?**
    a. Param b. Super30l c. Compaq Presario d. Cray YMP
    e. Blue Gene

33. **DBMS ensures data integrity by managing transactions through ACID test. What does ACID stands for in computer science?**
    a. Artistic, collaborative, inference, durability
    b. analytic, consistency, inference, duration
    c. Atomicity, consistency, isolation, durability
    d. Atomicity, collaborative, inference duration
    e. Adherence, consistency, isolation, durability

34. **Table of contents can be prepared by using:**
    a. macros b. headings as H1, H2, H3 and more in the document
    c. by table of contents in tools menu
    d. (b) and (c) e. By File menu

35. **Who developed the basic architecture of Computers?**
    a. Charles Babbage b. Blaise Pascal c. Steve Newton
    d. John Von Neumann e. Henery Johns

36. **Which bar is usually located below the Title Bar that provides categorized options?**
    a. Menu Bar b. Status bar c. Toolbar d. Scroll Bar
    e. None of the above

37. **Inheritance is the ability of an object to pass on its characteristics to its ________.**
    a. subclasses b. off-spring c. super classes d. parents
    e. none of the above

38. **What does the computer Motherboard contains that houses setting configurations and is powered by the onboard battery?**
    a. CMOS b. RAM c. DRAM d. CPU e. None of these

39. **Which type of system can learn and adjust to new circumstances by themselves?**
    a. Database management system b. Expert systems
    c. Geographical systems d. Neural networks
    e. File based systems

40. **The default and maximum size of text filed in Access is ______.**
    a. 266 characters & 6400 characters
    b. 288 characters & 6880 characters
    c. 299 characters & 6499 characters
    d. 50 and 255 characters
    e. None of these

41. Which among the following term is used for: Unauthorized copying of software to be used for personal gain instead of personal backups?
a. program thievery
b. data snatching
c. software piracy
d. program looting
e. data looting

42. Type _______ to start a numbered list, and then press SPACEBAR or the TAB key.
a. 1#
b. 1$
c. 1.
d. 1*
e. None of these

43. A/(n) __________ is an object embedded in a web page or email, which unobtrusively (usually invisibly) allows checking that a user has accessed the content.
a. email
b. virus
c. web beacon
d. spam
e. firewall

44. Non-physical components of the computer are referred to as _______.
a. CPU
b. Software
c. Hardware
d. Program
e. None of these

45. How many rows are there in latest version of MS Excel?
a. 65536
b. 16,384
c. 1,048,576
d. 1,050,000
e. 2,001,000

Section 2: Data Analysis and Interpretation

Direction for questions 46 – 50: Go through the data set given below and solve the questions based on it.
The following table provides information about the grades got by 15 students in six subjects namely Psychology, Sociology, Philosophy, English and History. The grades received by the students are A, B, C, D, E, F and G. Each student got only one out of the mentioned seven grades in each of the five subjects.

	Psychology	Sociology	Philosophy	English	History
Shefali	A	B	A	G	E
Taruna	B	C	A	E	B
Ram	G	E	C	F	D
Mohan	E	A	D	A	C
Sanjay	C	G	B	D	G
Ranjay	D	D	G	E	G
Suresh	F	D	G	B	F
Amit	G	E	F	D	E
Anshul	G	E	G	E	D
Nitisha	A	F	A	C	A
Aditi	B	A	D	G	C
Sushil	F	A	E	A	B
Arvind	D	B	C	A	E
Anand	C	C	D	B	F

Additional Information Given:
I. Grade A is better than grade B, grade B is better than grade C, grade C is better than grade D, grade D is better than grade E, grade E is better than grade F and grade F is better than grade G.

II. A student is said to be superior to another student if he/she has got better grades than a student in each of the five subjects.

III. Two students are said to be similar if they have got same grades in at least two subjects.

46. How many students got same grade in more than subject?
a. 10 b. 11 c. 12 d. 13 e. 9

47. How many students are superior to Suresh?
a. 0 b. 1 c. 2 d. 3 e. 4

48. How many pairs of students are similar?
a. 14 b. 13 c. 12 d. 10 e. 11

49. Which of the following students is not similar to any of the mentioned students?
a. Sushil b. Arvind c. Sanjay d. Aditi e. Anand

50. Which of the following students is superior to Ram?
a. Sanjay b. Arvind c. Anand d. Taruna e. Nitisha

Direction for questions 51 to 54: Go through the information given below and solve the questions based on it.

Five models – Ana, Bana, Ceena, Deena and Eeena were competing for Ms. World contest.

Each of them was rated on 5 different parameters, viz. Height, Body Language, Confidence, Presence of Mind, General Knowledge. The highest rating point being 5 and the lowest being 1. For each of the parameters, no two models got the same rating.

Overall scores for each of the models was the sum total of the rating points in each of the parameters.

Ana got the highest number of points, viz. 24

Ceena was consistent in her scores, i.e. she got the same number of points in 4 different parameters. Eeena got 5 in Presence of Mind and 3 in General Knowledge.

No two models got the same total score and the final rankings were as follows:
Ana, Bana, Ceena, Deena, and Eeena (Ana is best ranked)

51. The difference of total points for two pairs of models was the same. Which of the following is those two pairs?
a. Bana-Ceena, Ceena-Deena b. Ana-Bana, Bana-Ceena
b. Bana-Deena, Ceena-Eeena d. Ceena-Deena, Deena-Eeena
e. none of these

52. The numbers of points managed by Beena in Presence of Mind were?
a. 5 b. 4 c. 1 d. 2
e. Cannot be determined.

53. The number of points managed by Deena in General Knowledge were?
a. 5 b. 1 c. 3 d. 4 e. 2

54. The number of models who scored the same points in exactly 4 of the parameters was
a. 1 b. 2 c. 3 d. 4
e. Cannot be determined.

55. The numbers are respectively 30% and 40% of a third number. What percentage is the first number of the second number?
a. 25% b. 50% c. 75% d. 30% e. None of these

56. What is the probability that there are 53 Sundays and 53 Saturdays in a leap year?
a. 1/7 b. 2/7 c. 0 d. 1 e. None of these

57. In a mixture of milk and water of volume 30 litres, ratio of milk and water is 7: 3. Find the quantity of water to be added to the mixture make the ratio of milk and water 1: 2.
a. 30 b. 32 c. 33 d. 35 e. 40

58. By selling a CD for Rs. 150, a shop owner lost 1/16 of what it costs. What is the cost price of CP?
a. Rs. 120 b. Rs. 140 c. Rs. 150 d. Rs. 160 e. Rs. 200

59. Saurabh sold 250 cycles and had a gain equal to the selling price of 50 cycles. What is his profit percentage?
a. 25% b. 20% c. 10% d. 40% e. None of these

60. If x and y are consecutive natural numbers in increasing order, then which of the following is always true?
a. $x^y > y^x$ b. $y^x > x^y$ c. $x^x > y^y$ d. $y^y > x^x$ e. none of these

Direction for questions 61–67: Go through the data set given below and solve the questions based on it.

The following graphs provide data about four of the industrial sectors in the Republic of Reposia. Manufacturing constituted 20%, Mining & Quarrying 15%, Electricity 15% and Chemicals 10% of the Republic's total industrial production in 1989. For the period 90-98, the graphs give the percentage change in production over the previous year's production. 1989 production values has been assigned an index of 100 for each of the four sectors.

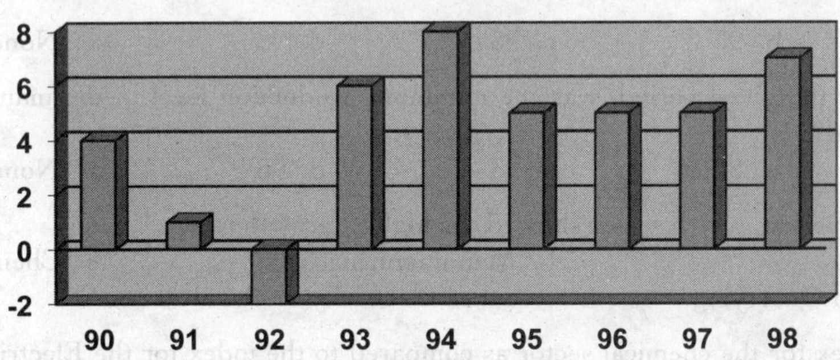

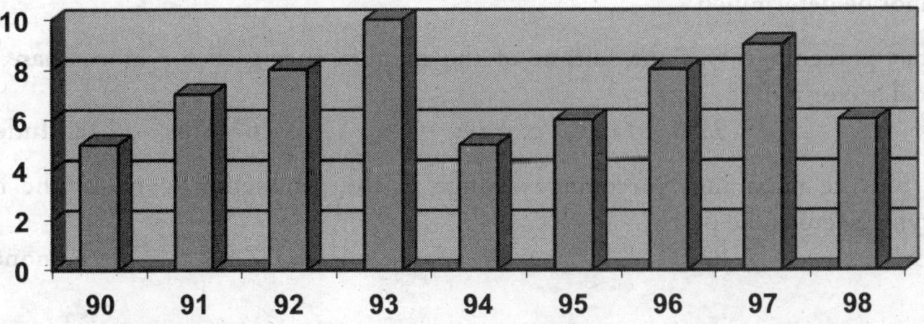

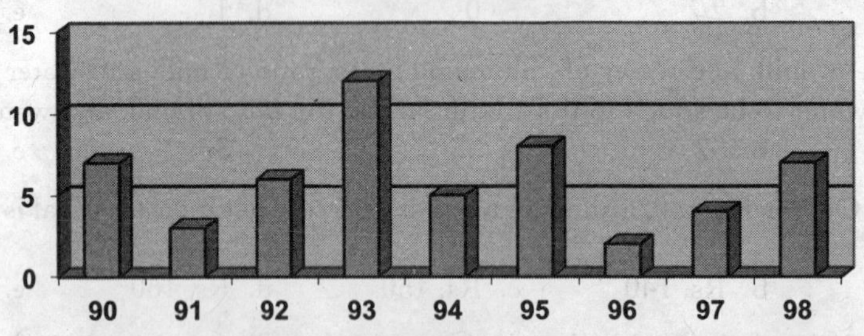

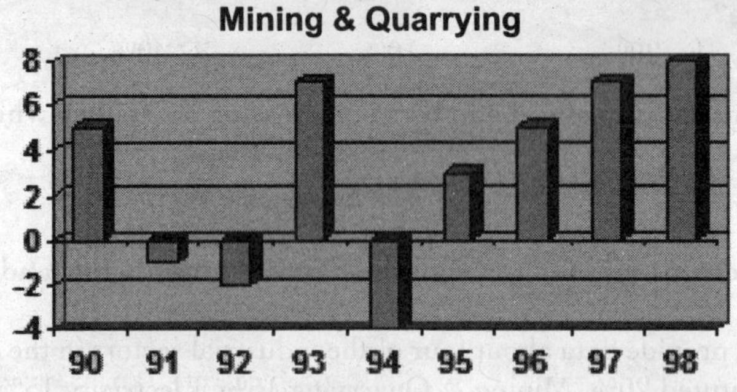

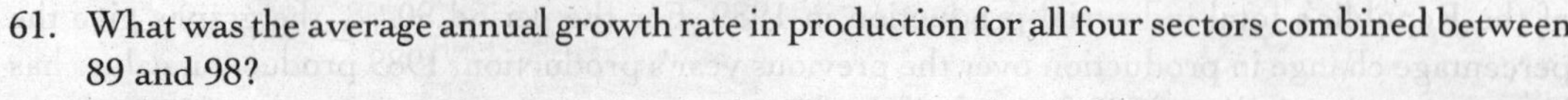

61. What was the average annual growth rate in production for all four sectors combined between 89 and 98?
    a. 1.2% b. 6% c. 56.6% d. 104% e. 22%

62. When during the given period, was the maximum production level in the electricity sector achieved?
    a. 89 b. 93 c. 95 d. 98 e. None of these

63. When, during the given period, was the minimum production level in the manufacturing sector achieved?
    a. 89 b. 90 c. 93 d. 98 e. None of these

64. For the given period, which sector showed the highest growth rate?
    a. Electricity b. Manufacturing c. Chemical
    d. Mining and Quarrying. e. either Electricity or chemical

65. In 92, the index for the chemical sector as compared to the index for the Electricity sector was
    a. greater by 6 b. less by 5 c. greater by 20 d. less by 20
    e. cannot be determined

66. By what percentage was the output of the manufacturing sector more than that of the chemical sector in 91?
    a. 84% b. 91% c. 98% d. 76% e. Indeterminate

67. When did the maximum percentage change in the production levels of the mining and Quarrying sector take place?
    a. 93-94 b. 92-93 c. 96-97 d. 97-98 e. none of these

Direction for questions 68 – 73: Go through the data set given below and solve the questions based on it.

Following grid presents the percentage composition of five verticals under different sectors.

Sector	Factories	Employment	Fixed Capital	Variable Cost	Value Added
Government	18	15	14	22	25
Central	8	6	5	7	10
State	4	6	4	8	3
Central/State	6	3	5	7	12
Public	12	8	6	19	8
Private	55	65	72	54	62
Joint	15	12	8	5	5
Total	100	100	100	100	100

68. If the total work force was 76 million whereas the total value added was 225 million, then which of the following had the maximum value addition per worker?
a. Central b. State c. Central/State d. Public e. Private

69. Which of the following sectors has the maximum fixed capital invested per factory?
a. Central b. State c. Central/State d. Public e. Joint

70. If the variable is proportional to the number of employees and the production per employee, then for which of the following is the production highest?
a. Government b. Private c. Joint d. Public e. Central

71. If the government has a fixed capital of $200 million in the Iron&Steel industry, which corresponds to 20.012% of its total investment as fixed capital, then how much did the government invest(in Rs. million) in Maruti Udyog Ltd. which forms 25% of the investment in the joint sector?(1US $ = Rs.45)
a. 6500 b. 2500 c) 143 d) 145 e) None of these

72. Maruti Udyog Ltd. is a joint project of the Indian Government and Suzuki Motors Japan, each having equal stake. One fine day, the Indian government decides to disinvest from the venture due to losses occurring from labour problems. How many money will be disinvested?
a. Rs.246 million b. Rs.6500 million c. $246 million
d. $ 6500 million e. None of these

73. Which of the following statements is true?
a. The number of government employees is more than that of the number of factories in the joint sector
b. The number of employees in the public is same as fixed capital of joint sector
c. Both [A] and [B] d. Neither A nor B
e. Cannot be determined

Direction for questions 74 – 78: Go through the data set given below and solve the questions based on it.

The following graph gives the data about foreign equity inflow index (FEII) for five countries for two years 1997 and 1998. FEII is taken as the ratio of foreign equity inflow (FEI) to the country's GDP. FEII is expressed as percentage in the graph.

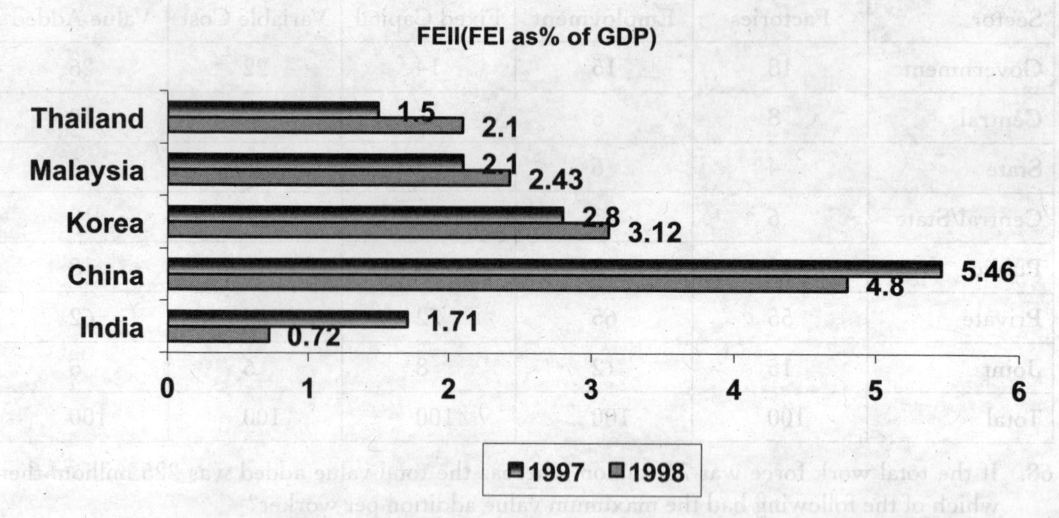

74. Which country has shown the maximum percentage change in FEII in 1998 relative to 1997?
    a. India b. China c. Korea d. Malaysia e. Malaysia

75. IF China's FEI is 10 times that of India in the year 1998, which of the following is true for 1998?
    a. China's GDP is 70% more than India.
    b. China's GDP is 40% more than India.
    c. China's GDP is 50% more than India.
    d. China's GDP is 20% more than India
    e. Nothing can be inferred.

76. If GDP of India increased by 5%, GDP of China increased by 7% and that of Korea decreased by 2% from year 1997 to 1998, which of the following is/are true?
    I. FEI to china was higher in 1998 than in 1997.
    II. FEI to china was lower in 1998 than in 1997.
    III. India's FEI has increases from 1997 to 1998.
    IV. FEI to Korea was lower in 1998 than in 1997.
    V. Korea's FEI has increased in 1998 from 1997.
    a. I and III b. II and V c. II,III and V d. I, II and IV
    e. All of the above.

77. Which of the following can be inferred from the given data?
    a. China's GDP is more than India. b. China's GDP is less than India
    c. India's GDP is less than Malaysia d. India's GDP is more than Malaysia
    e. Nothing can be deduced

78. In how many countries has the FEI increased from 1997 to 1998?
a. 1 b. 2 c. 3 d. 0
e. cannot be determined

79. A certain sum becomes 7/3 times itself in ten years under simple interest. Find the rate of interest.
a. $7\frac{1}{2}$% *p.a.* b. $13\frac{1}{3}$% *p.a.* c. 20% p.a. d. 10% p.a. e. 12.5 p.a.

80. $\frac{(3.134)^3 + (1.866)^3}{(3.134)^2 - 3.134 \times 1.868 + (1.866)^2} = ?$
a. 25 b. 2.68 c. 1.038 d. 5 e. 2.5

Section 3: General Awareness

81. With the aim of achieving Financial Inclusion, Reserve Bank Of India has issued guidelines permitting the banks to employ ____ to facilitate Business Development.
a. Business Correspondents
b. Franchisees
c. Business Facilitators
d. Both 'a' and 'c'
e. None of the above

82. In respect of CGTMSE (Credit Guarantee fund Trust for Micro and Small Enterprises) No collateral and no third party guarantee for fund based and non fund based credit facilities up to ____
a. Rs. 10.00 lakhs
b. Rs. 5.00 lakhs
c. Rs.100 lakhs
d. Rs. 5 lakhs
e. None of the above

83. SME Stands for:
a. Selling and Marketing Establishment
b. Selling and Managing Employee
c. Sales and Marketing entity
d. Small and Medium Enterprises
e. None of the above

84. Which of the following is the Regulator of the credit rating agencies in India?
a. RBI b. SBI c. SIDBI d. SEBI
e. None of the above

85. The branding line of Bank of Baroda is ____
a. International bank of India
b. India's International bank
c. Indian's Multinational Bank
d. World's local Bank
e. None of these

86. One of the major challenges banking industry is facing these days is money laundering. Which of the following acts/norms are launched by the banks to prevent money laundering in general?
a. Banking Regulation Act
b. Know Your Customer Norms
c. Negotiable Instrument Act
d. Narcotics and Psychotropic Substance Act
e. None of these

87. Which of the following is the Capital Market regulator?
a. RBI b. IRDA c. NSE d. BSE e. SEBI

88. We know that RBI is the apex bank of India. Similarly the apex Bank of the USA is:
a. Federal Reserve Bank
b. The Central Bank of USA
c. Bank of America
d. Central National Bank of USA
e. None of these

89. Sales above Breakeven point is called ___
a. Margin of Safety
b. Gross Profit
c. Net profit
d. b & c
e. None of the above

90. Authorized Dealers for foreign transactions are appointed by:
a. Reserve Bank of India
b. Government of India
c. Individual Banks
d. FEDAI
e. None of these

91. As per the report published in the newspaper, the banks, particularly public sector banks are tying up with various rating agencies for providing a qualitative assessment of the credit needs of the borrowers. Which amongst the following is/are such credit rating agencies in India?
A. CARE
B. CRISIL
C. ULIP
a. Only A b. Only B c. A and B d. Only C e. All A, B and C

92. As a practice, all banks now deduct some amount from their pre- tax income and set aside in a separate account to create a cushion for the loans which may go bad. This is called:
a. CRR b. SLR c. Provisioning d. PLR e. None of these

93. The power of the commercial banks to expand deposits through expanding their loans and advances is known as ____.
a. Capital Expansion
b. Credit Expansion
c. Credit control
d. Credit Creation
e. None of the above

94. The Securitization And Reconstruction of Financial Assets and Enforcement of Security Interest Act (SARFAESI) meant for recovery of loans which have become NPAis not applicable to:
a. Public Sector banks
b. Financial Institutes of the Govt.
c. Private Banks
d. Non – Banking Financial Companies
e. Small & Cooperative Banks

95. 'CEPI' stands for?
a. Council of Environmental Pollution of India
b. Comprehensive Environmental Pollution Index
c. Centre for Environmental Pollution in India
d. Centre for Environmental Pollution and Industries
e. None of these

96. Name the Indian cueist who has won the World 6-Red Snooker Championship in Karachi, his 13th world title.
a. Pankaj Advani
b. Manan Chandra
c. Aditya Mehta
d. Geet Sethi
e. None of these

97. Prime Minister Abdullah al-Thani has threaten to resign amid lingering peace talks in the country adding to the political chaos in
a. Iraq b. Syria c. Libya d. Yemen e. Jordan

98. Which of the following social networking majors has given benefits of around $21 million to Indian developers as part of one of its initiatives recently?
a. Twitter b. Facebook c. LinkedIn d. Myspace e. Google+

99. ________ has been accredited by the Green Climate Fund as an implementing entity for undertaking climate change related projects in India.
a. NABARD b. RBI c. SIDBI d. SEBI e. NHB

100. Who among the following has been roped in by the Maharashtra state govt as the state ambassador for the 'Save the Tiger' campaign and promote tiger tourism?
a. Dharmendra b. Sunny Deol c. Nana Patekar d. Amitabh Bachchan
e. Jackie Shroff

101. India has signed financing agreement with World Bank for NCRMP-II project. It is aimed at reducing vulnerability to cyclone and other similar hazards in
a. West Bengal b. Maharashtra c. Kerala d. Karnataka e. All the above

102. The Rajya Sabha committee on the land acquisition Bill has decided to seek an extension till the coming winter session. The committee is chaired by
a. SS Ahluwalia b. Pashupati Nath Singh c. KV Thomas
d. Kalyan Banerjee e. None of these

103. The govt has approved the setting up of All India Institute of Ayurveda (AIIA) for imparting MD and Ph.D level education. The AIIA will come up in
a. Ajmer b. Chennai c. Haridwar d. New Delhi e. Hyderabad

104. Identify the one who is NOT among the 17 sportspersons picked for this year's Arjuna awards?
a. PR Sreejesh (hockey) b. Dipa Karmakar (gymnastics)
c. Jitu Rai (shooting) d. Shikhar Dhawan (cricket)
e. K Srikanth (badminton)

105. As per the market research firm IDC, by 2017 India will overtake US to be the second-largest smartphone market globally. Which is the largest smartphone market in the world?
a. Russia b. China c. Japan d. France e. Brazil

106. Who is the governor of Karnataka?
a. V.P. Singh Badnore b. Vajubhai Vala
c. Chennamaneni Vidyasagar Rao d. S. C. Jamir
e. V. Shanmuganthan

107. Who is current Consumer Affairs, Food and Public Distribution Minister in Narendra Modi government?
a. Ananthkumar b. Kalraj Mishra c. Anant Geete
d. Ravi Shankar Prasad e. Ramvilas Paswan

108. Capital of Denmark is?
a. Tbilisi b. Copenhagen c. Conakry d. Djibouti e. Roseau

109. Bandipur National Park is situated in which of the following Indian state?
a. Karnataka b. Kerala c. West Bengal d. Uttar Pradesh
e. Madhya Pradesh

110. World Heritage Day is observed on which of the following date?
a. April 18 b. April 7 c. April 27 d. April 28 e. April 21

111. Which city is served by Swami Vivekananda Airport?
a. Tirupati b. Tezu c. Raipur d. Gangtok e. Agra

112. Which Indian city is also known as Financial Capital of India?
a. Mumbai b. Banglore c. Chennai d. New Delhi e. Kolkata

113. Name of the parliament of Vietnam is......
a. National Assembly b. Congress
c. Federal Assembly d. House of Assembly
e. National Parliament

114. Kodasalli Dam is in which of the following state?
a. Madhya Pradesh b. Uttar Pradesh
c. Himachal Pradesh d. Jammu and kashmir e. Karnataka

115. Headquarter of New Development Bank (NDB) is in which of the following city?
a. New Delhi b. Beijing c. Johannesburg d. Shanghai e. Rio de Janeiro

116. What is the Currency of Argentina?
a. Litas b. Euro c. Dram d. Peso e. Tenge

117. Mahatama Gandhi Marine National Park is situated in which of the following Indian state/UT?
a. Lakshadweep islands b. Daman and Diu
c. Andaman and Nicobar Islands d. Goa e. Kerala

118. Matki Dance is the folk dance of which of the following state?
a. Odisha b. Madhya Pradesh c. West Bengal
d. Maharashtra e. Gujarat

119. Mullaperiyar Dam is in which of the following state?
a. Karnataka b. Andhra Pradesh c. Kerala d. Maharashtra
e. Odisha

120. Who is the Chief Minister of Andhra Pradesh?
a. Pema Khandu b. Vajubhai Vala
c. Pawan Kumar Chamling d. Manik Sarkar
e. Chandrababu Naidu

Section 4: English Language

Directions (121-130): Read the following Comprehension and answer the following:

If India has survived as a secular, democratic nation, it is due in large measure to the moral authority exercised by the higher judiciary, which has intervened every so often to assert the country's core values. True, the same cannot be said of the lower courts: The sting operation that caught a magistrate issuing bail able warrants against the president and the chief justice is symptomatic of the degeneration of the justice system at the level of the ordinary citizen. But in shining contrast to this abysmal state of affairs, there is the Supreme Court, which, especially in recent decades, has always gone the extra mile to fulfil its role as the custodian of the people's interests. The trust in which the common citizen holds the apex court is, in fact, testified by the spurt in 'public interest litigation'. If anything, the court's frequent advocacy on behalf of the citizen has earned it many detractors: Purists raised on a text-book definition of democracy with its classic separation of the executive and the judiciary see this as judicial activism.

However, the short point is: The judiciary cannot both be accused of betraying the people and overdoing its role as their protector. Granted, there are areas where the apex court might appear to have expanded its domain: its stern directions to control pollution in Delhi being a case in point. And yet, isn't it plain for all to see that the judiciary has actually been forced to step into a role vacated by the executive. Finally, we have only to think of the many times the court has acted to pull the country back from the brink. Ayodhya would have been forcibly settled by now if it hadn't been for the court. Again, it is the court's hawk-like monitoring of the Gujarat situation that has delivered hope to victims of the communal carnage. If the lower court has not played fair by Zahira, it is the higher court that has restored her faith in the justice system.

121. Democracy and secularism in India would have been a part of history by now
   a. if the executive had failed to deliver.
   b. if the judiciary had not set the house in order at difficult times.
   c. if the higher judiciary had not banned other bodies from functioning.
   d. if the lower judiciary had delivered on people's expectations.
   e. if the executive had not been taken to task.

122. What does the increasing number of public interest litigations reflect?
   a. People are becoming more educated and aware of their rights.
   b. People are becoming more bold to fight for their cause.
   c. More ills and problems plague the society these days.
   d. People are showing much faith in the higher judiciary.
   e. None

123. Which of the following is true in the context of the passage?
   a. Higher judiciary has proved to be the caretaker of the people.
   b. Lower judiciary is closer to the people than the higher judiciary.
   c. Higher judiciary is equally responsible for the degeneration of the justice system.
   d. Executive has also at certain times intervened in the area of judiciary.
   e. None

124. Which of the following is the opposite in meaning of the word 'core' as used in the passage?
   a. inner b. trivial c. scant d. strange e. peripheral

125. Which of the following matches with the meaning of the word 'symptomatic' as used in the passage?
   a. outcome b. example c. indicator d. countdown e. reminder

126. According to the author, the judiciary has to intervene in certain matters only when
   a. there is a chance of social unrest.
   b. its supremacy is questioned.

c. the sovereignty of the country faces danger.
d. other organs of our system fail to deliver in a fair manner.
e. lower courts indulge in malpractices.

127. What will be the opposite in meaning of the word 'spurt' as used in the passage?
a. rapid decline b. slow downfall c. unintentional d. unusual e. broken pace

128. What do you mean by the expression 'hawk-like monitoring' as used in the passage?
a. intense hearing b. very careful observation
c. strict judgement d. sharp focus e. None

129. What is the meaning of the word 'carnage' as used in the passage?
a. violence b. riots c. hazard d. fire e. massacre

130. What do the purists expect from the judiciary?
a. It should not step outside its domain and intervene in the affairs of other bodies.
b. It should give up its habit of responding to each and every public interest litigation.
c. It must maintain friendly terms with the executive.
d. It must remain away from controversies.
e. None

Directions (131-135): Read each sentence to find out whether there is any error in it. The error, if any, will be in one part of the sentence. The number of that part is the answer. If there is error in number 1 so the answer is option a and so on, and if there is no error the answer is e). (Ignore the errors of punctuation, if any.)

131. A city which shall not 1)/ provide safety 2)/ to its citizens 3)/ is a failed one. 4)/ No error 5)
a. A city which shall not b. provide safety c. to its citizens
d. is a failed one e. No error

132. Even those entrusted 1)/ with the job of 2)/ protecting is sometimes 3)/ the culprits themselves. 4)/ No error 5)
a. Even those entrusted b. with the job of
c. protecting is sometimes d. the culprits themselves e. No error

133. Allergic diseases have 1)/ become very common 2)/ in most parts of the 3)/ world, also included India. 4)/ No error 5)
a. Allergic diseases have b. become very common
c. in most parts of the d. world, also included India e. No error

134. That car is 1)/ the most costliest 2)/ in the luxury car 3) / segment today. 4)/ No error 5)
a. That car is b. the most costliest c. in the luxury car
d. segment today e. No error

135. Just as the time taken by 1)/ different routes to reach a 2)/ particular destination varies, 3)/ each path of yoga takes its own time, 4)/ No error 5)
a. Just as the time taken by b. different routes to reach a
c. particular destination varies d. each path of yoga takes its own time
e. No error

Directions (136–140): Rearrange the following sentences in the proper sequence to form a meaningful paragraph; then answer the questions given below them.

136.

1. Although there are large regional variations, it is not infrequent to find a large number of people sitting here together and doing nothing.
2. Once in office, they receive friends and relatives who feel free to call any time without prior appointment.
3. While working, one is struck by the slow and clumsy actions and reactions, indifferent attitudes. Procedure rather than outcome orientation, and the lack of consideration for others.
4. Even those who are employed often come late to the office and leave early unless they are forced to be punctual.
5. Work is not intrinsically valued in India.
6. Quite often people visit ailing friends and relatives or go out of their way to help them in their personal matters even during office hours.

a. 531426 b. 514362 c. 514263 d. 126325 e. None of these

137.

1. But in the industrial era destroying the enemy's productive capacity means bombing the factories which are located in the cities.
2. So in the agrarian era, if you need to destroy the enemy's productive capacity, what you want to do is burn his fields, or if you're really vicious, salt them.
3. Now in the information era, destroying the enemy's productive capacity means destroying the information infrastructure.
4. How do you do battle with your enemy?
5. The idea is to destroy the enemy's productive capacity, and depending upon the economic foundation, that productive capacity is different in each case.
6. With regard to defence, the purpose of the military is to defend the nation and be prepared to do battle with its enemy.

a. 645213 b. 631254 c. 452136 d. 465213 e. None of these

138.

1. Michael Hofman, a poet and translator, accepts this sorry fact without approval or complaint.
2. But thanklessness and impossibility do not daunt him.
3. He acknowledges too—in fact he returns to the point often—that best translators of poetry always fail at Home level.
4. Hofman feels passionately about his work, and this is clear from his writings.
5. In terms of the gap between worth and reward, translators come somewhere near nurses and street - cleaners.

a. 51342 b. 14523 c. 51324 d. 43512 e. None of these

139.

1. Passivity is not, of course, universal.
2. In areas where there are no lords or laws, or in frontier zones where all men go armed, the attitude of the peasantry may well be different.
3. So indeed it may be on the fringe of the unsubmissive.
4. However, for most of the soil-bound peasants the problem is not whether to be normally passive or active, but when to pass from one state to another.

5. This depends on an assessment of the political situation.
   a. 25413 b. 34125 c. 54213 d. 12345 e. None of these

140.

1. The situations in which violence occurs and the nature of that violence tends to be clearly defined at least in theory, as in the proverbial Irishman's question: Is this a private fight or can anyone join in?'
2. So the actual risk to outsiders, though no doubt higher than our societies, is calculable.
3. Probably the only uncontrolled applications of force are those of social superiors to social inferiors and even here there are probably some rules.
4.. However binding the obligation to kill, members or feuding families engaged in mutual massacre will be genuinely appalled if by some mischance a bystander or outsider is killed.
   a. 4123 b. 1342 c. 3214 d. 4213 e. None of these

Directions (141-145). Read each sentence to find out whether there is any grammatical error or idiomatic error in it. The error, if any, will he in one part of the sentence. The number of that part is the answer. If there is 'No error', the answer is 'E'. (Ignore errors of punctuation, if any).

141. Should have been nice (A)/ if we could have (B)/ played this game before (C)/ the Australia one, would have (D)/ had a better idea of the conditions. (E).

142. The Constitution granted (A)/ the right to citizens (B)/ to join such bodies to (C)/ pursue their interest in (D) sports, religion, culture and art etc. (E).

143. We swap up to the drowning man, (A)/ caught hold of his clothes, (B)/ before he could go down (C)/ again and pulled him, (D)/ out safe to the shore. (E).

144. The scheme which (A)/ will be launched during (B)/ the next two years (C)/ require an additional investment (D)/ of one hundred crore. (E).

145. Household spends will support (A)/ real domestic growth of 2 percent or perhaps (B)/ more, because real earnings are rising at 2 percent (C)/, house prices are increasing (D)/ even faster in real terms and employment prospects are good. (E)/.

Directions (146-155): In the following passage, some of the words have been left out, each of which is indicated by a number. Find the suitable word from the options given against each number and fill up the blanks with appropriate words to make the paragraph meaningfully complete.

One indication of this would seem to be India's current approach towards different multilateral organisations and plurilateral groupings. Many are better known by their **(1)** such as NAM, SAARC, BRICS, BIMSTEC, etc. Multilateral fora have today become indispensable to the conduct of international diplomacy, and how a nation deals with, or adjusts to, the **(2)** soup of organisations that exist is important. This is so even if a case exists that some of the older ones have lost much of their **(3)** .

Since Independence, India has played a leading role in multilateral fora. It was a founder member of NAM (Non Aligned Movement), SAARC (South Asian Association for Regional Cooperation), BIMSTEC (Bay of Bengal Initiative for Multi-Sectoral Technical and Economic Cooperation), BRICS (Brazil, Russia, India, China and South Africa), and BCIM (Bangladesh, China, India and Myanmar). India has **(4)**membership of the NSG (Nuclear Suppliers Group) and the Wassenaar Arrangement (on Export Controls for Conventional Arms and Dual-use Goods and Technologies) and also full membership of ASEAN (Association of Southeast Asian Nations), the SCO (Shanghai Cooperation Organisation), etc, recognising the potential of being inside rather than outside such bodies. Even granting that the world is increasingly **(5)** towards the post-modern phenomenon of transactional politics, and that older institutions such as NAM are increasingly out of **(6)** with this, a proper study of the utility of participation in such fora — prior to treating many of them as of little consequence — would have been useful. To **(7)** its many advantages, India clearly needs to play on as many geopolitical chessboards as possible.

NAM may be a **(8)** shadow of what it was during an earlier period when towering personalities such as Nehru, Tito, Nasser and Castro dominated its proceedings. With non-alignment giving way to strategic alignment, organisations such as NAM may seem anachronistic, but it should not be lost sight of that it still resonates with many Third World countries. It also offers an alternative platform for putting forward a different viewpoint. It would, hence, be premature to **(9)** the death of NAM. The Indian Prime Minister's decision to skip the NAM Summit in Venezuela may well hasten its end, but does not take away from the fact that NAM still has some relevance and India could still utilise NAM — perhaps less ideological but more purposive than in the past — to **(10)** newer challenges such as China's not so 'peaceful rise'.

146. a. animus
b. diligent
c. Acronyms
d. palpable
e. tranquil

147. a. adverse
b. appalling
c. cataclysmic
d. alphabetic
e. analphabetic

148. a. fragile
b. relevance
c. impotence
d. invalidity
e. weakness

149. a. sought
b. sight
c. label
d. retrieve
e. ascertain

150. a. placid
b. serene
c. tranquil
d. conciliatory
e. tilting

151. a. diverge
b. sync
c. lash
d. differ
e. deviate

152. a. pertinent
b. depressed
c. optimise
d. gloomy
e. dejected

153. a. glowing
b. pale
c. bright
d. colourful
e. dazzle

154. a. assemble
b. vigilant
c. negligent
d. pronounce
e. preview

155. a. reverence
b. resemble
c. exist
d. counter
e. remember

ANSWER GRID

1. c	2. c	3. a	4. b	5. d	6. b	7. e	8. b	9. c	10. b
11. d	12. a	13. a	14. c	15. d	16. d	17. d	18. a	19. a	20. b
21. b	22. b	23. e	24. d	25. c	26. a	27. e	28. d	29. b	30. e
31. d	32. a	33. c	34. b	35. d	36. a	37. a	38. a	39. d	40. d
41. c	42. c	43. c	44. b	45. c	46. b	47. c	48. d	49. c	50. d
51. d	52. c	53. d	54. c	55. c	56. a	57. c	58. d	59. a	60. d
61. b	62. d	63. a	64. a	65. b	66. b	67. d	68. c	69. b	70. b
71. a	72. b	73. e	74. a	75. c	76. b	77. d	78. d	79. b	80. d
81. d	82. c	83. d	84. d	85. b	86. b	87. e	88. a	89. a	90. a
91. c	92. c	93. d	94. d	95. b	96. a	97. c	98. b	99. a	100. d
101. e	102. a	103. d	104. d	105. b	106. b	107. e	108. b	109. a	110. a
111. c	112. a	113. a	114. e	115. d	116. d	117. c	118. b	119. e	120. e
121. b	122. d	123.	124. e	125. c	126. d	127. a	128. b	129. e	130. a
131. a	132. c	133. d	134. b	135. e	136. a	137. a	138. c	139. d	140. a
141. c	142. a	143. b	144. d	145. a	146. c	147. d	148. b	149. a	150. e
151. b	152. c	153. b	154. d	155. d					

Solutions and Explanations

16.

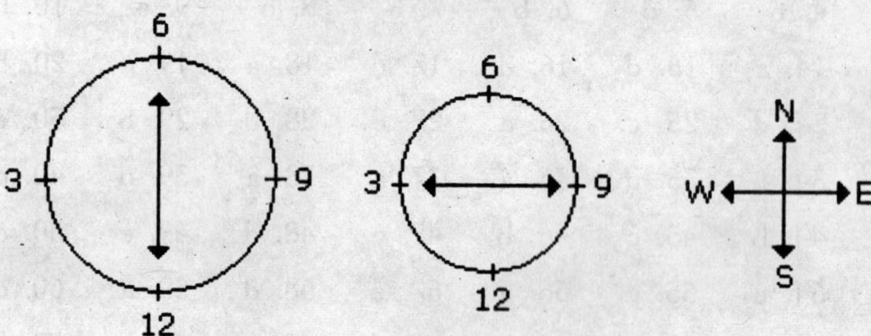

17.

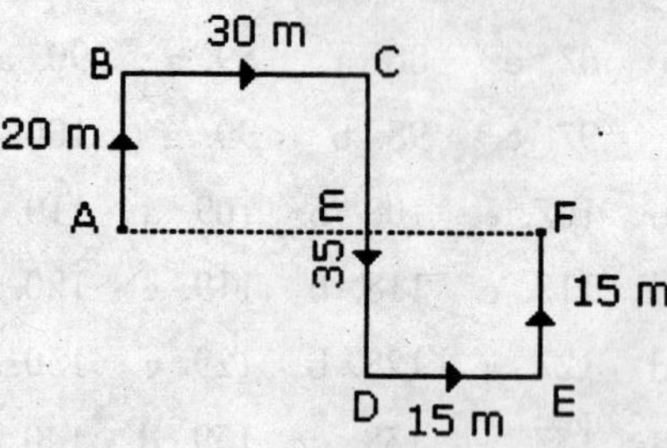

Required distance = AF
= 30 + 15
= 45 m

From the above diagram, F is in East direction from A.

Hence the required answer is '45 m East'.

18.

25 km.
A B
15 km.
25 km. 35km.
C D F E
150 km.
X Y

Required distance = DF
= 150 – (25 + 25 + 35)
= 150 – 85
= 65 km.

19.

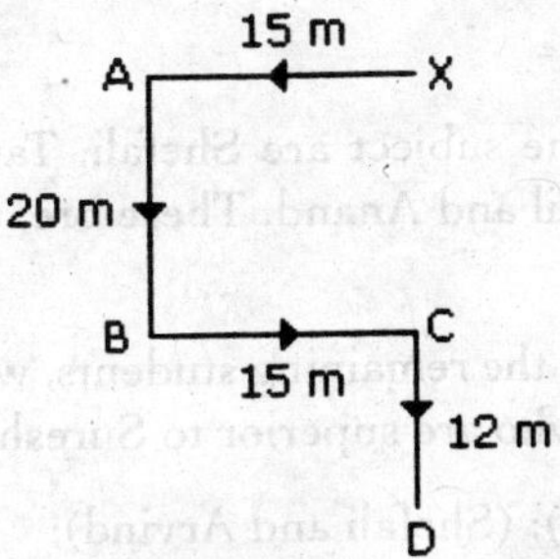

Required distance = 20 + 12

= 32 m in south direction

20.

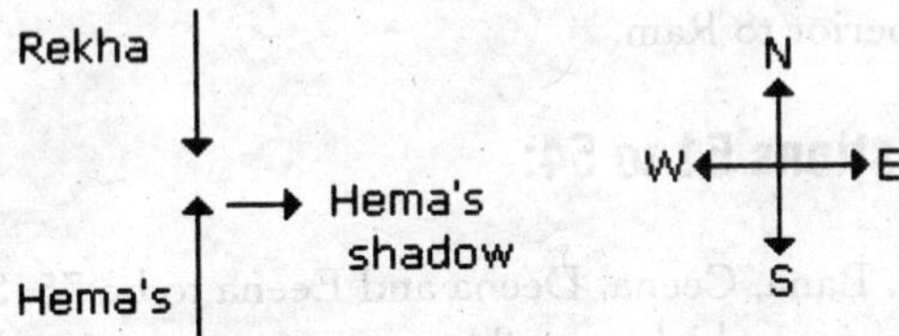

21.

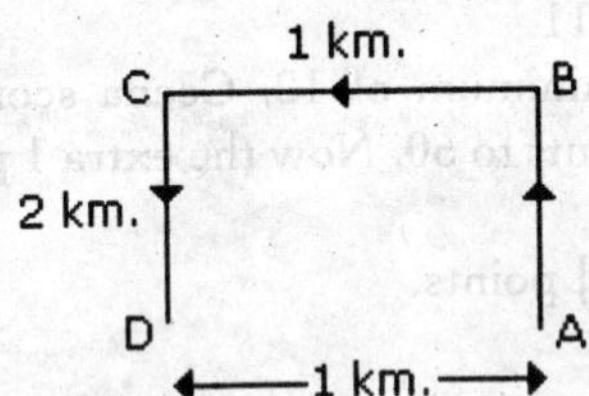

Solution to questions 22-26:

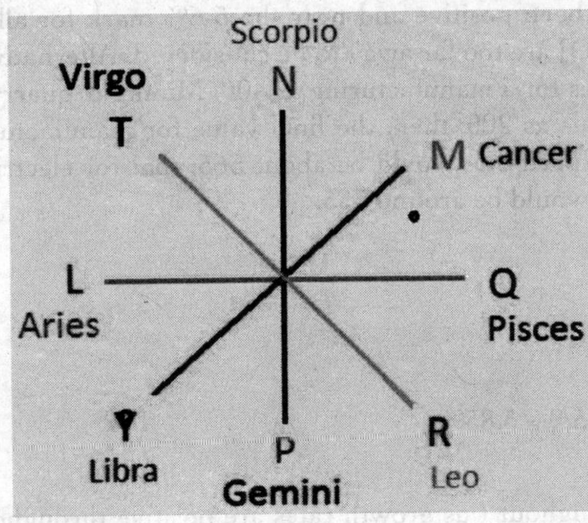

Solution to Questions 46–50:

46. The students who have got the same grade in more than one subject are Shefali, Taruna, Mohan, Sanjay, Ranjay, Suresh, Amit, Anshul, Nitisha, Sushil and Anand. Therefore, there are 11 such students.

47. By comparing the grades got by Suresh with the grades got by the remaining students, we get that there are only two students namely Mohan and Arvind who are superior to Suresh.

48. The pairs of students that are similar are (Shefali and Nitisha); (Shefali and Arvind); (Ram and Amit); (Ram and Anshul); (Mohan and Aditi); (Mohan and Sushil); (Ranjay and Suresh); (Ranjay and Anshul); (Suresh and Anand) and (Amit and Anshul) Therefore, there are 10 such similar pairs of students

49. Out of the mentioned students, Sanjay is not similar to any of the mentioned students.

50. Out of the options given, only Taruna is superior to Ram.

Solution to Questions 51 to 54:

We have the sum total of all the points with Ana, Bana, Ceena, Deena and Eeena to be 75. Since Ana was the one to score the highest number of points which were 24.

So the total of points scored by Bana, Ceena, Deena and Eeena was 51.

The minimum possible number of points scored by Eeena is 11.

If Eeena scores a minimum of 11, then Deena scores a minimum of 12, Ceena scores a minimum of 13 and Bana scores a minimum of 14. The total amounts to 50. Now the extra 1 point can be adjusted such that Bana scores 15 and the total will be 51.

Now for 24 to be possible there is just one set of {5, 5, 5, 5, 4} points.

Now all the questions can be answered.

61. [b]

You may note that apart from a few years for manufacturing and mining & quarrying, the annual growth rates in most years have been positive and near the 5-6% mark for all the sectors. The other options [A],[C], and [D] are too far away to be considered. Alternatively, for ease of calculation take the 1989 values for a manufacturing as 400, Mining & quarrying and Electricity as 300 each and Chemicals as 200. then, the final value for manufacturing would be nearly 580, that for mining & quarrying would be about 365; that for electricity would be around 550; and for Chemicals would be around 335.

=> Initial value of production

= 400 + 300 + 300 + 200 = 1200

Final value of production

= 580 + 365 + 550 + 335 = 1830

⇨ Overall % increase = 52.5%

⇨ Average annual growth = 52.5/9 = 5.85%

62. [d]

Electricity production has increased throughout (as growth rates are positive throughout) and the maximum production would be achieved in the last year, i.e. 98.

63. [a]

The production for manufacturing can be minimum either in 1989 or in 1992 (when the growth rate is negative).

If Manufacturing started with a production of 100 in 1989, then production in 1992 will be 100 × 1.04 × 1.01 × 0.97 >1

So, the production in 1989 was the least

64. [a]

Electricity has shown the highest growth rate in all the years and therefore, would have the highest growth rate for the entire period.

65. [b].

Electricity in 1992:

100 × 1.05 × 1.07 × 1.08 = 121.4

chemicals in 1992:

100 × 1.07 × 1.03 × 1.06 = 116.8

=> In 1992, the index of chemicals is less than that of electricity by approximately 5.

66. [b]

Let Manufacturing in 1989 = 200 and

Chemicals in 1989 = 100

=> Manufacturing in 1991:

200 × 1.04 × 1.01 = 210

and Chemicals in 1991:

100 × 1.07 × 1.03 = 110

$$\text{Required \%} = \frac{210 - 110}{110} \times 100 = 90.91\%$$

67. [d]

As can be seen directly from the graph, the highest increase(that of 8%) for Mining and Quarrying was in the year 1998, relative to 1997.

68. [c]

Values added per worker for various sectors will be proportional to following ratios:

Central	10/6
State	3/6
Central/state	12/3
Public	8/8/

69. [b]

Fixed capital per factory will be proportional to the following ratios:

Central	5/8
State	4/4
Central/state	5/6
Public	6/12

70. [b]
If the variables is proportional to the number of employees and the production per employees, then we can say that the variable cost is directly proportional to the production. Since the variable cost is maximum for private sector, it will also have the maximum production.

71. [a]
If 20% of govt. fixed capital is equal to $200 million => Total govt. sector fixed capital = $ 1000 m which is equivalent to 14% of the total fixed capital. Now, 25% of Govt. investment in joint sector i.e. 25% of the 8% of the total=2% 0f total fixed capital will be given by:
(1000 × 2) /14 = $ 143 million
Value in Rs. is given by:
143 × 45 = Rs.6450 million

72. [b]
From the above question the money disinvested will be Rs.6450 million.

73. [e]
Neither of the statements [A] or [B] can be inferred as we know only the percentages and not the actual values of the employees, factories or fixed capital.

74. [a]

Percentage change for India = $\frac{0.72 - 1.71}{1.71} > 50\%$

Percentage change for china = $\frac{5.46 - 4.8}{5.46} = 12\%$

Percentage change for Korea = $\frac{3.12 - 2.8}{2.8} = 11\%$

Percentage change for Malaysia = $\frac{0.33}{2.1} = 15\%$

Hence, maximum % change is for India

75. [c] For the year 1998

For China, $\frac{FEI_{China}}{GDP_{China}} = 0.048$ ....(1)

For India, $\frac{FEI_{India}}{GDP_{India}} = 0.0072$ ....(2)

$\frac{FEI_{China}}{FEI_{India}} = 10$

⇨ on dividing (1) by (2) :

$\frac{GDP_{India}}{GDP_{China}} \times 10 = \frac{0.048}{0.0072} = \frac{20}{3}$

=> $\frac{GDP_{China}}{GDP_{India}} = \frac{3}{2} = 1.5$

So percentage difference between china's GDP and India's GDP = 50%

76. [b]

Since the comparisons are for the same country in each case, assume the GDP as 100 in 1997 in all cases. So, GDP of china , India and Korea in 1998 is 105,107 and 98 respectively.

$$\frac{FEI_{1998}}{FEI_{1997}} = \frac{FEII_{1998} \times GDP_{1998}}{FEII_{1997} \times GDP_{1997}}$$

For China : $\frac{FEI_{1998}}{FEI_{1997}} = \frac{4.8 \times 107}{5.46 \times 100} < 1$

For India: $\frac{FEI_{1998}}{FEI_{1997}} = \frac{0.72 \times 105}{1.71 \times 100} < 1$

For Korea: $\frac{FEI_{1998}}{FEI_{1997}} = \frac{3.12 \times 98}{2.8 \times 100} > 1$

So, II and V are correct.

77. [d]

It can be seen that all the values (FEII) are expressed as a ratio of FEI to GDP, the absolute values of GDP cannot be determined.

78. [d]

Since only the ratios of GDP and FEI are known, the increase in one independent of other cannot be determined.

SBI PO Mains MOCK Test Paper 6

Structure of this MOCK Test

S. No.	Name of section	No. of Questions	Total marks	Allotted Time
1	Reasoning and Computer Aptitude	45	60	60 minutes
2	Data Analysis and Interpretation	35	60	45 minutes
3	English Language	35	40	40 minutes
4	General/ Economy/ Banking Awareness	40	40	35 minutes
Total		155	200	3 hours

- There is 1/4th Negative marking for every wrong answer.
- If a question is left blank, i.e. no answer is marked by the candidate, there will be no penalty for that question.

Section 1: Reasoning and Computer Ability

Directions (1–5): Read the given information carefully and answer the given questions.

Ten friends are sitting in two parallel rows containing five people. There is equal distance between adjacent persons.

In row 1, following people are seated: Samar, Irfan, Neil, Nitin and Nighy. All of them are facing North.

In row 2, following people are seated: Haider, Cosby, Tom, Johnny G and Bryan Dick. All of them are facing south (but not necessarily in the same order).

Each person also reads the Novel of different authors, namely Ruchir Sharma, Khaled Hosseini, James Joyce, J.R.R. Tolkien, Richard Bach , Jackie Collins, James Baldwin, James Frey, James Patterson and Jack London (not necessarily in the same order).

Consider following points regarding their seating arrangement:

- Nighy sits exactly in the centre of the row and faces the one who likes Richard Bach.
- Only one person sits between Johnny G and the one who likes Richard Bach.
- Johnny G faces one of the immediate neighbours of the one who likes Jackie Collins. Only two people sit between Irfan & the one who likes Jackie Collins.

- Irfan faces the one who likes James Frey.
- Haider faces one of the immediate neighbours of Neil.
- Haider does not like James Frey. Nitin is an immediate neighbour of Neil.
- The one who likes J.R.R. Tolkien is not an immediate neighbour of Neil.
- Bryan Dick is not an immediate neighbour of Haider and faces the one who likes Khaled Hosseini.
- Tom faces the one who likes James Patterson.
- The one who likes Jack London faces north.
- Haider does not face the one who likes Jack London.
- The one who likes Ruchir Sharma sits on the immediate right of the person who likes James Baldwin.
- Johnny G does not like Ruchir Sharma.

1. Which of the following pairs facing each other represent the people sitting third to person who sit at the extreme ends of two rows?
   a. Bryan Brown, Nitin b. Cosby, Nitin c. Haider, Nighy
   d. Cosby, Samar e. Tom, Samar
2. If the position of the persons sitting at the corners are interchanged with the person facing them then who sits third to the next of Nitin?
   a. Samar b. Haider c. Neil d. Tom e. Cosby
3. Who amongst the following is the immediate neighbour of the one who faces Neil, who is the immediate neighbor of one who likes Jack London?
   a. The one who likes Jackie Collins
   b. The one who like James Frey
   c. Irfan
   d. The one who likes Richard Bach
   e. Bryan Dick
4. Which of the following Novels does Irfan like when all persons of the both rows are arranged in the alphabetical order starting from left side of row 2 to right side of row 1?
   a. Ruchir Sharma b. Richard Bach c. Jackie Collins
   d. James Baldwin e. James Patterson
5. Who amongst the following sits second to the right of second to the left of Bryan Dick?
   a. Bryan Brown b. Tom c. Bryan Dick
   d. Irfan e. Cosby

Directions (6–10): Below is given a passage followed by several possible inferences which can be drawn from the facts stated in the passage. You have to examine each inference separately in the context of the passage and decide upon its degree of truth or falsity. Mark answer:
Sometimes the reaction is the real joke. Following demands for immediate arrest of comedian Tanmay Bhat, the Mumbai police are seeking legal opinion to find out whether there are enough grounds for registering an FIR against him. "A written application from the cinema wing of the Maharashtra Navnirman Sena has been received. We have taken a transcript of the contents of the video and are seeking legal opinion on further course of action. We have also contacted Facebook and YouTube authorities and asked them to block access to the video," said Mumbai police

Spokesperson Deputy Commissioner Sangramsinh Nishandar. Sanjay Raut of the Shiv Sena, for instance, decided to make it clear that people like Mr. Bhat "should be whipped in public". The video posted by Mr. Bhat on May 26, depicts morphed faces of singer Lata Mangeshkar and cricketer Sachin Tendulkar superimposed over his own in an imaginary conversation about cricketer Virat Kohli's batting skills. The video, the contents of which were found offensive by many, went viral, attracting the attention of political parties. The point here is to applaud his sense of humour — or to condemn it. When jokiness is curbed so menacingly — and for all the brave front they may put up, cartoonists and comedians are lonely people against the might of the state — the only response is to rally to defend freedom of expression. In an environment where possibly personal jokes are seen to warrant scrutiny and police action, no space can be available for shared humour, for comedy to evolve sufficiently so that the larger community internalizes what is truly, even mockingly, funny and what's not so progressive.

6. There should be enough grounds to arrest a person.
   a. if the inference is "definitely true", i.e. it properly follows from the statement of facts given.
   b. if the inference is "probably true "though not "definitely true" in the light of the facts given.
   c. if the "data are inadequate", i.e. from the facts given you cannot say whether the inference is likely to be true or false.
   d. if the inference is "probably false" though not "definitely false" in the light of the facts given.
   e. if the inference is "definitely false", i.e. it cannot possibly be drawn from the facts given or it contradicts the given facts.

7. Maharashtra Navnirman Sena has declared state bandh for 2 days in protest of Tanmay Bhatt's video.
   a. if the inference is "definitely true", i.e. it properly follows from the statement of facts given.
   b. if the inference is "probably true "though not "definitely true" in the light of the facts given.
   c. if the "data are inadequate", i.e. from the facts given you cannot say whether the inference is likely to be true or false.
   d. if the inference is "probably false" though not "definitely false" in the light of the facts given.
   e. if the inference is "definitely false", i.e. it cannot possibly be drawn from the facts given or it contradicts the given facts.

8. Tanmay Bhatt has good sense of humour.
   a. if the inference is "definitely true", i.e. it properly follows from the statement of facts given.
   b. if the inference is "probably true "though not "definitely true" in the light of the facts given.
   c. if the "data are inadequate", i.e. from the facts given you cannot say whether the inference is likely to be true or false.
   d. if the inference is "probably false" though not "definitely false" in the light of the facts given.
   e. if the inference is "definitely false", i.e. it cannot possibly be drawn from the facts given or it contradicts the given facts.

9. Political parties are giving their reaction on this incidence.
   a. if the inference is "definitely true", i.e. it properly follows from the statement of facts given.
   b. if the inference is "probably true "though not "definitely true" in the light of the facts given.
   c. if the "data are inadequate", i.e. from the facts given you cannot say whether the inference is likely to be true or false.

d. if the inference is "probably false" though not "definitely false" in the light of the facts given.
e. if the inference is "definitely false", i.e. it cannot possibly be drawn from the facts given or it contradicts the given facts.

10. Arresting of Tanmay Bhatt means arrest of freedom of expression.
a. if the inference is "definitely true", i.e. it properly follows from the statement of facts given.
b. if the inference is "probably true "though not "definitely true" in the light of the facts given.
c. if the "data are inadequate", i.e. from the facts given you cannot say whether the inference is likely to be true or false.
d. if the inference is "probably false" though not "definitely false" in the light of the facts given.
e. if the inference is "definitely false", i.e. it cannot possibly be drawn from the facts given or it contradicts the given facts.

Directions (11–15): Read the following information carefully and answer the questions given below:

(i) Seven teachers Ramesh, Neha, Sophia, Sanjay, Vivek, Mona and Divya teach in the B.Tech. at GEHU. They teach one of the following subjects Electrical Machine, Power Electronics, DCNS, Digital Electronics and Fluid Mechanics
(ii) Digital Electronics and DCNS are taught by two teachers.
(iii) Both the DCNS teachers and one from Electrical Machine and Fluid Mechanics each have cleared CAT.
(iv) Four female teachers are Neha, Sophia, Mona and Divya. Two of them are married. Two teachers are members of Sports council, out of which only one is male. However, none of the married teachers are its members.
(v) All the married teachers except one are class teachers of one class or the other. There are four married teachers Ramesh, Neha, Sanjay and Mona. There are three subject teachers.
(vi) None of the married women teachers have cleared CAT. Two male teachers have cleared CAT out of which one is married and he is Mr. Ramesh, a subject teacher. He teaches either Power Electronics or Electrical Machine.
(vii) The SPORTS members are subject teachers and not class teachers.
(viii) SPORTS members teach same subject.
(ix) Only Mrs. Neha teaches Power Electronics. Divya is a class teacher.

11. If one of the unmarried female teachers teaches Electrical Machine, one of the married female & one of the married male teacher teaches Fluid Mechanics and the unmarried male teacher teaches Power Electronics then how many married teachers teach Fluid Mechanics?
a. two b. three c. one d. none e. more than three

12. Which of the following combinations is correct?
a. Ramesh – CAT cleared – Married – Power Electronics
b. Neha – CAT not cleared – Married – Power Electronics
c. Sanjay – CAT cleared – Married – Digital Electronics
d. Vivek – CAT cleared – Married – DCNS
e. none of these

13. Who among the following are the CAT qualified sports council members?
    a. Sophia & Divya
    b. Divya & Ramesh
    c. Vivek & Sophia
    d. Vivek & Divya
    e. None of these

14. Who is the unmarried male class teacher?
    a. Vivek
    b. Sanjay
    c. Ramesh
    d. Either Sanjay or Vivek
    e. None of these

15. Which of the following combinations is incorrect?
    a. Vivek – Unmarried – male – DCNS
    b. Sophia – Unmarried – Female – DCNS
    c. Ramesh – Married – Male – Electrical Machine
    d. Neha – Married – Female – Power Electronics
    e. Divya – Married – Female – Fluid Mechanics

Directions (16–20): Solve the questions independently.

16. The committee on sexual discrimination has pointed that Dreamhouse Company is chief offender. Of the twenty senior executives in the firm, only one is a woman. And of the forty junior executives, only five are female. Dreamhouse could best defend itself against the charges by showing that
    a. male and female executives at the same level have the same qualifications
    b. they pay the same salary to senior men and senior women
    c. ten times more men than women apply for jobs with the company
    d. the work pressures and long hours make jobs with the company unattractive to married women
    e. all job applicants who were rejected had fewer qualifications than those accepted

17. Twenty percent of all energy consumed in the country is consumed by home appliances. If appliances that are twice as energy efficient as those currently available are produced, this figure will eventually be reduced to about ten percent. The argument above requires which of the following assumptions?
    a. Home-appliance usage would not increase along with the energy efficiency of the appliances.
    b. It would not be expensive to produce home appliances that are energy-efficient.
    c. Home appliance manufacturers now have the technology to produce appliances that are twice as energy efficient as those currently available.
    d. The cost of energy to the consumer would rise with increases in the energy efficiency of home appliances.
    e. None of these

18. Athletic director: "Members of our sports teams included, for the fall season, 80 football players and 40 cross-country runners; for the winter season, 20 wrestlers and 40 swimmers; for the spring season, 50 track-team members and 20 lacrosse players. Each team athlete participates in his or her sport five days a week for the whole three-month season, and no athlete is on two teams during any one season. Therefore, adding these figures, we find that our team sports program serves 250 different individual athletes."
    In drawing the conclusion above, the athletic director fails to consider the relevant possibility that
    a. athletes can be on more than one team in a single season
    b. athlete can be on teams in more than one season

c. some of the team sports require a larger number of athletes on the team than do others
d. more athletes participate in team sports during one season than during another
e. None of these

19. Sudhir has twenty years of data analyzing experience behind him. Hence if you are looking for an efficient data analyst, you should hire Sudhir.
The speaker assumes that:
a. Twelve years of practice ensures typing efficiency
b. The type of typing required for the new system is identical to what Sudhir has been doing
c. Sudhir's job profile is the best that the new employer is going to get
d. Sudhir is an outstandingly fast and accurate typist
e. Sudhir will fit well into the new office

20. As per a recent news article, most of the software companies have decided against increasing the salaries of their employees this year over previous years due to current economic situations. Which of the following assumptions is/are implicit in the statement?
(I) Majority of the employees may leave their job to protest against the decision.
(II) These companies may announce hike in salaries next year.
a. Only I b. Only II c. Both I and II
d. Either I or II e. Neither I nor II

Directions (21–24): Study the information given below and answer the given questions.
Historians have established that a particular copy of a rare painting was sold each year on New Year's Day for seven consecutive years, starting in 1931 and ending in 1937. Each person who bought that painting owned it only during that period and owned it for exactly a year. The seven owners of the painting during this period were J, K, L, M, N, O and P. The following are all additional facts the historians have discovered about the ownership during the period 1931-1937:

L sold it to O.

P sold it to M.

J owned it before O owned it.

N owned it before L owned it.

21. Which of the following could be true?
a. J sold it to O b. L sold it to M
c. N sold it to L d. O sold it to N

22. Which of the following must be true?
a. J owned it before L owned it.
b. L owned it before P owned it.
c. M owned it before P owned it
d. N owned it before M owned it.
e. None of these

23. Which of the following could have sold the painting to J on New Year's Day, 1932?
a. L b. M c. N d. O e J

24. Which of the following must have owned the painting before New Year's Day, 1936?
a. J b. K c. L d. M e. None of these

25. Five ships – J, K, L, M, and N – are to be unloaded on five consecutive days beginning on Monday and ending on Friday according to the following conditions:
Each ship takes exactly one day to unload.
K must be unloaded on a day preceding the days M and N are unloaded.
L cannot be unloaded on a Tuesday.
M must be the second ship unloaded after J is unloaded.
If M is unloaded on Friday, which of the following must be true?
a. J is unloaded on Wednesday
b. K is unloaded on Tuesday.
c. L is unloaded on Monday.
d. L is unloaded on Thursday.
e. None of these

Directions (26–30): Each of the questions below, consist a question and three statements numbered I, II and III. You have to decide whether the data provided in the statements are sufficient to answer the question. Read the three statements and Give answer

26. Among eight friends A, B, C, D, P, Q, R and S, who is sitting between B and R? (it is given that all the friends are sitting around circular table facing outside the centre of the table).
Statements:
I. S is seated third to the left of D, who is not near to A.
II. P is seated immediate right of D and third to the right of R, who is near to C.
III. Q is seated third to the left of A, who is second to the right of B, who is not near to C.
a. If the data in statement I and II together are sufficient to answer the question, while the data in statement III are not required to answer the question.
b. If the data in statement I and III together are sufficient to answer the question, while the data in statement II are not required to answer the question.
c. If the data in statement II and III are sufficient to answer the question, while the data in statement I are not required to answer the question.
d. If the data in all three statements I, II and III together are necessary to answer the question.
e. If the data in all the statements, I, II and III even together are not sufficient to answer the question.

27. What is the code for 'RUN' in a certain code language?
Statements:
I. In a certain code language 'run your business' is coded as 'lap duh pud' and 'mind your language' is coded as 'hpu dap lap'.
II. In a certain code language 'run fast and win' is coded as 'phl pud lph hap' and 'go and move ahead' is coded as 'hap pul pah lph'
III. In a certain code language 'move your legs' is coded as 'pah lap plh' and 'legs go on' is coded as 'pal plh pul'
a. If the data in statement I and II together are sufficient to answer the question, while the data in statement III are not required to answer the question.
b. If the data in statement I and III together are sufficient to answer the question, while the data in statement II are not required to answer the question.
c. If the data in statement II and III are sufficient to answer the question, while the data in statement I are not required to answer the question.
d. If the data in all three statements I, II and III together are necessary to answer the question.

e. If the data in all the statements, I, II and III even together are not sufficient to answer the question.

28. Point X is in which direction with respect to J?
Statements:
I. Point S is to the west of point T, which is in south of point J. Point X is to the north of point S.
II. Point J is to the east of point V, which is the south of point T. Point X is to the south of point W.
III. Point T is to the west of point Y, which is to the north of point W.
a. If the data in statement I and II together are sufficient to answer the question, while the data in statement III are not required to answer the question.
b. If the data in statement I and III together are sufficient to answer the question, while the data in statement II are not required to answer the question.
c. If the data in statement II and III are sufficient to answer the question, while the data in statement I are not required to answer the question.
d. If the data in all three statements I, II and III together are necessary to answer the question.
e. If the data in all the statements, I, II and III even together are not sufficient to answer the question.

29. Eight students A, B, C, D, E, F, G and H are sitting around a circle facing to the centre of the table. How many students are sitting between C and F?
Statements:
I. A is seated second to the right of H, who is seated third to the right of D. G is seated immediate left of F.
II. C is seated third to the right of A and is not near to E. F is seated second to the right B.
III. D is seated second to the left of E and is third to right of G. C is an immediate neighbor of H.
a. If the data in statement I and II together are sufficient to answer the question, while the data in statement III are not required to answer the question.
b. If the data in statement I and III together are sufficient to answer the question, while the data in statement II are not required to answer the question.
c. If the data in statement II and III are sufficient to answer the question, while the data in statement I are not required to answer the question.
d. If the data in all three statements I, II and III together are necessary to answer the question.
e. If the data in all the statements, I, II and III even together are not sufficient to answer the question.

30. Who earns highest salary among six members in a family? (six members A, B, C, D, E and F are earning different salaries)
Statements:
I. A earns more than only C and D. F earns more than B.
II. B earns less than E while D earns more than A and F.
III. C earns more than E but less than D. F earns more than two persons.
a. If the data in statement I and II together are sufficient to answer the question, while the data in statement III are not required to answer the question.

b. If the data in statement I and III together are sufficient to answer the question, while the data in statement II are not required to answer the question.
c. If the data in statement II and III are sufficient to answer the question, while the data in statement I are not required to answer the question.
d. If the data in all three statements I, II and III together are necessary to answer the question.
e. If the data in all the statements, I, II and III even together are not sufficient to answer the question.

Directions (31–35): Study the following information carefully and answer the questions given below.

UEFA Euro 2016 is being organized by France. Different teams are participating in the championship. Seven teams which are participating are – Spain, Slovakia, Sweden, France, Romania, Russia and Portugal. They will be playing their matches at different places, namely Bordeaux, Lens, Lille, Lyon, Marseille, Nice and Paris, but not necessarily in the same order, on different days of the week, starting from Monday.

- Spain will be playing at Lens, but neither on Friday nor on Monday.
- The host country will be playing on Thursday at Lyon.
- There is a gap of one day between Spain and France match.
- Russia will be playing the match before Portugal but after Romania at Marseille on Wednesday.
- Portugal will be playing on the last day of the week.
- Slovakia will be playing at Paris.
- No match will be played at Bordeaux on Monday.
- The match at Nice will be played on the last day of the week.
- The match at Lille will be played on Tuesday.
- No match will be played at Paris on Tuesday and Friday.

31. Slovakia will be playing the match on which day of the week?
a. Friday b. Tuesday c. Saturday d. Wednesday e. Monday

32. Which team will be playing the match between Thursday and Saturday?
a. Portugal b. Sweden c. France d. Romania e. Spain

33. Which of the following combinations is true?
a. France – Thursday Lyon
b. Romania – Wednesday Bordeaux
c. Portugal – Saturday Nice
d. Sweden – Monday Lens
e. Slovakia – Friday – Lille

34. If the venue of the team France and Slovakia are interchanged, which team will be playing in Lille?
a. Slovakia b. France c. Romania
d. Russia e. Portugal

35. Which of the following combinations is true?
a. Slovakia-Tuesday b. Russia-Sunday c. Romania-Thursday
d. Slovakia-Monday e. None of these

36. How can the user determine what programs are available on a computer?
  a. Checking the hard disk properties
  b. Viewing the installed programs during the booting process
  c. Checking the operating system for a list of installed programs
  d. Checking the existing files saved on the disk
  e. None of these

37. Apple Macintoshes (Macs) and PCs use different _________ to process data and different operating system.
  a. Language b. Methods c. CPUs
  d. storage devices e. None of these

38. _________ controls the way in which the computer system function and provides a means by which users can interact with the computer.
  a. The platform b. The operating system
  c. Application software d. The motherboard e. None of these

39. What happens when your boot up a PC?
  a. Portions of the operating system are copied from disk into memory
  b. Portions of the operating system are copied from memory onto disk
  c. Portions of the operating system are compiled
  d. Portions of the operating system are emulated
  e. None of these

40. Which of the following can handle most system functions that aren't handed directly by the operating system?
  a. Vertical market application b. Utilities c. Algorithms
  d. Integrated software e. Compilers

41. The device that assembles group of characters into complete messages prior to their entering the CPU is called
  a. An interpreter b. A compiler
  c. A communication processor d. An editor e. A translator

42. The subsystem of the kernel and hardware that cooperates to translate virtual to physical addresses comprises to translate virtual to physical addresses comprises
  a. Process management subsystem b. Memory management subsystem
  c. Input/output management subsystem
  d. All of the above e. None of these

43. Which of the following types of tables constraints will prevent the entry of duplicate rows?
  a. Primary key b. Unique c. Null d. Foreign Key e. None of these

44. Most application software today come with an interface called a (n) _____?
  a. Graphical User interface b. Character user interface
  c. Icon user interface d. Voice instructions system
  e. Button user interface

45. Which menu option can be used to split windows into two?
  a. Format > windows b. View > Windows > Split
  c. Windows > split d. View? Split e. None of these

Section 2: Data Analysis and Interpretation

Directions (46–50): Study the following graphs and answer the following questions:
The following pie chart shows the percentage of students admitted in different schools in 2010 – 2011
Total number of students admitted in 2010–2011 = 20,000

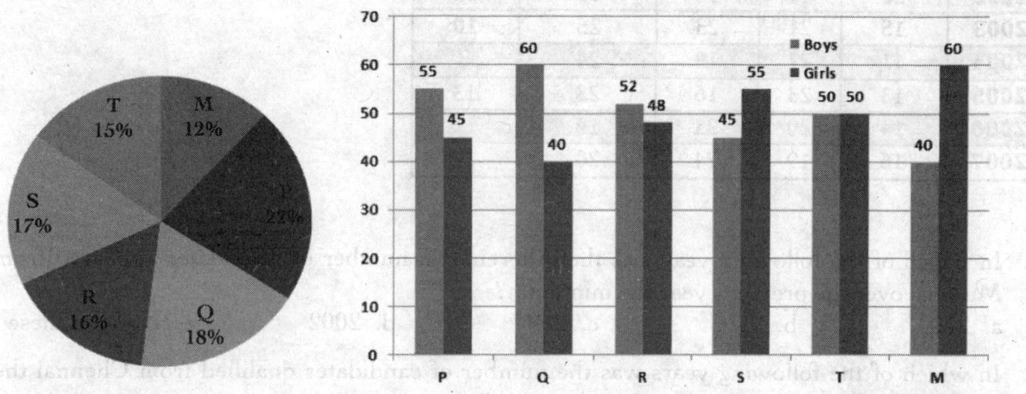

46. What is the total number of girls having taken admission in school R?
 a. 1664 b. 1536 c. 1648 d. 1694 e. None of these
47. The number of boys in schools M is what per cent of the number of girls in school S?
 a. 194.49% b. 113.54% c. 34.49% d. 51.33% e. 56.83%
48. What is the total number of boys admitted in all the schools in 2010–2011?
 a. 10,004 b. 9,766 c. 10,234 d. 11,405 e. None of these
49. The total number of boys taking admission in all schools is approximately what per cent more than the total number of girls taking admission in all schools in 2010 – 2011?
 a. 4.75% b. 4.50% c. 4.90% d. 5.04% e. 5.20%
50. The number of girls who have taken admission in school R is how many times the number of boy who have taken admission in school M?
 a. 0.625 b. 1.50 c. 1.60 d. 0.98 e. None of these

Directions (51–55): Study the following tables carefully and answer the questions given below:
Number and percentage of candidates qualified in a competitive examination
Number of candidates appeared in a competitive examination from five centers over the years

Centre / Year	Mumbai	Delhi	Kolkata	Hyderabad	Chennai
2001	35145	65139	45192	51124	37346
2002	17264	58248	52314	50248	48932
2003	24800	63309	56469	52368	51406
2004	28316	70316	71253	54196	52315
2005	36503	69294	69632	58360	55492
2006	29129	59216	64178	48230	57365
2007	32438	61345	56304	49178	58492

Percentage of candidates qualified in the competitive examination from five centers over the years

centre / Year	Mumbai	Delhi	Kolkata	Hyderabad	Chennai
2001	12	24	18	17	9
2002	10	28	12	21	12
2003	15	21	23	25	10
2004	11	27	19	24	8
2005	13	23	16	23	13
2006	14	20	21	19	11
2007	16	19	24	20	14

51. In which of the following year was the difference in number of candidates appeared from Mumbai over the previous year the minimum?
a. 2004 b. 2006 c. 2007 d. 2002 e. None of these

52. In which of the following years was the number of candidates qualified from Chennai the maximum among the given years?
a. 2007 b. 2006 c. 2005 d. 2003 e. None of these

53. Approximately what was the total number of candidates qualified from Delhi in 2002 and 2006 together?
a. 27250 b. 25230 c. 30150 d. 28150 e. 26250

54. Approximately how many candidates appearing from Kolkata in 2004 qualified in the competitive examination?
a. 13230 b. 13540 c. 15130 d. 15400 e. 19240

55. Approximately what was the difference between the number of candidates qualified from Hyderabad in 2001 and that in 2002?
a. 1680 b. 2440 c. 1450 d. 2060 e. 1860

Directions (56–60): Korona electronics sells only 5 types of products mobile, modem, router, laptop and printer. The total revenue generated in 1 year is 500 Cr. Given below is the percentage breakup of revenue earned by different products.

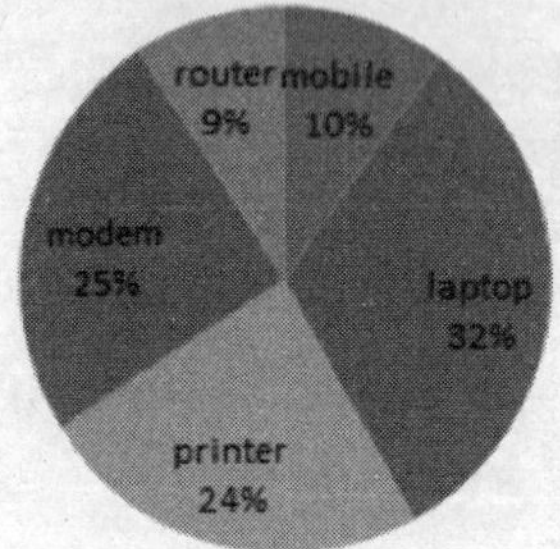

Percentage distribution of revenue of each product in different quarters of the year

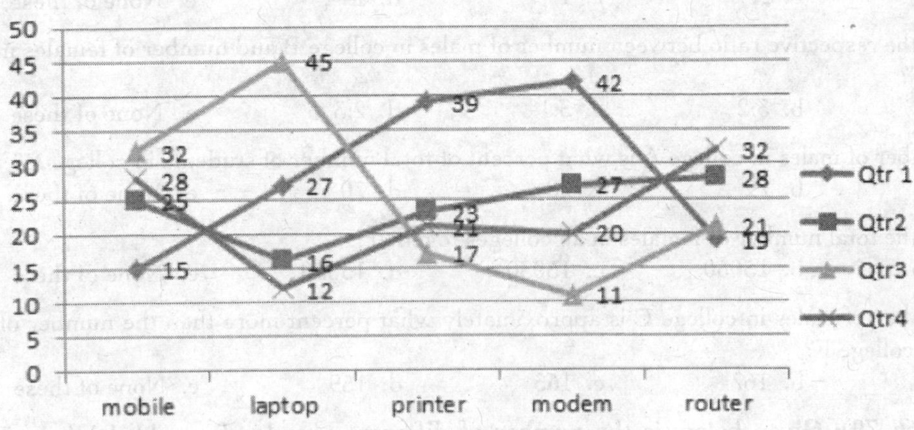

56. Revenue earned by laptop in 3rd quarter is what percent more than revenue of printer in 2nd and 4th quarter Together? (round off to two decimal places)
a. 36.36 b. 34.21 c. 38.86 d. 32.54 e. None of these

57. Find the respective ratio of revenue earned from mobiles in 2nd and 3rd quarter to revenue Of printer from 1st and 2nd quarter?
a. 283:744 b. 744:283 c. 285:744 d. 744:285 e. None of these

58. What is the difference between total revenue in quarter 2 and total revenue in quarter 3?
a. 16.85 b. 17.65 c. 19.25 d. 23.15 e. None of these

59. Revenue from Sales of printer in 1st 3rd and 4th quarter is approximately what times of revenue from sale of laptop in 2nd and 4th quarter?
a. 2.05 b. 1.85 c. 1.95 d. 3.22 e. 2.35

60. Revenue from sales of laptop and printer in quarter 1 is approximately what percent of revenue from sales of all Products together in quarter 2?
a. 80% b. 83% c. 63% d. 71% e. 86%

Directions (61–65): Read the following graph carefully and answer the questions given below:

Percentage distribution of total number of students who completed their graduation from different Colleges: Ratio of males and females

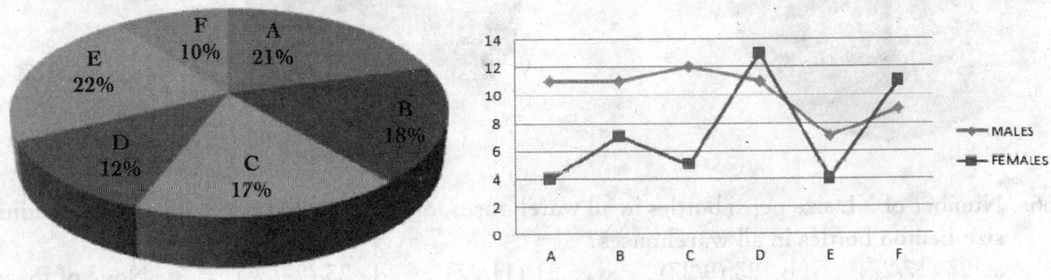

61. The number of males in college D is equal to number of females of which college?
a. C b. A c. F d. E e. None of these

62. What is the respective ratio between number of males in college B and number of females in college F?
a. 2:1 b. 3:2 c. 3:1 d. 2:3 e. None of these

63. The number of males in college A is what percent of total number of students in college E?
a. 74 b. 72 c. 78 d. 70 e. None of these

64. What is the total number of females in all colleges together?
a. 15045 b. 15050 c. 15030 d. 15020 e. None of these

65. The number of males in college C is approximately what percent more than the number of males in college F?
a. 152 b. 167 c. 163 d. 159 e. None of these

Directions (66–70): Given below is the number of different brands of a cold drink in 3 warehouses (warehouse 1, warehouse 2, warehouse 3) of a shop.

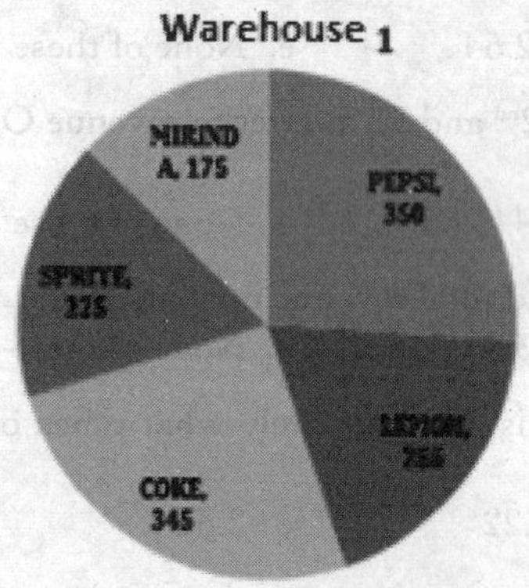

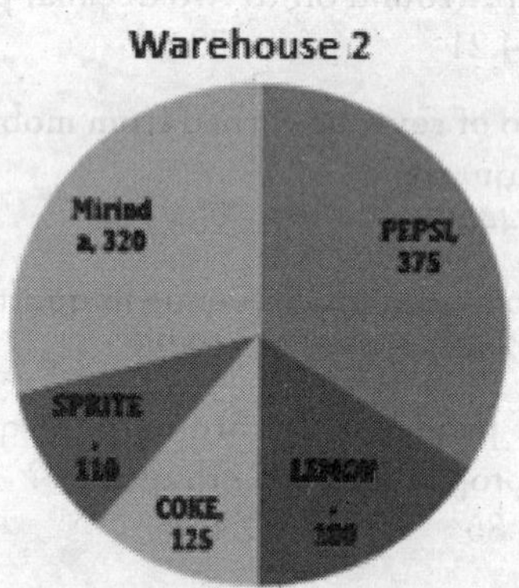

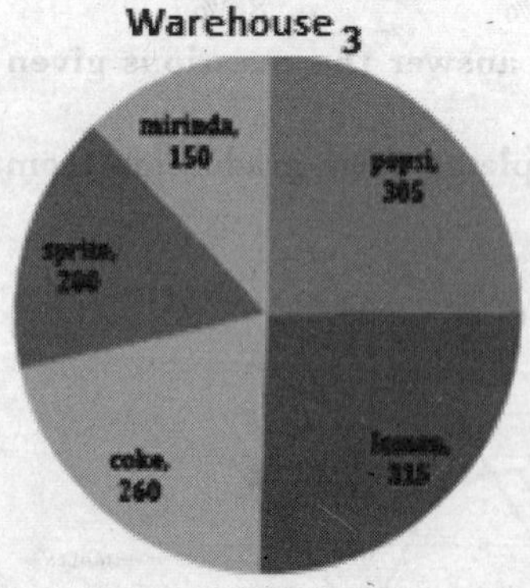

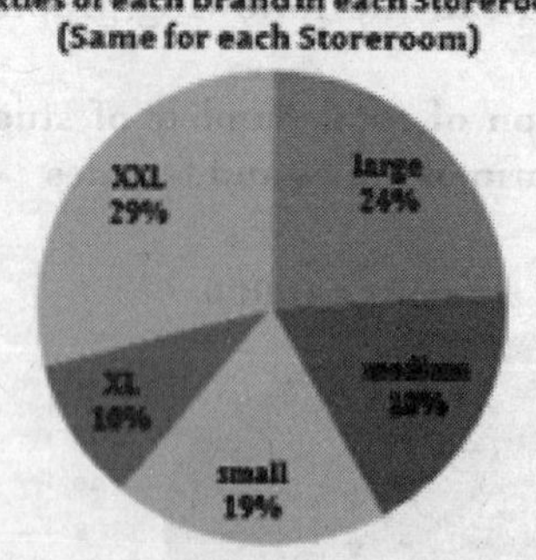

66. Number of XL size pepsi bottles in all warehouses together is what percent less than medium size Lemon bottles in all warehouses?
a. 23 (17/27) b. 23 (9/27) c. 21 (11/27) d. 23 (24/27) e. None of these

67. Number of medium size mirinda and lemon bottles together in warehouse 2 is what percent less than coke and Sprite bottles in lab 1and 3 together? (round off to two decimal places)
a. 91.26 b. 91.36 c. 91.16 d. 91.66 e. None of these

68. If three fourth of the XL mirinda bottles from store room 2 are taken out then find the ratio of remaining mirinda bottles in store room 2 the total number of bottles in warehouse 1?
a. 148:675 b. 8:45 c. 52:225 d. 233:135 e. None of these

69. What is half of the difference between average number of bottles in warehouse having maximum number of bottles to that of having minimum number of bottles?
a. 40 b. 48 c. 20 d. 24 e. 25

70. If all the coke bottles from store room 1 are excluded then lemon bottle from store 1 accounts for what percent of total number of bottles from warehouse1 and warehouse 2 together? (round off to 2 decimal places)
a. 12.06% b. 11.26% c. 11.36% d. 11.06% e. None of these

Directions (71–75): Given below are the graphs showing the respective income and expenditure of two companies A and B in different years. Answer the following question on the basis of these graphs

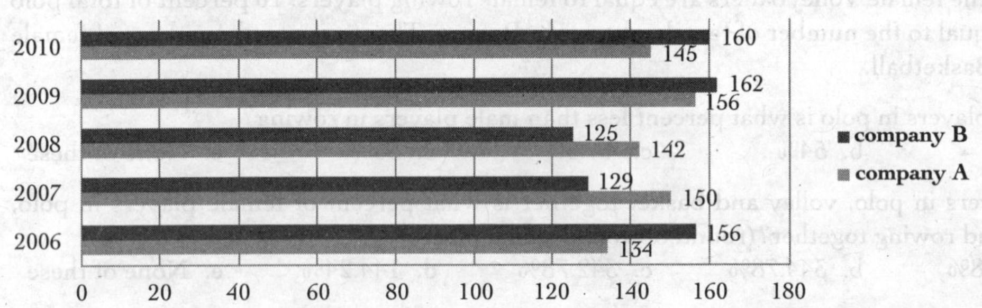

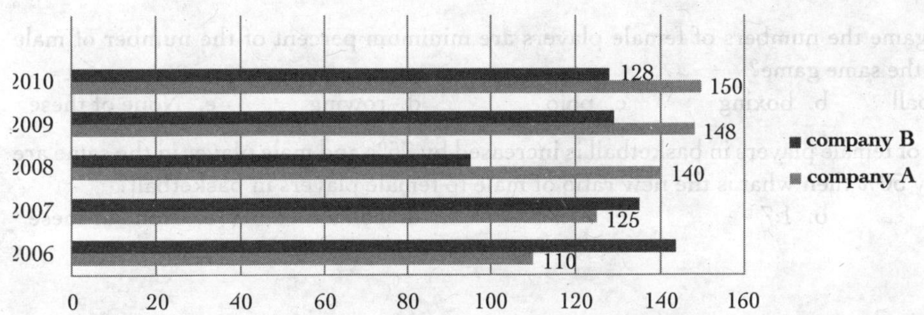

71. Average profit of company A from 2006 to 2008 is approximately what percent more/less than average profit of company B from year 2008 to 2010?
a. 46.32% less b. 46.32% more c. 53.68% more d. 53.68% less e. 54.58% less

72. What is the difference of profit percentage of company A in 2006 to profit percentage of B in 2009? (approximate)
a. 3.75% b. 5.75% c. 3.19% d. 3.85% e. 4.35%

73. In which year the profit percentage of company B is maximum?
a. 2006 b. 2007 c. 2009 d. 2010 e. None of these

74. Approximately what is the difference between the maximum profit percentage of company A over the years and loss percentage of company B in 2007?
a. 17.27% b. 17.37% c. 27.17% d. 19.13% e. 17.53%

75. If the expenditure of company B in 2011 is increased by 15% and income of the same is decreased by 8% in comparison of last year then what will be the profit /loss in 2011?
a. 2 cr loss b. 2 cr profit c. 4.2 cr profit d. 4.2 cr loss e. None of these

Directions (76–80): Study the information carefully to answer the question that follow:
In a sport event there are 5 sports viz. Polo, Volleyball, Boxing, Rowing and Basketball. There are total 800 players in the sports event. The ratio between female and male players is 1:3 respectively. Twenty five percent of the total players are in Volleyball. There are 110 Rowing players. 10 percent of the total players are in Boxing. Polo players are double the number of Rowing players. Remaining players are in Basketball. 30 percent of Volleyball players are female. Half the female Volleyballers are equal to female rowing players. 10 percent of total polo players are equal to the number of female players in Boxing. There are equal numbers of female in Polo and Basketball.

76. Female players in polo is what percent less than male players in rowing?
a. 45% b. 54% c. 44% d. 55% e. None of these

77 Male players in polo, volley and basket together is what percent of female players in polo, volley and rowing together? (round off to 2 decimal places)
a. 324.78% b. 344.78% c. 342.78% d. 144.24% e. None of these

78. What is the ratio of number of females in basket and rowing together to male player in polo and boxing together?
a. 117:37 b. 29:84 c. 28:97 d. 24:73 e. None of these

79. In which game the numbers of female players are minimum percent of the number of male players in the same game?
a. basketball b. boxing c. polo d. rowing e. None of these

80. If number of female players in basketball is increased by 75% and male player in the same are reduced by 50% then what is the new ratio of male to female players in basketball?
a. 73:77 b. 1:7 c. 77:73 d. 55:73 e. None of these

Section 3: English Language

Directions (81–85): Read each sentence to find out whether there is any grammatical error in it. The error, if any, will be one part of the sentence. The number of that part is the answer. If there is no error, the answer is (e). (ignore the errors of punctuation, if any.)

81. The auditions for India's first ever (a)/ reality based pop band hunt, is (b)/ going on in full swing, (c)/ with numerous entries coming in. (d)/ No error (e)

82. To curbing the spread of violence, (a)/ authorities brought under curfew (b)/ more areas in the State, where (c)/ three youths were killed. (d)/ No error (e)

83. Demand for diesel cars, which has (a)/ been on the rise for the last few years, (b)/ may dip as the government is increasing the price (c)/ of the fuel, bringing it closer to that of petrol. (d)/ No error (e)

84. Not only was the actress over the Moon (a)/ as winning an award, but was (b)/ also deeply touched by the support (c)/ she got from the industry. (d)/ No error (e)

85. The protestors went on a rampaging (a)/ and set ablaze three shops (b)/ resulting in injuries to 30 people (c)/ including women and children. (d)/ No error (e)

Directions (86–90): Rearrange the following six sentences (A), (B), (C), (D), (E) and (F) in the proper sequence to form a meaningful paragraph and then answer the questions given below.

A. In 2011, he presented the Leonard Hastings Schoff Memorial Lectures at Columbia, and these form the basis of this posthumous book, an analysis of plot in drama and fiction.

B. Foundational largesse on such a scale certainly reinforces the impression that the life of a tenured professor at a major university resembles one long holiday, some of it spent with a beautiful view of Lake Como.

C. Not to sound philistine, but this seems an inordinate amount of money and time off, especially given the relatively small scholarly return.

D. According to the introduction by Russian scholar Robin Feuer Miller, "Plots," though brief, reflects many years of thought and research.

E. A prefatory note by Belknap duly thanks "the Woodrow Wilson Fellowship Program, the Bellagio Center, the Kennan Institute at the Smithsonian Institute, the John Simon Guggenheim Foundation, the National Endowment for the Humanities, and the International Research and Exchanges Board."

F. Robert L. Belknap was a longtime Columbia University professor and the author of two important studies of Dostoevsky's "Brothers Karamazov."

86. Which of the following should be the FIRST sentence after rearrangement?
    a. A b. B c. C d. D e. F

87. Which of the following should be the FIFTH sentence after rearrangement?
    a. A b. B c. C d. D e. F

88. Which of the following should be the THIRD sentence after rearrangement?
a. A b. B c. C d. D e. F

89. Which of the following should be the FOURTH sentence after rearrangement?
a. A b. B c. C d. D e. E

90. Which of the following should be the SIXTH (last) sentence after rearrangement?
a. A b. B c. C d. D e. E

Directions (91–95): The Following questions have two blanks, each blank indicating that something has been omitted. Choose the set of words for each blank that best fits the meaning of the sentence as a whole.

91. The old man could not have been accused of _____ his affection; his conduct toward the child betrayed his __________ her.
a. lavishing. .fondness for
b. sparing. .tolerance of
c. rationing. .antipathy for
d. stinting. .adoration of
e. increasing - apparently

92. A leading chemist believes that many scientists have difficulty with stereochemistry because much of the relevant nomenclature is ____, in that it combines concepts that should be kept ____
a. obscure. .interrelated
b. specialized. .intact
c. subtle. .inviolate
d. imprecise. .discrete
e. concentration . . incidental

93. Among the many _________ of the project, expense cannot be numbered; the goals of the project's promoters can be achieved with impressive __________.
a. highlights. .efficiency
b. features. .savings
c. disadvantages. .innovation
d. defects. .economy
e. escalating - joyfully

94. Social scientists have established fairly clear-cut __________ that describe the appropriate behavior of children and adults, but there seems to be _____ about what constitutes appropriate behavior for adolescents.
a. functions. .rigidity
b. estimates. .indirectness
c. norms. .confusion
d. regulations. .certainty
e. disagreement . . incongruous

95. Although Mount Saint Helens has been more ------ during the last 4,500 years than any other volcano in the coterminous United States, its long dormancy before its recent eruption ------ its violent nature.
a. awe-inspiring. .restrained
b. gaseous. .confirmed
c. explosive. .belied
d. familiar. .moderated
e. collaboration . . predictable

Directions (96–105): Read the following passage carefully and certain words in the passage are printed in bold letters to help you locate them easily while answering some of these questions.

A star's life cycle is inversely determined by its mass. A star's mass is determined by the amount of matter that is available in its nebula, the giant cloud of gas and dust from which it was born. Over time, the hydrogen gas in the nebula is pulled together by gravity and it begins to spin. As the gas spins faster, it heats up and becomes as a proto star. Eventually the temperature reaches 15,000,000 degrees and nuclear fusion occurs in the cloud's core. The cloud begins to glow brightly, contracts a little, and becomes stable. It is now a main sequence star and will remain in this stage, shining for millions to billions of years to come. This is the stage our Sun is at right now. As the main sequence star glows, hydrogen in its core is converted into helium by nuclear fusion. When the hydrogen supply in the core begins to run out, and the star is no longer generating heat by nuclear fusion, the core becomes unstable and contracts. The outer shell of the star, which is still mostly hydrogen, starts to expand. As it expands, it cools and glows red. The star has now reached the red giant phase. It is red because it is cooler than it was in the main sequence star stage and it is a giant because the outer shell has expanded outward. In the core of the red giant, helium fuses into carbon. All stars evolve the same way up to the red giant phase. For low-mass stars, after the helium has fused into carbon, the core collapses again. As the core collapses, the outer layers of the star are **expelled**. A planetary nebula is formed by the outer layers. The core remains as a white dwarf and eventually cools to become a black dwarf. Like low mass stars, high mass stars are born in nebulae and evolve and live in the Main Sequence. However, their life cycles start to differ after the red giant phase. A massive star will undergo a supernova explosion. If the **remnant** of the explosion is 1.4 to about 3 times as massive as our Sun, it will become a neutron star. The core of a massive star that has more than roughly 3 times the mass of our Sun after the explosion will do something quite different. The force of gravity overcomes the nuclear forces which keep protons and neutrons from combining. The core is thus swallowed by its own gravity. It has now become a black hole which readily attracts any matter and energy that comes near it. What happens between the red giant phase and the supernova explosion is described below. Once stars that are 5 times or more massive than our Sun reach the red giant phase, their core temperature increases as carbon atoms are formed from the fusion of helium atoms. Gravity continues to pull carbon atoms together as the temperature increases and additional fusion processes proceed, forming oxygen, nitrogen, and eventually iron. When the core contains essentially just iron, fusion in the core ceases. This is because iron is the most compact and stable of all the elements. It takes more energy to break up the iron nucleus than that of any other element. Creating heavier elements through fusing of iron thus requires an input of energy rather than the release of energy. Since energy is no longer being radiated from the core, in less than a second, the star begins the final phase of gravitational collapse. The core temperature rises to over 100 billion degrees as the iron atoms are crushed together. The **repulsive** force between the nuclei overcomes the force of gravity, and the core recoils out from the heart of the star in a shock wave, which we see as a supernova explosion. As the shock encounters material in the star's outer layers, the material is heated, fusing to form new elements and radioactive isotopes. While many of the more common elements are made through nuclear fusion in the cores of stars, it takes the unstable conditions of the supernova explosion to form many of the heavier elements. The shock wave propels this material out into space. The material that is exploded away from the star is now known as a supernova remnant. The hot material, the radioactive isotopes, as well as the leftover core of the exploded star, produce Xrays and gammarays.

96. According to the passage, a supernova.....
A. ends up being a black dwarf.
B. ends up being a neutron star.
C. ends up being a black hole.
a. A or B b. A, B and C
c. A or B or C d. B or C
e. None of (A), (B) and (C)

97. It can be deduced from the passage that after the giant molecular cloud, a Black Hole has
a. Three clearly defined stages including the supernova in its evolution.
b. Four clearly defined stages including the supernova in its evolution.
c. Five clearly defined stages including the supernova in its evolution.
d. Six clearly defined stages including the supernova in its evolution.
e. None of these

98. The passage supports all these inferences EXCEPT:
A. At about a 100 billion Celsius, iron molecules are fused into heavier elements.
B. The larger a star's mass, the shorter its life cycle.
C. Main sequence stars are sustained by nuclear fission for millions or billions of years.
D. The sun would most likely end up as black dwarf.
a. A and B b. C and D c. A and C d. B, C, and D e. B and D

99. Which of the following best describes the explosion of a supernova?
a. A massive star may run out of fuel, ceasing to generate fusion energy in its core, and collapsing inward under the force of its own gravity to form a neutron star or a black hole.
b. A massive star may run out of fuel, it may undergo sudden gravitational collapse into a neutron star or black hole, releasing energy that heats and expels that star's outer layers.
c. After the core of an aging massive star ceases to generate energy from unclear fusion, it may undergo sudden gravitational collapse into a neutron star or black hole.
d. After the core of an aging star may undergo sudden gravitational collapse releasing gravitational potential energy that heats and expels the star's outer layers.
e. None of these

100. The author expects which of the following to be his/ her readers?
a. Astronomy professors. b. Training astrophysicists.
c. Secondary school students. d. Stellar scientists. e. veteran scientists

101. The writer does not make use of which of the following in the construction of this essay?
a. Specific examples. b. Definitions of specific vocabulary.
c. Comparison of different phenomena.
d. Explanation of physical laws. e. All the above options have been used

102. The style of expression adopted by the writer can be best describes as
a. Factual and elucidative b. Speculative and instructional
c. Revelatory and educative d. Scientific and edifying
e. Sarcastic and ironic

Directions (103–104): Choose the word/group of words which is MOST SIMILAR in meaning to the word/group of words printed in bold as used in the passage.

103. EXPELLED
a. Allow b. Absorb c. Take in d. Imbibe e. Evacuate

104. REMNANT
a. Whole b. Vestige c. Base d. Need e. Unabridged

Directions (105): Choose the word/group of words which is MOST OPPOSITE in meaning to the word/group of words printed in bold as used in the passage.

105. REPULSIVE
a. Abhorrent b. Hateful c. Abominable d. Agreeable e. Vile

Directions (106–115): In the following passage there are blanks, each of which has been numbered. These numbers are printed below the passage and against each, five words are suggested, one of which fits the blank appropriately. Find out the appropriate word in each case.

Hundreds of plants and animals are **(106)** every day due to deforestation and urbanization what might happen if this continues in future? The last mass extinction of plant and animal species occurred 65 million years ago with the Dinosaurs. In all, five mass extinctions have occurred and scientists **(107)** earth is in sixth mass extinction. The world as it is now is threatened, including people, who are responsible for earth's **(108)**. Pesticides contaminating water; overharvesting of animals and plants; air pollution; illegal fishing and the clearing of land are direct results of urbanization and deforestation. People have **(109)** and damaged almost half a earth's land, at a very unsustainable rate.

Global warming is having a serious impact as well. A six-degree Celsius increase in global temperature killed 95% of all species on Earth 251 million years ago. An increase of six-degree Celsius is forecast this century if a change is not made to **(110)** the damage done to earth. Humans will be one of the 95% of species lost. Noticeable, changes of global warming include migration **(111)** and the change in season timings. Migrating birds are migrating earlier, which in turn is causing them to hatch eggs and **(112)** young earlier than they did at the beginning of this century. While this is just the tip of the iceberg many other **(113)** regarding the extinction of plant and animal species need addressing. It is more important now than ever before to pull our heads out of the sand and make changes for the **(114)** of the earth. Future generations are **(115)**, as they are a species as well.

106.	a. killing	b. alive	c. born	d. left	e. lost
107.	a. speak	b. told	c. estimation	d. believe	e. consider
108.	a. shape	b. development	c. deterioration	d. warmth	e. expansion
109.	a. altered	b. created	c. produced	d. made	e. brought
110.	a. void	b. dissipate	c. augment	d. reverse	e. increase
111.	a. delay	b. birds	c. slowdown	d. hasten	e. acceleration

112. a. spare b. bear c. destroy d. amend e. generation

113. a. animals b. difficulty c. issues d. humans e. problem

114. a. extinction b. better c. wealth d. stigma e. demand

115. a. endangered b. threaten c. evaluated d. living e. compared

Section 4: General Awareness

116. What is the name of Global Positioning System (GPS) system developed by India?
a. PATH b. NAVIC c. KIRAN d. IRNS e. ISSNA

117. Which RBI Governor had the largest tenure?
a. C D Deshmukh b. Benegal Rama Rau
c. R N Malhotra d. Bimal Jalan e. C Rangarajan

118. The World Day against Child Labour is celebrated each year on?
a. 15 June b. 10 June c. 12 June d. 11 June e. None of these

119. Multilateral Investment Guarantee Agency (MIGA) is a part of the
a. IMF b. World Bank c. United Nations
d. World Economic Forum e. None of these

120. Foreign Currency Non Resident Account can be opened in the form of?
a. Current Account b. Term deposit only
c. Saving deposit only d. Recurring deposit e. None of these

121. The process of transformation of Physical Shares, Commercial paper or Certificate of deposit into electronic form is called as______
a. Dematerialization b. Electronic Clearing Service
c. Truncation d. Securitization e. None of these

122. What is the full form of FATCA?
a. Foreign Account Tax Compliance Act
b. Finance Account Tax Compliance Act
c. Financial Accounting Tax Compliance Act
d. Foreign Account Tax Code Act
e. Foreigners Account Tax Compliance Act

123. Mr. Urjit Patel is the ___________ Governor of RBI.
a. 23rd b. 24th c. 21st d. 20th e. 19th

124. Who among the following has been appointed as Principle Adviser for social sector in NITI Aayog?
a. Rajiv Mehrishi b. Ratan P Watal
c. Hasmukh Adhia d. Arvind Mayaram e. None of these

125. Government has enforced the decision of retirement fund body _________ to almost double the maximum sum assured under its insurance scheme from 3.6 lakh to 6 lakh rupees. It will benefit around four crores subscribers.
a. LIC b. NIACL c. EPFO d. UIICL e. None of these

126. The 2016 Global Bamboo Summit will be hosted by which city of India?
a. Bhopal b. Indore c. Jaipur d. Pune e. None of these

127. The securities that are purchased by banks with the intention to take advantage of price movement or interest movement are classified as:
a. Held till maturity b. Available for sale
c. Held for trading d. Fluctuating securities e. None of these

128. The market for short term financial for short term financial assets/instruments, that are close substitutes of money, is called:
a. Money market b. capital market c. forex market
d. financial market e. None of these

129. Under the marginal standing facility (MSF), the eligible entities can avail the facility, up to ______ per cent of their respective Net Demand and Time Liabilities (NDTL) outstanding at the end of the second preceding fortnight.
a. 1% b. 2% c. 3% d. 5% e. None of these

130. Non Convertible Denominations with a min of_____ (face value) and in multiples of______:
a. Rs. 1 lakh, Rs. 1 lakh b. Rs. 5 lakh, Rs. 1 lakh
c. Rs. 5 lakh, Rs. 5 lakh d. Rs. 5 lakh, Rs. 10 lakh e. None of these

131. What happens if a cheque is post dated?
a. Bank on whom it is drawn will not honour the cheque before the date of the cheque
b. Bank on whom it is drawn has to honour the cheque before the date of the cheque
c. Bank on whom it is drawn has to refer to court to honour the cheque before the date of the cheque
d. Bank on whom it is drawn has to refer to RBI to honour the cheque before the date of the cheque
e. None of these

132. When a smaller company folds into a larger one through exchange of shares or cash, it is termed as
a. Diversification b. Collaboration c. Joint Venture
d. Merger e. None of these

133. The amount invested by a single investor in the Commercial Paper(CP)should not be less than __________
a. Rs. 5 lakh b. Rs. 10 lakh c. Rs. 15 lakh d. Rs. 25 lakh e. None of these

134. The ethically questionable practice of a salesperson misrepresenting or misleading an investor about the characteristics of a product or service is termed as
a. Over the counter sale b. Misbehavior c. Miss-selling
d. Persuasion e. None of these

135. The depositories of India, which have the mandate to help firms convert their physical shares or securities into dematerialized demat forms are regulated by
a. RBI b. FMC c. SEBI d. NPCI e. None of these

136. The Urban cooperative banks are controlled by two entities. One of them is the Reserve Bank of India (RBI) and the other is/are
a. Union Finance Ministry b. State Govt c. NABARD
d. SIDBI e. None of these

137. As per the prevailing rules, microfinance institution can lend to a single borrower a sum of Rs.______

a. Rs. 25,000 b. Rs. 50,000 c. Rs.1 lakh d. Rs. 2 lakh e. None of these

138. The lending by the scheduled commercial banks, on a fortnightly average basis, should not exceed what percent of their owned fund (paidup capital and reserves)?

a. 20% b. 15% c. 50% d. 25% e. None of these

139. Which of the following pairs of international organizations and their headquarters is NOT matched correctly?

a. Bank of International Settlements (BIS) Basel Switzerland
b. OECD –Paris, France
c. Swift – La Hulpe, Belgium
d. WTO Zurich, Switzerland
e. None of these

140. Even if you do not have any of the documents listed by the govt to show your 'proof of identity' you can open a bank account with a bank named

a. Micro account b. BSBDA
c. No frills account d. Small account e. None of these

141. The term 'Gully' is associated with which of the following sports?

a. Cricket b. Baseball c. Football d. Hockey e. Baseball

142. A Transaction in which the real beneficiary is not the one in whose name a property has been purchased is defined as

a. Fraud b. Benami
c. Proprietary d. Insider Trading e. None of these

143. Which bank launched Bangalore's first ATM that accepts Aadhaar number and Aadhaar fingerprint (biometric) instead of ATM/Debit Card and PIN to dispense cash?

a. DCB Bank b. HDFC Bank c. Yes Bank
d. RBL Bank e. None of these

144. Kotak Mahindra Bank said that its customers will continue to enjoy 6% interest rate on savings account for balance above how much amount, and 5% interest rate pa on savings account for balance up to how much amount?

a. Rs. 75,000 b. Rs. 50,000 c. Rs. 1 lakh d. Rs. 2 lakh e. None of these

145. President Pranab Mukherjee has been presented National Order of the ________ Coast. This is the highest award of the West African country and was conferred on him during his two days visit to the nation.

a. Cape Verde b. Ghana c. Namibia
d. Republic of Ivory e. None of these

146. The Reserve Bank of India (RBI) has come up with a new scheme for Sustainable Structuring of Stressed Assets (S4A) of the large project. The Scheme for S4A will cover those projects which have started commercial operations and have an outstanding loan of over ____________?

a. Rs. 100 cr. b. Rs. 200 cr. c. Rs. 300 cr. d. Rs. 400 cr. e. Rs. 500 cr.

147. The Centre has constituted a team of senior officials to assess the irrigation facilities and implementation of Pradhan Mantri Krishi Sinchayee Yojana (PMKSY) at selected districts of western in which of the following state recently?
a. Bihar
b. Madhya Pradesh
c. Uttar Pradesh
d. West Bengal
e. None of these

148. The Union Cabinet gave its nod to BIMSTEC Convention on Mutual Legal Assistance in Criminal Matters recently. Which of the following is NOT a member of BIMSTEC?
a. Sri lanka
b. Thailand
c. Myanmar
d. China
e. None of these

149. The Project Mausam, promoted by the Union Ministry of Culture, focuses on?
a. Maritime trade routes
b. Coastal landscapes
c. Monsoon patterns
d. All of the above
e. None of these

150. Which of the following is not correctly matched?
a. MSF – Marginal Standing Facility
b. CRR – Cash Reserve Ratio
c. SLR – Statutory Liquidity Ratio
d. LAF – Liquidity Adjustment Facility
e. None of these

151. Which private sector lender has received a 'Custodian of Securities' licence from the markets regulator SEBI to allows the entity to offer custodial services to financial market participants, including FIIs and foreign portfolio investors (FPIs)?
a. HDFC Bank
b. YES Bank
c. ICICI Bank
d. State Bank of India
e. None of these

152. India and Bangladesh conducted a five-day dialogue in which place over a host of security issues, including drug trafficking and cattle smuggling across the border between the two neighbors?
a. New Delhi
b. Bangalore
c. Dhaka
d. Mirpur
e. None of these

153. Name the Indian American Sikh woman from California who has been elected as the newest national committee woman of the Republican National Committee.
a. Harmeet Kaur Dhillon
b. Jasmine kaur
c. Bobby Jindal
d. Nikki Haley
e. None of these

154. "Multicurrency basket" means?
a. A number of international currencies to which the value of SDRs is linked
b. Number of major international currencies to which the external value of the Indian rupee is linked
c. The name given to a group of West European currencies.
d. An inflationary situation where the external forces are the primary contributing factors
e. None of these

155. The Union Information and Broadcasting ministry has framed a New Print Media Advertisement Policy for DAVP. What is the full form of DAVP?
a. Directorate of Audio Visual Publicity
b. Directorate of Advertising and Visual Publicity
c. Department of Audio-Visual Publicity
d. Doctrinal Audio-Visual Program
e. None of these

ANSWER GRID

1. e	2. d	3. d	4. e	5. a	6. a	7. e	8. b	9. a	10. b
11. a	12. b	13. c	14. e	15. e	16. e	17. a	18. c	19. a	20. e
21. c	22. a	23. c	24. a	25. a	26. c	27. a	28. e	29. c	30. c
31. e	32. b	33. a	34. c	35. d	36. b	37. c	38. b	39. c	40. b
41. c	42. b	43. d	44. a	45. c	46. b	47. d	48. c	49. a	50. c
51. c	52. a	53. d	54. b	55. e	56. a	57. c	58. e	59. a	60. a
61. c	62. a	63. d	64. e	65. b	66. e	67. a	68. a	69. d	70. a
71. a	72. a	73. e	74. b	75. e	76. a	77. b	78. e	79. c	80. a
81. b	82. a	83. e	84. b	85. a	86. e	87. c	88. d	89. e	90. b
91. d	92. d	93. d	94. c	95. c	96. d	97. c	98. c	99. b	100. c
101. d	102. a	103. e	104. b	105. d	106. e	107. d	108. c	109. a	110. d
111. e	112. b	113. c	114. c	115. a	116. b	117. b	118. c	119. b	120. b
121. a	122. a	123. b	124. b	125. c	126. b	127. c	128. a	129. a	130. b
131. a	132. d	133. a	134. c	135. c	136. b	137. b	138. d	139. d	140. d
141. a	142. b	143. a	144. c	145. d	146. e	147. c	148. d	149. d	150. e
151. b	152. c	153. a	154. b	155. b					

Solution to Questions 11–15:-

Name	sex	Marital status	CAT	subject	Subject teacher or class teacher
Ramesh	M	Y	Y	Electrical Machine	ST
Neha	F	Y	N	Power Electronics	CT
Sophia	F	N	Y	DCNS	ST
Sanjay	M	M	N	Digital Electronics	CT
Vivek	M	N	Y	DCNS	ST
Mona	F	M	N	Digital Electronics	CT
Divya	F	N	Y	Fluid Mechanics	CT

Solutions to questions 21–24:

21. N owned it before L owned it. Hence option A cannot be true, as J owned it before O owned it. Similarly, options B and D are not true, as it is not related to the conditions given. Hence the answer is option C.

22. The answer is option A, that is, J owned it before L owned it. Option B cannot be true as it is violating the conditions. Similarly, options, C and D, are incorrect, as it is not related to the conditions. Hence the answer is option A.

23. N sold it to J on New Year's Day, 1932, that is option C. As it is given that, "L sold it to O, J owned it before O owned it, N owned it before L owned it". According to these conditions, option C is correct.

24. Following diagram can be drawn:

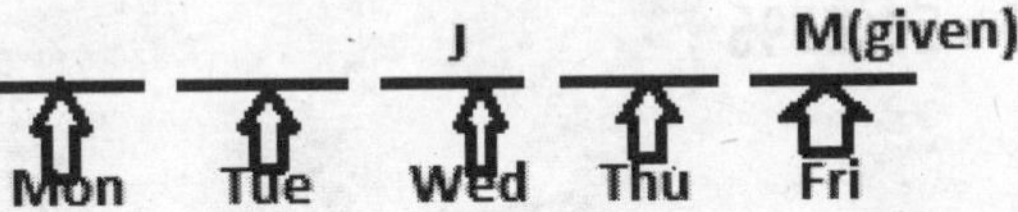

As it is given that - M must be the second ship unloaded after J is unloaded. Since, M is unloaded on Friday, J must be unloaded on Wednesday. Option B is not true as K can be unloaded on either on Tuesday or on Monday. Similarly, option C cannot be true as it is not fixed when to L is unloaded. Also, option D is not true. Hence the answer is option A.

25. Following diagram can be drawn:

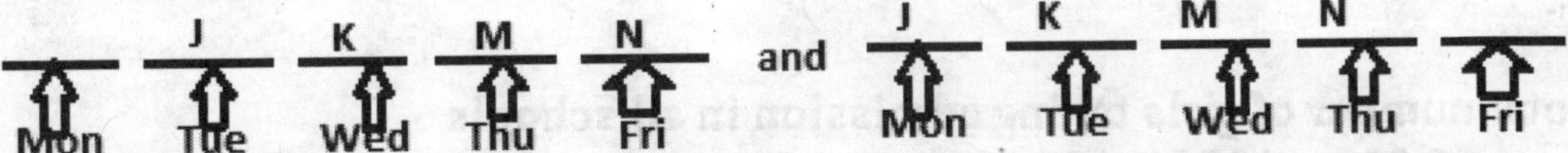

As per the conditions given, we can see that J can be unloaded on Monday or Tuesday. Since, it is given that – K must be unloaded on a day preceding the days M and N are unloaded and M must be the second ship unloaded after J is unloaded, therefore, the answer is option A. Hence the answer is option A.

(31—35):-

Team	Venue	Day
Slovakia	Paris	Monday
Romania	Lille	Tuesday
Russia	Marseille	Wednesday
France	Lyon	Thursday
Sweden	Bordeaux	Friday
Spain	Lens	Saturday
Portugal	Nice	Sunday

46:-

Total number of those who have taken the admisssion in school R

$= 20,000 \times \frac{16}{100} \times \frac{48}{100} = 1536$

47:-

$$\therefore \text{Required per cent} = \frac{20000 \times \frac{12}{100} \times \frac{40}{100}}{20000 \times \frac{17}{100} \times \frac{55}{100}} \times 100$$

$$= \frac{12 \times 40}{17 \times 55} \times 100 = 51.33\%$$

48:-

Total number of boys taking admission in all the schools $= \frac{20000}{100 \times 100}$

$[22 \times 55 + 18 \times 60 + 16 \times 52 + 17 \times 45 + 15 \times 50 + 12 \times 40] = 2 \times 5117 = 10234$

49:-

Total number of girls taking admission in all schools

$= 20,000 - 10234 = 9766$

Required per cent

$$= \frac{10234 - 9766}{9766} \times 100 \approx 4.75\%$$

50:-

Required answer

$$=\frac{20000\times\frac{16}{100}\times\frac{48}{100}}{20000\times\frac{12}{100}\times\frac{40}{100}}=\frac{16\times48}{12\times40}=1.60\text{ times}$$

53:-

(d) Number of candidates passed from delhi in 2002 & 2006 = (58248 * 28/100) + (59216 * 20 / 100) = 16309 + 11843 = 28152 ≈ 28150

54:-

Required No of passed candidates = 71253 * 19/ 100 = 13540

55:-

Required difference = 50248 * 21/100 – 51124 * 17/100
= 10551 – 8691 = 1860 Approx

61:-

No. of males in D $=\frac{11}{24}\times\frac{12}{100}\times 40000 = 2200$

No. of females in A $=\frac{4}{15}\times\frac{21}{100}\times 40000 = 2240$

No. of females in B $=\frac{7}{18}\times\frac{18}{100}\times 40000 = 2800$

No. of females in C $=\frac{5}{17}\times\frac{17}{100}\times 40000 = 2000$

No. of females in D $=\frac{13}{24}\times\frac{12}{100}\times 40000 = 2600$

No. of females in E $=\frac{4}{11}\times\frac{22}{100}\times 40000 = 3200$

No. of females in F $=\frac{11}{20}\times\frac{10}{100}\times 40000 = 2200$

So, no. of males in D is equal to no. of females in F.

62:-

No. of males in B = $\frac{11}{18} \times \frac{18}{100} \times 40000 = 4400$

No. of females in F = $\frac{11}{20} \times \frac{10}{100} \times 40000 = 2200$

Ratio = $\frac{4400}{2200} = 2:1$

63:-

No. of males in A = $\frac{11}{15} \times \frac{21}{100} \times 40000 = 6160$

No. of students in E = $\frac{22}{100} \times 40000 = 8800$

% age = $\frac{6160}{8800} \times 100 = 70\%$

64:- Total no. of females = 2240 + 2800 + 2000 + 2600 + 3200 + 2200 = 15040

65:-

; No. of males in C = $\frac{12}{17} \times \frac{17}{100} \times 40000 = 4800$

No. of males in F = $\frac{9}{20} \times \frac{10}{100} \times 40000 = 1800$

% age = $\frac{4800-1800}{1800} \times 100 = 166.67 \approx 167\%$

66:-

Number of XL size Pepsi bottles in all Warehouse $= \frac{10}{100} \times (350 + 375 + 305) = 103$

Medium size lemon bottles in all Warehouse $= \frac{18}{100}(255 + 315 + 180) = 135$

Required percentage = $\frac{135-103}{135} \times 100 = 23\frac{19}{27}\%$

67:-

Medium size Mirinda and lemon bottles in Warehouse 2 = $\frac{18}{100}(320 + 180) = 90$

Coke and sprite in Warehouse 1 and Warehouse 3 together = 225 + 345 + 200 + 260 = 1030

Required percentage = $\frac{1030-90}{1030} \times 100 = 91.26\%$

68:-

XL Mirinda bottles in Warehouse $2 = \frac{10}{100} \times 320 = 32$

$\frac{3}{4}$ th are excluded $= \frac{3}{4} \times 32 = 24$

Remaining Mirinda bottles in Warehouse $2 = 320 - 24 = 296$

Total number of bottles in Warehouse $1 = 1350$

Ratio = 148 : 675

69:-

Warehouse 1 has maximum number of bottles = 1350

Warehouse 2 has minimum number of bottles = 1110

Half of difference between average no. of bottles $= \frac{1}{2}\left(\frac{1350}{5} - \frac{1110}{5}\right) = 24$

70:-

Required % age $= \frac{255}{350+255+225+175+320+375+180+125+110}$

$= \frac{255}{2115} \times 100 = 12.06\%$

71:-

Average profit of company A from 2006 to 2008 $= \frac{24+25+2}{3} = 17$ cr

Average profit of company B from 2008 to 2010 $= \frac{30+33+32}{3} = \frac{95}{3}$ cr

Required percentage $= \frac{\frac{95}{3}-17}{\frac{95}{3}} \times 100$

$\approx 46.32\%$ less

72:-

Profit percentage of A in 2006 $= \frac{134-110}{110} \times 100 \approx 21.81\%$

Profit percentage of B in 2009 $= \frac{162-129}{129} \times 100 \approx 25.58\%$

Difference $\approx 3.75\%$

73:-

Profit percentage of B in 2006 = $\frac{156-144}{144} \times 100 = 8.33\%$

Profit percentage in 2007 = $\frac{129-135}{135} \times 100 = -4.44\%$ (loss)

In 2008 = $\frac{125-95}{95} \times 100 = 31.58\%$

In 2009 = $\frac{162-129}{129} \times 100 = 25.58\%$

In 2010 = $\frac{160-128}{128} \times 100 = 25\%$

So maximum profit percentage of company B is in 2008.

74:-

Company A has maximum profit percentage in year 2006 that is $\frac{134-110}{110} \times 100 = 21.81\%$

Loss percentage of company B in 2007 = $\frac{135-129}{135} \times 100 = 4.44\%$

Difference = 17.37%

75:-

expenditure of B in 2011 = $\frac{115}{100} \times 128 = 147.2$ cr

Income of B in 2011 = $\frac{92}{100} \times 160 = 147.2$ cr

Income = expenditure

No profit no loss.

(76–80):-

Directions (Q.76-80) :

Sports	Total Player	Female	Male
Volleyball	200	60	140
Rowing	110	30	80
Boxing	80	22	58
Polo	220	44	176
Basketball	190	44	146
Total	800	200	600

76:-

Required % age = $\frac{80-44}{80} \times 100 = 45\%$

77:-

Male players in Polo, Volley and Basket = $140 + 176 + 146 = 462$

Female players in Polo, Volley and Rowing = $60 + 30 + 44 = 134$

Required % age = $\frac{462}{134} \times 100 = 344.78\%$

78:-

No. of females in basket and rowing = $44 + 30 = 74$

No. of male players in Polo and Boxing = $176 + 58 = 234$

Required ratio = $37 : 117$

79:-

% of female players to male players in Volley ball = $\frac{60}{140} \times 100 = 42.85\%$

Rowing = $\frac{30}{80} \times 100 = 37.5\%$

Boxing = $\frac{22}{58} \times 100 = 37.93\%$

Polo = $\frac{44}{176} \times 100 = 25\%$

Basketball = $\frac{44}{146} \times 100 = 30.13\%$

So Polo is the required answer.

80:-

New number of females in basketball = $\frac{100+75}{100} \times 44 = 77$

New number males of males in Basketball = $\frac{100-50}{100} \times 146 = 73$

Required ratio = $73 : 77$

91. Stinting means restrict amount of someone. Besides, statement given in the question is divided into two parts by semi colon so they are now two different parts. In option A lavishing means give someone in generous amount which the sentence does not indicate, also options B and C both are mot going with the sentence. Hence the answer is option **D.**

92. Sentence is talking about a chemist who believes that many scientists found difficulty with stereochemistry. In option A, obscure means not clear which the author does not indicate as the author is talking about difficulty. Option B does not match with the sentence at all and in option C subtle means ultrafine which does not go with the sentence talking about. Option D imprecise means indefinite and is the answer because in other part of the sentence discrete means distinct which clearly defines the sentence. Hence the answer is option **D.**

93. The sentence is divided in two parts by semicolon so have two different meanings, option A highlight for 1st blank don't fit(positive trait)for expense ,options B and C does not fit in the sentence and option D defects is fit for 1st blank and economy for 2nd blank fits as it contradicts the expense where economy means cheaply. Hence the answer is option **D.**

94. Sentence is talking about the social scientists that have established and describe the appropriate behavior of the children and adults. In option A, rigidity means quality found in people and objects which the author is not talking about, 'but' in the sentence indicates that the sentence is in negative tone, option B also does not match with sentence, similarly option D. Hence the answer is option **C.**

95. Sentence is comparing Mount Saint Helens of last 4,500 years with respect to any other volcano in US. Option C is the answer as volcano is explosive which the author indicated in the sentence and belied means contradicting the 'violent nature' fits in the sentence. In case of option (a), both awe inspiring (meaning amazing) and restrained do not fit together. Similarly option B gaseous (related to gas) also does not fit in the sentence. Option D familiar also cannot be the answer. Hence the answer is option **C.**

SBI PO Mains MOCK Test Paper 7

Structure of this MOCK Test

S. No.	Name of section	No. of Questions	Total marks	Allotted Time
1	Reasoning and Computer Aptitude	45	60	60 minutes
2	Data Analysis and Interpretation	35	60	45 minutes
3	General/Economy/ Banking Awareness	40	40	35 minutes
4	English Language	35	40	40 minutes
Total		155	200	3 hours

- There is 1/4th Negative marking for every wrong answer.
- If a question is left blank, i.e. no answer is marked by the candidate, there will be no penalty for that question.

Section 1: Reasoning and Computer Aptitude

Directions (1-5): Read each statement carefully and answer the following questions:

Input: 40 made butter 23 37 cookies salt extra 52 86 92 fell now 19

Step I: butter 19 40 made 23 37 cookies salt extra 52 86 92 fell now

Step II: Cookies 23 butter 19 40 made salt 52 86 92 fell now

Step III: extra 37 cookies 23 butter 19 40 made salt 52 86 92 fell now

Step IV: fell 40 extra 37 cookies 23 butter 19 made salt 52 86 92 now

Step V: made 52 fell 40 extra 37 cookies 23 butter 19 salt 8692 now

Step VI: now 86 made 52 fell 40 extra 37 cookies 23 butter 19 salt 92

Step VII: salt 92 now 86 made 52 fell 40 extra 37 cookies 23 butter 19

Step VII is the last step of the above arrangement as the intended arrangement is obtained.

As per the rules followed in the given steps, find out the appropriate steps for the given input.

Input: 32 proud girl beautiful 48 55 97 rich family 61 72 17 nice life

1. How many steps will be required to complete the given input?
   a. Five b. Six c. Seven d. Eight e. Nine

2. Which of the following is the third element from the left end of step VI?
   a. beautiful b. life c. 61 d. nice e. 17

3. Which of the following is step III of the given input?
   a. Proud 72 girl 48 family 32 beautiful 17 55 97 rich 61 nice life
   b. life 55 girl 48 family 32 beautiful 17 proud 97 rich 61 72 nice
   c. girl 48 family 32 beautiful 17 proud 55 97 rich 61 72 nice life
   d. family 32 beautiful 17 proud girl 48 55 97 rich 61 72 nice life
   e. girl 48 life 55 family 32 beautiful 17 proud 97 rich 61 72 nice

4. What is the position of 'nice' from the left end in the final step?
   a. Fifth b. Sixth c. Seventh d. Eighth e. Ninth

5. Which element is third to the right of 'family' in Step V?
   a. Beautiful b. 17 c. proud d. 97 e. 32

Directions (6–10): Study the information and answer the following questions:
A, B, C, D, E, F, G and H are sitting around a square table in such a way that four of them sit at four corners of the square while fore sit in the middle of each of the four sides. The ones who sit at the four corners face the centre while those who sit in the middle of the sides face outside. Two females sit in the middle of the sides and two at the corners. A sits second to the left of G. G sits in the middle of one of the sides. C sits fourth to the right of his wife and his wife is not an immediate neighbour of A or G. B sits third to right of her husband. B does not sit at any of the corners. Only D sits between B and H. H is husband of A. E is a male.

6. Which of the following is true with respect to given seating arrangement?
   a. No two males are immediate neighbours of each other.
   b. G and H face each other in the seating arrangement.
   c. A sits in the centre of one of the sides of the square table.
   d. F is a male and sits diagonally opposite to E.
   e. E and D are immediate neighbours of each other.

7. Who amongst the following is B's husband?
   a. C b. G c. F d. E
   e. cannot be determined

8. How many people sit between B and C when counted in anti-clock wise direction from B?
   a. None b. One c. Two d. Three e. Four

9. Who amongst the following is the wife of C?
   a. D b. F c. B d. G
   e. cannot be determined

10. What is the position of E with respect to C?
    a. Immediately to the right b. Second to the left
    c. Third to the right d. Immediately to the left
    e. Second to the right

Directions (11–15): Read each statement carefully and answer the following questions:

11. Which of the following expression's will be true if the expression R > O = A > S < T as definitely true?
a. O>T b. S < R c. T>A d. S=O e. T < R

12. Which of the following symbols should replace the questions mark (?) in the given expression in order to make the expression 'P > A' as well as 'T < L' definitely true? P>L?A e" N = T
a. < b. > c. < d. > e. either < or <

13. Which of the following symbols should be placed in the blank spaces respectively (in the same order from left to right) in order to complete the given such a manner that makes the expressions 'B > N' as well 'D < L' definitely true ? B _ L_ O _N _D
a. =, = , >, > b. >, >, = > c. >, <, =, < d. >, = , =, < e. >, = , >, >

14. Which of the following should be placed in the blank spaces respectively (in the same order from left to right) in order to complete the given express in such a manner that makes the expression A<P definitely false? __ < __ < __ > __
a. L, N, P, A b. L, A, P, N c. A, L, P, N d. N, A, P, L e. P, N, A, L

15. Which of the following symbols should be placed in the blank spaces respectively (in the same order from left to right) in order to complete the given expression in such a manner that makes the expression 'F > N' and 'U > D' definitely false? F__O__U__N__D
a. <, <, >, = b. <, =, =, > c. <, =, =, < d. >, = , =, > e. >, >, =, <

Directions (16–18): Read the information carefully and answer the following questions

X # y means y is at 1 metre to the right of x.
X $ B means B is at 1 metre to the North of X.
X * B means B is at 1 metre to the left of X.
X @ B means B is at 1 metre to the south of X.
In each question first person from the left is facing north.

16. According to X @ B * P, P is in which direction with respect to X?
a. North b. South c. North-East d. South-West e. None of these

17. According to M # N $ T, T is in which direction with respect to M?
a. North-West b. North-East c. South-West d. South-East e. None of these

18. According to P # R $ X * U, in which direction is U with respect to P?
a. East b. West c. North d. South e. None of these

19. Rahul put his timepiece on the table in such a way that at 6 P.M. hour hand points to North. In which direction the minute hand will point at 9.15 P.M.?
a. South-East b. South c. North d. West e. None of these

20. Maddy starts from his house towards West. After walking a distance of 30 metres, he turned towards right and walked 20 metres. He then turned left and moving a distance of 10 metres, turned to his left again and walked 40 metres. He now turns to the left and walks 6 metres. Finally he turns to his left. In which direction is he walking now?
a. East b. South c. North d. South west e. South west

Directions (21–25): In each of the questions below are given two/three statements followed by two conclusions numbered I & II. Assuming the statements to be true find the conclusions which follow and mark the correct option.

21. **Statements:** All Games are Crickets.
    No Cricket is a Football.
    All Footballs are Kabaddi.
    Conclusions: I. No Game is a Football.
    II. Some Kabaddi is Crickets.
    a. If only (II) conclusion follows
    b. If either (I) or (II) follows
    c. If neither (I) nor (II) follows
    d. If only (I) conclusion follows
    e. If both (I) and (II) follow

22. **Statements:** All Lions are Goats.
    All elephant are Goats.
    Some Goats are Monkey.
    Conclusions: I. some elephants are Lions.
    II. Some Monkey is elephant.
    a. If both (I) and (II) follow
    b. If only (II) conclusion follows
    c. If only (I) conclusion follows
    d. If either (I) or (II) follows
    e. If neither (I) nor (II) follows

23. **Statements:** All kings are Queens.
    All Jokers are kings.
    All Aces are Queens.
    Conclusions: **I.** All Ace is kings
    II. All Joker is Queens.
    a. If both (I) and (II) follow
    b. If neither (I) nor (II) follows
    c. If either (I) or (II) follows
    d. If only (II) conclusion follows
    e. If only (I) conclusion follows

24. **Statements:** All Plays are Interesting.
    All Drama is Plays.
    All Worse are Drama.
    Conclusions: I. Some Plays being not worse is a possibility.
    II. All Worse are Interesting.
    a. If only (I) conclusion follows
    b. If only (II) conclusion follows
    c. If either (I) or (II) follows
    d. If neither (I) nor (II) follows
    e. If both (I) and (II) follow

25. **Statements:** Some cars are bikes.
    Some bikes are buses.
    All buses are trucks.
    Conclusions: **I.** No bus is a car.
    II. Some trucks are bikes.
    a. If only (I) conclusion follows
    b. If only (II) conclusion follows
    c. If either (I) or (II) follows
    d. If neither (I) nor (II) follows
    e. If both (I) and (II) follow

Directions (26–30)

These data sufficiency problems consist of a question and two statements, labelled (1) and (2), in which certain data are given. You have to decide whether the data given in the statements are sufficient for answering the question. Choose the correct option which follow.

26. How is A related to B?

Statements:

1. B and C are children of D who is wife of A.
2. E's sister A is married to B's father.

a. 1 alone is sufficient while 2 alone is not sufficient
b. 2 alone is sufficient while 1 alone is not sufficient
c. Either 1 or 2 is sufficient
d. Neither 1 nor 2 is sufficient
e. Both 1 and 2 are sufficient

27. What is the code for 'water' in the code language?

Statements:

1. In the code language, 'water is wet' is written as 'la min tu'.
2. In the same code language, 'water is wet' is written as 'la ja go'.

a. 1 alone is sufficient while 2 alone is not sufficient
b. 2 alone is sufficient while 1 alone is not sufficient
c. Either 1 or 2 is sufficient
d. Neither 1 nor 2 is sufficient
e. Both 1 and 2 are sufficient

28. What will be the total weight of 10 boxes, each of the same weight?

Statements:

1. One-fourth of the weight of each box is 5 kg.
2. The total weight of three boxes is 20 kilograms more than the total weight of two boxes.

a. 1 alone is sufficient while 2 alone is not sufficient
b. 2 alone is sufficient while 1 alone is not sufficient
c. Either 1 or 2 is sufficient
d. Neither 1 nor 2 is sufficient
e. Both 1 and 2 are sufficient

29. Which is the smallest number out of the three numbers, a, b and c?

1. ac = 12, bc = 20|
2. a,b,c are positive integers, ab = 15.

a. If the data in statement I alone is sufficient to answer the question, while the data in statement II alone is not sufficient to answer the question.
b. If data in statement II alone is sufficient to answer the question, while the data in statement I alone is not sufficient to answer the question
c. If the data either in statement I or in statement II alone is sufficient to answer the question
d. If the data even in both statements I and II together are not sufficient to answer the question
e. If data in both statements I and II together are necessary to answer the question.

30. Among T, V, B, E and C, who is the third from the top when arranged in the descending order of their weights?

1. B is heavier than T and C and less heavier than V who is not the heaviest.
2. C is heavier than only T.
 a. if the data in statement I alone are sufficient to answer the question, while the data in statement II alone are not sufficient to answer the question;
 b. if the data in statement II alone are sufficient to answer the question, while the data in statement I alone are not sufficient to answer the question;
 c. if the data either in statement I alone or in statement II alone are sufficient to answer the question;
 d. if the data given in both statement I and II together are not sufficient to answer the question;
 e. if the data given in both statement I and II together alone are necessary to answer the question.

Directions (31–45) answer the questions:

31. The first step to get started with Tally is to create a
 a. account b. company c. file d. folder e. None of these
32. It is the primary online document for recording transactions
 a. file b. entry c. voucher d. receipt e. None of these
33. Which of the following is not a property of fiber optic cabling?
 a. Transmits at faster speeds than copper cabling
 b. Easier to capture a signal from than copper cabling
 c. Very resistant to interference
 d. Carries signals as light waves
 e. None of these
34. What does fiber use to transmit data?
 a. Vibrations b. Sound c. Electrical current d. Light
 e. None of these
35. Which of the following network cabling would you choose to install around a noisy room where machines were constantly running?
 a. Fiber b. STP c. Coax d. UTP e. None of these
36. You've been told about radio frequency eavesdropping and want to protect your network from this threat. Which of the following media types would you choose in this situation?
 a. UTP b. STP c. Coax d. Fiber e. None of these
37. Which of the following statements in false?
 a. Secondary storage is non-volatile
 b. Primary storage is volatile
 c. When the computers is turned off, data and instructions stored in primary storage are erased
 d. All of the above
 e. None of these
38. What does OCR stands for
 a. Optical Character Reader
 b. Operational Character Reader

c. Optical Character Recognition
d. Only Character Reader
e. None of these

39. Dot Matrix is a type of
a. Tape b. Disk c. Printer d. Bus e. None of these

40. The secondary storage devices can only store data but they cannot perform
a. arithmetic operations b. fetch operations
c. logic operations d. Either of these
e. None of these

41. In computer science by information we mean
a. any output coming out from computer b. processed data put in an intelligent form
c. a report printed by the computer d. plural of data
e. None of these

42. Which keys can be pressed quit without saving in DOS?
a. Ctrl + A b. Ctrl + B c. Ctrl + C d. Ctrl + D e. None of these

43. Which command is used to get the current date only?
a. Date b. Time c. Second d. All of these e. None of these

44. Generally, the DATE is entered in the form
a. DD-YY-MM b. YY-DD-MM c. MM-YY-DD d. MM-DD-YY e. None of these

45. The extensions .gov, .edu, .mil, and .net are c
a. mail to addresses b. add-ons c. domain codes
d. DNSs e. e-mail targets

Section 2: Data Analysis and Interpretation

Directions (46–50): Study the data given below and answer the given questions.
Production of different plastics materials

Months	Polypropylene Production (in thousand tones)		Polyethylene Production (in thousand tones)		Nylon filament yarn production (in thousand tones)	
	2009-10	2010-11	2009-10	2010-11	2009-10	2010-11
April	35.2	41.6	208	80	6300	5800
May	32.8	41.2	200	176	6100	5700
June	32.0	42.8	160	192	6000	5800
July	30.8	38.4	176	160	5040	5600
August	32.0	38.4	180	168	5200	5400
September	33.2	42.8	188	160	5300	5500
October	32.8	41.6	196	168	5000	5300

Months	Polypropylene Production (in thousand tones)		Polyethylene Production (in thousand tones)		Nylon filament yarn production (in thousand tones)	
	2009-10	2010-11	2009-10	2010-11	2009-10	2010-11
November	35.6	46.0	200	160	4400	6000
December	32.8	45.2	208	184	4000	5900
January	35.2	43.6	216	176	4500	6000
February	40.0	40.0	192	200	5500	4700
March	39.4	35.6	40	192	5200	4500

46. The average production of polypropylene in 2010-11 is approximate what percent of the average production of Nylon filament yarn in 2009-10.
a. 0.4% b. 0.8% c. 0.1% d. 1.2% e.. 1.6%

47. In 2009-10, the ratio of the difference between the maximum and the minimum production of Polypropylene, to the difference between the maximum and minimum production of Polyethylene, is nearly
a. 0.05 b. 0.90 c. 0.09 d. 0.50 e. 0.4

48. Of all three products from 2010-11 is maximum from which month?
a. January b. February c. March d. October e. November

49. Production of polyethelene from 2009-10 in June, October and January together is approximately what percent of the production of polyproylene from 2010-11 in October, November and February together?
a. 350% b. 450% c. 300% d. 400% e. 500%

50. The minimum production of Nylon filament yarn in 2010-11 is how many times of the difference between the maximum production of Polypropylene in 2010-11 and the minimum production of polyethylene in 2009-10?
a. 800 b. 750 c. 700 d. 850 e. 600

Directions (51–55): Study the table carefully to answer the questions that follow it. Number of students appeared (App) and qualified (Qua), for an examination in six states over the years

Years	States											
	A		B		A		B		A		B	
	App	Qua	App	Qua	App	Qua	App	Qua	App	Qua	App	Qua
2001	1567	124	1745	156	1684	150	1440	165	1564	162	1886	142
2002	1673	110	1897	178	1550	178	1390	172	1575	188	1764	186
2003	1785	156	1674	162	1754	210	1364	114	1510	214	1738	194
2004	1630	234	1986	154	1806	186	1478	138	1654	196	1644	182

Years	States											
	A		B		A		B		A		B	
	App	Qua	App	Qua	App	Qua	App	Qua	App	Qua	App	Qua
2005	1805	256	2107	193	1666	198	1560	189	1690	180	1680	162
2006	1922	234	2080	245	1884	254	1672	193	1432	206	1572	222
2007	1790	198	2095	220	1728	202	1778	195	1864	216	1444	218

51. The number of candidates qualified from state C in 2002 and 2005 together is what per cent of the number of candidates appeared from state F in 2003 and 2004 together? (rounded off to two digits after decimal)
a. 10.65% b. 12.44% c. 14.86% d. 11.11% e. None of these

52. The percentage of candidates qualified over appeared in 2004 is the highest for which of the following states?
a. B b. D c. A d. E e. None of these

53. The percentage of candidates qualified over appeared from state B is the lowest during which of the following years?
a. 2007 b. 2004 c. 2001 d. 2005 e. None of these

54. Approximately what is the percentage of candidates qualified over appeared from state D over the given years?
a. 11% b. 21% c. 27% d. 15% e. None of these

55. Approximately what is the average number of candidates qualified from state D over the given years?
a. 132 b. 116 c. 167 d. 192 e. None of these

Directions (56–60): Study the following graphs carefully and answer accordingly. Performance of TV's surveyed is represented by the following chart:

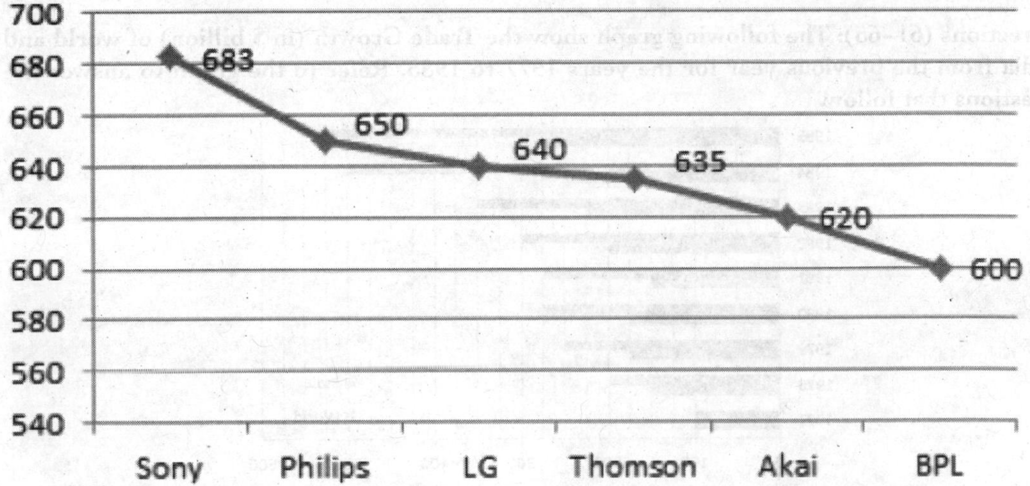

Of the total points received assume that the following is the percentage breakup of points received due to each of the parameters listed below:

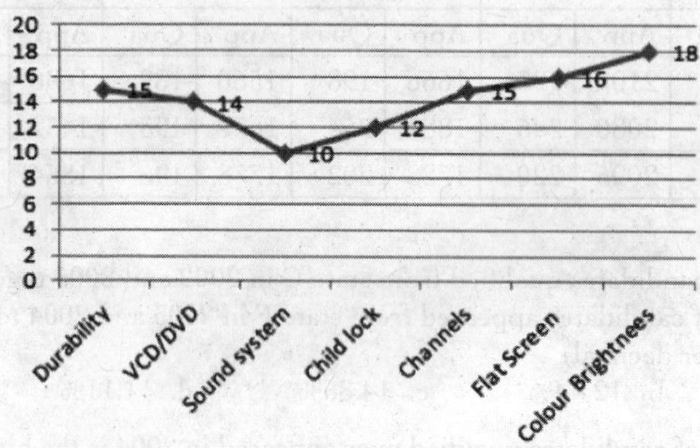

56. The points obtained by Thomson for durability is equal to which of the following?
   a. LG sound system
   b. Akai colour brightness
   c. BPL flat screen
   d. Thomson channels
   e. None of these

57. What is the total number of points earned by all the TV's for channels?
   a. 490.42 b. 573.72 c. 553.70 d. 572.70 e. None of these

58. What are the average points per TV earned for Child lock?
   a. 80.34 b. 76.56 c. 70.42 d. 86.23 e. None of these

59. The sound system of LG is approximately what per cent of the flat screen of Sony?
   a. 52% b. 171% c. 59% d. 64% e. None of these

60. The points earned by BPL for VCD/DVD is what per cent more/less than the points earned by BPL for colour brightness?
   a. 15.22% (less)
   b. 15.74 (more)
   c. 22.22% (more)
   d. 22.22% (less)
   e. None of these

Directions (61–65): The following graph show the Trade Growth (in $ billion) of world and India from the previous year for the years 1977 to 1985. Refer to the graph to answer the questions that follow.

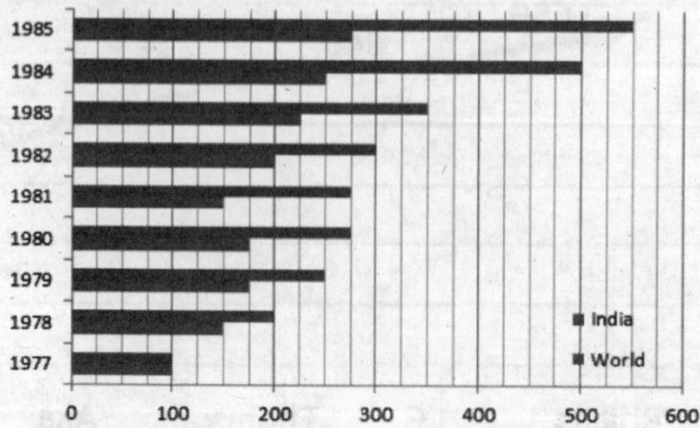

61. If the total trade of world in the year 1976 is $ 5267 billion, what it will be in the year 1985?
a. $ 6176 billion b. $ 6967 billion c. $ 6965 billion d. $ 6987 billion e. None of these

62. If the total trade of India in the year 1979 is $ 1200 billion, what it will be in the year 1985?
a. $ 3456 billion b. $ 3786 billion c. $ 3954 billion d. $ 3450 billion e. None of these

63. What is the Approx ratio of the total World trade to total trade of India in the year 1985, if the total trade of world in 1976 is $ 5267 billion and total trade of India in 1979 is $ 1200 billion?
a. 2 : 1 b. 3 : 1 c. 2 : 3 d. 3 : 2 e. 4 : 3

64. Average world trade growth is how much per cent more or less than the average trade growth of India during the entire shown period?
a. more, 25 % b. less, 30 % c. less, 39% d. 80 % e. None of these

65. What is the per cent increase in trade growth of India in the year 1980 over that of the same in 1979?
a. 70 % b. 10 % c. 17 % d. more, 35% e. None of these

Directions (66–70): Study the following graph carefully to answer these questions – Details about the distribution of employees and expenditure of an organization (Distributed proportionately across the departments)

Annual expenditure on different items, Total Expenditure = Rs. 12 crores

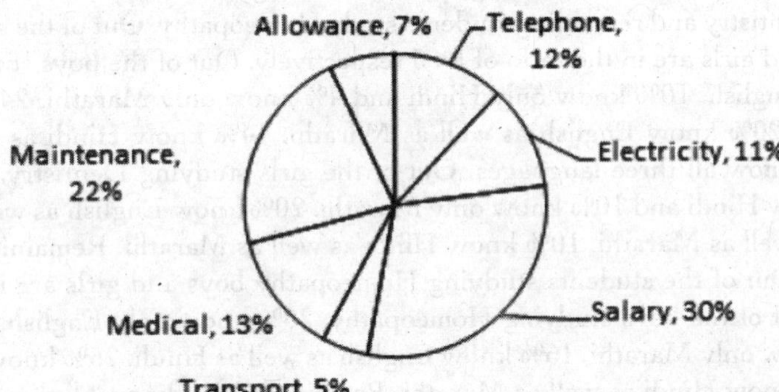

Department wise distribution of employees, Total number of employes-1200

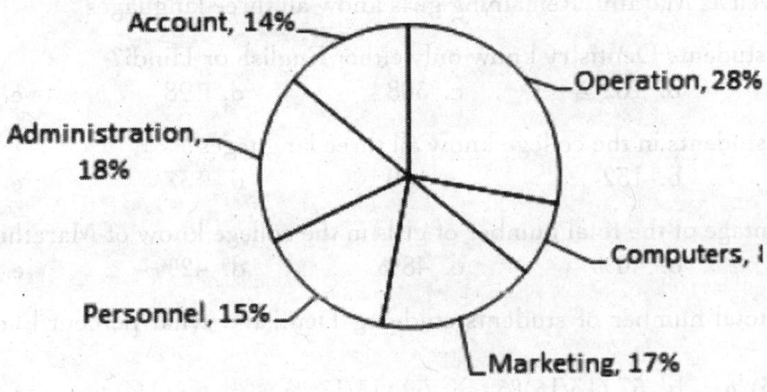

66. What was the total expenditure on Accounts, marketing and administrative departments together?
a. Rs. 57.2 lakhs b. Rs. 58.2 lakhs c. Rs. 57.8 millions
d. Rs. 58.8 millions e. None of these

67. What was the per employee expenditure on medical?
a. Rs. 12000 b. Rs. 13000 c. Rs. 12500 d. Rs. 13500 e. None of these

68. What was the approximate expenditure on salary of employees in Marketing department?
a. Rs. 6.12 lakhs b. Rs. 61.2 millions c. Rs. 6.12 millions
d. Rs. 176 lakhs e. None of these

69. Amount spent on electricity is what percent to the amount spent on maintenance and allowance together?
a. 37.93% b. 37.83% c. 37.97% d. 37.87% e. None of these

70. What was the ratio of expenditure on telephone for employees in computer department to the expenditure on transport for employee in computer department?
a. 3:8 b. 12:5 c. 8:3 d. 5:12 e. None of these

Directions (71–75): Study the following information carefully to answer the given questions. In a medical college, there are 1600 students studying Dentistry and Homeopathy. Each student from each course knows one or more languages out of English, Hindi and Marathi. 45% of the students study Dentistry and remaining students study Homeopathy. Out of the students studying Dentistry, boys and girls are in the ratio of 5 : 3 respectively. Out of the boys studying Dentistry, 16% know only English, 10% know only Hindi and 4% know only Marathi. 24% know English as well as Hindi. 20% know English as well as Marathi. 14% know Hindi as well as Marathi. Remaining boys know all three languages. Out of the girls studying Dentistry, 20% know only English, 10% know Hindi and 10% know only Marathi. 20% know English as well as Hindi. 20% know English as well as Marathi. 10% know Hindi as well as Marathi. Remaining girls know all three languages. Out of the students studying Homeopathy boys and girls are in the ratio of 4 : 7 respectively. Out of the boys studying Homeopathy, 20% know only English, 15% know only Hindi and 5% know only Marathi, 15% know English as well as Hindi. 25% know English as well as Marathi. 10% know Hindi as well as Marathi. Remaining boys know all three languages. Out of the girls studying Homeopathy, 15% know only English, 15% know only Hindi and 5% know only Marathi. 20% know English as well as Hindi, 20% know English as well as Marathi. 15% know Hindi as well as Marathi. Remaining girls know all three languages.

71. How many students Dentistry know only either English or Hindi?
a. 166 b. 162 c. 308 d. 198 e. 248

72. How many students in the college know all three languages?
a. 108 b. 132 c. 169 d. 137 e. 142

73. What percentage of the total number of girls in the college know of Marathi?
a. 45% b. 40% c. 48% d. 42% e. 50%

74. Out of the total number of students studying Dentistry, what percent knows at least two languages?
a. 61 (12/13)% b. 57 (13/16)% c. 59 (13/17)% d. 66 (1/4)% e. 62 (12/19)%

75. What percent of the total number of girls in the college do not know Hindi? (Rounded off to nearest integer)
a. 38% b. 46% c. 48% d. 36% e. 43%

Directions (76–80): Study the following graphs and answer the given questions.

Number of Students Playing Chess, Cricket and Hockey from Different Schools

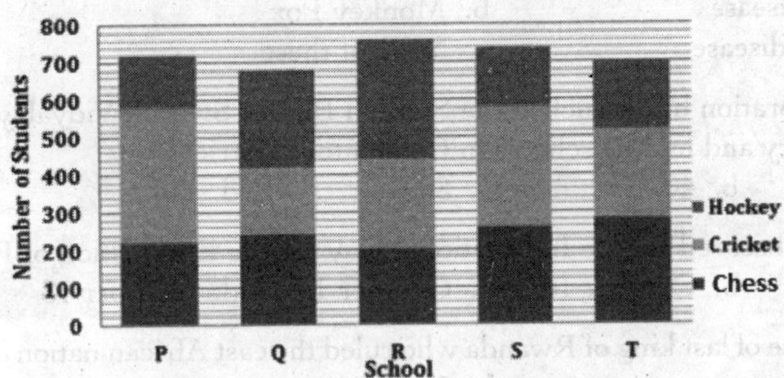

76. Total number of students playing Chess and Hockey together from school P is what percent of the total number of students playing these two games together from school R?
a. 68.18% b. 64.23% c. 69.23% d. 63.23% e. 62.23%

77. Number of students playing each game in school S is increased by 15% and the number of students playing each game in school Q is decreased by 5%. What will be the difference between number of students in schools S and Q?
a. 54 b. 218 c. 356 d. 224 e. 205

78. If out of the students playing Cricket from schools Q, S and T 40%, 35% and 45% respectively got selected for state level competition, what was the total number of students got selected for State level competition from these schools together?
a. 346 b. 241 c. 292 d. 284 e. 268

79. Total number of students playing Hockey from all schools together is approximately what percent of the total number of students playing Cricket from all schools together?
a. 84% b. 74% c. 72% d. 79% e. 70%

80. From school P, out of the students playing Chess, 40% got selected for State level competition. Out of which 25% further got selected for National level competition. From school T, out of the students playing Chess, 45% got selected for State level competition, out of which two-third further got selected for National level competition. What is the total number of students playing carom from these two schools who got selected for National level competition?
a. 106 b. 98 c. 112 d. 108 e. 96

Section 3: General and Banking Awareness

81. The 2016 SAARC Sufi festival was organised annually by the Foundation of SAARC Writers And Literature (FOSWAL) was held at which place?
a. Bhubaneshwar b. Udaipur c. New Delhi
d. Jaipur e. None of these

82. The Indian Silk Export Promotion Council organized 5th India International Silk Fair was held at which city?
a. Bose Maidan, Salem
b. Azad Maidan, Mumbai
c. Gandhi Maidan, Patna
d. Pragati Maidan, New Delhi
e. None of these

83. What is the name of disease has killed over 150 children and taken epidemic proportions in Malkangiri district due to negligence in Japan?
a. Zika virus disease
b. Monkey Pox
c. Encephalitis
d. Ebola virus disease
e. None of these

84. The City Corporation has launched the Swacch Bharat Swacch Vidyalaya campaign in how many elementary and middle schools in Coimbatore district?
a. 55 b. 40 c. 50 d. 60 e. None of these

85. Which date is observed as The International Day for the Eradication of Poverty every year?
a. October 17 b. October 16 c. October 15 d. October 18 e. None of these

86. What is the name of last king of Rwanda who ruled the east African nation died at an age of 80?
a. King Tut II
b. King Tut
c. Bhumibol Adulyadej
d. Kigeli V
e. None of these

87. What is the name of cyclone that battered wide areas of Chennai?
a. Vardah b. Vardan c. Varda d. Vaardah e. None of these

88. India's ODI against which country at Dharamshala is the team's 900th making it the world first side to achieve a milestone?
a. Sri Lanka b. New Zealand c. South Africa d. Bangladesh e. None of these

89. Which magnificent species could finally get some protection with the IUCN is all set to declare it a 'critically endangered' species?
a. Asiatic Lion b. Bengal Tiger c. Hangul d. Red Panda e. None of these

90. What is the name of largest freshwater lake is situated in North America?
a. Lake Tanganyika
b. Lake Baikal
c. Lake Superior
d. Lake Mansarovar
e. None of these

91. Which organisation has launched the skill development digital platform "UNO Learn" to offer skill development courses from industry experts and universities?
a. Ideal Way International
b. Game Changer International
c. Success Life International
d. Positive Shift International
e. None of these

92. Which institute group of students has been developing drones using indigenous hardware and software under the initiative of its Aerial Robotics?
a. IIT New Delhi b. IIT Mumbai c. IIT Chennai d. IIT Kharagpur e. None of these

93. Which country has successfully launched a spacecraft carrying two astronauts, in its longest-ever manned space mission?
a. United States b. Japan c. China d. India e. None of these

94. Which Senior diplomat was appointed Ambassador to United Arab Emirates on October 18 2016 by the External Affairs Ministry?
a. Navdeep Singh Suri
b. Sudeep Singh
c. Anoop Singh
d. Ashish Mehta
e. None of these

95. Who took charge as the member of the ICC's powerful Finance and Commercial Affairs committee after completion of the global cricket body's board meeting in Cape Town?
a. J Balakrishnan
b. N Srinivasan
c. Anurag Thakur
d. Shashank Manohar
e. None of these

96. Who has been appointed as Member Secretary of Law Commission of India by the President Pranab Mukherjee?
a. Sanjay Singh
b. Anil Singh
c. Rajnath Singh
d. Ravindar Singh
e. None of these

97. Which company is the India's most valuable company with a market capitalization of Rs. 4.66 trillion, followed by Reliance Industries Ltd?
a. Cognizant b. TCS c. Wipro d. HP e. None of these

98. Which country has opened the first sanctuary with Guida and Maia for elephants to provide a home for an estimated 50 circus animals from across the region?
a. Brazil
b. Australia
c. Philippines
d. Indonesia
e. None of these

99. Who have been nominated as Member of Rajya Sabha and have taken oath in the presence of Rajya Sabha Chairman Md. Hamid Ansari in the Parliament House?
a. Roopa Ganguly and Ganeshan
b. Mallika Pooja and Ilangesan
c. Roopa Devi and Ilanganesan
d. Malika Ganguly and Ganeshan
e. None of these

100. Approx __ % of Indian population is still Agriculturist.
a. 46% b. 50% c. 58% d. 64% e. None of these

101. Contribution of agriculture to Gross National Product is approximately?
a. 14% b. 15% c. 16.5% d. 17.5% e. None of these

102. How much population is living below poverty line in India?
i. Approx 24% ii. Approx 25% iii. Approx 26% iv. Approx 27% v. None of these

103. The best indicator of economic development of any country is?
i. Its agriculture
ii. Its transport
iii. Its gross production
iv. Its per capita income
v. None of these

104. What is the mainstay of Indian economy?
i. Manufacturing
ii. Business
iii. Public sector
iv. Agriculture
v. None of these

105. Modi Government came up with an "Income Disclosure Scheme" to unearth the black money. What was the last date to do so?
a. 15 September 2016
b. 30 September 2016
c. 31 October 2016
d. 7 November 2016
e. Date was different for Individuals and corporate

106. Who was the father of Operation Flood?
a. Dr. Norman Borlaug
b. Dr. M.S. Swaminathan
c. Dr. Verghese Kurien
d. Dr. William Gande
e. None of these

107. National Agriculture Insurance Scheme was implemented on
    a. Oct. 1997 b. Oct. 1998 c. Oct. 1999 d. Oct. 2000 e. None of these

108. Which is not a Kharif Crop?
    a. Jowar b. Maize c. Groundnut d. Wheat e. None of these

109. The data of estimation of India's National income is issued by?
    a. Planning Commission b. National Data Centre
    c. Central Statistical Organisation d. None of above
    e. Both A and B

110. Which is not the characteristic of socialist or planned economy?
    a. Government is the owner of resources
    b. Production decisions are determined by the government
    c. Profit motive
    d. None of the above
    e. Both A and C

111. The main feature of mixed economy is—
    a. Combination of free market economy and centrally planned economy
    b. Production is carried out by private individuals and government
    c. Both of the above
    d. None of the above
    e. Either A or B

112. What per cent of GDP at 2004-05 prices was contributed by agriculture and related sectors in 2009-10?
    a. 14.6% b. 17.6% c. 19.0% d. 19.8% e. None of these

113. According to World Development Report 2010, Low income economies are those whose per-capita gross national income is—
    a. $ 975 or less than this b. Less than $ 11905
    c. Less than $ 4526 d. None of the above e. Both B and C

114. Which of the following country's economy is known as high income economy?
    a. USA b. U.K. c. Singapore
    d. All of the above e. None of these

115. Doing away with the more than six-decade practice of Planning Commission, present government came up with a think-tank approach to economic strategy named NITI aayog. What is the full form of NITI?
    a. National Institution for Transforming Industry
    b. National Institution for Transforming India
    c. National Industrial Transforming Institution
    d. National Interstate Institution for Transforming India
    e. None of these

116. Which policy of economic system has been adopted by India for its economic development?
    a. Capitalist Economy b. Mixed Economy
    c. Socialist Economy d. Centralised Planned Economy
    e. None of these

117. A positive aspect of economic development after independence is—
   a. Creation of a large industrial base
   b. Proportion of population living below poverty line has declined
   c. Self sufficient in the production of food grains
   d. All of the above
   e. None of these

118. The negative aspect of economic development after independence is—
   a. Problems of poverty and unemployment have not been eliminated
   b. Industrialisation did not take place as expected
   c. Many public sector enterprises started making losses
   d. All of the above
   e. None of these

119. Reasons for the privatisation and liberalisation of public sector after 1991 are—
   a. Corruption
   b. Lack of efficiency in work
   c. Ineffective management
   d. All of the above
   e. None of these

120. The main strategy adopted in the new economic policy of 1991 is—
   a. Liberalisation
   b. Privatisation
   c. Globalisation
   d. All of the above
   e. None of these

Section 4: English Language

Directions (121–130): Read the following passage carefully and answer the questions given below it. Certain words/phrases are given in bold to help you locate them while answering some of the questions.

The main idea conveyed by the report is that our children do not get a chance to enjoy learning at school because the syllabus are irrationally organised, teaching is text-book, centred, and the system of examinations instils fear and encourages mechanical repetition. Textbooks developed along the lines of reconceptualised syllabus can attempt to integrate positive values, life skills, aesthetic sensibility and concern for the environment. They are interactive and make a conscious effort to point both children and the teachers towards other sources of learning such as neighbourhood, nature etc. In addition two parallel challenges deserve attention. The first is examination reforms. Rigid indifference to individual differences is the major flaw of the present system. From the quality of questions to the manner of evaluation, it favours drilled preparedness and ignores independent thought while the unrealistically high cut-offs in coveted colleges are a further sign of systemic inefficiency. It is hardly, surprising that the very thought of examinations makes the young depressed. Moreover, practices of splitting unified topics into arbitrary bits carrying small marks value encourage teachers to concentrate on scoring topics overlooking the importance of perspective and overall understanding. Little surprise that many elite high fee schools are opting for International Baccalaureate not because it offers status with its global certification but for its flexibility and respect for individual differences in learning.

The second area is teacher training, which suffers from obsolete notions. Most teachers are trained mainly to cover the syllabus in a mechanical exam-oriented manner. By insisting that every child move at the same pace in all subjects teachers encourage rote learning and ridicule for those who fall behind. Teacher training, whether for nursery or secondary school teachers, should be embedded in courses which have the capacity to develop both the teacher's personality and perspective on society by linking subject learning with reflective and creative project work. The ultimate responsibility lies with universities and institutes of higher learning to ensure the quality of all teachers. Initiatives to improve the content of teacher training courses will ensure utilisation, of desolate university campuses during summer vacations which conceal an enormous waste of infrastructure and expertise. The quality of education is a reflection of the quality of teachers and major improvements in their training and working conditions will motivate the young to pursue a teaching career, determine how India fares in the pursuit of economic and social development in the years to come.

121. According to the author, what is the major weakness of the present examination system?
 a. Teachers do not take into account the nature of questions asked in the examination.
 b. Teachers are subjective in their assessment of papers.
 c. Cut-off standards for admissions to good institutions need to be raised.
 d. It distinguishes between a creative student and a rote learner.
 e. It does not consider, unique learning patterns of students.

122. Which of the following factors is responsible for children's dislike of learning?
 I. Rigid, logical, systematic organisation of syllabus.
 II. Teaching methodology which does not focus on text books.
 III. Examination pattern which rewards rote learning.
 a. Only I b. Both I & II c. Only III d. All e. None

123. What is the drawback of teacher training courses?
 a. They are held during summer vacations so attendance is low.
 b. Content is being constantly changed so teachers cannot keep up.
 c. Their focus is on imparting education only from an exam ination perspective.
 d. They focus on making syllabi interactive rather than focusing on examination patterns.
 e. None

124. Which of the following is NOT TRUE in the context of the passage?
 a. Examinations arouse negative emotions in students.
 b. Weak students are at a disadvantage if teachers force students to learn at same speed.
 c. Holding teacher training courses only during the academic year will help teachers cover the syllabus in an exam-oriented manner.
 d. The responsibility for improving the quality of teachers lies in the hands of universities.
 e. In the present educational system rote, learning is encouraged.

125. According to the author, which of the following conditions will influence India's future development?
 I. Replacing traditional educational systems with globally accepted foreign systems
 II. Improving employment conditions of teaching staff
 III. Getting global accreditation for Indian college courses
 a. Only I b. Both I & II c. Both II & III d. Only II e. None

126. What will be the impact of having an interactive syllabus?
 a. Teachers, and students will explore sources other than the textbook.
 b. Students may get distracted and perform poorly in examinations.
 c. Weaker students may get left behind.
 d. Teachers may not be able to cover the entire syllabus for the examination.
 e. Students and teachers alike will be over-burdened.

127. Which of the following is essential to improve the quality of education?
I. Focus on encouraging educational systems like international Baccalaureate
II. Reducing the number of examinations students have to take
III. Lowering the cut-offs for expensive colleges so that all students have access
a. None b. Both I & II c. All d. Only I e. Both II & III

128. Why do teachers focus on "scoring" topics?
a. Pressure from colleges who want to maintain high cut-offs
b. Faulty examination pattern which divides topics into smaller sections
c. It is an objective of teacher training programmes
d. To reduce the nervousness of students curing examinations
e. None

129. What is the author's recommendation to universities?
a. Encourage only creative project work for primary school teachers.
b. Enforce strict rules so that only those truly interested take up teaching as a profession.
c. Utilise their infrastructure during the academic year for teacher training.
d. Pass on responsibility for improving teacher training content to a government body.
e. None

130. Why is the International Baccalaureate gaining popularity?
a. It is a rigid well-defined system.
b. It has a good reputation.
c. Fees and other educational systems are too high for the quality of education given.
d. It allows students some scope to learn at their own pace.
e. None

Directions (131–133): Choose the word which is most nearly the SAME in meaning as the word given in bold as used in the passage.

131. COVETED
a. desired b. priceless c. necessary d. private e. valid

132. INSTILS
a. teach b. causes c. orders d. inserts e. invites

133. CHALLENGES
a. fears b. questions c. disputes d. obstacles e. conflicts

Directions (134–135): Choose the word which is most OPPOSITE in meaning of the word given in bold as used in the passage.

134. DESOLATE
a. happy b. occupied c. dejected d. repaired e. cheerful

135. OBSOLETE
a. stylish b. fashion c. present d. useless e. novel

Directions (136–140). Read each sentence to find out whether there is any grammatical error or idiomatic error in it. The error, if any, will he in one part of the sentence. The number of that part is the answer. If there is 'No error', the answer is 'E'. (Ignore errors of punctuation, if any).

136. There will be no scrutiny a)/ or enquiry of money declared, neither b)/ under the Income-Tax Act or the Wealth Tax Act c)/ and the declarents will have immunity d)/ from prosecution. No error. e)/.

137. The government have a)/ decided to open a one-time b)/, four-month compliance window c)/ for domestic black d)/ money- holders. e).

138. The victim was persuaded a)/ to recall back what had b)/ happened with her but c)/she was unable to d)/ recollect anything. e).

139. The process to be adopted by the government a)/ for these activities has to be defined b)/ because the government is responsible for c)/ any objects put up in space and for d)/ what happens to it in orbit or because of it. e).

140. The carbonic acid a)/ thus produced leads to b)/ ocean acidification by decreasing the pH of the ocean c), reducing the concentration of d)/ the carbonate ion. e).

Directions (141- 145): Rearrange the following six sentences in the proper sequence to form a meaningful paragraph; then answer the questions given below them.

A. Some people believe that at present its importance is decreasing because of rapid economic and social changes.

B. The extent of its importance may be slightly less in cities as compared to rural communities.

C. Some even go to the extreme and say that it will soon become obsolete because of these changes.

D. The family is an important socialisation agency both in rural and city communities.

E. The difference in the degree of importance does not matter much and therefore has no significance.

F. There are others who believe that the family has survived such storms in the past and it will do so in the future also.

141. Which of the following should be the FIRST sentence after rearrangement?
a. F b. E c. D d. C e. B

142. Which of the following should be the SIXTH (LAST) sentence after rearrangement?
a. F b. E c. D d. C e. B

143. Which of the following should be the FIFTH sentence after rearrangement?
a. F b. E c. D d. C e. B

144. Which of the following should be the THIRD sentence after rearrangement?
a. F b. E c. D d. C e. B

145. Which of the following should be the SECOND sentence after rearrangement?
a. F b. E c. D e. C e. B

Directions (146–155): In the following passage, some of the words have been left out, each of which is indicated by a number. Find the suitable word from the options given against each number and fill up the blanks with appropriate words to make the paragraph meaningfully complete.

The (1) increase in the number of vehicles on Indian roads has also led to an increase in road accidents. India (2) for 10 per cent of the global road crash (3). Statistics show that (4) more than a million people die due to road accidents every year; if we do not do (5) about it by 2020 this (6) will double. Vehicular safety standards are a (7) area.

Hence, the United Nations has (8) 2011-20 as the "Decade of Action for Road Safety" with the (9) to reduce fatalities by 50 per cent. The UN has (10) five pillars to achieve this target, ie Road Safety Management, Safer Roads and Mobility, Safer Road Users, Post Crash Response and Safer Vehicles.

146.
a. fantastic b. tremendous c. awesome d. excellent e. terrible

147.
a. calculates b. registers c. targets d. wishes e. accounts

148.
a. lethality b. numbers c. fatalities d. disaster e. mortality

149.
a. globally b. always c. entirely d. finally e. lastly

150.
a. anymore b. whatever c. all things d. anything e. everything

151.
a. total b. sum c. character d. amount e. figure

152.
a. complication b. dispute c. problem d. question e. difficulty

153.
a. announced b. disclosed c. released d. circulated e. told

154.
a. aspiration b. wish c. scheme d. aim e. course

155.
a. classified b. identified c. established d. selected e. separated

ANSWER KEY

1. c	2. d	3. c	4. a	5. b	6. c	7. d	8. c	9. a	10. e
11. b	12. b	13. d	14. e	15. c	16. d	17. b	18. c	19. d	20. c
21. a	22. d	23. b	24. e	25. b	26. c	27. d	28. c	29. e	30. a
31. b	32. c	33. b	34. d	35. a	36. d	37. d	38. a	39. c	40. d
41. b	42. c	43. a	44. a	45. c	46. b	47. a	48. a	49. b	50. b
51. d	52. c	53. b	54. a	55. c	56. d	57. e	58. b	59. c	60. d
61. b	62. d	63. a	64. c	65. b	66. d	67. b	68. d	69. a	70. b
71. d	72. c	73. e	74. d	75. e	76. c	77. e	78. c	79. d	80. a
81. d	82. d	83. c	84. d	85. a	86. d	87. a	88. b	89. c	90. c
91. d	92. d	93. c	94. a	95. c	96. a	97. b	98. a	99. a	100. c
101. d	102. c	103. d	104. d	105. b	106. c	107. c	108. d	109. c	110. c
111. c	112. a	113. a	114. d	115. b	116. b	117. d	118. d	119. d	120. d
121. e	122. c	123. d	124. c	125. d	126. a	127. a	128. b	129. e	130. d
131. a	132. b	133. d	134. b	135. e	136. b	137. a	138. b	139. d	140. e
141. c	142. a	143. d	144. b	145. e	146. b	147. e	148. c	149. a	150. d
151. e	152. c	153. a	154. d	155. b					

Explanations

Section I

(6-10) Answers:

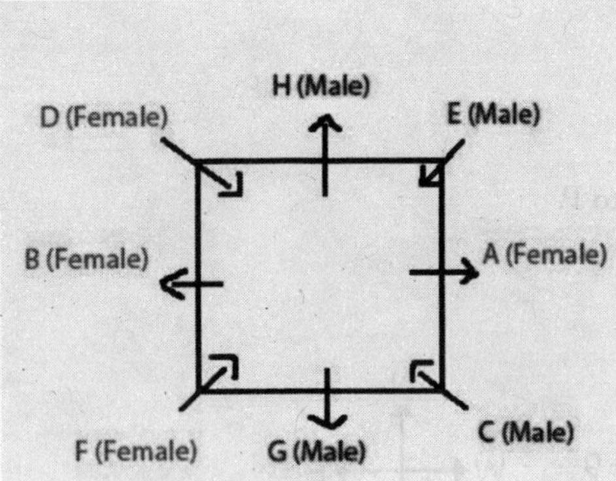

6. c.
7. d.
8. c.
9. a.
10. e.

(16-19) Answers:

16. According to X @ B * P

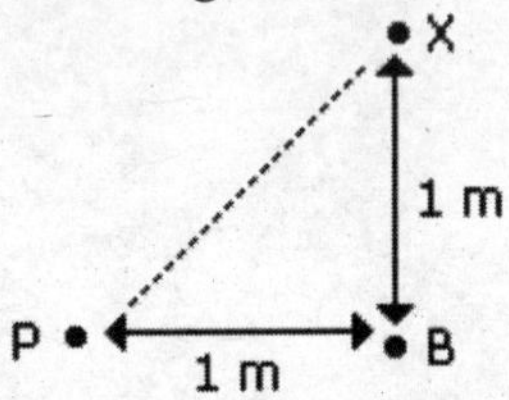

Hence P is in South-West of X

17. According to M # N $ T

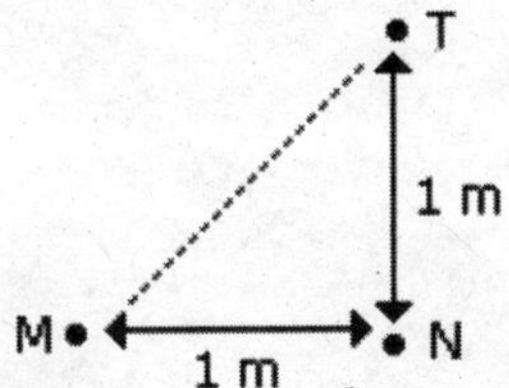

Hence T is in the North-East of M.

18. According to P # R $ A * U

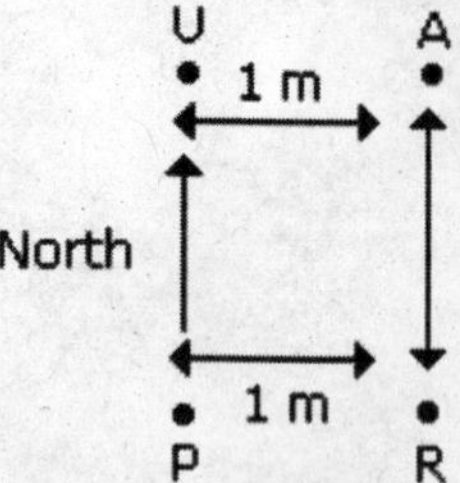

Hence U is in North direction with respect to P.

19.

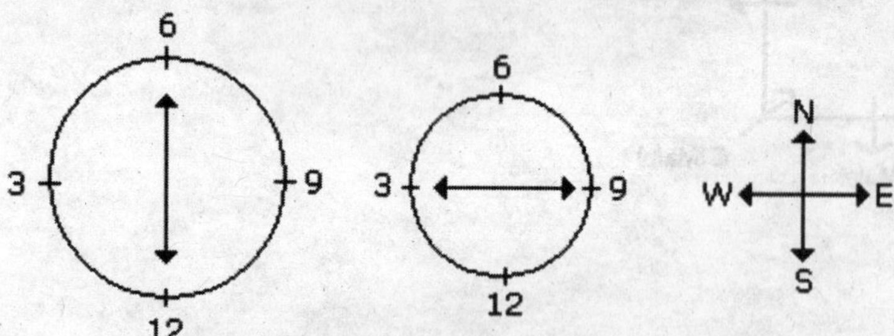

At 9.15 P.M., the minute hand will point towards west.

21.

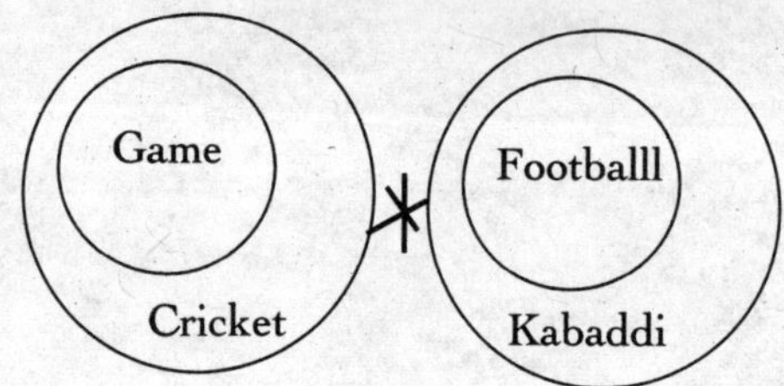

22.

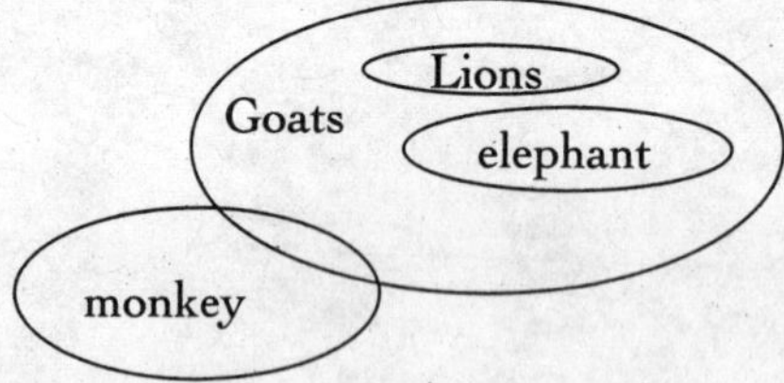

23.

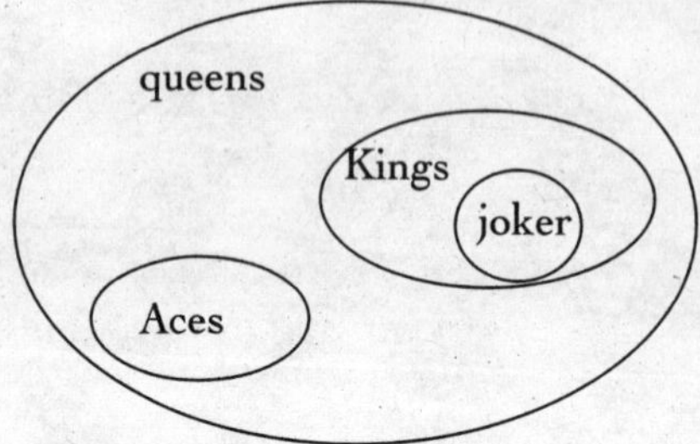

24.

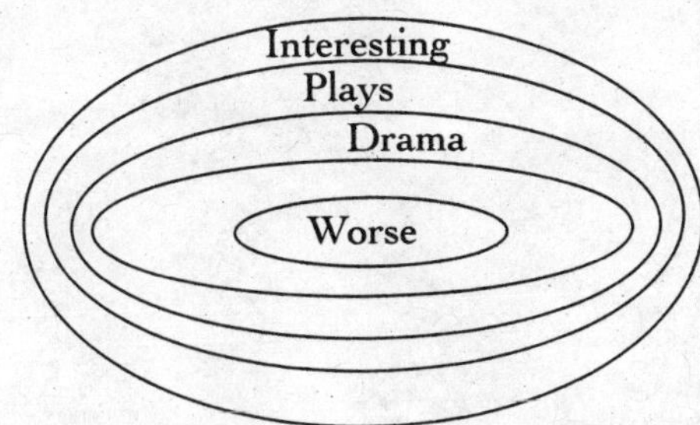

25.

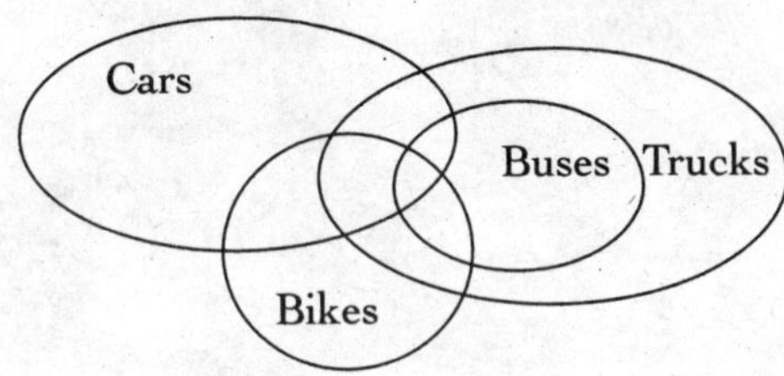

26. From 1, we conclude that B is the child of D who is wife of A i.e. A is B's father.
From 2, A is married to B's father. This implies that A is B's mother.

27. The only word common to 1 and 2 is 'wet' and as such, only the code for 'wet' can be ascertained from the given information.

28. From 1, we conclude that weight of each box = (4x5) kg = 20 kg.
So, total weight of 10 box = (20 x 10) kg = 200 kg.
From 2, we conclude that:
Weight of each box = (weight of 3 boxes) - (weight of 2 boxes) = 20 kg.
So, total weight of 10 boxes = (20 x 10) kg = 200 kg

30. From I, we have: B > T, B > C, V > B.
Thus, V is heavier than each one of B, T and C. But V is not the heaviest. So, E is the heaviest.
Thus, we have the order: E > V > B > T > C or E > V > B > C > T.
Clearly, B is third from the top.

136. b. Neither should be replaced by Either.

137. a. Has.

138. b. Back will be removed.

139. d. Objects will be removed by object.

140. e. "The" will be removed.

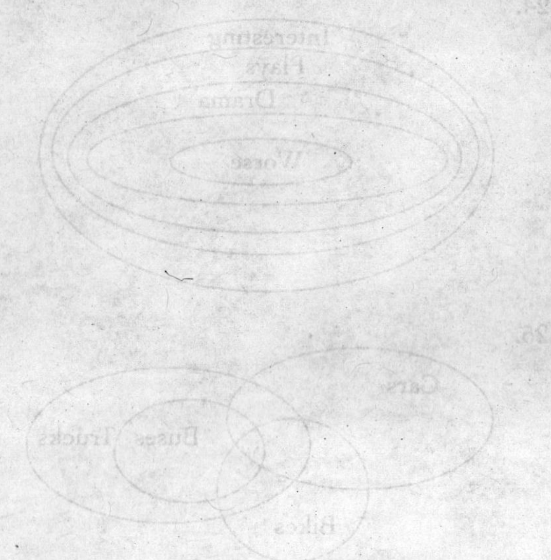

SBI PO Mains MOCK Test Paper 8

Structure of this MOCK Test

S.No.	Name of section	No. of Questions	Total marks	Allotted Time
1	Reasoning and Computer Aptitude	45	60	60 minutes
2	Data Analysis and Interpretation	35	60	45 minutes
3	General/ Economy/ Banking Awareness	40	40	35 minutes
4	English Language	35	40	40 minutes
Total		155	200	3 hours

- **There is $1/4^{th}$ Negative marking for every wrong answer.**
- **If a question is left blank, i.e. no answer is marked by the candidate, there will be no penalty for that question**

Section 1: Reasoning and Computer Ability

Directions (1–7): Study the following information carefully to answer the given questions:
Eight persons from different banks, viz UCO Bank, Syndicate Bank, Canara Bank, PNB, Dena Bank, Oriental Bank of Commerce, Indian Bank and Bank of Maharashtra, are sitting of two parallel rows containing four people each, in such a way that there is an equal distance between adjacent persons. In row 1 Raghuram Rajan, Shikha Sharma, Chanda Kochhar and HR Khan are seated and all of them are facing south. In row 2 Urjit Patel, SS Mundra, Rakesh Sethi and Rana Kapoor are seated and all of them are facing north. Therefore in the given seating arrangement each member seated in a row faces another member of the other row. (All the information given above does not necessarily represent the order of seating as in the final arrangement.)

- Chanda Kochhar sits second to right of the person from Bank of Maharashtra. Rakesh Sethi is an immediate neighbour of the person who faces the person from Bank of Maharashtra.
- Only one person sits between Rakesh Sethi and the person from PNB. The immediate neighbour of the person from PNB faces the person from Canara Bank.
- The person from UCO bank faces the person from oriental Bank of Commerce. Rakesh Sethi is not from Oriental Bank of Commerce. Urjit Patel is not from PNB. Urjit Patel does not face the person from Bank of Maharashtra.

- SS Mundra faces the person from Dena Bank. The one who faces Rana Kapoor sits to the immediate left of Raghuram Rajan.
- Shikha Sharma does not sit at any of the extreme ends of the line. The person form Bank of Maharashtra does not face the person from Syndicate Bank.

1. Which of the following is true regarding Raghuram Rajan?
   a. The person from UCO Bank faces Raghuram Rajan
   b. The person from Bank of Maharashtra is an immediate neighbour of Raghuram Rajan
   c. Raghuram Rajan faces the person who sits second to the right of Rakesh Sethi
   d. Raghuram Rajan is from Oriental Bank of Commerce
   e. Raghuram Rajan sits at one of the extreme ends of the line

2. Who is seated between Rakesh Sethi and the person from PNB?
   a. The person form Oriental Bank of Commerce
   b. Urjit Patel
   c. SS Mundra
   d. The person from Syndicate Bank
   e. Rana Kapoor

3. Who amongst the following sit at extreme ends of the rows?
   a. HR Khan and the person from PNB
   b. The persons from Indian Bank of UCO Bank
   c. The persons from Dena Bank and Urjit Patel
   d. The persons from Syndicate Bank and HR Khan
   e. Chanda Kochhar, SS Mundra

4. Who amongst the following faces the person from Bank of Maharashtra?
   a. The person form Indian Bank
   b. Urjit Patel
   c. Rakesh Sethi
   d. The persons form Syndicate Bank and HR Khan
   e. The person from Canara Bank

5. If Urjit Patel is related to Dena Bank in the same way as Shikha Sharma is related to PNB based on the given arrangement. Who amongst the following is HR Khan related to, following the same pattern?
   a. Syndicate Bank
   b. Canara Bank
   c. Bank of Maharashtra
   d. Indian Bank
   e. Oriental Bank of Commerce

6. Four of the following five are alike in a certain way based on the given seating arrangement and thus form a group. Which is the one that does not belong to the group?
   a. Canara Bank
   b. Rakesh Sethi
   c. Syndicate Bank
   d. SS Mundra
   e. Oriental Bank of Commerce

7. Who amongst the following is from Syndicate Bank?
   a. Chanda Kochhar
   b. Rakesh Sethi
   c. Urjit Patel
   d. HR Khan
   e. Raghuram Rajan

Directions (8–10): Study the following information carefully and answer the questions given below:

Eight persons Smith, Putin, Xinping, Jack, Robert, Farooq, James and Alisha are sitting in a straight line facing north, but not necessarily in the same order. Putin sits second to the left of Smith. Three persons are sitting between James and Putin. James sits on the extreme left end of the row. Jack is an immediate neighbor of James. Farooq and Putin are not neighbours. Xinping sits second to the right of Jack but is not the immediate neighbor of Robert. There are three persons between Xinping and Farooq.

8. Who among the following sits between Xinping and Jack?
   a. Farooq b. Robert c. Putin
   d. Alisha e. None of the above

9. Who among the following sits third to the left of Farooq?
   a. Putin b. Smith c. Xinping
   d. Robert e. None of the above

10. Who among the following sits on the extreme ends of the row?
    a. Jack, Smith b. James, Robert c. James, Farooq
    d. Alisha, Farooq e. None of the above

Directions (11–15): Each of the questions below consists of a question and two statements numbered I and II given below it. You have to decide whether the data provided in the statements are sufficient to answer the question. Read both the statements and give answer.

a. If the data in statement I alone are sufficient to answer the question, while the data in statement II alone are not sufficient to answer the question.
b. If the data in statement II alone are sufficient to answer the question, while the data in statement I alone are not sufficient to answer the question.
c. If the data either in statement I alone or in statement II alone are sufficient to answer the question.
d. If the data in both statements I and II together are not sufficient to answer the question.
e. If the data in both statements I and II together are necessary to answer the question.

11. How many students are enrolled in a classroom?
    I. A total of 36 students are present today in the class according to attendance register.
    II. 4 students are not present in the class today.

12. What is the total of number of runs scored by a team?
    I. Rahul correctly remembers that the team scored a grand total of above 185 runs but below 194 runs.
    II. Robin correctly remembers that the team scored a total of above 180 runs and below 187 runs.

13. How will 'PREDIAL' be coded in a certain language?
    I. In the code language, each consonant in the word is replaced with the next letter in the English alphabetical series.
    II. In the code language, each vowel in the word is replaced with the previous letter in the English alphabetical series.

14. U, V, W, X and Z are seated around a circular table facing the centre, such that there is equal space between each of the adjacent members. Who sits on the immediate right of Z?
    I. V sits second to the right of Z and X sits second to the left of Z.
    II. W is not an immediate neighbour of either U or V.

15. Which direction is Gautam facing at this moment?
    I. After walking 10 metres early in the morning from point P, Gautam is facing away from the sun.
    II. Gautam takes two consecutive right turns after covering 15 metres to reach point P.

Directions (16-20): Study the following information to answer the given question:-
In a certain code, 'come and join us' is written as '6894', 'join to get success ' is written as '7539','come to prepare' is written as '243', and 'prepare and success' is written as '728'.

16. Which of the following is the code for 'come'?
    a. 9 b. 8 c. 4 d. 6 e. Either 4 or 6
17. Which of the following can be coded as 285374?
    a. come and prepare to get success
    b. join us to get success for you
    c. to us come get
    d. prepare to get come success for
    e. None of these
18. Which of the following represents "Join us to get success"?
    a. 879636 b. 96743 c. 34768 d. 21578 e. 76359
19. What does '8' represent in this code?
    a. get b. to c. and d. us e. join
20. Which of the following is the code for 'success'?
    a. 5 b. 2 c. 7 d. 8 e. 2

Directions: (21–25): Study the following information carefully and answer the questions given below:

T-20 World Cup is being organized by India. Different teams are participating in the T-20 World Cup. There are some new teams which are also participating in this T-20 for the first time. Seven new teams which are participating for the first time are – Afghanistan, Nepal, UAE, India, Netherlands, Hong-Kong and Ireland. They will be playing there practice matches at different places, namely Mumbai, Chennai, New Delhi, Dharamshala, Bengaluru, Kolkata and Mohali, put not necessarily in the same order, on different days of the week, starting from Monday.

- Afghanistan will be playing at Chennai, but neither on Friday nor on Monday.
- The host country will be playing on Thursday at Bengaluru.
- There is a gap of one day between Afghanistan and India match.
- Hong-Kong will be playing the match before Ireland but after Netherlands at New Delhi on Wednesday.
- Ireland will be playing on the last day of the week.
- Nepal will be playing at Mohali.
- No match will be played at Mumbai on Monday.
- The match at Kolkata will be played on the last day of the week.
- The match at Dharamshala will be played on Tuesday.
- No match will be played at Mohali on Tuesday and Friday.

21. Nepal will be playing the match on which day of the week?
    a. Friday b. Tuesday c. Saturday d. Wednesday e. Monday
22. Which team will be playing the match between Saturday and after Thursday?
    a. Ireland b. UAE c. India d. Netherlands e. Afghanistan

23. Which of the following combinations is true?
a. India – Thursday – Bengaluru
b. Netherlands – Wednesday – Mumbai
c. Ireland – Saturday – Kolkata
d. UAE – Monday – Chennai
e. Nepal – Friday – Dharamshala

24. Which team will be playing in Dharamshala?
a. Nepal
b. India
c. Netherlands
d. Hongkong
e. Ireland

25. Which of the following combinations is true?
a. Nepal – Tuesday
b. Hongkong – Sunday
c. Netherlands – Thursday
d. Nepal – Monday
e. None of the above

Directions (26-30): Read the following information carefully and answer the questions given below:

Ten businessmen Prashant Pandey, roshni Singh, Ashish Gupta, Swati Gupta, Vandana Sharma, Gopal Anand, Mansi Viswas, Shivam Dhar, Narendra Kumar and Pooja Saini are travelling by ten different airlines to ten different destinations. The Airlines are – Air India, Lufthansa, Virgin Airlines, British Airways, Go Air, Qatar Airways, Cathay Pacific, Thai Airways, Fly Emirates and Air Arabia. The ten destinations are Brazil, South Africa, Sydney, New York, Hong Kong, Seoul, Myanmar, Durban, Dubai and Paris, but not necessarily in the same order.

- Roshni Singh is travelling to South Africa.
- Vandana Sharma is travelling by Go Air and going to Hong Kong.
- The person travelling by Air Arabia is going to Paris.
- Mansi Viswas is travelling by Cathay Pacific.
- Narendra Kumar is travelling to Dubai.
- Shivam Dhar is travelling to Durban.
- Gopal Anand is travelling to Seoul by Qatar Airways.
- Swati Gupta is travelling by British Airways to New York.
- Neither Prashant Pandey nor Roshni Singh is travelling by Fly Emirates.
- Narendra Kumar is not travelling by Air India or Lufthansa.
- Prashant Pandey travels neither by Air India nor by Thai Airways.
- The person who travels to Sydney is using Virgin Airlines.
- Prashant Pandey is travelling to Brazil.
- Ashish Gupta is travelling by Virgin Airlines and Shivam Dhar by Thai Airways.

26. Narendra Kumar is travelling by which airline?
a. Thai Airways
b. Go Air
c. Air India
d. Other than given options
e. Virgin Airlines

27. Mansi Viswas is travelling to which destination?
a. Myanmar
b. Dubai
c. Paris
d. South Africa
e. Hong Kong

28. Which of the following pairs is correct?
a. Pooja Saini – Air Arabia – Hong Kong
b. Shivam Dhar – Thai Airways – Sydney
c. Ashish Gupta – British Airways – Sydney
d. Gopal Anand– Qatar Airways – Seoul
e. Mansi Viswas –Go Air – Myanmar

29. Roshni Singh is travelling by which airline?
a. Air India b. Lufthansa c. Thai Airways d. Fly Emirates
e. Either Air India or Lufthansa

30. Prashant Pandey is travelling by which airline and to which destination?
a. Qatar Airways – Seoul b. British Airways – New York
c. Lufthansa – Sydney d. Lufthansa – Brazil
e. Virgin Airlines -Sydney

31. OSI model has how many layers?
a. Two layers b. Five Layers c. Seven Layers d. Six Layers e. Eight Layers

32. Network __________ is the arrangement of the various elements (links, nodes, etc.) of a computer network.
a. memory b. topology c. mainframe d. protocol e. devices

33. Which of the following terms is associated with Internet?
a. Plotter b. Slide presentation c. Bookmark
d. Pie Chart e. Microsoft Excel

34. Which of the following is contained at the end of the file name and helps to determine the type of file?
a. File property b. The nomenclature c. The name
d. File subname e. File extension

35. How can you access the font size tool on font dialog box in MS Word?
a. Ctrl + S b. Ctrl + Shift + S c. Ctrl + P
d. Ctrl + Shift + P e. Alt + P

36. Which of the following is not a binary number?
a. 1010101 b. 0101010 c. 2020202 d. 1110011 e. 111111

37. What is a small arrow or blinking symbol i.e. a movable indicator on desktop is called?
a. Logo b. Mouse c. Cursor d. Palm e. Hand

38. Which among the following is not legitimate type of computer virus?
a. Boot Virus b. File infector Virus c. Resident Virus
d. Hangout Virus e. Macro Virus

39. An __________ address is a numerical label assigned to each device (e.g., computer, printer) participating in a computer network.
a. IP b. RIP c. EP d. TCP e. ARP

40. What is the attempt to acquire sensitive information such as usernames, passwords, and credit card details (and sometimes, indirectly, money) by masquerading as a trustworthy entity in an electronic communication?
a. Phishing b. Spoofing c. Identity theft
d. Authentication e. Spamming

41. Which of the following is the correct option that allows users to bring together copies of workbooks that other users have worked on independently in MS Excel?
a. Copying b. Merging c. Pasting d. Compiling e. None of these

42. EBCDIC stands for?
    a. Extended Binary Coded Decimal Interchange Code
    b. Enlarged Binary Code Digital Interchange Code
    c. Extended Bilingual Coded Decimal Interchange Code
    d. Encoded Bilingual Coded Division Interchange Code
    e. None of the above is correct

43. If your computer keeps rebooting itself, then it is likely that ________.
    a. It has a virus
    b. It does not have enough memory
    c. There is no printer
    d. There has been a power surge
    e. It needs a CD-ROM

44. In PROM, P stands for?
    a. Plausible b. Program c. Programmable d. Proper e. Preferred

45. __________ ports connect special types of music instruments to sound cards.
    a. MIDI b. CPU c. USB d. BUS e. OCR

Section 2: Data Analysis and Data Interpretation

Direction for questions 46 – 51: Read the information given below and solve the questions based on it.

Chef Sudhir is preparing orders of toast for three customers A, B and C.

Assume that all the three customers ordered at exactly the same time, and the time to place bread in and remove toast from the toaster is negligible.

Sudhir has two toasters that can each toast 2 pieces of bread at the same time, and 1 knife to apply both butter and jam.

- It takes 1 minute to lightly toast 2 pieces of bread
- It takes 1 minute 30 seconds to moderately toast 2 pieces of bread
- It takes 2 minutes to darkly toast 2 pieces of bread
- It takes 10 seconds to apply butter to a piece of toast
- It takes 15 seconds to apply jam to a piece of toast

Following are the orders:

Customer A wants 4 pieces of toast, moderately toasted, with butter on each piece

Customer B wants 2 pieces of toast, lightly toasted, with butter and jam on each piece

Customer C wants 3 pieces of toast, darkly toasted, with butter on 1 piece, nothing on the others.

Waiting time for any customer is the total time taken by Sudhir to serve that particular customer. For example, if A had to wait for 2 minutes, and after serving A, B is served in another 1 minute, then total waiting time for B will be 3 minutes.

Overall objective of Sudhir is to minimize the total combined waiting time. Total combined waiting time = Individual waiting time of A + individual waiting time of B + Individual waiting time of C.

46. Who will be served first?
    a. A b. B c. C d. A or B or C
    e. cannot be determined

47. Who will be served second?
a. A b. B c. C
d. A or B or C e. cannot be determined

48. Who will be served third?
a. A b. B c. C
d. A or B or C e. cannot be determined

49. What is the combined total waiting time?
a. 9 minutes 20 seconds b. 8 minutes 55 seconds
c. 8 minutes 40 seconds d. None of these
e. cannot be determined

50. What is the individual waiting time of A?
a. 4 minutes 20 seconds b. 4 minutes 10 seconds
c. 4 minutes 40 seconds d. None of these
e. cannot be determined

51. What is the waiting time of C?
a. 2 minutes 10 seconds b. 4 minutes 20 seconds
c. 2 minutes 30 seconds d. None of these
e. cannot be determined

Directions for questions 52 to 55: Answer the questions on the basis of the information given below.

Mr. Fruit has six different types of fruits with him namely Mangoes, Apples, Oranges, Peaches, Guavas and Litchis. The following table provides information about the minimum and the maximum price of each of the mentioned fruits. The table also provides information about the number of fruits of each type and the average price of each fruit.

Assume that the price of each fruit is an integer. There is only one mango that has the minimum price and there is only one mango that has the maximum price. The same holds true for each type of fruit.

	Minimum Price	Maximum Price	Average Price	Number of Fruits
Mango	20	28	23	16
Apple	40	50	46	24
Orange	4	8	7	40
Peach	16	26	20	34
Guava	3	8	5	28
Litchi	10	18	16	30

52. Find the approximate average price of fruits with Mr. Fruit.
a. Rs. 18 b. Rs. 20 c. Rs. 23 d. Rs. 15 e. Rs. 22

53. The number of mangoes whose price is more than Rs. 21 is at least
a. 3 b. 4 c. 5 d. 6 e. 2

54. Given that the price of four peaches with Mr. Fruit is Rs. 22 each and there are exactly 10 peaches whose price is Rs. 18. The number of peaches with Mr. Fruit whose price is at least Rs. 25 is at most

a. 13 b. 12 c. 11 d. 9 e. 15

55. Total number of guavas with Mr. Fruit whose price is less than the average price of the guavas with Mr. Fruit is at least

a. 17 b. 18 c. 19 d. 20 e. 24

Directions (56-60): The following table shows the revenue generated from sales of monthly magazine from January to June 2016, in 5 different states (PV – Printed version, OV – Online version) (The revenue given in the table is in rupees thousands)

	Haryana		Delhi		U.P.		Gujarat		Rajasthan	
	PV	OV	PV	OV	PV	OV	PV	OV	PV	OV
January	169	163	201	145	136	141	152	209	131	184
February	144	171	157	139	156	149	186	217	98	190
March	129	148	204	144	152	174	116	185	118	219
April	163	139	232	139	168	207	129	156	174	236
May	113	152	128	151	196	209	187	139	168	111
June	172	141	142	163	178	243	154	144	151	194

56. What is the ratio between the revenue generated from the printed version of magazine in Haryana in all the months to the revenue generated from online version of magazine in the same state in all months together ?

a. 435 : 458 b. 458 : 435 c. 482 : 481 d. 435 : 457 e. None of these

57. In Delhi state, which month revenue from the online version of magazine is highest as compared to the total revenue from online version and printed version of magazine together?

a. March b. April c. May d. June e. None of these

58. Find the difference (in rupees) between the revenue from the state having highest revenue (from both online and printed version) and the revenue from the state having lowest revenue in the month of May.

a. 2.4 lakh b. 0.24 lakh c. 1.6 lakh d. 16 lakh e. None of these

59. Total revenue generated from Haryana, Delhi and U.P. in April from the printed version is approximately what percent of the total revenue generated from Gujarat and Rajasthan in the same month from printed version and online version of Magazine ?

a. 84% b. 83% c. 82% d. 81% e. 80%

60. Find the average total revenue (revenue from printed version + revenue from online version) from Rajasthan, over the months.
a. 3,96,800 b. 3,96,600 c. 3,96,500 d. 3,29,000 e. None of these

Directions (61–65) : An electronics company sells only 5 types of products refrigerator, TV, cooler, AC and washing machine. The total revenue generated in 1 year is 500 Cr. Given below is the percentage breakup of revenue earned by different products.

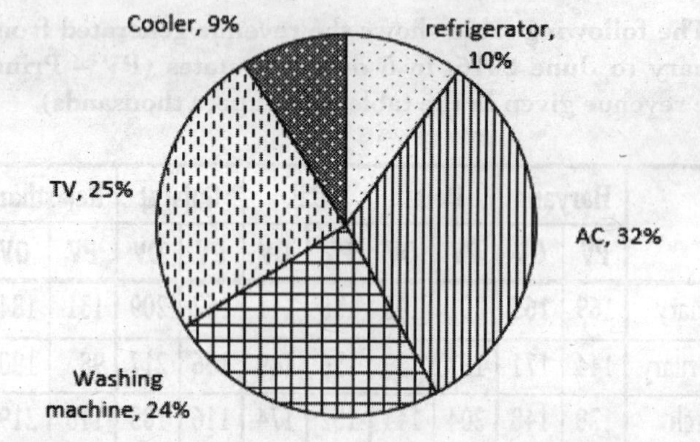

Percentage distribution of revenue of each product in different quarters of year

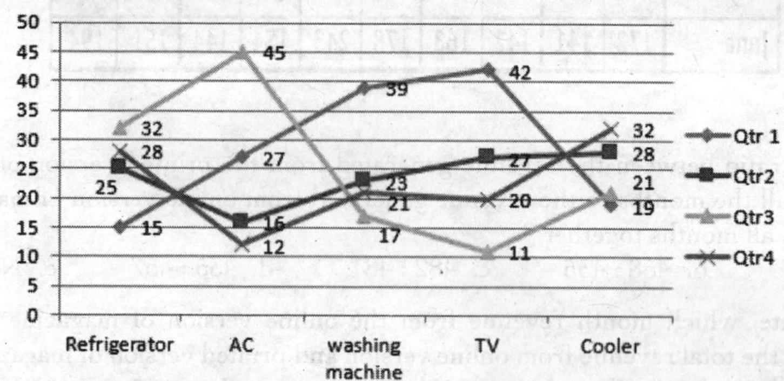

61. Revenue earned by AC in 3rd quarter is what percent more than revenue of washing machine in 2nd and 4th quarter Together? (round off to two decimal places)
a. 36.36 b. 34.21 c. 38.86 d. 32.54 e. None of these

62. Find the respective ratio of revenue earned from refrigerators in 2nd and 3rd quarter to revenue of washing machine from 1st and 2nd quarter?
a. 283:744 b. 744:283 c. 95:248 d. 744:285 e. None of these

63. What is the difference between total revenue in quarter 2 and total revenue in quarter 3?
a. 16.85 cr b. 17.65 cr c. 19.25 cr d. 23.15 cr e. None of these

64. Revenue from Sales of washing machine in 1st 3rd and 4th quarter is approximately what times of revenue from sale of AC in 2nd and 4th quarter?
a. 2.05 b. 1.85 c. 1.95 d. 3.22 e. 2.35

65. Revenue from sales of AC and washing machine in quarter 1 is approximately what percent of revenue from sales of all Products together in quarter 2?
a. 80% b. 83% c. 63% d. 71% e. 86%

66. Anuj can do a piece of work in certain number of days. To do the same piece of work, Bhanu takes thrice the number of days as Anuj takes whereas Chandu takes thrice as many days as Bhanu does and Dodo takes thrice as many days as Chandu does. Now they are paired and two groups are formed. The first pair takes one-third the time taken by the second pair to complete the work. Which is the first pair?
a. Anuj and Dodo b. Anuj and Chandu
c. Chandu and Bhanu d. Bhanu and Dodo e. None of these

67. A train traveling at 100 kmph overtakes a motorbike traveling at 64 kmph in 40 seconds. What is the length of the train in meters?
a. 200m b. 400 m c. 600 m d. 800m e. 1000m

68. The average weight of seven members of a family is 18 kgs. If the head of the family is not considered, the average weight of the others would be 5 kgs less. The weight of the head of the family is
a. 42 years b. 52 years c. 48 years d. 36 years e. 45 years

69. Ram completes 60% of a task in 15 days and then takes the help of Rahim and Rachel. Rahim is 50% as efficient as Ram and and Rachel is 50% as efficient as Rahim. In how many more days will they complete the work?
a. $13\frac{1}{3}$ b. $8\frac{1}{3}$ c. $5\frac{5}{7}$ d. $7\frac{5}{7}$ e. None of these

70. At CI, a sum of money amounts to 3 times in 5 years. In how many years, will the same sum amount to 9 times the original value at the same rate of CI?
a. 8 years b. 10 years c. 12 years d. 15 years e. 20 years

71. Two men A and B walk from P to Q, a distance of 24 km, at 11 and 13 km an hour respectively. B reaches Q, returns immediately and meets A at R. Find the total distance travelled by B.
a. 26 km b. 28 km c. 30 km d. 32 km e. none of these

72. The length of room is 1½ times its breadth. The cost of carpeting it at Rs. 150 per sq metres is Rs. 14400 and the cost of white washing the four walls at Rs. 5 per sq metre is Rs. 625. Find the length, breadth and height of the room.
a. 12m, 8m, 3 1/8m b. 12 1/2m, 8 1/8m, 3 1/8m
c. 12 3/4m, 8 2/3m, 3 2/4m d. Data inadequate e. none of these

73. An 8 members committee is to be selected out of 18 members team. In how many ways can the selection be made so that 2 particular members are always included?
a. 8800 b. 8008 c. 8088 d. 9800 e. none of these

74. If p men working p hours per day for p days produce p unit of work, then units produced by q men working q hours a day for q days is
a. p^2/q^2 b. p^2/q^2 c. q^2/p^2 d. q^2/p^2 e. None of thesc

75. A bag contains 6 red and 4 white balls. Four balls are drawn out one by one and not replaced. What is the probability that they are alternatively of different colours?
a. 2/7 b. 4/7 c. 1/7
d. Data inadequate e. none of these

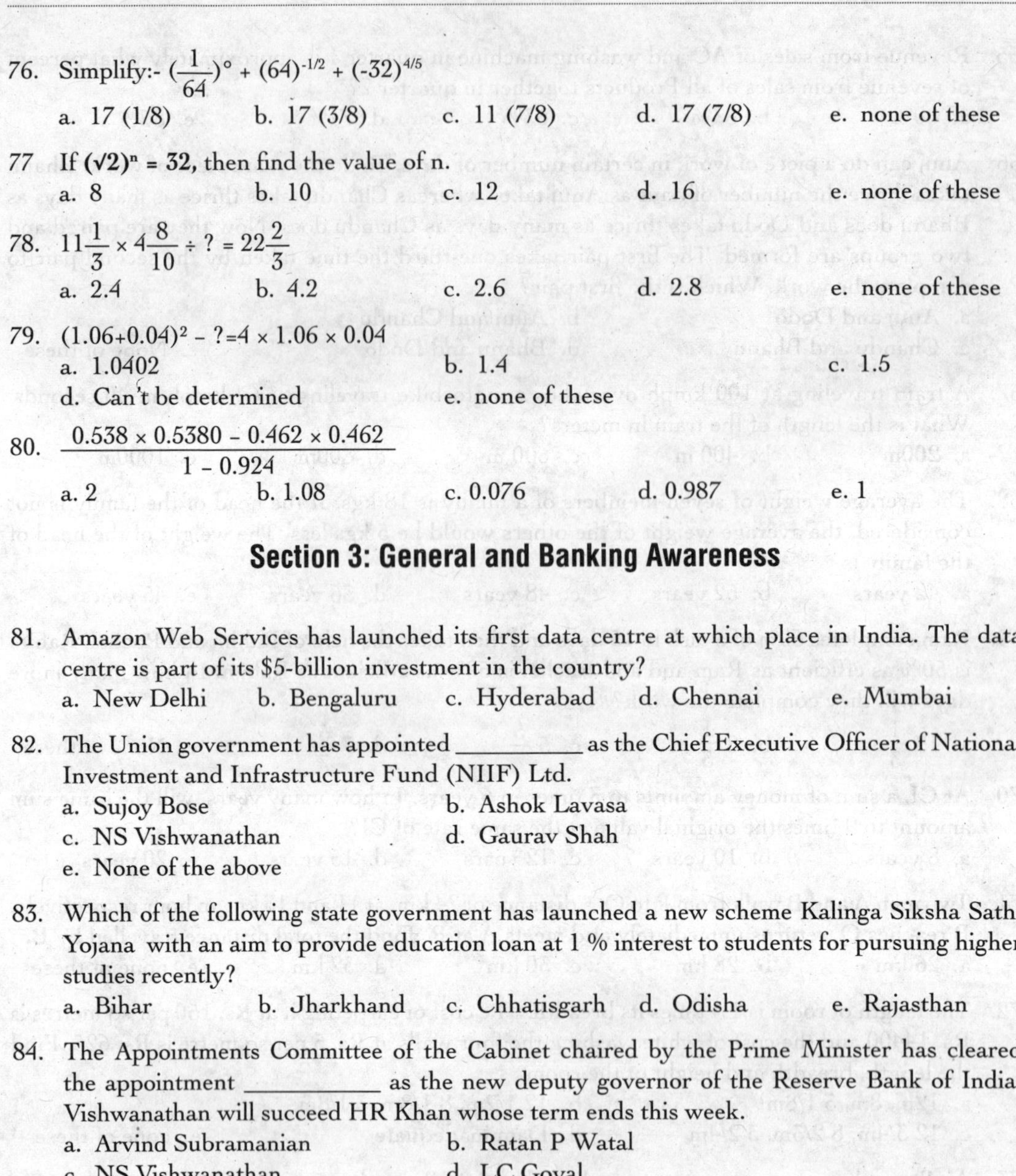

76. Simplify:- $(\frac{1}{64})^{o} + (64)^{-1/2} + (-32)^{4/5}$

a. 17 (1/8) b. 17 (3/8) c. 11 (7/8) d. 17 (7/8) e. none of these

77 If $(\surd 2)^n = 32$, then find the value of n.

a. 8 b. 10 c. 12 d. 16 e. none of these

78. $11\frac{1}{3} \times 4\frac{8}{10} \div ? = 22\frac{2}{3}$

a. 2.4 b. 4.2 c. 2.6 d. 2.8 e. none of these

79. $(1.06+0.04)^2 - ? = 4 \times 1.06 \times 0.04$

a. 1.0402 b. 1.4 c. 1.5

d. Can't be determined e. none of these

80. $\dfrac{0.538 \times 0.5380 - 0.462 \times 0.462}{1 - 0.924}$

a. 2 b. 1.08 c. 0.076 d. 0.987 e. 1

Section 3: General and Banking Awareness

81. Amazon Web Services has launched its first data centre at which place in India. The data centre is part of its $5-billion investment in the country?

a. New Delhi b. Bengaluru c. Hyderabad d. Chennai e. Mumbai

82. The Union government has appointed ___________ as the Chief Executive Officer of National Investment and Infrastructure Fund (NIIF) Ltd.

a. Sujoy Bose b. Ashok Lavasa

c. NS Vishwanathan d. Gaurav Shah

e. None of the above

83. Which of the following state government has launched a new scheme Kalinga Siksha Sathi Yojana with an aim to provide education loan at 1 % interest to students for pursuing higher studies recently?

a. Bihar b. Jharkhand c. Chhatisgarh d. Odisha e. Rajasthan

84. The Appointments Committee of the Cabinet chaired by the Prime Minister has cleared the appointment ___________ as the new deputy governor of the Reserve Bank of India. Vishwanathan will succeed HR Khan whose term ends this week.

a. Arvind Subramanian b. Ratan P Watal

c. NS Vishwanathan d. LC Goyal

e. None of the above

85. Name the Indian social entrepreneur who has been named among 10 "champions and pioneers" by United Nation chief Ban Ki-moon under the world's largest corporate sustainability initiative that calls on companies to align with universal principles of human rights, environment and anti-corruption.

a. Zubaida Bai b. Malala Yousafzai

c. Taslima Nasrin d. All of the above

e. None of the above

86. Lionel Messi sensationally announced his retirement from international football. He played for which country?
a. Russia b. USA c. Argentina d. Brazil e. Chile

87. Which of the following state government has declared that all natural calamities including unseasonal heavy rain, lightning, Loo and storm etc will be treated as state disaster?
a. Odisha b. Uttar Pradesh c. Bihar d. Maharashtra e. Gujarat

88. ____________ transformation into a global R&D hub is epitomised by the strides the country is making in attracting R&D investments in the electronics and IT segment, beating the likes of US and Germany.
a. China b. Russia c. India
d. France e. None of the above

89. Majuli is to become India's first river island district by August this year. At present the island is a sub-division under Jorhat district in which of the following state?
a. Assam b. West Bengal c. Tripura
d. Bihar e. Jharkhand

90. The ______________ got the Cabinet approval, paving the way for auction of 100 prospective mineral blocks and boosting the country's mining potential.
a. Aadhaar Bill b. The National Mineral Exploration Policy (NMEP)
c. Child protection policy d. All of the above
e. None of the above

91. Minister of Human Resource and Development Smriti Irani is launching the teacher education portal ___________ for District Institutes of Education and Training (DIETs) in New Delhi on 30th June 2016.
a. Prashikshak b. Shikshak
c. Adhyapak Samvarg d. Masterjee
e. None of the above

92. Central government announced an overall increase of 23.5 per cent for over one crore government employees and pensioners in line with the Seventh Pay Commission's recommendations, which left most services dissatisfied. The hikes will come with the August paychecks and be paid with effect from __________
a. September 1, 2016 b. January 1, 2016
c. January 1, 2017 d. April 1, 2016 e. June 1, 2017

93. Cabinet Committee on Economic Affairs (CCEA) approval of road projects in which of the following two states recently and this project will help improve the infrastructure and connectivity in these states?
a. Bihar and West Bengal b. Jharkhand and Haryana
c. Uttar Pradesh and Madhya Pradesh
d. Rajasthan and Gujarat e. Odisha and Punjab

94. Washington DC-based the International Monetary Fund (IMF) has cleared the payment of how much for Pakistan recently?
a. $501 million b. $4501 million c. $7501 million
d. $2501 million e. $1501 million

95. An Australia-based construction giant has cracked a deal worth $169.5 million with Indian company to build a retail and hospitality development project in which place?
a. New Delhi b. Pune c. Mumbai d. Kolkata e. Hyderabad

96. What does FSDC stand for?
a. Financial Security and Development Council
b. Financial Stability and Development Council
c. Fiscal Security and Development Council
d. Fiscal Stability and Development Council
e. None of the above

97. ________ has been declared the first 'total banking state' in India, successfully implementing the total financial inclusion thereby ensuring banking facility to all households.
a. Maharashtra b. Kerala
c. Himachal Pradesh d. Uttarakhand e. Gujarat

98. RBI has introduced "Marginal Standing Facility" with the objective of:
a. Controlling Inflation
b. Containing instability in long term inter-bank rates
c. Containing instability in the overnight inter-bank rates
d. All of the above e. None of the above

99. ____________ are the beneficiaries of the "Reverse Mortgage Scheme".
a. Government employees b. Senior citizens
c. Unemployed persons d. Persons of BPL category
e. None of the above

100. RBI was nationalized in the year-
a. 1949 b. 1952 c. 1955 d. 1964 e. 1935

101. Which of the following is/are associated with the fiscal policy?
1. Marginal Standing Facility
2. Devaluation of Currency
3. Market Stabilization Scheme
a. 1 & 2 b. Only 3 c. 2 & 3
d. Only 2 e. None of the above

102. _____ is the percentage of total deposits of a bank which it has to keep with itself in the form of liquid assets.
a. Statutory Liquidity Ratio (SLR) b. Cash Reserve Ratio (CRR)
c. Statutory Reserve Ratio d. Cash Ratio
e. Marginal Standing Facility (MSF)

103. The exchange rate in India is dependent upon:
1. Government policy
2. Demand-supply forces
3. Monetary policy objectives
a. Only 2 b. 2 & 3 c. 1 & 2
d. 1, 2 & 3 e. None of the above

104. Collateralized Borrowing and Lending Obligation (CBLO) is a/an ________.
a. Money Market Instrument
b. Instrument of Monetary Policy
c. Type of Risk Cover
d. Stock Market Instrument
e. None of the above

105. Often, we read in newspapers that the RBI has changed the Repo rate and the Reverse Repo rate by a few basis points. What is a basis point?
a. Ten % of one hundredth point
b. One hundredth of 1
c. One tenth of 1%
d. Ten % of 100
e. None of the above

106. Banks generally don't pay interest on money deposited in which of the following accounts?
a. Savings account
b. Current account
c. Fixed deposit account
d. All of the above
e. None of the above

107. 'Fiat Money' is defined as the money which is
a. Accepted internationally
b. Accepted temporarily in lieu of gold
c. Issued by keeping gold or silver as deposit
d. Decreed as money by the government
e. None of the above

108. Demand-pull inflation can be caused by which of the following?
a. A decline in consumption expenditure
b. A sharp increase in lending rates
c. A steep decline in income tax
d. An increase in direct taxation
e. None of the above

109. RBI isn't expected to perform the role of-
a. Acting as a clearing house
b. Working as a banker to the government
c. Managing Forex
d. Accepting deposits from general public
e. None of the above

110. Who decided on the quantity of coins to be minted?
a. The Government of India
b. RBI
c. Either (a) or (b)
d. All of the above
e. None of the above

111. Who was the first administrator-statesman to attempt planning as a means for economic development?
a. Sir CP Ramaswami Aiyyar
b. M Viswesvarayya
c. VT Krishnamachari
d. C Rajagopalachari
e. None of the above

112. An economy is at the take off stage on its path to development when it
a. becomes stagnant
b. begins steady growth
c. is liberalized
d. gets maximum foreign aid
e. None of the above

113. Which of the following is the basic characteristic of Oligopoly?
a. a few sellers, one buyer
b. a few sellers, many buyers
c. a few sellers, a few buyers
d. many sellers, a few buyers
e. None of the above

114. The aim of which of the Five Year Plans was to correct the disequilibrium in the economy?
a. First Five Year Plan
b. Second Five Year Plan
c. Third Five Year Plan
d. Fourth Five Year Plan
e. None of the above

115. Which of the following Five Year Plans recognized human development as the core of all developmental efforts?
a. Eighth Five Year Plan
b. Seventh Five Year Plan
c. Fifth Five Year Plan
d. Third Five Year Plan
e. None of the above

116. Which of the following plans aimed at improving the standard of living?
a. Third Plan
b. Fourth Plan
c. Fifth Plan
d. Sixth Plan
e. None of the above

117. At which of the following places was the mining of coal started in 1774?
a. Chhindwara
b. Dhanbad
c. Ranchi
d. Raniganj
e. None of the above

118. In which of the following years were the cocking coals and non-cocking coal mines in India nationalized?
a. 1971 and 1972 repetitively
b. 1972 and 1973 respectively
c. 1973 and 1974 respectively
d. 1970 and 1972 respectively
e. None of the above

119. Which Indian state has the largest number of cotton textile mills?
a. Madhya Pradesh
b. Maharashtra
c. Gujarat
d. West Bengal
e. None of the above

120. Minor ports like Kakinada, Machilipatnam, Bheemunipatnam and Krishnapatnam are in which of the following states?
a. Tamil Nadu
b. Andhra Pradesh
c. Maharashtra
d. Karnataka
e. None of the above

Section 4: English Language

Directions (121-130): Read the following passage carefully and answer the questions given below.

Ethics concern an individual's moral judgements about right and wrong. Decisions taken within an organisation may be made by individuals or groups, but whoever makes them will be influenced by the culture of the company. The decision to behave ethically is a moral one; employees must decide what they think is the right course of action. This may involve rejecting the route that would lead to the biggest short-term profit. Ethical issues include the rights and duties between a company and its employees, suppliers, customers and neighbours, its **fiduciary** responsibility to its shareholders.

Issues concerning relations between different companies include hostile take-over and industrial **espionage**. Related issues include governance; corporate; political contributions; legal issues such as the ethical debate over introducing a crime of corporate manslaughter; and the marketing of corporations' ethics policies. Business ethics reflects the philosophy of business, one of whose aims is to determine the fundamental purposes of a company. If a company's purpose is to maximise shareholder returns, then sacrificing profits to other concerns is a violation of its fiduciary responsibility. Business ethics is also known as corporate ethics, a form of applied ethics or professional ethics that examines ethical principles and moral or ethical problems that arise in a business environment. It applies to all aspects of business conduct and is relevant to the conduct of individuals and entire organisations. Business ethics has both normative and descriptive dimensions. As a corporate practice and a career specialisation, the field is primarily normative.

Academics attempting to understand business behaviour employ descriptive methods. The range and quantity of business ethical issues reflects the interaction of profit-maximising behaviour with non-economic concerns. Ethical behaviour and corporate social responsibility can bring significant benefits to a business. For example, they may: attract customers to the firm's products, thereby boosting sales and profits. It makes employees want to stay with the business, reduce labour turnover and therefore increase productivity. It attracts more employees wanting to work for the business, reduce recruitment costs and enable the company to get the most talented employees and also attract investors and keep the company's share price high, thereby protecting the business from takeover. While unethical behaviour or a lack of corporate social responsibility, by comparison, may damage a firm's reputation and make it less appealing to stakeholders. Unethical behaviour can also result in bad publicity, resulting in a bad name that will always be associated with the company even if they attempt to utilise a more ethical code of conduct. If a company has unethical behaviour and is charged by the courts, they can wind up paying fines, court fees and may even receive some jail time, many companies eventually go bankrupt and close their doors due to the high cost of unethical behaviours. Unethical behaviour also decreases productivity of a company. If you are working in a company with bad ethical behaviours, it is difficult for the employees to trust each other, or their supervisors. When people work in an environment where they do not trust anyone, they are not going to do their best work, if they continue to work there at all. Unethical behaviour can cause employees to lose the faith in the company and become more likely to call it sick more often or not even show up at all. Once a company is known for having unethical behaviours, the effects can be permanent. All of the years spent on building a good reputation can be quickly **torn down** with only one unethical incident, destroying the company's reputation possibly forever.

121. What is meant by manslaughter ?
   a. A kind of heinous crime
   b. It's all about employees.
   c. Legally killing of one human being by another.
   d. Killing without malicious forethought
   e. None of these

122. What is/are the dimensions of Business ethics?
   a. Corporate ethics
   b. Applied ethics or professional ethics
   c. Normative and descriptive
   d. 1) and 2)
   e. None of these

123. What can be the worst impact of unethical behaviour in corporate world?
   a. It can reduce the loyalty of customer towards the product.
   b. It will reduce productivity.
   c. It may damage firm's reputation and make it less appealing to stake holders.
   d. A company can be charged by the counts and order to close down it with a fine or jail or both. Thus it becomes insolvent.
   e. Both 1) and 3)

124. Once a company is known for having unethical behaviours, the effect can be-
a. Permanent b. Negligible c. Temporary d. Partial e. None of these

125. Which of the following is definitely true in the context of the passage ?
a. Profit maximisation directly is proportional to ethical behaviour.
b. People having ethical behaviour are always in loss at their workplace.
c. Corporate culture does not understand business behaviour.
d. Both 2) and 3) e. None of these

Directions (126 - 128) : Choose the word which is most nearly the SAME in meaning as the word printed in bold as used in the passage.

126. FIDUCIARY
a. Employee b. Guardian c. Minimum d. Collector e. Store keeper

127. ESPIONAGE
a. Spying b. Information c. Reforms d. Norms e. Requirement

128. TORN DOWN
a. Restore b. Reject c. Initiate d. End e. Demolish

Directions (129- 130): Choose the word which is most OPPOSITE in meaning of the word printed in bold as used in the passage.

129. WIND-UP
a. Start b. Air c. Conclude d. Unsettle e. Normalise

130. BANKRUPT
a. Successful b. Saved c. Rich d. Solvent e. Complete

Directions (131-135): Find the error in the given sentences and mark the appropriate option as your correct answer.

131. Death is preferable than life.
a. Death b. is c. preferable d. than life. e. No error

132. Ramu closely resembles to his father not only in physical features but also in habits.
a. Ramu closely b. resembles to his father
c. not only in physical features d. but also in habits. e. No error

133. After he had read the two first chapters of the novel, he felt like reading the book at one sitting.
a. After he had read the two first chapters b. of the novel,
c. he felt like reading d. the book at one sitting. e. No error

134. If it snowed tomorrow, we'll go skating.
a. If b. it snowed tomorrow c. we'll go
d. skating. e. No error

135. A quarrel arose between the five members and for a time it appeared as if the party had been heading for a split.
a. A quarrel arose between the five members

b. and for a time c. it appeared as if the party
d. had been heading for a split. e. No error

Directions (136-138): In the given paragraph, the first and last sentence is given, Rearrange the following five sentences (A), (B), (C), (D), (E) in the proper sequence to form a meaningful paragraph; then answer the questions given below them.

136. The need to identify a suitable mate is such a strong biological urge that the animal kingdom has spawned a bewildering array of courtship rituals.
A. Humans also use dance as part of courtship but is has been difficult for scientists to pin down exactly what it is about a dance that appeals to members of the opposite sex.
B. Such competitive displays depend on the speed, strength and size of an animal, which is why they convey a measure of reproductive fitness.
C. Scorpions and sand hill cranes, for instance, dance to impress.
D. Hippo males fling their faeces, and humpback whales sing and leap above the ocean surface.
E. Dancing is popular among animals for similar reasons.
This is because factors such as facial attractiveness, height and even social status tend to confound any attempt to judge the relative merits of a person's gyrations.
a. ABCDE b. DEBCA c. CBDEA d. EDBCA e. DBECA

137. A. Carbon fibre is an expensive alternative to making things in steel or aluminium, but besides being extremely strong it is also very light.
B. When his Formula 1 can be cart-wheeled in a spectacular 306 kph crash at the recent Valencia Grand Prix, what helped him to escape unscathed was the immensely strong carbon-fibre "tub" that racing drivers now sit in.
C. But if work by Germany's BMW proves successful, it could also become the material of choice to mass-produce electric cars.
D. It is found in high-performance parts, like aircraft wings, bits of supercars and the frames of pricey mountain bikes.
E. Mark Webber has a lot to thank tiny strands of carbon for.
a. EBADC b. DABCE c. CAEBD d. DCEBA e. EABDC

138. Arguments for legalising prostitution depend on the strength of two arguments: that prostitution is a choice for those in it and that the harms of prostitution are decreased if it is legalised. There is little evidence that either of these arguments is true.
A. They usually have options for escape.
B. For most, prostitution is not a freely-made choice because the conditions that would permit genuine choice are not present: physical safety, equal power with buyers, and real alternatives.
C. But zombie theories about prostitution never seem to die no matter how many facts we beat them down with.
D. The few who do choose prostitution are privileged by class or race or education.
E. Only a tiny percentage all women in prostitution are there because they choose it.
Most women in prostitution do not have viable alternatives. They are coerced into prostitution by sex inequality, race/ethnic inequality, and economic inequality.
a. BDCEA b. ABDCE c. CEBDA d. CEDAB e. DECBA

Directions (139-148): Fill in the blanks choosing the word that is most appropriate in the context of the passage.

One of the (1) we have to face is that of unemployment. It is a big problem, a human problem, which we cannot (2). Yet in looking (3) it, it has to be remembered that merely giving some kind of occupation to a large number of people does not ultimately increase employment or lessen unemployment. Employment comes by newer and more effective means of wealth production. The whole experience and history of the past 200 years shows that it comes (4) the growth of technological methods. Do not imagine that we can effectively deal (5) the problem of unemployment without (6). Every country which boasts of (7) employment is a country which is technologically advanced. Every country which is not technologically advanced has unemployment or under-employment. Therefore, if India is to advance, she must advance in science and technology. The fact is that our poverty is (8) our backwardness in science and technology. If we (9) that backwardness, we create not only wealth (10) employment.

139.
a. major problem b. major problems c. main problem
d. serious problem e. only problem

140.
a. ignore b. avoid c. overlook d. neglect e. shun

141.
a. into b. after c. at d. on e. above

142.
a. by b. through c. for d. form e. beyond

143.
a. in b. off c. about d. with e. over

144.
a. technological progress b. technical progress
c. technological temper d. technical temper e. technical bend

145.
a. complete b. total c. full d. ultimate e. final

146.
a. due to b. owing to c. because of d. on account of e. in relation to

147.
a. treat b. remedy c. remove d. eradicate e. estimate

148.
a. but b. but also c. but even d. and also e. in spite of

Directions (149–155) : In the following passage some of the words have been left out each of which is indicated by a number. Find the suitable word from the options given against each number and fill up the blanks with appropriate words to make the paragraphs meaningfully complete.

When we discuss about discrimination then in our country, we find discrimination even in the game of chess, as the white piece is moved first. People are not disabled ...*(1)*... their choice. It occurs. Congenital since birth or progressive degeneration is a medical condition or due to an accident. This disabled with ...*(2)*... support from family and doctors learn to ...*(3)*... with the new reality and fit in a society which is not compatible both attitudinally and infrastructural.

I am suffering from an injury and a permanent disability due to an accident. More than 2 million people in India are suffering from this devastating, life- altering injury due to accidents. There is no cure, only lifelong rehabilitation can allow us to have a ...*(4)*... quality of life.

At no point could I go to a store and ask, "Could you please give a ...*(5)*... of kilos of dignity?" In exchange for some money. No one can buy dignity or self-respect or expect it to be ...*(6)*... out to us. ....*(7)*... take is that as soon as we ask, expect or demand, we become smaller, lower, inferior and weaker.

149.
a. derange b. by c. with d. to e. through

150.
a. spotless b. segregate c. elegant d. immense e. Avow

151.
a. cope b. play c. trench d. curtail e. flow

152.
a. slander b. drudge c. thwart d. unused e. threshold

153.
a. ascetic b. innate c. couple d. sobriety e. stern

154.
a. doled b. ease c. officious d. stout e. convene

155.
a. Restore b. My c. Hazy d. Naive e. Lessen

ANSWERS AND EXPLANATIONS:-

1. b 2. e 3. d 4. a 5. d 6. d 7. c 8. d 9. a 10. c
11. e 12. e 13. e 14. 15. a 16. c 17. a 18. e 19. c 20. c
21. e 22. b 23. a 24. c 25. d 26. d 27. a 28. d 29. a 30. d
31. c 32. b 33. c 34. e 35. d 36. c 37. c 38. d 39. a 40. a
41. b 42. a 43. a 44. c 45. a 46. c 47. b 48. a 49. b 50. b
51. a 52. a 53. d 54. d 55. b 56. e 57. c 58. a 59. d 60. d
61. a 62. c 63. e 64. a 65. a 66. b 67. b 68. c 69. c 70. b
71. a 72. a 73. b 74. d 75. c 76. a 77. b 78. a 79. e 80. e
81. e 82. a 83. d 84. c 85. a 86. c 87. b 88. c 89. a 90. b
91. a 92. b 93. e 94. a 95. c 96. b 97. b 98. c 99. b 100. a
101. c 102. a 103. c 104. a 105. b 106. b 107. d 108. c 109. d 110. a
111. b 112. b 113. b 114. a 115. a 116. b 117. d 118. b 119. b 120. b
121. d 122. c 123. d 124. a 125. a 126. b 127. a 128. e 129. a 130. d
131. d 132. b 133. a 134. b 135. a 136. e 137. a 138. c 139. b 140. a
141. c 142. b 143. d 144. a 145. c 146. a 147. d 148. b 149. b 150. d
151. a 152. e 153. c 154. a 155. b

1-7)

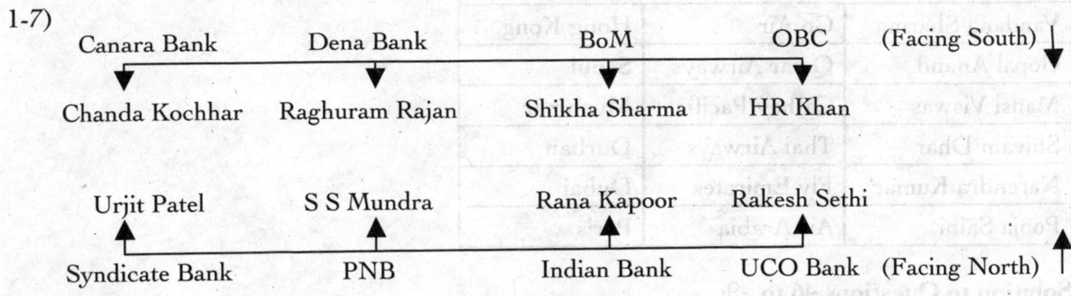

8-10)

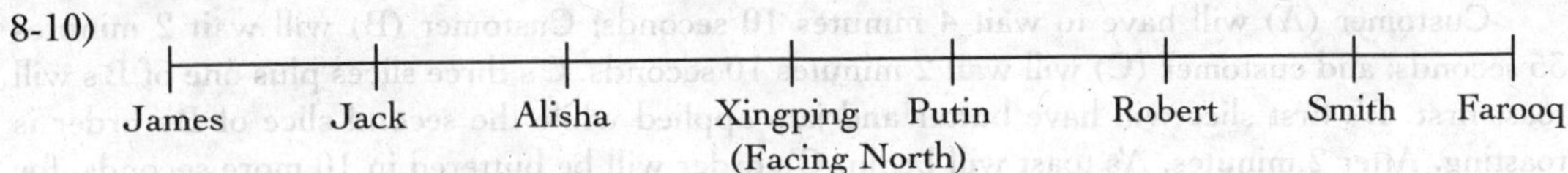

11) Statement I gives the No. of students present today=36
Statement II, tell us about absent students=4

12) Rahul→186 to 193
Robin→181 to 186,
Total=186

13) The word has vowels and consonants both.

15) Statement I-Gautam faces west.
Statement II-No clue to direction.

21-25)

Days	Team	Venue
Monday	Nepal	Mohali
Tuesday	Netherlands	Dharamshala
Wednesday	Hongkong	New Delhi
Thursday	India	Bengaluru
Friday	UAE	Mumbai
Saturday	Afghanistan	Chennai
Sunday	Ireland	Kolkata

26-30)

Name	Airline	Destination
Prashant Pandey	Lufthansa	Brazil
Roshni Singh	AirIndia	South Africa
Ashish Gupta	Virgin Airline	Sydney
Swati Gupta	British Airways	New York

Vandana Sharma	Go Air	Hong Kong
Gopal Anand	Qatar Airways	Seoul
Mansi Viswas	Cathay Pacific	Myanmar
Shivam Dhar	Thai Airways	Durban
Narendra Kumar	Fly Emirates	Dubai
Pooja Saini	Air Arabia	Paris

Solution to Questions 46 to 49:

Total Combined waiting time = 8 minutes 55 seconds

Customer (A) will have to wait 4 minutes 10 seconds; Customer (B) will wait 2 minutes 35 seconds; and customer (C) will wait 2 minutes 10 seconds. C's three slices plus one of B's will toast first. B's first slice will have butter and jam applied while the second slice of B's order is toasting. After 2 minutes, A's toast will begin. C's order will be buttered in 10 more seconds, for a total of 2 minutes 10 seconds. Then, B's last slice will be buttered and jam applied, for a total waiting time of 2 minutes 35 seconds. After A's order is toasted and 1 slice buttered, 4 minutes 10 seconds will have elapsed.

46. Customer C will be served 1st after 2 minutes 10 seconds. Hence option (c) is the answer.

47. Customer B will be served 2nd. Hence option (b) is the answer.

48. Customer A will be served 3rd. Hence option (a) is the answer.

49. Combined total waiting time = Waiting time of A + Waiting time of B + Waiting time of C = 4:10 + 2:35 + 2:10 = 8 minutes 55 seconds. Hence option (b) is the answer.

50. As obvious from the explanation above, A will wait for 4 minutes 10 seconds. Hence option (b) is the answer.

52. Total price of fruits with Mr. Fruit is 23 x 16 + 46 x 24 + 7 x 40 + 20 x 34 + 5 x 28 + 16 x 30 = Rs. 368 + Rs. 1104 + Rs. 280 + Rs. 680 + Rs. 140 + Rs. 480 = Rs. 3052. Total number of fruits with Mr. Fruit is 16 + 24 + 40 + 34 + 28 + 30 = 172. Average price of fruits with Mr. Fruit = (3052/172) = Rs. 17.74

53. The total price of mangoes with Mr. Fruit is 16 x 23 = Rs. 368.
Total price of 14 mangoes = 368 – (20 + 28) = Rs. 320
Out of the given 14 mangoes assume that maximum number of mangoes have price equal to Rs. 21.
The maximum price of any mango out of these 14 mangoes is Rs. 27
So, 9 x 21 + 1 x 23 + 4 x 27 = Rs. 320
Therefore, the number of mangoes whose price is more than Rs. 21 is 1 + 4 + 1 = 6.

54. The price of the 18 peaches with Mr. Fruit whose price is not known to us = X
X = 20 x 34 – (16 + 26 + 4 x 22 + 10 x 18) = Rs. 370
Assume that maximum number of peaches have price equal to Rs. 17
370 = 25 x 8 + 17 x 10. Number of peaches with Mr. Fruit whose price is at least Rs. 25 is at most 8 + 1 = 9.

55. The total price of the guavas with Mr. Fruit is 5 x 28 = 140
The total price of the 26 guavas whose price is not known is 140 – (3 + 8) = Rs. 129.
Assume maximum number of guavas have price equal to Rs. 7
129 = 8 x 7 + 1 x 5 + 17 x 4. Therefore, the number of guavas with Mr. Fruit whose price is less than the average price of the guavas with Mr. Fruit is at least 17 + 1 = 18.

126. Fiduciary means Law involving trust or a trustee or a guardian.

127. Espionage is the practice of spying or using spies.

128. Torn down is a phrase which means to demolish.

129. Wind-up is to conclude so the opposite is start.

130. Bankrupt is a person who is judged by a court to be insolvent, whose property is taken and disposed of, so the opposite is solvent.

131. Use preposition 'to' in place of 'than'. 'to' is used with 'prefer

132. Preposition 'to' will not be used with 'resembles'.

133. Write 'the first two' in place of 'the two first'.

134. Write 'snows' in place of 'snowed'.

135. Use 'among' in place of 'between'. For more than two person or things, we write 'among'.

139. 'major problems' is correct. We use plural noun after the structure "One + of".

140. 'ignore'. The problem of unemployment cannot be ignored.

141. Look at- is phrasal verb. Hence preposition 'at' is correct.

142. 'through'. Is correct preposition in this context.

143. "deal with" is correct phrase.

144. 'technological progress' fits in the context correctly. According to the meaning we need positive phrase to express the complete meaning.

145. 'full employment'.

146. 'due to' is correct phrase.

147. eradicate- destroy completely; put an end to.

148. Not only, but also – is a correlative conjunction. Always used in a pair.

SBI PO Mains MOCK Test Paper 9

Structure of this MOCK Test

S. No.	Name of section	No. of Questions	Total marks	Allotted Time
1	Reasoning and Computer Aptitude	45	60	60 minutes
2	Data Analysis and Interpretation	35	60	45 minutes
3	General/ Economy/ Banking Awareness	40	40	35 minutes
4	English Language	35	40	40 minutes
Total		155	200	3 hours

- There is 1/4th Negative marking for every wrong answer.
- If a question is left blank, i.e. no answer is marked by the candidate, there will be no penalty for that question

Section 1: Reasoning and Computer Aptitude

A word and number arrangement machine when given an input line of words and numbers rearranges them following a particular rule in each step. The following is an illustration of input and rearrangement.

Input: *go now 53 39 18 for again 66*
Step 1 : 66 go now 53 39 18 for again
Step 2 : 66 again go now 53 39 18 for
Step 3 : 66 again 53 go now 39 18 for
Step 4 : 66 again 53 for go now 39 18
Step 5 : 66 again 53 for 39 go now 18
Step 6 : 66 again 53 for 39 go now 18
Step 7 : 66 again 53 for 39 go 18 now

As per the rule followed in the following questions the appropriate step for the given input.

1. Input: chanoyu wink 24 44 57 Heinz beech 71.
How many steps will be required to complete the rearrangement?
a. Three b. Four c. Five
d. Six e. Cannot be determined

2. Input: *trees 18 27 desk are 91 hour zero 31 16 chairs.*
Which of the following will be step 4 ?
a. 91 are 31 trees 18 27 desk hour zero 16 chairs
b. 91 trees 18 27 desk are hour zero 31 16 chairs
c. 91 are 31 chairs trees 18 27 desk hour zero 16
d. 91 are 31 chairs 27 desk 18 trees hour zero 16
e. None of these

3. Step 2 of an input is: *94 car 86 window shut 52 31 house*
Which of the following is definitely the input?
a. 94 car window 86 shut 52 31 house
b. 86 window 94 car shut 52 31 house
c. Car shut window 86 52 31 house 94
d. Cannot be determined
e. None of these

4. Input: *show 51 37 now for 82 49* goot
Which of the following steps will be the last but one?
a. Step 7 b. Step 8 c. Step 6 d. Step 5 e. None of these

5. Input: *how two 38 23 87 43 room over*
which of the following steps will be the last?
a. Step 4 b. Step 5 c. Step 6 d. Step e. None of these

6. **Directions (6–10): Study the information and answer the questions that follow:**
If A + B means A is the mother of B;
A – B means A is the brother B;
A % B means A is the father of B and
A x B means A is the sister of B,
which of the following shows that P is the maternal uncle of Q?
a. Q – N + M x P b. P + S x N – Q
c. P – M + N x Q d. Q – S % P e. None of these

7. If A + B means A is the brother of B;
A – B means A is the sister of B and
A x B means A is the father of B.
Which of the following means that C is the son of M?
a. M – N x C + F
b. F – C + N x M
c. N + M – F x C
d. M x N – C + F
e. None of these

8. Pointing to a photograph Lata says, "He is the son of the only son of my grandfather." How is the man in the photograph related to Lata?

a. Brother
b. Uncle
c. Cousin
d. Data is inadequate
e. None of these

9. If A + B means A is the father of B;
A – B means A is the brother B;
A % B means A is the wife of B and
A x B means A is the mother of B,
which of the following shows that M is the maternal grandmother of T?
a. M x N % S + T
b. M x N – S % T
c. M x S – N % T
d. M x N x S % T
e. None of these

10. If A + B means A is the sister of B; A x B means A is the wife of B, A % B means A is the father of B and A – B means A is the brother of B. Which of the following means T is the daughter of P?
a. P x Q % R + S – T
b. P x Q % R – T + S
c. P x Q % R + T – S
d. P x Q % R + S + T
e. None of these

Directions (11–14):-
Marks A as answer if statement I alone is sufficient to answer the question
Marks B as answer if statement II alone is sufficient to answer the question
Marks C as answer if statement I and II together are sufficient to answer the question but neither statement alone is sufficient to answer the question
Mark D as the answer if the answer cannot be determined by both the statements
Mark E as the answer if either of the statement can answer the question

11. How many people are there in the plain?
Statement I : 25% passengers are women and 35% are children.
Statement II : There are 24 men in the plain

12. What is the difference between monthly income of Ram and Chaaru?
Statement I : Ram earns Rs. 6000 less than Shaam
Statement II : Chaaru earns Rs. 6000 more than Shaam.

13. Is x divisible by 28 ?
Statement I : x is divisible by 20
Statement II : x is divisible by 84

14. P,Q,R,S and T are five friends. Their mean age is 18. What is the age of R ?
Statement I : P's age is 18
Statement II : Q's age is 2 years less than T and T's age is 6 years less than S.
Statement III : R's age is 6 years more than B's age and 4 years more than T's age.

Directions (15–20): Study the information and answer the following questions:
'P $ Q' means 'P is not smaller than Q'
'P @ Q' means 'P is neither smaller than nor equal to Q'
'P # Q' means 'P is neither greater than nor equal to Q'
'P & Q' means 'P is neither greater than nor smaller than Q'
'P * Q' means 'P is not greater than Q'

15. Statements:
H @ T, T # F, F& E, E * V
Conclusions:
I. V $ F
II. E @ T
III. H @ V
IV. T # V
a. Only I II and III are true
b. Only I II and IV are true
c. Only II III and IV are true
d. Only I III and IV are true
e. All I II III and IV are true

16. Statements::
D # R, R * K, K @ F, F $ J
Conclusions:
I. J # R
II. J # K
III. R # F
IV. K @ D
a. Only I II and III are true
b. Only II III and IV are true
c. Only I III and IV are true
d. All I II III and IV are true
e. None of these

17. Statements:
N & B, B $ W, W # H, H * M
Conclusions:
I. M @ W
II. H @ N
III. W & N
IV. W # N
a. Only I is true
b. Only III is true
c. Only IV is true
d. Only either III or IV are true
e. Only either III or IV and I are true

18. Statements:
R * D, D $ J, J # M, M @ K
Conclusions:
I. K # J
II. D @ M
III. R # M
IV. D @ K
a. None is true
b. Only I is true
c. Only II is true
d. Only III is true
e. Only IV is true

19. Statements:
M $ K, K @ N, N * R, R # W
Conclusions:
I. W @ K
II. M $ R

III. K @ W
IV. M @ N
a. Only I and II are true
b. Only III and IV are true
c. Only III or IV are true
d. Only II III and IV are true
e. None of these

Directions (20–26) Study the information carefully and answer the question that follows

A, B, C, D, E, F, G and H are eight sportspersons, each of them playing a different game, viz Cricket, Football, Golf, Hockey, Chess, Baseball, Badminton and Tennis (not necessarily in the same order). All of them are seated around a circular table facing the centre. A, who plays Golf, sits third to the left of E. The one who plays Baseball sits second to the right of D. D, who plays Badminton, sits second to the right of B, who cannot sit adjacent to E. C, who plays Football, sits between the players of Chess and Baseball. G is a Tennis player, and sits second to the left of H, who is a Cricketer.

20. Who among the following pairs represent immediate neighbours of the Badminton player?
a. GA b. AH c. BH d. AE e. None of these

21. Which of the following is definitely true in the context of F?
a. F sits second to the left of the Cricketer.
b. F sits third to the right of A.
c. F is a Hockey player.
d. The one who plays Golf is not an immediate neighbour of F.
e. None of these

22. What is the position of B with respect to the Chess player?
a. Fourth to the right
b. Third to the left
c. Second to the right
d. Fourth to the left
e. Second to the left

23. How many persons are sitting between A and the one who plays Hockey, if counted clockwise from A?
a. One b. Two c. Three d. Four e. Six

24. Which of the following games is played by the one who sits second to the left of the Baseball player?
a. Chess b. Tennis c. Cricket d. Football e. None of these

25. The one who sits between the Tennis player and the cricketer plays which of the following games?
a. Hockey b. Golf c. Badminton d. Chess e. None of these

26. In which of the following pairs the player of first game (of the pair) sits on the immediate left of the player of the second game (of the pair)?
a. Tennis-Football b. Cricket-Hockey c. Baseball-Golf
d. Football-Chess e. Chess-Golf Directions

Directions (27–30): Go through the information given below and solve the questions based on it.
In a certain code, her idea has 'merit' is written as 'fo la bu na', 'merit list has been displayed' is written as 'jo ke la si na', 'her name displayed there' is written as 'ya si bu zo' and 'name in merit list' is written as 'na ya go ke'.

27. What does 'ke stand for?
a. been b. has c. merit d. name e. list

28. What is the code for 'idea'?
a. fo b. la c. bu
d. na e. Either bu or na

29. Which of the following represents 'name has been displayed'?
a. ya la ke si b. jo Si ya Ia c. si jo ke na
d. bu ya ke la e ya si jo zo

30. In a certain code 'PLANT' is written as '$@2*©' and 'YIELD' is written as 'β64@%'. How is 'DELAY' written in that code?
a. β4*2% b. β4@2% c. %42@β
d. %4@2β e. None of these

Directions (31–45) Answer the questions based on your knowledge of computers.

31. A process known as ____________ is used by large retailers to study trends.
a. data mining b. data selection c. POS
d. data conversion e. None of these

32. terminals (formerly known as cash registers) are often connected to complex inventory and sales computer systems.
a. Data b. Point-of-sale (POS)
c. Sales d. Query e. None of these

33. A/An ____________ system is a small, wireless handheld computer that scans an item's tag and pulls up the current price (and any special offers) as you shop.
a. PSS b. POS c. inventory d. data mining e. None of these

34. ____________ tags, when placed on any object, can be used to record and track in a database all of the animal's movements.
a. POS b. RFID c. PPS d. GPS e. None of these

35. Technology no longer protected by copyright, available to everyone, is considered to be:
a. proprietary b. open c. experimental
d. in the public domain e. None of these

36. Computers process data into information by working exclusively with:
a. multimedia b. words c. characters d. numbers e. None of these

37. What term describes explanatory text attached to a cell?
a. Comment b. Type c. Hyperlink d. Dialog e. Put

38. Which language is most suited for commercial applications?
a. Fortran b. Cobol c. Basic d. Prolog e. None of these

39. How many margins are on a page?
a. Two (header and footer) b. Four (top, bottom, right, left)
c. Two (landscape and portrait) d. Two (top and bottom) e. None of these

40. Nibble describes a bits combination of?
a. 5 bits b. 6 bits c. 7 bits d. 4 bits e. None of these

41. The ________ becomes different shapes depending on the task you are performing?
a. Active tab b. Insertion point c. Mouse pointer
d. Ribbon e. None of these

42. A key that will erase information from the computer's memory and characters on the screen
a. Edit b. Delete key c. Dummy out
d. Trust key e. None of these

43. Screen that comes on when you turn on your computer that shows all the icons _____
a. Desktop b. Face to face c. Viewer
d. View space e. None of these

44. With which of the following all formulas in excel starts ?
a. / b. + c. = d. # e. it can vary

45. A byte can hold one ____________ of data.
a. bit b. binary digit c. character d. kilobyte e. None of these

Section 2: Data Analysis and Interpretation

Directions for questions 46–50: Go through the data set given below and solve the questions based on it.

The following pie charts show the break-up of the annual expenditures of two private sector companies:

SYNERGY LTD (TOTAL EXPENDITURE IN 2008 = Rs. 100000)

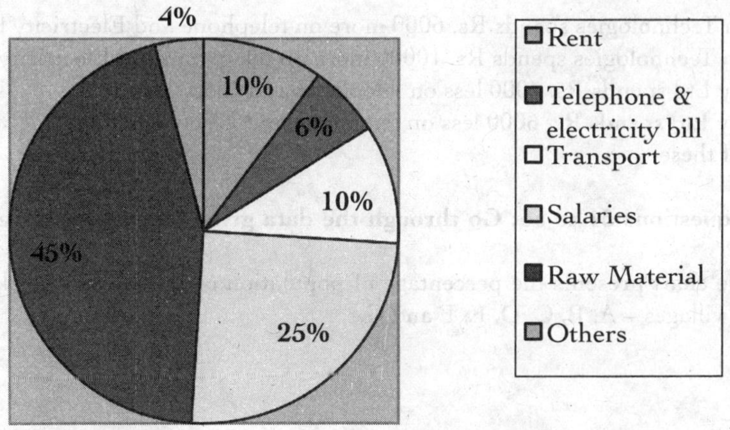

PODIUM TECHNOLOGIES (TOTAL EXPENDITURE IN 2008 = Rs. 80000)

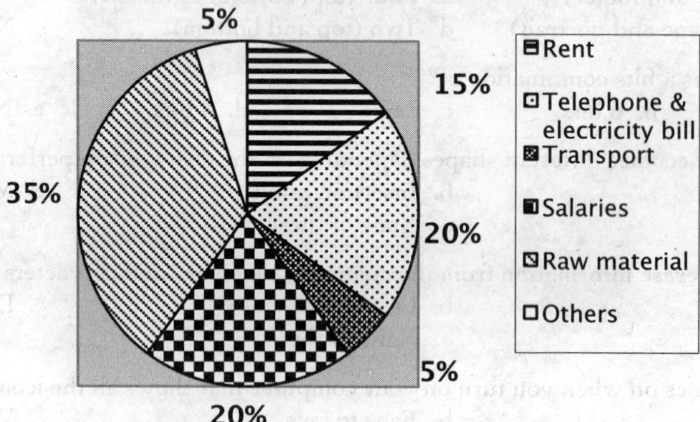

46. The amount spent on transport by Podium technologies is what percentage of the amount spent by Synergy Ltd on transport?
a. 30% b. 35% c. 40% d. 45% e. 60%

47. The expenditure on raw material for both companies taken together, is what fraction of the total expenditure in 2008?
a. 0.2 b. 0.25 c. 0.3 d. 0.4 e. 0.6

48. Both Synergy Ltd and Podium Technologies spend the same amount on which category?
a. Rent b. Transport c. Salaries d. Others e. None of these

49. For which category the difference in expenditure is maximum?
a. Telephone & Electricity Bill b. Transport c. Salaries
d. Raw Material e. Others

50. What is the difference in the amount spent by the two companies on telephone and Electricity bills?
a. Podium Technologies spends Rs. 6000 more on telephone and Electricity bills.
b. Podium Technologies spends Rs. 10000 more on telephone and Electricity bills.
c. Synergy Ltd spends Rs. 4000 less on telephone and Electricity bills.
d. Synergy Ltd spends Rs. 6000 less on telephone and Electricity bills.
e. None of these

Direction for questions 51 to 55: Go through the data given below and solve the questions based on it.

Below given pie chart presents the percentage of population of Bachwaran block comprising of the following 7 villages – A, B, C, D, E, F and G.

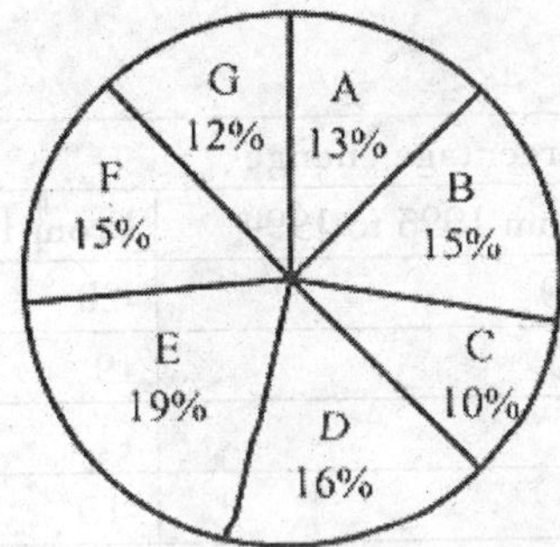

Table gives the percentage of the population in that particular village below poverty line:

Village	% population below poverty line
A	55
B	48
C	36
D	60
E	42
F	43
G	49

51. In 1996, the population of villages A as well as B is increased by 10% from the year 1995. If the population of village A in 1995 was 5000 and the percentage of population below poverty line in 1996 remains same as in 1995, find the population of village B below poverty line in 1996.
a. 3128 b. 3264 c. 3168 d. 3100 e. 3200

52. If in 1997 the population of village D is increased by 10% and the population of village G is reduced by 5% from 1995 and the population of village G in 1995 was 9000, what is the total population of village D and G in 1997?
a. 21750 b. 21670 c. 22000 d. 22500 e. 23000

53. If in 1995 the total population of the seven villages together was 55,000 approximately, what will be population of village F in that year below poverty line?
a. 3000 b. 3600 c. 3700 d. Cannot be determined e. 2500

54. If the population of village C below poverty line in 1995 was 1520, what was the approximate population of village F in 1995?
a. 5800 b. 6100 c. 6400 d. 6500 e. 5500

55. The population of village C is 2000 in 1995. What will be the ratio of population of village C below poverty line to that of the village E below poverty line in that year?
a. 2/7 b. 4/7 c. 6/7 d. 3/7 e. 1/7

Direction for questions 56 to 60: Go through the data given below and solve the questions based on it.

The percentage change in sales of six departmental stores from 1993 to 1995 is shown in the following table:

Store	Percentage change	
	From 1993 to 1994	From 1994 to 1995
UCB	+20	-20
Van	-20	+9
Wrangler	+5	+12
X-tra	-7	-15
Yo	+17	-8
Zodiac	+21	+9

56. In 1995 which of the stores had greater sales than any of the other stores?
a. Van b. Wrangler c. Zodiac d. cannot be determined e. Yo

57. In store Yo the sales for 1994 amounted to about what percentage of the sales for 1995?
a. 117 b. 109 c. 101 d. 113 e. 121

58. If in 1993 the sales in store Wrangler amounted to Rs. X, the sales for that store in 1995 amounted to:
a. 1.5x b. 1.17x c. 1.32x d. 1. 61x e. 1.23x

59. Which of the following has the maximum percentage increase in the sales in 1995 over 1993 ?
a. Van b. Wrangler c. Zodiac d. cannot be determined e. Yo

60. For how many of the stores given in the table can we definitely determine that if that particular store's sales in 1995 is more than the its sales in 1993?
a. 0 b. 1 c. 2 d. 3 e. None of these

Direction for questions 61 to 64: Go through the data given below and solve the questions based on it.

Table 1 give the transportation cost of a product from six factories F1, F2, F3, F4, F5 and F6 to five warehouses W1, W2, W3, W4 and W5.

	W1	W2	W3	W4	W5
F1	60	25	45	40	80
F2	85	40	45	60	75
F3	80	20	45	50	90
F4	90	40	55	25	70
F5	95	20	40	45	80
F6	85	35	50	50	75

Table 2 give the transportation cost of the same product from five warehouses W1, W2, W3, W4 and W5 to six retailers R1, R2, R3, R4, R5 and R6.

	R1	R2	R3	R4	R5	R6
W1	40	20	40	30	85	25
W2	50	50	45	60	70	30
W3	20	10	50	50	80	35
W4	40	30	45	40	90	40
W5	50	30	50	40	70	30

61. What is the minimum transportation cost incurred in transferring the product from any factory to any retailer?
    a. Rs. 45 b. Rs. 50 c. Rs. 55 d. Rs. 60 e. Rs. 65

62. What is the maximum transportation cost incurred in transferring the product from any factory to any retailer?
    a. Rs. 175 b. Rs. 180 c. Rs. 170 d. Rs. 190 e. None of these

63. What is the minimum transportation cost at which the product can be supplied to R4 from any factory?
    a. Rs. 45 b. Rs. 50 c. Rs. 65 d. Rs. 70 e. Rs. 80

64. What is the maximum transportation cost at which the product can be supplied to Rs.3 from any factory?
    a. Rs. 145 b. Rs. 150 c. Rs. 140 d. Rs. 130 e. None of these

Direction for questions 65–69: Go through the data set given below and solve the questions based on it.

The following table gives the point scored by each of the ten teams of F1 racing in five races i.e. Spanish G.P., Italian G.P., American G.P., Malaysian G.P., Australian G.P.

Team	Races				
	Spanish	Italian	American	Malaysian	Australia
Ferrari	71	84	94	72	50
McLaren	74	70	96	54	76
Honda	78	72	90	52	75
BMW Sauber	82	80	69	81	68
Toyota	90	68	64	77	48
Renault	68	57	84	63	44
Red Bull	69	56	74	58	79
William	66	52	77	61	53
Super Agubi	85	58	81	68	58
Force India	92	62	60	60	61

The performance of a team, A is said to be better than that of any other team, B, if A scored more marks than B in at least three of the five given races.
Answer the following questions on the basis of the table given above.

65. The team whose performance is better than that of all the other teams is
a. BMW Sauber b. Ferrari c. McLaren d. Toyota e. Force India

66. The performance of how many teams is better than that of Red Bull but not better than that of BMW Sauber?
a. 4 b. 3 c. 5 d. 7 e. 2

67. If the scores of the teams in the Spanish G.P are not considered due to foul play, which team is better than BMW Sauber?
a. Honda b. McLaren c. Renault d. Ferrari e. Force India

68. The team whose performance is better than that of Super Agubi, even though it scored less than Super Agubi in Australian G.P. ?
a. Honda b. Ferrari c. Toyota d. Renault e. Red Bull

69. Which of the following is/are true?
i. The performance of Red Bull is better than that of William.
ii. Performance of BMW Sauber is better than that of Red Bull even though Red Bull scored more in the Australian G.P.
iii. The performance of only one team is better than that of William.
a. Only (i) b. Only (ii) c. Only (iii) d. (i) &(ii) e. All three

70. Length of a rectangle is increased by 30% and breadth is decreased by 20%. What is the percentage change in the perimeter of the rectangle due to this?
a. 5% increase b. 10% increase c. 5% decrease
d. Cannot be determined e. 10% decrease

71. What is the probability that there are 53 Sundays and 53 Tuesdays in a leap year?
a. 0 b. 1 c. 0.5 d. 1/3 e. None of these

72. By multiplying with which of the following numbers does the product of 8 x 9 x 10 x 11 x 12 become a perfect square?
a. 55 b. 11 c. 165 d. 310 e. 22

73. Find the height of the cylinder whose volume is 511 cm^3 and the area of the base 36.5 cm^2.
a. 3. 5 cm b. 10.5 cm c. 14 cm d. 11 cm e. None of these

74. Hoppers' Stop stocks four styles of trousers. For each style, there are ten different possible waist sizes, six different trousers lengths and four colour choices. How many different types of trousers could the store have?
a. 1024 b. 960 c. 921 d. 924 e. 124

75. There are three inlet taps whose diameters are 1 cm, 2 cm and 3 cm respectively. Rate of flow of water is directly proportional to the square of the diameter. It takes 9 mins for the smallest pipe to fill an empty tank. Find the time taken to fill an empty tank when all the three taps are opened.
a. 9/14 b. 14/9 c. 3 d. 1 e. None of these

76. Likhit earns x% on the first Rs. 2000 and y% on the rest of his income. If he earns Rs. 700 from Rs. 4000 income and Rs. 900 from Rs. 5000 income, find x%.
a. 20% b. 15% c. 25% d. 10% e. None of these

77. If a number is divided by 15, it leaves a remainder of 7. If thrice the number is divided by 5, then what is the remainder?
a. 5 b. 6 c. 7 d. 1 e. 2

78. The greatest possible number of points of intersection of 8 straight lines and 4 circles is
a. 32 b. 64 c. 76 d. 104 e. 28

79. If x and y are positive integers for which $2^x3^y = 1296$, what is the value of x + y?
a. 8 b. 9 c. 10 d. 11 e. 7

80. If 4 whole numbers are taken at random, and multiplied together, then the probability that the last digit in the product is 1, 3, 7 or 9 will be:
a. 13/976 b. 17/529 c. 16/625 d. 13/625 e. None of these

Section 3: General and Banking Awareness

81. According to the data released by the Registrar General and Census Commissioner on 25 Aug, the population growth rate of India in the decade 2001-2011 was found to be
a. 24.6 per cent b. 17.7 per cent c. 16.8 per cent
d. 15.5 per cent e. 8.4 per cent

82. Who won the women's 100 m gold at the IAAF World Championships, Beijing 2015?
a. Shelly-Ann Fraser-Pryce b. Gelete Burka
c. Blessing Okagbare d. Tori Bowie e. Dafne Schippers

83. Rana Kapoor has received the RBI approval for his re-appointment as MD and CEO of which of the following private banks for 3 years effective from Sep 1, 2015?
a. Bandhan Bank b. IDFC Bank c. YES Bank
d. Federal Bank e. Kotak Mahindra Bank

84. The govt on 25 Aug launched a health service called SEHAT. The term SEHAT stands for
a. Social Enterprise for Health And Treatment
b. Social Entity for Health And Telemedicine
c. Social Endeavour for Health And Treatment
d. Social Endeavour for Health And Telemedicine
e. None of these

85. Retired judge ML Tahaliyani was on 24 Aug sworn in as the new Lokayukta of which of the following states?
a. Uttar Pradesh b. Delhi c. Gujarat
d. Maharashtra e. Andhra Pradesh

86. The govt on 25 Aug launched a health service called SEHAT along with ________ to provide healthcare access to citizens irrespective of geographical location connecting Common Service Centres (CSCs)?

a. Sahara Hospital b. Max Healthcare c. Surya Clinic
d. Dr Reddy's Laboratories e. Apollo Hospitals

87. Who among the following are the winners of the men's doubles title of 2015 Cincinnati Masters tennis tournament, the oldest tennis tournament in the US?
a. Marcin Matkowski and Nenad Zimonjic
b. Daniel Nestor and Edouard RogerVasselin
c. Vasek Pospisil and Jack Sock
d. Stan Wawrinka and Leander Paes
e. None of these

88. India and _______ on 24 Aug agreed on a joint financial commitment of up to AUS$ one mn and signed an MoU to strengthen existing partnerships in higher education and research.
a. UK b. Sweden c. Norway d. Germany e. Australia

89. The birth centenary celebrations of Rani Gaidinliu were held by the central govt recently. She was a legendary freedom fighter from
a. Assam b. Nagaland c. Tripura d. Kerala e. Puducherry

90. When RBI was established in 1935, its headquarter was at:
a. Mumbai b. Delhi c. Kolkata d. Chennai e. Shimla

91. In the case of granting loan against a life insurance policy, the banker should see:
a. The existence of insurable interest
b. The surrender value
c. The admission of age
d. All of the above
e. None of the above

92. In Mutual Funds, NAV is the price of ___
a. Entire fund value b. One unit of a fund c. Surrender value
d. Average value of shares e. Dividends paid in a year

93. New Lending Rate on Bank Loans is now calculated as per:
a. Bench Mark Prime Lending Rate (BPLR)
b. Base Rate
c. Prime Lending Rate (PLR)
d. Marginal Cost of Funds based Lending Rate (MCLR)
e. Risk Based Rate

94. According to new norms anyone would be able to register a company in India in how many days?
a. 5 b. 4 c. 7 d. 1 e. 3

95. Naina Lal Kidwai is an independent non-executive director of:
a. Altico Capital
b. Reliance Capital
c. Infrastructure Development Finance Company
d. Shriram Transport Finance
e. None of the above

96. Which Indian bank has launched iWork@Home programme for its women employees?
a. HDFC b. Axis bank c. ICICI Bank d. IDBI Bank e. SBI

97. Who is the present MD and CEO of Multi Commodity Exchange?
a. Balasubramaniam Venkatramani
b. Mrugank Paranjape
c. Manoj Vaish
d. Praveen Kumar Singhal
e. Mansi Aggarwal

98. Flipkart has launched an online wallet-Flipkart Money. What purpose does E-wallet serve?
a. E-wallet is an online prepaid account under which user can deposit money in advance and can be used as payment
b. E-wallet is an offline prepaid account where one can stock money to be used when required
c. E-wallet is an online prepaid account under which user can purchase online and they can pay later.
d. E-wallet is a feature of web browser that allows a user to store personal details for identification purpose
e. None of the above

99. The bank does not open a saving account in the name of:
a. Government Departments b. Municipal Corporations/ Committees
c. Panchayat Samities d. State Housing Boards e. All the above

100. The Reserve Bank of India publishes the classification of demand deposits with the commercial banks. Which of the following are included in demand deposits?
a. Fixed deposits held as security for advances is a classification of time deposits
b. Deposits held as security for advances which are repayable on demand
c. Current deposits
d. Demand liabilities portion of saving bank deposits
e. b, c and d

101. Time deposits include:
a. Fixed deposits
b. Cash certificates, recurring deposits
c. Time liabilities portion of saving bank deposits
d. Staff security deposits
e. All of the above

102. Which of the following is included in the banking reforms in India?
a. To strengthen risk management
b. Providing easy credit to all
c. Provide guaranteed subsidy from the government
d. Both b and c
e. None of the above

103. Which of the following Nation is not a member country of Shanghai Cooperation Organization (SCO)?
a. Peru b. Kazakhstan c. Tajikistan d. China e. Russia

104. What is the purpose for RBI allowing RRBs to open their branches in tier-II cities without asking for permit?
  a. To empower RRBs with the powers that RBI has
  b. To increase the reach of banking service in tier-II cities.
  c. To generate money from tier-II cities
  d. To increase the number of RRBs more than other commercial bank in tier-II cities
  e. None of the above

105. Which of the following is not associated with risks related to risk management in banks?
  a. Credit risk b. Market risk c. Fund risk
  d. Operational risk e. None of these

106. Which was the first Indian commercial bank wholly owned and managed by Indians opened in the year 1911?
  a. Bank of Madras
  b. Central Bank of India
  c. State Bank of India
  d. Hindustan Bank
  e. Union Bank of India

107. Financial activities tax and Financial stability contribution is proposed by ?
  a. G-8 b. SAARC Summit (second) c. G-20
  d. SAARC Summit (First) e. None of the above

108. Which of the following statement(s) is/are true about promissory note?
  a. It is always in writing
  b. It has an unconditional undertaking called promise
  c. The promise is to pay money
  d. The money is to be pay money
  e. All of the above

109. On recommendation in which of the following committee NABARD was established?
  a. C. Rangarajan Committee
  b. Vijay Kelkar Committee
  c. Sivaraman Committee
  d. Chelliah Committee
  e. None of the above

110. Money lent in the money market for one day is referred as:
  a. Notice money b. Long term loan
  c. Short term loan d. Call money e. None of these

111. If the customer can do all transactions only in a branch and the branch has no online access, it is called............
  a. Online Banking b. Internet Banking
  c. Virtual Banking d. Brick and Mortar Banking e. None of these

112. As a part of financial inclusion, Bank on Wheels is a banking kiosk in a mobile van which goes to various rural villages as per the predetermined schedule to provide the banking services to the rural Indians. This Vehicle Tracking through GPRS. GPRS stands for ....

a. General Packet Radio Service
b. General Packet Running Service
c. Gross Packet Radio Service
d. Gain Packet Radio Service
e. General Packet Radio Store

113. A collection of investment tools such as stocks, shares, mutual funds, bonds, cash and so on depending on the investor's income, budget and convenient time frame. The art of selecting the right investment policy for the individuals in terms of minimum risk and maximum return is called as ....

a. Portfolio management
b. Credit creation
c. Amortized management
d. Zero account
e. None of these

114. Which bank has launched the country's first contactless debit and credit cards on 7 January 2015?

a. HDFC
b. SBI
c. ICICI
d. Union Bank of India
e. Yes Bank

115. On 7 May 2015, RBI said with effect from September 1, 2015 all new cards issued - debit and credit, domestic and international - by banks shall be EMV chip and pin based cards. EMV stands for ....

a. Europay, Mastro and Visa
b. Euro, Master Card and Visa
c. Europay, Master Card and Visulas
d. Entitlement of Master Card and Visa
e. Europay, Master Card and Visa

116. Which is the first bank to get ISO certificate?

a. Corporation Bank
b. UBI
c. Canara Bank
d. Syndicate Bank
e. ICICI

117. Kisan Credit Card (KCC) scheme introduced in .... has emerged as an innovative credit delivery mechanism to meet the production credit requirements of the farmers in a timely and hassle - free manner.

a. 1998
b. 2000
c. 2001
d. 1991
e. 2004

118. To make KCC a Smart Card cum Debit Card, Government of India had constituted a Working Group under the Chairmanship of ....

a. C. Ranga Rajan
b. Chanda Kocchar
c. Arundhathi Bhattacharya
d. D. Subba Rao
e. T.M. Bhasin

119. In 2014, Competition Commission of India probed the merger between regional rural banks sponsored by Punjab National Bank and ....

a. Andhra Bank
b. Union Bank of India
c. State Bank of India
d. Syndicate Bank
e. None of these

120. A personal loan is a kind of unsecured loan which can be used for any purpose that the borrower deems necessary. The loan backed only by promise to repay, and for this reason the personal loan also called.........

a. Signature loans
b. Secured loans
c. Priority sector loan
d. Transfer loan
e. None of these

Section 4: English Language

Directions: Read the following passage carefully and answer the questions given below it. Certain words are given in bold to help you locate them while answering some of the questions.

The subject "Good Governance" is both topical and timely. It is an axiom of political science that a State comes into being for life but it exists for good life. The duty of the state is not only to protect life and liberty but goes further, to enable the people to live in a measure of physical and mental comfort. Democracy is a government by the citizens themselves. The people should realise that they are responsible for choosing the right and proper persons to represent them in national affairs. In colonial administration the government was different from the people. Those governments ruled but without the consent and concurrence of the people. This old concept still persists in the masses today. They do not realise that the general election is the occasion for them to choose a government for themselves. On the contrary, the masses feel that the franchise is a patronage to be conferred on their kith and kin, or the local candidate, or one of their caste and religious fraternity. In mature democracies, a person who changes his party affiliation or crosses the floor, seldom gets re-elected by the electorate. They do not trust him to stand firm by the policies and programmes proposed by him. In India a person who was in the Congress Government and immediately thereafter in the Janata Government and then in Chandrashekhar Government was re-elected and came once again into the Congress Government!

The electorate votes for a criminal or a corrupt candidate, and bemoans that the country has a bad government. The electorate does not realise that even as it contributes to its own household expenditure, it has to contribute to the country's governance. It is easily misled by the unscrupulous promises of political parties of free food, free clothes, free electricity, free everything. Even enlightened people plead for tax concessions, subsidies and incentives oblivious of the fact that they are met by borrowings which in turn impose burdens indirectly on themselves. Besides, in a true democracy, the people voluntarily observe the laws, rules and regulations as they are forged by themselves in the interest of good governance. It is only because 90% of the people abide by the laws and 10% transgress them that the state is able to maintain order and harmony. If the situation were reversed with 90% transgressing the law and 10% abiding by it, there can be no organised society, no peace and harmony. Some of the advanced countries, notably Switzerland, have perhaps the highest degree of compliance. A mere board stating that the road is closed will be complied with by almost 100% of the people.

121. Which of the following is supposed to be the most relevant duty of the state?
   a. to ensure sovereignty of the region
   b. to ensure prosperity of the region
   c. to look after the welfare of its people
   d. to develop better terms with other nations
   e. None of these

122. What is the basic difference between democracy and colonial rule?
   a. In a democracy, people's will prevails, whereas in a colonial rule, ruler's will prevails.
   b. Democracy is a rule by different parties whereas a colonial rule is a single-party rule.

c. Democracy can be opposed by the people but such is not the case with colonial rule.
d. A colonial rule can be converted into a democracy but the same cannot happen with a democracy.
e. None of these

123. If the people want to have a responsible government in a democracy
a. they must call for free and fair elections.
b. they should take charge of the elections.
c. they should elect educated and experienced representatives.
d. they should look for single-party rule.
e. they should elect desirable candidates.

124. Why does a person changing his party find it hard to get re-elected in mature democracies?
a. Because political parties suspect his fidelity.
b. Because he loses his image in the political circle.
c. Because his eligibility for fighting elections gets questioned.
d. Because he has to depend upon the stand of his new party.
e. None of these

125. In a country like India, who is mainly responsible for good or bad governance?
a. The system of electing our representatives
b. The political parties
c. The voters
d. The political party in power
e. None of these

126. Which of the following is true in the context of the passage?
a. Good governance is related to the welfare of the people.
b. We have a mature democracy in India.
c. The leaders who change parties face hurdles in getting re-elected in our country.
d. Colonial rule was much better than the present democracy.
e. None of these

127. What makes Switzerland a successful democracy?
a. Clear instructions regarding public concerns marked on boards, even on roadsides
b. High rate of literacy among the populace
c. Law-abiding citizens
d. Governance with a mission
e. None of these

128. Which of the following suggestions may not be necessary to make India a mature democracy?
a. The voters should elect candidates with clean image.
b. The voters should not entertain candidates who frequently change their party and ideology.
c. The voters should shun their narrow interests while voting for their candidates.
d. The people should respect the law of the land.
e. None of these

129. With which stream does the author seem to be related?
a. Sociology
b. History
c. Political Science
d. Constitution of India
e. None of these

Directions: Choose the word which is the same in meaning as the word given in bold as used in the passage.

130. CONCURRENCE
    a. satisfaction b. agreement c. participation d. loyalty e. dependence

131. FRATERNITY
    a. society b. groups c. background d. ethnicity e. brotherhood

132. VOLUNTARILY
    a. basically b. generally c. systematically d. willingly e. unwieldy

Directions: Choose the word which is the opposite in meaning as the word given in bold as used in the passage.

133. SELDOM
    a. hardly b. unopposed c. generally d. majority e. convincingly

134. BEMOAN
    a. laud b. accept c. approve d. weep e. debate

135. OBLIVIOUS
    a. arguing b. veteran c. expert d. aware e. orator

Directions (136–140): Rearrange the following sentences (A), (B), (C), (D), (E. and (F) in the proper sequence to form meaningful paragraph and then answer the questions given below.

a. Knowledge has given him enough power.
b. Man is a rational animal
c. Due to their knowledge philosophers and religious preachers have exercised tremendous influence on the minds of gullible people.
d. He has the power of reasoning, critical judgement and analysis.
e. Thus, in spite of being physically weak, he has succeeded in establishing his supremacy over the animal kingdom.
f. In fact, knowledge helps a man vanquish even a physically stronger being who is ignorant.

136. Which of the following should be the FIRST sentence after rearrangement?
    a. A b. F c. E d. D e. B

137. Which of the following should be the THIRD sentence after rearrangement?
    a. B b. A c. D d. E e. C

138. Which of the following should be the SECOND sentence after rearrangement?
    a. C b. B c. A d. F e. D

139. Which of the following should be the FIFTH sentence after rearrangement?
    a. A b. F c. B d. C e. E

140. Which of the following should be the SIXTH (LAST) sentence after rearrangement?
    a. E b. D c. C d. B e. A

Directions (141–145): Each question below has two blanks, each blank indicating that something has been omitted Find out which option can be used to fill up the blank in the sentence in the same sequence to make it meaningfully complete.

141. Healthy scepticism, a vital __________ for any journalist, has given __________ to credulity, or worse, naiveté.
a. factor, up
b. role, them
c. attribute, way
d. thing, away
e. task, chance

142. 'Samar' ________ about all kinds of people became more and more _________ and even if there was a grain of truth in any of them, there was just no evidence.
a. statements, attacking
b. ideas, scathing
c. pronouncements, outdated
d. allegations, outlandish
e. defamations, severe

143. Every time Vidya went about repeating "Entertainment, entertainment, entertainment!" audiences at awards nights went into _________ as if Voltaire had _________ from his grave.
a. raptures, quipped
b. dark, came
c. silence, grown
d. hallucination, risen
e. enjoy, awaken

144. Whether one believes it or not, there are still some people __________ us who could have become powerful__________ in strength and in financial means.
a. about, either
b. surrounding, neither
c. above, here
d. over, there
e. around, both

145. When politicians became _________ and the bureaucracy __________ it is to the media that people turn for some guidance.
a. corrupt, helpful
b. venal, unresponsive
c. dishonest, strong
d. careless, dictator
e. powerful, autocrat

Directions(146–155):- In the following passage, some of the words have been left out, each of which is indicated by a number. Find the suitable word from the options given against each number and fill up the blanks with appropriate words to make the paragraph meaningfully:

Mohit was born in a small coastal village near Ahmedabad. He always loved reading but the small library in his town was inadequate. There weren't ...*(1)*... many books and many of those had the pages ...*(2)*... out. So he ...*(3)*... to finish those stories. His debut novel was my sweet memories. It is a story about a Man›s journey ...*(4)*... the past, a family drama, ...*(5)*... ...(6)... of secrets. It is an ...*(7)*... to Ahmedabad. And much of this book has been drawn from his own ...*(8)*... up years in the city. He grew up in Ahmedabad and worked for a while in Pune. He had been posted to UK, ...*(9)*... that time so he did a creative writing course there – something he always wanted to do. He went on to publish stories in publications. All his stories start ...*(10)*... a picture he create in his mind. This one had two girls, were sharing secrets with each other. He was now working on his second novel, based on real life story.

146.
a. that b. to c. so d. the e. too

147.
a. torn b. moribund c. released d. signed e. controlled

148.
a. has b. have c. had d. is e. suppose

149.
a. of b. into c. at d. in e. for

150.
a. a b. an c. all d. almost e. the

151.
a. ridiculous b. unearthing c. contradict d. keep e. access

152.
a. owe b. agitate c. cynical d. ode e. imprisoned

153.
a. growing b. giving c. set d. cover e. end

154.
a. offered b. convention c. around d. negotiating e. humiliating

155.
a. get b. dangle c. secure d. with e. betrayed

ANSWER KEY

1. b	2. c	3. d	4. c	5. c	6. c	7. d	8. a	9. a	10. b
11. c	12. d	13. c	14. c	15b.	16. e	17. e	18. a	19. e	20. b
21. e	22. c	23. b	24. e	25. a	26. d	27. e	28. a	29. b	30. d
31. a	32. b	33. a	34. b	35. b	36. d	37. a	38. c	39. b	40. d
41. d	42. d	43. a	44. c	45. c	46. c	47. d	48. d	49. d	50. b
51. c	52. a	53. d	54. b	55. d	56. d	57. b	58. b	59. c	60. 5
61. b	62. b	63. c	64. c	65. a	66. b	67. d	68. b	69. d	70. d
71. a	72. c	73. c	74. b	75. a	76. b	77. d	78. d	79. a	80. c
81. b	82. a	83. c	84. d	85. d	86. e	87. b	88. e	89. b	90. c
91. d	92. b	93. d	94. d	95. a	96. c	97. b	98. a	99. e	100. a
101. e	102. b	103. a	104. b	105. c	106. b	107. c	108. e	109. c	110. d
111. d	112. a	113. a	114. c	115. e	116. c	117. a	118. c	119. d	120. b
121. c	122. a	123. e	124. e	125. c	126. a	127. c	128. e	129. c	130. b
131. e	132. d	133. c	134. a	135. d	136. e	137. b	138. e	139. b	140. a
141. c	142. d	143. a	144. e	145. b	146. e	147. a	148. c	149. b	150. e
151. b	152. d	153. a	154. c	155. d					

Solutions and Explanations:

2. Step 1 : 91 trees 18 27 desk are hour zero 31 16 chairs
Step 2 : 91 are trees 18 27 desk hour zero 31 16 chairs
Step 3 : 91 are 31 trees 18 27 desk hour zero 16 chairs
Step 4 : 91 are 31 chairs trees 18 27 desk hour zero 16
Step 5 : 91 are 31 chairs 27 trees 18 desk hour zero 16
Step 6 : 91 are 31 chairs 27 desk trees 18 hour zero 16
Step 7 : 91 are 31 chairs 27 desk 18 trees hour zero 16
Step 8 : 91 are 31 chairs 27 desk 18 hour trees zero 16
Step 9 : 91 are 31 chairs 27 desk 18 hour 16 trees zero
Step 10 : 91 are 31 chairs 27 desk 18 hour 16 trees zero

4. Step 1 : 82 show 51 37 now for 49 goot
Step 2 : 82 for show 51 37 now 49 goot
Step 3 : 82 for 51 show 37 now 49 goot
Step 4 : 82 for 51 goot show 37 now 49
Step 5 : 82 for 51 goot 49 show 37 now
Step 6 : 82 for 51 goot 49 now show 37
Step 7 : 82 for 51 goot 49 now 37 show

5. Step 1 : 87 how two 38 23 43 room over
Step 2 : 87 how 43 two 38 23 room over
Step 3 : 87 how 43 over two 38 23 room
Step 4 : 87 how 43 over 38 two 23 room
Step 5 : 87 how 43 over 38 room two 23
Step 6 : 87 how 43 over 38 room 23 two

6.

Answer: Option C
P – M → P is the brother of M
M + N → M is the mother of N
N x Q → N is the sister of Q
Therefore, P is the maternal uncle of Q.

7.

Answer: Option D
M x N → M is the father of N
N – C → N is the sister of C
and C + F → C is the brother of F.
Hence, M is the father of C or C is the son of M.

8.

Answer: Option A
The man in the photograph is the son of the only son of Lata's grandfather i.e., the man is the son of Lata's father. Hence, the man is the brother of Lata.

9.

Answer: Option A
M x N → M is the mother of N
N % S → N is the wife of S
and S + T → is the father of T.
Hence, M is the maternal grandmother of T.

10.

Answer: Option B
P x Q → P is the wife of Q
Q % R → Q is the father of R
R – T → R is the brother of T
T + S → T is the sister of S.
Therefore, T is the daughter of P.

11. From Statement I we can conclude that there are 40% men in the plain but we can't find the exact number of passengers
From Statement two: Number of men passengers = 24
By combining both the statements we get, total number of passengers = 24 * 100/40 = (you don't need to calculate the answer)

13. Using statement I - x is divisible by 4 and 5
Using statement II - x is divisible by 3,4, and 7.
By using both statements we can conclude that x is divisible by 28 (4*7), hence answer is C.

14. P+Q+R+S+T = 90
From Statement I: Q+R+S+T = 72
From Statement II: Q = T - 2 and T=S - 6
So S = T + 6
Statement III: R = Q+6 and R = T + 4
Age of every friend can be defined in terms of T's age by using all three statements. So we can reach the answer using all three statements. Hence answer is C.

20-26.

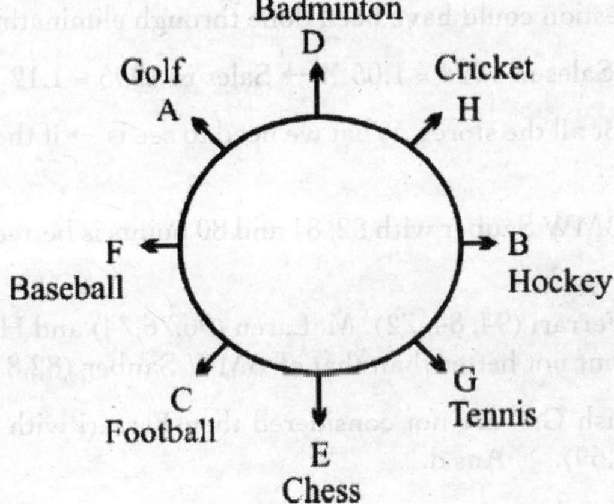

Solution to questions 46–50:

46. Amount spent by podium technologies on transport = 5% of Rs. 80000 = Rs. 4000
Amount spent by Synergy Ltd on transport = 10% of Rs. 100000 = Rs. 10000
Hence, (4000 × 100) / 10000 = 40%. Hence, answer option is (3).

47. (45 + 35) / 200 = 0.4. Hence, answer option is (4).

48. Others for both the companies = Rs. 4000. Hence, answer option is (4).

49. For the category, raw material the difference is maximum = 45000 – 28000 = Rs. 17000. Hence, answer option is (4).

50. Synergy technologies spends 6% of Rs. 100000 = Rs. 6000 on telephone and Electricity bills while Podium Technologies spends 20% of Rs. 80000 = Rs. 16000 on telephone and Electricity bills. Hence, answer option is (2).

51. Population of village B in 1995 = $5000 \times \frac{15}{12.5} = 6000$
Population of B in 1996 = 6600
Population below poverty line = 6600 × 48% = 3168

53. Population figure is approximate. So cannot calculate the population.

54. Population of village F in 1995 = $1520 \times \frac{100}{36} \times \frac{14.5}{10} = 6100$

55. Population of village E in 1995 = $\frac{2000}{10} \times 20 = 4000$
Therefore required ratio = $\frac{2000 \times 36\%}{4000 \times 42\%} = \frac{3}{7}$

Solution to Q56 – Q60:

56. We don't have the initial figures for all the stores. So cannot be calculated that which store has the largest sales in 1995.

57. If the sales in 1993 was 100 → sales in 1994 = 117 → sales in 1995 = 0.92 × 117 = 107. 5 (approx.)
Required percentage = [117/107.5] × 100 = 109% (approx)
Alternatively if x is the amount of sales for store Y in 1994, then 0.92x is the amount of sales for 1995. So, the answer is: 1/0.92
Alternatively this question could have been done through eliminating the options too.

58. Sales in 1993 = X → Sales in 1994 = 1.05 X → Sales in 1995 = 1.12 × 1.05X = 1.17X

60. It can be calculated for all the stores. What we need to see is → if the final percentage change is positive or negative.

65. The performance of BMW Sauber with 82, 81 and 80 points is better than all the other teams. Ans (1)

66. The performance of Ferrari (94, 84, 72), McLaren (96,76,74) and Honda (90,78,75) is better than that of red bull but not better than that of BMW Sauber (82,81,80). Hence, Ans (2)

67. If the points of Spanish G.P. are not considered then Ferrari with 94, 84, 72 is better than BMW Sauber (81,80,69). Ans d.

68. The performance of Ferrari with (94, 84, 72) is better than that of Super Agubi although it scored less than Super Agubi in the Australian G.P. Ans (2)

69. (i) Red bull (79, 74, 69) while William (77, 66, 61) Hence, True.
(ii) Performance of BMW Sauber (82, 81 ,80) is better than that of Red Bull(79, 74, 69) even though Red bull scored more than BMW Sauber in the Australian G.P. (True)
(iii) False Ans (4)

SBI PO Mains MOCK Test Paper 10

Structure of this MOCK Test

S.No.	Name of section	No. of Questions	Total marks	Allotted Time
1	Reasoning and Computer Aptitude	45	60	60 minutes
2	Data Analysis and Interpretation	35	60	45 minutes
3	General/ Economy/ Banking Awareness	40	40	35 minutes
4	English Language	35	40	40 minutes
Total		155	200	3 hours

- There is 1/4th Negative marking for every wrong answer.
- If a question is left blank, i.e. no answer is marked by the candidate, there will be no penalty for that question

Section 1: Reasoning & Computer Aptitude

Direction for questions 1–5: In the following questions some symbols are used with the following meanings as illustrated below:

X * Y means 'X is neither greater than or equal to Y'

X∑ Y means 'X is not smaller than Y'

X@Y means 'X is not greater than Y'

X©Y means 'X is neither greater than nor smaller than Y'

X#Y means 'X is neither smaller than nor equal to Y'

Now in each of the following questions assuming the given statements to be true, find which of the two conclusions 1 and 2 given below them is/are definitely true and give answer accordingly

a) If only conclusion 1 is true

b) If only conclusion 2 is true

c) If either conclusion 1 or 2 is true

d) If neither conclusion 1 nor 2 is true

e) If both conclusion 1 and 2 are true

1. **Statements:** R @ J, F ∑ J, C ∑F
Conclusions:
1. R @ C 2. C # R

2. **Statements:** W @ P, W # E, E * V
Conclusions:
1. P # E 2. V © W

3. **Statements:** J © R, P ∑ R, Z # P
Conclusions:
1. R * Z 2. J @ P

4. **Statements:** G @ O, N © O, H # G
Conclusions:
1. O * H 2. G © N

5. **Statements:** Q * B, M ©B, K ∑ M
Conclusions:
1. K © B 2. Q * K

(6–10). Study the following information carefully and answer the questions given below

Three ladies and four men are a group of friends i.e. R, M, T, S, L, W and Z. Each one has different profession i.e. lawyer, travel agent, air hostess, doctor, professor, consultant and jeweller and each one owns a different car i.e. Alto, Corolla, Santro, Lancer, Ikon, Scorpio, Esteem, not necessary in that order. None of the ladies is a Consultant or a Lawyer. T is an Air Hostess and she owns an Ikon car. R owns a Scorpio. M is not a Doctor. L is a jeweller and he owns Corolla. W is a Lawyer and does not own Alto. Z is a consultant and owns Santro. The Doctor owns Esteem car whereas thee Professor owns Scorpio. The Travel Agent owns an Alto. None of the ladies own a Scorpio.

6. Which car does S own?
a. Alto b. Santro c. Lancer d. Esteem e. None of these

7. Who owns the car Lancer?
a. Z b. M c. W d. Data inadequate
e. None of these

8. What is the profession of R?
a. Professor b. Travel Agent c. Doctor d. Data inadequate
e. None of these

9. Who is the Doctor?
a. R b. S c. L d. Data inadequate
e. None of these

10. Who are the three ladies in the group?
a. T, R, L b. T, M, S c. W, T, M d. Data inadequate
e. None of these

(11–15). Each of the questions below consists of a question and two statements numbered 1 and 2 given below it. You have to decide whether the data given below in the statements are sufficient to answer the questions. Read both the statements and give answer.

a. If statement 1 alone is sufficient but statement 2 is alone not sufficient
b. If statement 2 alone is sufficient but statement 1 is alone not sufficient

c. If each statement alone (either 1 or 2) is sufficient
d. If statement 1 and 2 together are not sufficient
e. If both statement together are sufficient, but neither statement alone is sufficient.

11. What is code for 'is' in that code language?
 a. In that code language 'shi tu ke' means 'pen is blue'
 b. in that code language 'ke si re' means 'this is wonderful'

12. Which train did Harish catch to go to office?
 a. Harish missed his usual train of 10:25 am. A train comes in every 5 minutes.
 b. Harish did not catch the 10:40 am train or any train after that time.

13. How is Vandana related to Prabha?
 a. Mallika's sister Vandana is Rajnesh's wife. Prabha is Rajnesh's good friend.
 b. Prabha is Rajnesh's brother's wife and Vandana is Rajnesh's wife.

14. Who earns the highest among the five friends?
 a. Priya earns more than Pinky and Sheetal and less than only Shilpa.
 b. Sheetal earns more than Neetu but less than Pinky.

15. Who is sitting immediate right of Tanvi among five friends sitting around a circle facing the center?
 a. Ansh is sitting exactly between Bindu and Suresh and Neel is sitting to the immediate right of Suresh
 b. Tanvi is sitting exactly between Bindu and Neel and Ansh is sitting to the immediate right of Bindu

(16–20). Study the following information carefully and answer the questions given below.
Seven people N, K, T, B, M, W and R have their weekly offs on different days of the week i.e. Sunday, Monday, Tuesday, Wednesday, Thursday, Friday, Saturday not necessary in that order. Each of them has a liking for different cuisine i.e. Indian, Italian, Mexican, Chinese, Spanish, Continental, and Thai, not necessary in same order. K likes Thai food and gets his weekly off on Thursday. B likes Italian food and does not have off on Sunday. M has weekly off on Saturday and R has his weekly off on Tuesday. W likes continental food whereas the one who has weekly off on Monday likes Mexican cuisine. T does not like Spanish cuisine and has weekly off on Wednesday. The one who likes Indian food does not have a weekly off on Tuesday or Wednesday.

16. Who has weekly off on Friday?
 a. T b. R c. W d. Data inadequate
 e. None of these

17. What cuisine does R like?
 a. Continental b. Indian c. Italian d. Spanish e. None of these

18. On which day N have weekly off?
 a. Tuesday b. Friday c. Monday d. Sunday e. None of these

19. Who likes Chinese cuisine?
 a. T b. B c. R d. N e. None of these

20. On which day does W have weekly off?
 a. Monday b. Sunday c. Wednesday d. Data Inadequate
 e. None of these

(21–25). Study the following information carefully and answer the questions given below.

Point AB is 14 m towards the West of point CD

Point NH is 4 m towards the South of point AB.

Point KL is 9 m towards the south of point AB

Point IJ is 7 m towards the East of point NH.

Point WX is 4 m towards the North of point IJ

Point UV is 4 m towards the South of point CD

21. Which of the following points are in a straight line?

a. AB, IJ, CD b. IJ, UV, WX c. AB, NH, UV d. IJ, UV, NH e. KL, NH, WX

22. CD is in which direction with respect to WX?

a. East b. West c. North d. South

e. Can't be determined

23. NH is in which direction with respect to IJ?

a. East b. west c. North d. South

e. Can't be determined

24. If a person walks 5m towards North from point KL and then takes right turn and walk some distance, which of the following points would he reach first?

a. UV b. AB c. IJ d. CD e. WX

25. What is the distance between point AB and CD?

a. 14m b. 10m c. 12m d. 8m

e. Can't be determined

26. Pointing to Seema, Sonu said,'i am the son of her father's only daugher'. How is Seema related to Sonu?

a. Brother b. self c. Cousin-sister d. Data Inadequate

e. None of these

27. In a certain code TSGC is written as 5%3$ and EGIT is written as $1@8. How is TPOSQ written in that code?

a. 85%8 b. 8@51 c. 8%31 d. Data Inadequate

e. None of these

28. In a certain code COMPLETE is written as PDDKOLFU. How is MAGAZINE written in that code?

a. TBODMNHS b. BOBTMNHS c. BNHYZFFO

d. BIBMIGTR e. None of these

29. In a row of thirty children facing north, Veena is fifth to the right of Reena, who is twenty first from the right end of the row. What is Veena's position from the right end of the row?

a. Eleven b. Tenth c. Sixteenth d. Data Inadequate

e. None of these

30. Among Priya, Faruk, Juhi and Kareena each having different height, Priya's height is more than Faruk and Intaqab. Juhi's height is less than Intaqab. Kareena is not the tallest. Who is the tallest among them?

a. Intaqab b. Faruk c. Priya d. Juhi e. Kareena

31. Consider the following:
1. C 2. C++ 3. COBOL
Which among the above is/ are high-level languages (HLL)?
a. Only 1 b. 1 & 2 c. 2 & 3 d. 1, 2 & 3 e. None of these

32. Which among the following is NOT a search engine?
a. Google b. Baidu c. Wolfram Alfa d. Yahoo e. None of these

33. A Digital Certificate can identity
1. an individual
2. a server
3. a company Choose the correct option:
a. Only 1 b. 1 & 2 c. 2 & 3 d. 1, 2 & 3 e. None of these

34. What do we call an input/output device on a computer, reserved for communication between the computer operator or maintenance engineer and the computer?
a. EDP Device b. Console c. Jokey d. Link Device e. None of these

35. Which among the following is a high-level language used to develop software applications in compact, efficient code that can be run on different types of computers with minimal change?
a. FORTRAN b. C c. COBOL d. ALGOL e. None of these

36. While browsing internet, what do we call the area of storage that compensates for the different speeds of data flow or timings of events by temporarily holding a block of data that is waiting to be processed?
a. Cache b. Buffer c. Flash d. Trash e. None of these

37. Which among the following has been standardized in the IEEE 802.3 specification?
a. Ethernet b. Bluetooth c. WiMAX d. All of them e. None of these

38. Dynamic Ad-hoc Wireless Networks (DAWN) usually come under?
a. 2G b. 3G c. 4G d. 5G e. All of these

39. What do we call a CPU that is designed specifically to handle the communications processing task with main purpose is to off-load communications processing task from the host computer so that the host computer can be dedicated for applications and data processing jobs?
a. Backend processor b. Front-end processor
c. Node processor d. File Server e. None of these

40. The peak cell rate (PCR), sustainable cell rate (SCR), and maximum burst size (MBS) are used for measurement of ?
a. Bandwidth b. Channel Capacity
c. Frequency Modulation d. Amplitude distortion e. All of these

41. What do we call the pictorial representation that uses predefined symbols to describe either the logic of a computer program or the data flow and processing steps of a system?
a. Algorithm b. Flowchart c. Block diagram d. Loop e. None of these

42. What do we call a storage device where the access time is effectively independent of the location of the data?
a. Direct Access Storage Device b. Secondary Storage Device
c. Primary Storage Device d. Gateway Device e. None of these

43. What do we call the automatic execution of high-priority computer programs that have been designed to pre-empt the use of computer resources?
   a. Foreground processing. b. Background processing.
   c. Black processing. d. White processing. e. None of these

44. What would be the number of bytes, transferred at the rate of 1 Kilobit per second?
   a. 100 b. 108 c. 125 d. 140 e. None of these

45. Which among the following is the time period during which a computer is malfunctioning or not operating correctly due to machine failures?
   a. Downtime b. Uptime c. Response time d. Runtime e. None of these

Section 2: DATA Analysis and Interpretation

Directions for questions 46 to 49: Go through the data given below and solve the questions based on it.

Below given table gives the cost structure for packaged food products – Potato chips, Jam and Packaged Juice. All the data pertains to the 'N' grams packet of each of the three products. MRP = Maximum retail price = the price at which the retailer sells the article to the customer. All the questions pertain to this table only.

Cost structure for select packaged food products			
	Potato Chips INR	**Jam INR**	**Packaged Juice INR**
MRP	**10**	**50**	**68**
Retailer's Margin + discount	0.83	7.20	11.80
Distributor's Margin	0.44	2.18	3.50
Sales Tax	**0.94**	**5.37**	**8.20**
Excise Duty	**1.04**	**0.00**	**0.00**
Distribution	0.41	2.81	2.70
Returns	0.27	1.06	0.68
Manufacturing Cost	1.10	0.87	5.10
Packaging Cost	1.50	6.18	12.60
Raw Material Cost	1.25	9.52	5.80

46. For which of the following items, raw material cost as a percentage of MRP maximum?
   a. Potato chips b. Jam c. Packaged juice
   d. Potato chips and Jam e. None of these

47. A distributor sells 5 packets of potato chips, 12 packets of Jam and 8 packets of packaged juice (each of N grams each). What is his total margin for these items (INR)?
   a. 48.7 b. 56.36 c. 28.52 d. 38.24 e. 64.12

48. If there is no sales tax, then which of the following products price will come down over MRP by maximum percentage?
a. Potato chips b. Jam c. Packaged juice
d. Potato chips and Jam e. It will come down equal in all the three cases

49. What percentage of the MRP is the retailers' margin in case of packaged juice?
a. 8.3% b. 7.2% c. 19.8%
d. 16.2% e. Cannot be determined

Directions for Questions 50 to 55: Answer these questions based on the data provided in the table below:

Year	Production (in lacs)	Workers	Assets (Rs. Millions)	Sales (Rs Crores)
2005	12	80	200	16
2006	14	85	220	18
2007	13.5	90	220	21
2008	15	102	240	22
2009	17.5	120	250	25

Asset Utilization Factor (AUF) = Sales value/Assets
Worker productivity = Production in units/Number of workers
Assume that whatever is produced in a given year is sold in the same year.
All sales are of produced units only.

50. In which year is the worker productivity the highest?
a. 2005 b. 2007 c. 2008 d. 2006

51. Which year has the highest AUF?
a. 2005 b. 2006 c. 20007 d. 2009

52. In which year is the average selling price of a unit sold the highest?
a. 2005 b. 2008 c. 2007 d. 2009

53. In which year is the average selling price of a unit sold the second lowest?
a. 2005 b. 2008 c. 2007 d. 2006

54. Worker Turnover is defined as the average sales (value) per worker in a given year. In which year is the worker turnover the highest?
a. 2007 b. 2006 c. 2008 d. 2005

55. The average cost of production in 2008 was Rs. 120/unit. What was the approximate profit percentage on a unit sold in the same year?
a. 17% b. 23% c. 31% d. 42%

Directions for questions 56 to 60: Answer these questions based on the data provided in the table below:

The following table is the details of 5 companies who have taken corporate subscription of mobile phones for their employees. NO employee can have more than one connection. The details are on monthly basis.

Company	Mobile phone service provider	No. of employees covered	Rentals per employee (in Rs.)	Free calls per employee	Per call charge (in Rs.)	Per SMS charge (in Rs.)
A	BSNL	400	500	500	2.00	1.00
B	Reliance	700	0	250	2.50	0.75
C	Airtel	250	300	250	3.00	0
D	Aircel	400	400	500	2.50	0.50
E	Virgins	625	500	500	2.00	1.50

NOTE: Per call charges become effective only after free calls are exhausted.

56. Which company has made highest payment towards total bill of all the employees if, on an average, each employee has made 700 calls, no sms? (call charges = Rentals + charges after free calls)
a. A b. B c. D d. E e. C

57. If each employee sends a total of 1000 SMS per month, then what is the total annual SMS bill of company A and company B put together excluding the monthly rentals? (in Rs. Lakhs)
a. 212 b. 175 c. 111 d. 626 e. None of these

58. If another company F estimates that its 1000 employees will make 600 calls and send 200 SMS per month, then which mobile phone service provider should it opt for, such that its payout is least?
a. BSNL b. Reliance c. Aircel d. Virgins e. Airtel

59. What is the total bill for mobile phones of E if its employees send 200 SMS's each and make 500 phone calls each in a particular month?
a. Rs. 312500 b. Rs. 500000 c. Rs. 812500 d. Rs. 625000 e. None of these

60. If employees of both C and D send 100 SMS and make 600 calls each, then by what percentage has the revenue of Airtel exceeded that of Aircel from these 2 clients respectively?
a. 50% b. 80% c. 20% d. 17.75% e. None of these

Directions for questions 61 to 64: Answer these questions based on the data provided in the table below:

The following table gives the sales of various sections of three departmental stores which began operations in 2005. All values are in Rs. crores.

	2009	2008	2007	2006	2005
Shopper's Top:					
Men	12.5	11.5	9.8	12.5	13.5
Women	18.7	16.2	12.2	8.8	14.5
Others	25.2	21.7	25.6	16.2	21.2
Jivestyle:					
Men	15.4	18.5	17.2	18.5	21.5
Women	12.7	11.5	10.8	9.5	8.2
Others	21.5	22.7	21.5	18.5	16.5
Eastside:					
Men	9.5	11.2	8.6	5.4	4.3
Women	11.8	10.8	9.2	7.5	6.5
Others	7.5	6.5	6.8	7.2	6.5
Total	**134.8**	**130.6**	**121.7**	**104.1**	**112.7**

61. For which year did sales increase the most, relative to the previous year for the Men's section of Jivestyle?
    a. 2008 b. 2007 c. 2006 d. 2005
    e. Cannot be determined

62. The total sales of Men's sections of the three departmental stores lay between 30 and 40 percent of total turnover of the three stores, in the year/s…
    a. 2009, 2008, 2006 b. 2006 and 2005 only
    c. 2008, 2006, 2005 d. 2001, 2000, 2006 e. None of these

63. The highest percentage growth in sales of the three stores together, relative to previous year was achieved in…
    a. 2005 b. 2008 c. 2006 d. 2007
    e. Either 2005 or 2006

64. Which of the following statements is correct?
    a. During 2006 to 2009, sales of Women's section of Shopper's Top declined steadily whereas that of 'others' sections steadily increased.
    b. The Women's section sales at Eastside have always been higher than average sales of the three sections of Eastside.
    c. 'Others' section has contributed to more than 50% of sales for shopper's Top for all the years.
    d. None of the above statements are true.
    e. All are true

65. Three Englishmen and three Frenchmen work for the same company. Each of them knows a secret not known to others. They need to exchange these secrets over person-to-person

phone calls so that eventually each person knows all six secrets. None of the Frenchmen knows English, and only one Englishman knows French. What is the minimum number of phone calls needed for the above purpose?

a. 5 b. 10 c. 9 d. 15 e. None of these

Direction for questions 66 – 69: Go through the passage given below and solve the questions based on it.

In the table below is the listing of players, seeded from highest (#1) to lowest (#32), who are due to play in an Association of Tennis Players (ATP) tournament for women. This tournament has four knockout rounds before the final, i.e., first round, second round, quarterfinals, and semi-finals. In the first round, the highest seeded player plays the lowest seeded player (seed # 32) which is designated match No.1 of first round; the 2nd seeded player plays the 31st seeded player which is designated match No.2 of the first round, and so on. Thus, for instance, match No. 16 of first round is to be played between 16th seeded player and the 17th seeded player. In the second round, the winner of match No.1 of first round plays the winner of match No. 16 of first round and is designated match No.1 of second round. Similarly, the winner of match No.2 of first round plays the winner of match No. 15 of first round, and is designated match No.2 of second round. Thus, for instance, match No.8 of the second round is to be played between the winner of match No.8 of first round and the winner of match No.9 of first round. The same pattern is followed for later rounds as well.

Seed #	Name of Player	Seed #	Name of Player	Seed #	Name of Player
1	Maria Sharapova	12	Mary Pierce	23	Silvia Farina Elia
2	Lindsay Davenport	13	Anastasia Myskina	24	Tatiana Golovin
3	Amelie Mauresmo	14	Alicia Molik	25	Shinobu Asagoe
4	Kim Clijsters	15	Nethalie Dechy	26	Francesca Schiavone
5	Svetlana Kuznetsova	16	Elena Bovina	27	Nicole Vaidisova
6	Elena Dementieva	17	Jelena Jankovic	28	Gisela Dulko
7	Justine Henin	18	Ana Ivanovic	29	Flavia Pannetta
8	Serena Williams	19	Vera Zvonareva	30	Anna Chakvetadze
9	Nadia Petrova	20	Elena Likhovtseva	31	Ai Sugiyama
10	Venus Williams	21	Daniela Hantuchova	32	Anna-lena Groenefeld
11	Patty Schnyder	22	Dinara Safina		

66. If Elena Dementieva and Serena Williams lose in the second round, while Justine Henin and Nadia Petrova make it to the semi-finals, then who would play Maria Sharapova in the quarterfinals, in the event Sharapova reaches quarterfinals?

a. Dinara Safina b. Justine Henin c. Nadia Petrova
d. Patty Schnyder e. None of these

67. If the top eight seeds make it to the quarterfinals, then who, amongst the players listed below, would definitely not play against Maria Sharapova in the final, in case Sharapova reaches the final?

a. Amelie Mauresmo b. Elena Dementieva c. Kim Clijsters
d. Lindsay Davenport e. None of these

68. If there are no upsets (a lower seeded player beating a higher seeded player) in the first round, and only match Nos. 6, 7, and 8 of the second round result in upsets, then who would meet Lindsay Davenport in quarter finals, in case Davenport reaches quarter finals?
a. Justine Henin b. Nadia Petrova
c. Patty Schnyder d. Venus Williams e. None of these

69. If, in the 1st round, all even numbered matches (and none of the odd numbered matches) result in upsets, and there are no upsets in the second round, then who could be the lowest seeded player facing Maria Sharapova in semi-final?
a. Anastasia Myskina b. Nadia Petrova
c. Flavia Pennetta d. Svetlena Kuznetsova e. None of these

Direction for questions 70 – 74: Go through the data set given below and solve the questions based on it.

The following table gives the break-up of the revenue earned by Phistream Private Limited over a period of five years. All figures in the table are in Rs. Crores.

	1994-95	1995-96	1996-97	1997-98	1998-99
Hardware					
(a) Domestic	68	54	52	66	35
(b) Exports	540	600	730	1770	1827
Software					
(a) Domestic	142	127	150	320	422
(b) exports	1100	1200	1339	2500	2215
Peripherals	25	10	25	20	37
Training	140	106	160	240	161
Maintenance	21	19	25	92	126
Others	12	10	19	40	24
Total	2048	2126	2500	5048	4847

70. In which years the hardware Exports lie been between 35-40% of the total revenues for Phistream?
a. 97-98,98-99 b. 98-99,95-96 c. 97-98,94-95 d. 95-96,96-97 e. None of these

71. Which of the following is true?
a. The revenues from Training consistently increased over the given period.
b. Hardware exports consistently increased over the given period.
c. Software exports consistently increased over the given period.
d. None of the above
e. cannot be determined

72. In how many years during the given period, was the total revenue from training and Maintenance less than ten percent of the total revenue for the corresponding years?
a. 2 b. 3 c. 4 d. 5 e. either 2 or 3

73. In which of the following years was the revenue from Hardware business more than 50% of that from the software business done by Phistream?
a. 94-95 b. 95-96,96-97 c. 97-98, 94-95 d. 95-96 e. None of these

74. If in 99-00, the total revenue earned by Phistream decreases by five percent from the previous year but the revenue from software increases to Rs.2437 crores, then what is the approximate percentage decrease in the combined revenue from the rest of the heads (excepting software) in 99-00?
a. 1.0% b. 1.8% c. 2.1% d. 3.3% e. 4.5%

75. One brick is one kilogram and half a brick heavy. How heavy is one brick?
a. 1 kg b. 1.5 kg c. 2 kg d. 2.5 kg e. 3 kg

76. A survey shows that 63% of the Americans like cheese whereas 76% like apples. If x% of the Americans like both cheese and apples then find the range of x?
a. $0\% \leq x \leq 23\%$ b. $0\% \leq x \leq 39\%$ c. $4\% \leq x \leq 35\%$
d. $39\% \leq x \leq 63\%$ e. cannot be determined

77. The number of solutions of the equation $2x + y = 40$ where both x and y are positive integers and $x \leq y$ is:
a. 7 b. 13 c. 14 d. 18 e. 19

78. The number of employees is a prime number and is less than 300. The ratio of the number of employees who are graduates and above, to that of employees who are not, can *possibly* be:
a. 101 : 88 b. 87 : 100 c. 110 : 111 d. 97 : 84 e. None of these

79. There are 6 tasks and 6 persons. Task 1 cannot be assigned either to person 1 or to person 2, task 2 must be assigned to either person 3 or person 4. Every person is to be assigned one task. In how many ways can the assignment be done?
a. 144 b. 180 c. 192 d. 360 e. 240

80. First six Prime Ministers of the country had an average tenure of 6 years. What is the approximate tenure of the 7th Prime Minister if the average tenure of the first nine Prime Ministers is 5.25 years and the duration of the tenure of the 7th, 8th and 9th Prime Minister are in the ratio 1:2:3?
a. 1 year 3 months 18 days b. 1 year 10 months 15 days
c. 2 years d. 1 year 6 months e. None of these

Section 3: General and Banking Awareness

81. The maximum amount of the total Revenue earned by the government of India comes from:
a. Income Tax b. Customs Duty c. Excise Duty
d. Value Added Tax e. Corporate Tax

82. Capital Market Regulator is
a. RBI b. IRDA c. NSE d. BSE e. SEBI

83. IMPS stand for
a. Immediate Payment Service
b. Internet Money Payment Service
c. Internal Market Payment Service
d. Important Payment Service
e. None of These

84. Which of the following bank launches India's first Mobile ATM?
a. HDFC Bank b. Axis Bank c. ICICI Bank d. SBI e. None of These

85. India's first "talking" Automated Teller Machine (ATM) for visually impaired located in?
a. Ahmedabad b. Pune c. Kolkata d. New Delhi e. None of These

86. Which of the following bank has launched 'mVisa' – a mobile-based payments solution?
a. HSBC Bank b. ICICI Bank c. SBI d. Canara Bank e. Yes Bank

87. Who was known as the "Father of Economics"?
a. Amartya Sen
b. Karl Marx
c. Adam Smith
d. George Loewenstein
e. None of These

88. What is Gross Domestic Product(GDP)?
a. It is the market value of all final goods and services made in the country.
b. It is the Cost production of all final goods and services made in the country.
c. It is the Cost services of all final goods and services made in the country.
d. It is the market value of all final goods and services made within the borders of a country in a year.
e. None of These

89. Name the country's first small finance bank which started its operations recently?
a. Capital Local Area Bank
b. Disha Microfin Private Limited
c. Au Financiers (India) Limited
d. Ujjivan Financial Services
e. Utkarsh Micro Finance

90. Which Bank has opened its first branch in South Korea that is to play an important role in strengthening economic partnership between the two nations?
a. ICICI b. SBI c. PNB d. HDFC e. None of These

91. NBFCs are an important part of the Indian financial system. what is meant by this term?
a. New Banking Financial Companies
b. Non Banking Financial Companies
c. Neo Banking Financial Confederation
d. Non banking Fiscal Companies
e. None of these

92. What is a stale cheque?
a. A cheque issued without drawer's signature.
b. A cheque with only signature of the drawer.
c. A cheque which has completed 3 months from the date of its issue.
d. Any one of the above.
e. None of these

93. Where is the head office of Insurance Regulatory Development Authority?
a. Kolkata b. Mumbai c. Hyderabad d. Chennai e. Delhi

94. USSD stands for?
a. Unstructured Supplementary Service Data
b. Universal Supplementary Service Data
c. Unstructured Standard Service Data
d. Unstructured Supplementary Service Dairy
e. Unstructured Supplementary Stolen Data

95. A cheque returned for insufficiency of funds. Payee will have right to notice and approach court of law for justice under section 138 of which act?
a. Indian Penal Code
b. Negotiable Instrument Act
c. Criminal Procedure Code
d. Payment and Settlement Act
e. Indian Contract Act

96. Which of the following is not a primary function of a Bank?
a. Granting loans
b. Collecting cheques/ drafts of Customers
c. Arranging VISA for students for abroad education
d. Issuing bank drafts
e. Selling Gold/Silver Coins.

97. Which of the following is not classified as a Commercial Bank?
a. Public Sector Bank
b. Foreign Bank
c. Private Sector Bank
d. Regional Rural Bank
e. Urban Cooperative Bank

98. The name 'Bluetooth' gets its name from a 10th century king of?
a. China b. Denmark c. Greece d. Thailand e. Spain

99. Which of the following tools is used by the RBI to control credit and monetary situations of the markets?
a. RTGS
b. NEFT
c. ECS
d. CRR
e. Balance of trade

100. Which of the following is not a banking term?
a. Letter of credit
b. MIBOR
c. Factoring services
d. Entry load
e. None of these

101. The basic functions of the bank are?
a. Acceptance of Deposits from the public
b. Lending or investing the funds so collected from the customers
c. Lending to customers
d. (a) and (b)
e. (a) and (c)

102. Functions of Banks are governed by?
a. Indian Contract Act
b. FEMA
c. Traditions in India
d. Banking Regulation Act
e. Indian Trust Act

103. Electronic banking has opened new banking channels like?
a. Internet banking
b. Telephone banking
c. Branch Banking
d. ATM banking
e. (a), (b) and (d)

104. Illiterate Persons are allowed to open?
a. Current account
b. Savings account
c. only savings account (without cheque facility) or fixed deposit account
d. Any type of account
e. Not allowed to open bank account

105. The effect of a valid nomination is that?
a. on death of the sole depositor /all depositors, the amount will be returned to the nominee after further legal formality.
b. on death of the sole depositor, the amount will be returned to the nominee
c. on death of the sole depositor / all depositors, the amount will be returned to the nominee without any further legal formality.
d. None
e. (a), (b) and (c)

106. Fixed deposits cannot be
a. Renewed for a further period on maturity date
b. Transferred to third parties
c. Pre-paid before the maturity date
d. Only a&c
e. Any of the above

107. Minimum period of fixed deposit is__days and maximum period for which a bank can accept a deposit presently is__years?
a. 10 – 10 b. 7 – 10 c. 7 – 20 d. Any period e. 1 – 10

108. Flexi deposits means?
a. Floating Rate of Interest deposits b. Fixed deposits
c. Hybrid deposits d. Call Deposit e. None of these

109. When the bank lends money to the customer, the relationship, of the customer and banker is
a. Creditor and Debtor, b. Debtor and Creditor
c. Principle - Agent d. Either a or b e. None of these

110. Debt refers to?
a. Outstanding Loan Balance
b. Present and future dues from customer of any nature say locker rent
c. a sum of money owed by one person or entity(debtor) to an-other person or entity (creditor)
d. a sum of money owed by one person or entity (Creditor) to another person or entity (Debtor)
e. None of these

111 The world's largest seating capacity cricket stadium will come up in which state of India ?
a. Gujarat b. West Bengal c. Karnataka d. Tamil Nadu e. None of these

112. What is the theme of 2016 Human Rights Day (HRD)?
a. Our Rights, Our Freedoms, Always
b. Stand up for someone's rights today
c. My Voice Counts d. Human Rights 365 e. None of these

113. Which union minister has launched Digidhan campaign to promote digital transactions?
a. Narendra Modi
b. Rajnath Singh
c. Ravi Shankar Prasad
d. Venkaiah Naidu
e. None of these

114. Who has won the 2016 Presidential election of the Republic of Ghana?
a. Paa Kwesi Nduom
b. Ivor Greenstreet
c. John Dramani Mahama
d. Nana Akufo-Addo
e. None of these

115. Who has become the acting president of South Korea?
a. Hwang Kyo-ahn
b. Park Jong-sun
c. Kim So-yeon
d. Moon Jae-in
e. None of these

116. What is the India's rank in the 2016 Global Terrorism Index (GTI)?
a. 9th
b. 7th
c. 11th
d. 13th
e. None of these

117. The book "Dipa Karmakar: The Small Wonder" has been authored by whom?
a. Vimal Chauhan
b. Dipa Karmakar
c. Bishweshwar Nandi
d. Shikha Sabharwal
e. None of these

118. The 2016 Serendipity Arts Festival (SAF) will be held in which state?
a. Maharashtra
b. Uttar Pradesh
c. Rajasthan
d. Goa
e. None of these

119. Which committee has been constituted by Internet and Mobile Association of India (IAMAI) to fight against the menace of online piracy?
a. D B Shekatkar committee
b. Ratan Watal committee
c. Nagana Gowda committee
d. Ajit Mohan committee
e. None of these

120. Which committee has recently submitted its final report on digital payments to Union Government?
a. H R Khan committee
b. Ratan Watal committee
c. Indrajeet Sarkar committee
d. Salil Kapoor committee
e. None of these

Section 4: English Language

121-130 Read the following passage carefully and answer the questions given below it. Certain words have been printed in bold to help you locate them while answering the questions.

Globalization liberalization and free market are some of the most significant modern trends in an economy. Most economists in our country seem captivated by the spell of the free market. Consequently nothing seems good or normal that does not accord with the requirements of the free market. A price that is determined by the seller or, for that matter, established by anyone other than the aggregate of consumers teems **pernicious**.

Accordingly, it requires a major act of will to think of price-fixing as both normal and having a valuable economic function. In fact, price fixing is normal in all industrialized societies because the industrial system itself provides, as an effortless consequence of its own development, the price fixing that is required. Modern industrial planning requires and rewards great size. Hence, a comparatively small number of large firms will be competing for the same group of consumers. That each large firm will act with considerations of its own needs and thus avoid selling its product for more than its competitors charge, is commonly recognized by advocates of free market economic theories. But each firm will also act with full consideration of the needs that it has in common with the other large firm competing for the same consumer. Each large firm will thus avoid significant stable price cutting because price cutting will be **prejudicial** to the common interest in a stable demand for products. Most economists do not see price fixing when it occurs because they expect it to be brought about by a number of explicit agreements among the large firms; it is not moreover, those economists who argue that allowing the free to operate without interference is the most efficient method of establishing prices have not considered the economics of non-socialist countries. Most of these economies employ intentional price-fixing, usually in an overt fashion. Formal price-fixing by cartel and informal price-fixing by agreements covering the members of an industry are common place. Were there something peculiarly efficient about the free market and inefficient about price-fixing, the countries that have avoided the first and used the second would have suffered drastically in their economic development. There is no indication that has.

Socialist industry also works within a framework of controlled prices. In the early 1970s the Soviet Union began to give firms and industries some flexibility in adjusting prices that a more informal evaluation has accorded the capitalist system. Economists in the USA have hailed the change as a return to the free market. But the Soviet firms were not in favour of the price established by a free market over which they exercised little influence; rather, Soviet firms acquired some power to fix price.

121. The author's primary objective of writing the passage seems to
   a. Belie the popular belief that the free market helps enhance development of industrial societies
   b. Advocate that price-fixing is unavoidable and it is beneficial to the economy of any industrialize society
   c. Explain the methodology of fixing price to stabilize free-market
   d. Prove that price-fixing and free-market are compatible and mutually beneficial to industrialized societies
   e. None of these

122. Which of the following statement is /are tyre in the context of the information given in the passage?
   1. Know some of the ways in which prices can be fixed
   2. Identify the products foe which price fixing can be more beneficial
   3. Differentiate between the economies of various countries
   a. Only 1   b. Only 2   c. Only 3
   d. Only 1 and 2   e. All of the above

123. Considering the literal meaning and connotations of the word used in the passage, the author's attitude towards 'most economists' can best be described as
   a. Derogatory and antagonistic   b. Impartial and unbiased
   c. Spiteful and envious   d. Critical and condescending
   e. Sympathetic and caring

124. The author feels that price fixed by seller seems pernicious because
   a. People don't have faith in large firms
   b. People don't want the Government to fix prices
   c. Most economists believe that no one group should determine prices
   d. Most economists believe that no one group should determine price
   e. All expect option (d)

125. According to the passage, price-fixing in non-socialistic countries is generally
 a. International and widespread b. Illegitimate but beneficial
 c. Conservative and inflexible d. Legitimate and innovative e. All of the above

126. What was the result of the Soviet Union's change in economic policy in 1970s?
 1. They showed greater profits
 2. They had less control over the free market
 3. They were able to adjust to technological advancement
 a. Only 1 b. Only 2 c. Only 1 and 2
 d. Only 1 and 3 e. None of the above

127. The author's primary concern seem to
 a. Summarise conflicting viewpoints
 b. Make people aware of recent discoveries
 c. Criticize a point of view
 d. Predict the probable result of a practice
 e. Both option (a) and (b)

128. Which of the following statements about the socialist industry is/are false?
 1. It has work under certain price restrictions
 2. It has no authority to determine price
 3. It hails the strategy of price fixing, as a major deviation
 a. Only 1 b. Only 2 c. Only 3 d. Only 2 and 3 e. Only 1 and 3

129. Choose the word most similar in the meaning to the word printed in bold, as used in the passage
 Pernicious
 a. Preferred b. Fair c. Inferior d. Cheap e. Devastating

130. Choose the word which is most nearly the opposite in the meaning as the word printed in bold as used in the passage
 Prejudicial
 a. Favoured b. Advantage c. Beneficial d. Inimical e. Deleterious

(131-155). Rearrange the following sentences 1, 2, 3, 4, 5 and 6 in the proper sequence to form a meaningful paragraph, than answer the questions given below them.

1. However, while the SEBI paper does seek to reduce the allotment for institutional investors, it simply does not go far enough.
2. Which allows small and medium enterprises (SMEs) to list and issue capital without an initial public offering (IPO)
3. At present, the norms stipulate that 75 percent of the net offer needs to be allocated to institutional investors, with remaining 25 percent earmarked for the non-institutional type
4. With start-ups, tech entrepreneurship and new business models growing by the day, the capital market regulator, SEBI, has put out a discussion paper seeking to revamp rules for the Institutional Trading Platform (ITP)
5. SEBI has sought to revise this to 'not less than 50 percent' for non institutional investors
6. The ITP framework makes possible trading in specified securities of SMEs for informed investors, either institutional or non institutional, to arrive at better valuation

131. Which of the following is the Last sentence after rearrangement?
a. 4 b. 3 c. 5 d. 6 e. 2

132. Which of the following is the Fourth sentence after the rearrangement?
a. 4 b. 6 c. 5 d. 2 e. 1

133. Which of the following is the Second sentence after the rearrangement?
a. 5 b. 4 c. 2 d. 6 e. 1

134. Which of the following is the First sentence after the rearrangement?
a. 2 b. 3 c. 5 d. 4 e. 1

135. Which of the following is the fifth sentence after the rearrangement?
a. 4 b. 3 c. 5 d. 6 e. 1

(136-145). Read each part of the sentence to find out if there is any error in it. The error, if any, will be in one part of the sentence. The number of that part is an answer. If there is no error mark your answer as (e)

136. With an aim to develop corporate bond market in India, an (1)/ expert panel suggested easing (2)/ of norms to foreign investors, a corporate bond index on the lines of Sensex or Nifty, and making it mandatory of large (3)/ corporate to tap this market for funds beyond a threshold. (4)/ No error (5)
a. 1 b. 2 c. 3 d. 4 e. No error

137. It is only in the recent past that many temples (1)/ has got into the (2)/ practice of closing the shrine for as long as (3)/ six months to one year under the pretext of renovation. (4)/ No error (5)
a. 1 b. 2 c. 3 d. 4 e. No error

138. It is welcome that the recent past that the government is paying more attention to pulses, (1)/ which may multiple roles ranging from providing much needed protein to Indians (2)/ which do not eat meat either because they cannot afford it (3)/ or foe cultural reasons (4)/ no error (5)
a. 1 b. 2 c. 3 d. 4 e. No error

139. Mainly confined to temples and courts, singing at the (1)/ places of worship gave exposure to (2)/ many talented artists to reach out to the (3)/ mass at large thus gaining recognition and fame (4)/ No error (5)
a. 1 b. 2 c. 3 d. 4 e. No error

140. When *carnatic* music moved to city *sabhas*, a western educated (1)/ mostly high caste audience constituted the new listening public (2)/ and they wanted to represent their music (3)/ tradition to their colonial masters, giving it a textual history and theoretical paradigm(4)/ No error (5)
a. 1 b. 2 c. 3 d. 4 e. No error

141. After the brief appearance before the waiting crowds (1)/ he was taken (2)/ to the Governor chamber (3)/ for the swearing in ceremony (4)/ No error(5)
a. 1 b. 2 c. 3 d. 4 e. No error

142. The theory of relativity is (1)/ so complicated (2)/ as we cannot describe (3)/ it in a few sentences (4)/ No error (5)

a. 1 b. 2 c. 3 d. 4 e. No error

143. Congress dissidents and (1)/ a wide range among the (2)/ opposition has mounted a (3)/ campaign to have the President re-nominated (4)/ No error (5)

a. 1 b. 2 c. 3 d. 4 e. No error

144. The crisis they are facing (1)/ is the most critical (2)/ natural disaster whatever (3)/ happened in Thai history (4)/ No error (5)

a. 1 b. 2 c. 3 d. 4 e. No error

145. Many times the news (1)/ has been published (2)/ in the papers that the end of the world (3)/ will be certain if the nuclear war breaks out (4)/ No error (5)

a. 1 b. 2 c. 3 d. 4 e. No error

(146-150). Which of the following phrase given below should replace the phrase printed in bold in the sentence to make it grammatically correct. If the sentence is correct, as it is given, and no correction is required, mark (e) as the answer.

146. The attack on military base at Uri, close to the line of control separating Pak-held area of Kashmir from the rest of India, is yet another instalment in the covert war that Pakistan **has been waged against India.**

a. has wage against India b. had waged against India
c. has been waging for India d. has been waging against India
e. No correction required

147. There are many things India can do, covert and overt, **apart from a diplomatic offensive** against Pakistan at a time when the world has little patient with terror apologists.

a. apart from a diplomacy offensive b. apart from a diplomat offensive
c. apart from a diplomatic offend d. apart from diplomat offense
e. No correction required

148. Non uniform rates have worked in the EU **there value added tax rates varied across** member states, and there is no reason why they cannot work in India.

a. there value added taxation rate vary across
b. where value added tax rates vary across
c. where value added tax ratings vary across
d. where value added tax rates vary apart
e. No correction required

149. The class 'special category' does not exist anymore, after the 14th Finance commission (FFC) **removing the distinction between** general and special category states, given that it had factored in levels of backwardness to devolve funds to states.

a. removed the distinct between b. removed the distinction between
c. removed the distinction between d. removing the distinction for
e. No correction required

150. With 17 states passing the 122nd Constitution Amendment Bill already passed by Parliament, the move to a goods and service tax (GST) **that will subsumed mostly indirect taxes** other than import duty has begun in earnest.

a. that will subsume most indirect taxes
b. that would subsume most indirect taxation
c. which will subsuming most indirect taxes
d. that will subsume mostly indirect taxes
e. No correction required

(151-155). In the following passage there are blanks each of which has been numbered. These numbers are printed below the passage and against each five words have been suggested. One of which fits the blank appropriately. Find out the appropriate word in each case.

The survey said safety concerns related to hybrid and genetically modified (GM) seeds need to be debated and tested so that their introduction is facilitated in the next six months. It also said the regulatory process needs to be (31) to address safety concerns of GM crops. The economic survey for 2015-16, which was tabled in Parliament on Friday suggested the policies must incentivise raising of production of pulses and oilseeds, for which the country is heavily dependent on imports.

It is said that agriculture requires a 'new paradigm' shift by focusing on raising yields with less inputs, prioritising cultivation of less water intensive crops, especially pulses and oilseeds, supported by favourable MSP (32) and backed by better procurement system and research. Pointing out deep segmentation in agri-market, the survey said unified national market would boost farmer's income. On controversial GM crops, it said "concerns about affordability of hybrid and GM seeds, environmental and ethical issue in cultivation of GM crops, risk to the food-chain, disease spread and cross pollination have resulted in their non-introduction. These issues need to be debated, tested, evaluate, so that introduction of hybrid is facilitated in next six months".

The adoption of hybrid and high yielding variety seeds is one definite (33) to raising productivity in Indian agriculture, it added. Stating that a host of studies have demonstrated significant net benefit of GM crops, the survey said "nonetheless there are good reasons for some of the public apprehensions on GMO, therefore the regulatory process in India needs to evolve so as to address the concerns in a way that does not come in the way adapting high (34) technologies and rapidly moving towards the world's agro-technological frontier". The Government has allowed only Bt cotton for commercial cultivation and there is a moratorium on Bt brinjal. Currently, it is examining a proposal on GM mustard seeds despite there being severe (35) to it among green activities.

151. a. block b. leave c. decrease d. evolved e. stop

152. a. failure b. regime c. mismanagement d. ignorance e. inefficiency

153. a. conclusion b. stoppage c. exit d. egress e. pathway

154. a. yielding b. hard c. rigid d. solid e. strong

155. a. kindness b. calm c. friend d. opposition e. harmony

ANSWER GRID WITH EXPLANATIONS:

1. c	2. a	3. e	4. d	5. b	6. d	7. c	8. a	9. b	10. b
11. e	12. d	13. b	14. a	15. c	16. e	17. d	18. c	19. a	20. b
21. d	22. a	23. b	24. c	25. a	26. c	27. d	28. c	29. c	30. c
31. d	32. c	33. d	34. b	35. b	36. b	37. a	38. d	39. b	40. a
41. b	42. a	43. a	44. c	45. a	46. b	47. b	48. c	49. e	50. d
51. d	52. c	53. a	54. a	55. b	56. b	57. c	58. c	59. b	60. c
61. a	62. c	63. d	64. b	65. c	66. c	67. d	68. d	69. a	70. a
71. b	72. d	73. d	74. c	75. c	76. d	77. b	78. d	79. a	80. b
81. c	82. e	83. a	84. c	85. a	86. c	87. c	88. d	89. a	90. b
91. b	92. c	93. c	94. a	95. b	96. c	97. e	98. b	99. d	100. d
101. d	102. d	103. e	104. c	105. c	106. b	107. b	108. c	109. b	110. c
111. a	112. b	113. e	114. d	115. a	116. b	117. c	118. d	119. d	120. b
121. b	122. a	123. b	124. c	125. a	126. e	127. a	128. c	129. e	130. c
131. c	132. e	133. c	134. d	135. b	136. c	137. e	138. d	139. d	140. e
141. c	142. c	143. c	144. c	145. e	146. d	147. e	148. b	149. c	150. a
151. d	152. b	153. e	154. a	155. d					

Solution to 6–10:

Friends	Profession	Car
R(Male)	Professor	Scorpio
M(Female)	Travel Agent	Alto
T(Female)	Air Hostess	Ikon
S(Female)	Doctor	Esteem
L(Male)	Jeweller	Corolla
W(Male)	Lawyer	Lancer
Z(Male)	Consultant	Santro

16-20. Puzzle

People	Weekly Off	Cuisine
N	Monday	Mexican
K	Thursday	Thai
T	Wednesday	Chinese
B	Friday	Italian
M	Saturday	Indian
W	Sunday	Continental
R	Tuesday	Spanish

70. [a]

Hardware exports as percentage of total revenues for corresponding years are:

1994-95: $\frac{540}{2048} \times 100 < 33\%$

1995-96: $\frac{600}{2126} \times 100 < 33\%$

1996-97: $\frac{730}{2500} \times 100 < 33\%$

1997-98: $\frac{1770}{5048} \times 100 = 35.06\%$

1998-99: $\frac{1827}{4847} \times 100 = 37.7\%$

So, Hardware Exports lie between 35-40% of total revenue in the last 2 years.

71. [b]

Checking the values from the tables, you can verify that [B] is true.

72. [d]

The combined revenue from Training and Maintenance is never greater than 10% of total revenue for the corresponding year throughout the given period.

73. [d]

Year	50% of software Revenue	Hardware Revenue
1994-95	1242x0.5=621	608
1995-96	1327x0.5=663	654
1996-97	1484x0.5=744	782
1997-98	2820x0.5=1410	1836
1998-99	2637x0.5=1318	1862

Hardware business provides revenues> 50% of the revenue from software business in 96-97, 97-98 and 98-99.

74. [c]

In 99-00:
Total revenue = 0.95 x 4847 = 4600
Software revenue = 2437
Remaining revenue = 4600- 2437 = 2163
In 98-99, Revenue from heads other than Software = 4847 – 2637 = 2210
% Decrease = (2210 – 2163)/2210 x 100 = 2.12%

SBI PO Mains MOCK Test Paper 11

Structure of this MOCK Test

S.No.	Name of section	No. of Questions	Total marks	Allotted Time
1	Reasoning and Computer Aptitude	45	60	60 minutes
2	Data Analysis and Interpretation	35	60	45 minutes
3	General/ Economy/ Banking Awareness	40	40	35 minutes
4	English Language	35	40	40 minutes
Total		155	200	3 hours

- There is $1/4^{th}$ Negative marking for every wrong answer.
- If a question is left blank, i.e. no answer is marked by the candidate, there will be no penalty for that question

Section 1: Reasoning and Computer Aptitude

Direction for questions 1 – 5: Study the following information carefully to answer the given questions.

Eight members P, Q, R, S, T, U, V and W of a family are sitting around a circular table with all of them facing outwards. Each one of them likes different brand of bikes viz. TVS, Yamaha, Hero, Honda, SUZUKI, KTM, Bajaj and Royal Enfield. Three married couples are there in the family.

P who is the father of U and uncle of V, sits to the left of the person who likes TVS. U is an immediate neighbour of her aunty W who does not sit next to S. R does not like Royal Enfield or Bajaj. W is the only sister-in-law of P whereas Q likes KTM and daughter-in-law of R. The two youngest members sit next to each other. The one likes the Yamaha sits between V and the one who likes SUZUKI. V is third to the left of S. The one who likes KTM sits between the persons who like Bajaj and Royal Enfield Respectively. S's husband and son sit next to her. Honda is not liked by V's father. V does not like Hero or Bajaj. S is the mother of P and T, and sits second to the left of T.

1. Which of the following statements is true regarding the family?
   a. P is the brother of W
   b. R is the father-in-law of P
   c. Q is the aunty of V
   d. U and V are married couple
   e. None of the Above

2. Who among the following sits between Q and the one who likes Yamaha?
   a. P b. T c. S d. V e. W

3. What is the position of the person who likes Honda with respect to the one who likes KTM?
   a. Third to the right
   b. Second to the left
   c. Immediate left
   d. Third to the left
   e. Fourth to the left

4. Who among the following likes Hero?
   a. W b. U c. V d. X e. T

5. Which of the following options represent a pair?
   a. Y, X
   b. W, T
   c. W, R
   d. S, U
   e. None of the above

(6–10). In each of the questions below are given statements followed by conclusions. You have to take the given statements to be true (even if they seem to be at variance from commonly known facts). Read all the conclusions and then decide which of the given conclusions logically follows.

6. **Statements:**
   Some P are Q.
   Some Q are R.
   All R are S.
   Some S are T.
   Conclusions:
   I. Some P are not R.
   II. Some S are R.
   III. Some P are S.
   IV. At least some R are T.
   a. Only II and III follow
   b. All follow
   c. Only II follows
   d. None follows
   e. None of these

7. **Statement:**
   Some grapes are fruits.
   No fruits is a apples.
   All apples are mangoes.
   Conclusions:
   I. Some fruits are definitely not mangoes.
   II. Some apples are not grapes.
   III. Some grapes being not mangoes is a possibility.
   a. Only conclusion I do not follow.
   b. Only conclusion II does not follow.
   c. Only conclusion III does not follow.
   d. Conclusions I and III do not follow.
   e. Only conclusion III follows

8. **Statements:**
No student is teacher.
No teacher is HM.
No HM is Professional.
Conclusions:
I. Some students are professionals.
II. Some teachers being professionals is a possibility.
a. if only conclusion I follows.
b. if only conclusion II follows.
c. if either conclusion I or conclusion II follows.
d. if neither conclusion I nor conclusion II follows.
e. if both conclusions I and II follow.

9. **Statements:**
All water are juice.
All juices are liquids.
No liquids is a milk.
No milk is a curd.
Conclusions:
I. All water are liquids.
II. At least some juices are curd.
III. No liquid is a curd.
IV. No Juice is a milk.
a. All follow
b. Only I,II and IV follow
c. Only I and IV follow
d. None follows
e. None of these

10. **Statements:**
Some pen are pencil.
Some pencil are paper.
All paper are eraser.
No eraser is box.
Conclusions:
I. No box is paper.
II. Some pencil are Eraser.
III. Some box are Pen.
IV. No box is pen.
a. Only I and II follow
b. Only either III or IV follows
c. Only I and either III or IV follow
d. Only I, II and either III or IV follow
e. None of these

(11–15). Study the following information carefully to answer the given questions.

Ten persons from ten different cities viz. Delhi, Jaipur, Patna, Indore, Mangaluru, Chennai, Hyderabad, Bengaluru, Raipur and Sri Nagar are sitting in two parallel rows containing five people each, in such a way that there is an equal distance between adjacent persons. In row 1- A, B, C, D and E are seated and all of them are facing south. In row 2 – P, Q, R, S and T are seated and all of them are facing north. Therefore in the given seating arrangement, each member seated in a row faces another member of the other row. (All the information given above does not necessarily represent the order of seating in the final arrangement.)

The person from Indore sits to the immediate right of Q. P faces one of the immediate neighbours of the person from Jaipur. D faces one of the immediate neighbours of the person from Patna. S is not from Patna. D is not from Mangaluru. R sits second to the left of the persons from Sri Nagar. A sits third to the right of person from Chennai. Only One person sits between the person from Raipur and Q. C sits to the immediate left of the person who faces Q. Only two people sit between B and E. The person from Mangaluru sits second to the right of the one who faces S. S does not sit at an extreme end of the line. One of the immediate neighbours of the person from Mangaluru faces Raipur. P does not face A. The person from Delhi sits second to the right of the person from Bengaluru.

11. Who amongst the following faces the person from Hyderabad?
a. The person from Delhi b. D
c. The person from Chennai d. The person from Raipur e. B or E

12. T is from which of the following Cities?
a. Patna b. Indore c. Hyderabad d. Raipur e. Mangaluru

13. Which of the following is true regarding C?
a. C sits an extreme end of the line
b. None of the given options is true
c. C is from Bengaluru
d. The person from Indore faces C
e. The person from Hyderabad is an immediate neighbour of C

14. R is related to Indore in the same way as C is related to Jaipur based on the given arrangement, To who amongst the following is T related to the following same pattern?
a. Delhi b. Sri Nagar c. Patna d. Hyderabad e. Raipur

15. Who amongst the following sit at extreme end of the row?
a. The person from Delhi and R
b. The persons from Bengaluru and A
c. A and the person from Patna
d. The persons from Chennai and Patna
e. A, E

(16–20). Study the following information carefully and answer the given questions.

When a word and number arrangement machine is given an input line of words and numbers, it arranges them following a particular rule. The following is an illustration of Input and rearrangement.

INPUT: expect 30 more funny 41 52 sea 61 ring 36 89 joy
STEP 1 : expect funny 30 more 41 52 sea 61 ring 36 89 joy
STEP 2 : expect funny 89 61 30 more 41 52 sea ring 36 joy
STEP 3 : expect funny 89 61 joy more 30 41 52 sea ring 36
STEP 4 : expect funny 89 61 joy more 52 41 30 sea ring 36
STEP 5 : expect funny 89 61 joy more 52 41 sea ring 30 36
STEP 6 : expect funny 89 61 joy more 52 41 ring sea 36 30

And step VI is the last step of the above input. As per the rules followed in the above step, find out the appropriate step for the given output.

Input: best 11 all 25 my 47 81 equal 49 strength 16 and

16. Which of the following term exactly comes between 49 and equal in step 3 ?
a. my b. 11 c. strength d. best e. None of these

17. How many elements are there between 25 and 16 in step 5 ?
a. One b. Three c. Two d. Five e. None of these

18. In step 6, equal and my, 11 and 49 are interchanged then which will be placed between 49 and equal?
a. Two b. Three c. Four d. Six e. None of these

19. What is the position of 25 in step 4 from the right end?
a. Third b. Fourth c. Sixth d. Fifth e. None of these

20. Which of the following will be the final step of the given input?
a. all and 16 11 best equal 25 47 my strength 49 81
b. my and 49 81 equal best 47 25 all strength 16 11
c. all and 81 49 best equal 25 47 my strength 11 16
d. all best 81 49 and equal 47 25 my strength 16 11
e. None of these

(21–25). Study the following information carefully to answer the given questions.
Eight players – P, Q, R, S, T, U, V and W sit around a square table in such a way that four of them sit on the four sides while the rest at corners. They play different sports like Chess, Football, Kabaddi, Tennis, Badminton, Boxing, Hockey and Cricket. Some of them are facing the centre while some are facing facing outside. (i.e. away from the centre)

Note: Same directions means that if one person facing the centre then the other person also faces the centre and vice versa. Opposite direction means if one person is facing the centre then the other person faces outside and vice versa.

Q faces the centre of the table and does not sit on any corner. V sits on one of the corner between the Cricketer and boxer. W sits second to the right of Football player who faces centre.

The Badminton player sits third to the left of Q. S sits opposite to W. P sits on the corner exactly opposite to T. The Football player sits third to the right of hockey player. The chess player does not facing the centre.

The boxer sits opposite to Q, also faces in opposite direction of Q and sits between hockey and badminton player. T who is the Badminton player sits immediate right to the tennis player.

The Tennis player faces the same direction of the U. The immediate neighbours of Q are facing opposite directions. The Hockey player sits exactly opposite to Kabaddi player.

The one who is on the immediate left of U is facing the same direction as W. R sits third to the left of W.

21. Who among the following is a boxer?
a. P b. U c. T
d. Can't be determined e. None of these

22. R is related to which of the following Sports?
a. Kabaddi b. Chess c. Hockey
d. Can't be determined e. None of these

23. Which of the following sits exactly between R and the chess Player?
a. The person who plays Cricket b. The person who plays Hockey
c. The person who plays Football d. Boxer e. None of these

24. How many persons sit facing the centre?
a. None b. One c. Two d. Three e. Four

25. Which of the following pairs is the immediate neighbour of the cricketer?
a. P, V b. P, R c. V, R d. Q, R e. V, Q

(26–30). In each of the questions below are given statements followed by conclusions. Read all the conclusions and then decide which of the given conclusions logically follows.

26. Statements: $P \geq Q$; $R > M$; $P \geq O$; $Q \geq R$; $N = Q$
Conclusions:
I. $R > O$
II. $O > Q$
III. $Q > M$
IV. $N > P$
a. Only I is true
b. Only II is true
c. Either I or II true
d. Neither I nor II is true
e. Only III is true

27. Statements: $A \geq B$; $C = B$; $E > F$; $A \leq D$; $B \geq F$
Conclusions:
I. $C < E$
II. $D \geq B$
III. $A \geq F$
IV. $E > D$
a. Only II is true
b. Only III is true
c. Either I or II true
d. II and III are true
e. I and II are true

28. Statements: $P > Q$; $S \geq U$; $Q \leq T$; $R = S$; $R < T$
Conclusions:
I. $P \geq U$
II. $U < T$
III. $S \leq P$
IV. $P < T$
a. Only I is true
b. Only II is true
c. Either I or II true
d. Neither I nor II is true
e. III and IV are true

29. Statements: $A=B$; $C \leq D$; $E>C$; $B<D$
Conclusions:
I. $D < B$
II. $D > E$
III. $A > E$
IV. $A > C$
a. None is true
b. Only II is true
c. Only I and II are true
d. Only II and III are true
e. Only IV is true

30. Statements: $Q \geq P$; $R = S$; $U < T$; $Q < R$; $Q < V$; $S \geq T$
Conclusions:
I. $S < U$

II. P > R
III. T < V
IV. P < R

a. Only I is true b. Only IV is true c. Only III is true
d. None is true e. All are true

31. Computers that control processes accept data in a continuous _________
a. feedback loop b. finite loop c. infinite loop
d. All of the above e. None of the above

32. Which of the following involves creating a single cell by combining two or more selected cells?
a. Combining b. Formatting c. Splitting
d. Merging e. None of the Above

33. Which of the following contains buttons and menus that provide quick access to commonly used commands?
a. Scroll bar b. Menu bar c. Tool bar
d. All of the Above e. None of the Above

34. A removable disk module that contains a single hard disk platter or a floppy disk is known as _______
a. Virtual Device Driver b. Floppy Disk c. PCMCIA Card
d. Disk Cartridge e. None of the Above

35. _________ allows you to take a presentation and put it onto another computer.
a. Save As b. Pack and go
c. Save as HTML d. Slide Transition
e. None of the Above

36. Which of the following is used to create charts in MS Excel?
a. Chart Wizard b. Slide Transition
c. Create New d. Optical Bar Code Reader
e. None of the Above

37. The period of time for which a process is allowed to run uninterrupted in a pre-emptive multitasking operating system is known as _______
a. throughput b. time slice c. time quantum
d. Both (B) and (C) e. Both (A) and (B)

38. SGML stands for
a. Standardized General Markup Language
b. Standard Generalized Marking Language
c. Standardized Generalized Markup Language
d. Standard General Marking Language
e. Standard Generalized Markup Language

39. Pre defined and built in formulas in Excel are known as _______
a. Chart b. Table c. Function
d. Diagram e. None of the Above

40. In M.S Word, we can use ______ to format your documents
a. Styles b. Text c. Table
d. All of the Above e. None of the Above

41. ________ characters can be entered in a single command line.
a. 140 b. 127 c. 60
d. 254 e. None of the above

42. How many function keys are available in the modern keyboard?
a. 10 b. 12 c. 8
d. 6 e. None of the Above

43. The key F12 opens a
A. Save As dialog box B. Open dialog box
C. Save dialog box D. Close dialog box E. None of these

44. Which of the following number system was used by ENIAC?
a. Decimal Number System b. Binary Number System
c. Octal Number System d. Hexadecimal Number System
e. None of the Above

45. A 64 bit microprocessor has the word length equal to ______
a. 4 byte b. 8 byte c. 16 byte
d. 2 byte e. None of the Above

Section 2: Data Analysis and Interpretation

Direction for question 46–50: Go through the data set given below and solve the questions based on it.

Name of Stock	Date of Auction	Date of Issue	Notified amount	Devolvement on PDs	Cut off price (in Rs.)	Cut off yield (%)	Date of Maturity
7.56% GS 2014	02-Apr-09	06-Apr-09	8000	0	103.47	6.80	03-Nov-14
7.94% GS 2021	02-Apr-09	06-Apr-09	4000	567	102.5	7.62	24-May-21
6.05% GS 2019	09-Apr-09	13-Apr-09	8000	0	95.05	6.75	02-Feb-19
7.50% GS 2034	09-Apr-09	13-Apr-09	4000	0	97.35	7.74	10-Aug-34
7.56% GS 2014	17-Apr-09	20-Apr-09	8000	0	106.75	6.10	03-Nov-14
8.24% GS 2027	17-Apr-09	20-Apr-09	4000	0	107.82	7.44	15-Feb-27
6.05% GS 2019	24-Apr-09	27-Apr-09	8000	0	99.38	6.13	02-Feb-19

46. For how many stocks, date of maturity is minimum 5 years ahead of date of auction?
a. All but 1 stock b. All but 2 stocks c. All but 3 stocks
d. None of these e. cannot be determined

47. Nomenclature of the stocks is done in the following way:
7.56% GS 2014 - It means that desired yield from the Government stock (GS) in 2014 is 7.56%.
For how many of the stocks Desired yield is more than cut-off yield?
a. 3 b. 4 c. 5 d. 2 e. 1

48. How many stocks with a cut-off price of more than Rs. 100 have their cut-off yield more than its desired yield (use definition from above question if required)?
a. 0 b. 1 c. 2 d. 3 e. 4

49. Mr. Robert is quite an ambitious person. He wants to obtain a minimum desired yield of 8%. For that to happen, he buys exactly two stocks in different ratio. How many combinations can he have, out of 7 stocks given, such that his minimum desired yield is atleast 8% (use information from previous qs)?
a. Not possible b. 6 c. 7 d. 2 e. None of these

50. If we arrange the stocks in the ascending order of their cut-off price, which stock will be ranked third?
a. 7.50% GS 2034 b. 6.05% GS 2019 c. 7.94% GS 2021
d. 7.56% GS 2014 e. None of these

Direction for question 51–53: Go through the data set given below and solve the questions based on it.

Five women decided to go shopping to M.G. Road, Bangalore. They arrived at the designated meeting place in the following order: 1. Arhcana, 2. Chellamma, 3. Dhenuka, 4. Helen, and 5. Shahnaz. Each women spent at least Rs.1000. below are some additional facts about how much they spent during their shopping spree.

i. The women who spent Rs.2234 arrived before the lady who spent Rs.1193.
ii. One women spent Rs.1340 and she was not Dhenuka.
iii. One women spent Rs.1378 more than Chellamma.
iv. One women spent Rs.2517 and she was not Archana.
v. Helen spent more than Dhenuka.
vi. Shahnaz spent the largest amount and Chellamma the smallest.

51. What was the amount spent by Helen?
a. Rs. 1193 b. Rs. 1340 c. Rs. 2234 d. Rs. 2517 e. None of these

52. Which of the following amount was spent by one of them?
a. Rs. 1139 b. Rs. 1378 c. Rs. 2571 d. Rs.2718 e. None of these

53. The women who spent Rs.1193 is
a. Archana b. Chellamma c. Dhenuka d. Helen e. Shahnaz

Direction for question 54–56: Go through the data set given below and solve the questions based on it.

Five friends meet every morning at Sree sagar restaurant for an idli-vada breakfast. Each consumes a different number of idli and vada. The number of idli consumed are 1,4,5,6 and 8; while the number of vadas consumed are 0,1,2,4 and 6. Below are some more facts about who eats what and how much:

i. The number of vadas eaten by Ignesh is three times the number of vadas consumed by the person who eats four idlis.
ii. Three persons, including the one who eats four vadas eat without chutney.
iii. Sandeep does not take any chutney.
iv. The one who eats one idli a day does not eat any vadas or chutney. Further, he is not Mukesh.
v. Daljits eats idli with chutney and also eats vada.
vi. Mukesh, who does not take chutney, eats half as many vadas as the person who eats twice as many idlis as he does.
vii. Bimal eats two more idlis than Ignesh, but Ignesh eats two more vadas than Bimal.

54. Which of the following statement is true?
 a. Daljit eats 5 idlis b. Ignesh eats 8 idlis
 c. Bimal eats 1 idli d. Bimal eats 6 idlis. e. None of these

55. Which of the following statement is true?
 a. Sandeep eats 2 vadas. b. Mukesh eats 4 vadas.
 c. Ignesh eats 6 vadas. d. Bimal eats 2 vadas. e. None of these

56. Which of the following statements is true?
 a. Mukesh eats 8 idlis and 4 vada but not chutney
 b. The person who eats 5 idlis and 1 vada does not take chutney.
 c. The person who eats equal number of vadas and idlis also takes chutney.
 d. The person who eats 4 idlis and 2 vada also takes chutney.
 e. None of these

Direction for question 57–61: Go through the data set given below and solve the questions based on it.

The table below presents data on percentage data on percentage covered by drinking water and sanitation facilities in selected Asian countries.

Population covered by drinking water and sanitation facilities (Percentage Coverage)

	Drinking water			Sanitation Facilities		
	Urban	Rural	Total	Urban	Rural	Total
India	85	79	81	70	14	29
Bangladesh	99	96	97	79	44	48
China	97	56	67	74	7	24
Pakistan	82	69	74	77	22	47
Philippines	92	80	86	88	66	77
Indonesia	79	54	62	73	40	51
Sri-Lanka	88	52	57	68	62	63
Nepal	88	60	63	58	12	1

Country A is said to dominate B or A>B if A has higher percentage in total coverage for both drinking water and sanitation facilities, and, B is said to be dominated by A, or B<A.

A country is said to be on coverage frontier if no other country dominates it. Similarly, a country is not on the coverage frontier if it is dominated by at least one other country.

57. Which countries are the countries on the coverage frontier?
 a. India and China b. Sri Lanka and Indonesia
 c. Philippines and Bangladesh d. Nepal and Pakistan
 e. Indian and Nepal

58. Which of the following statements are true?
 a. India>Pakistan and India>Indonesia
 b. India>China and India> Nepal
 c. Sri Lanka>China
 d. China>Nepal
 a. A and C b. B and D c. A,B and C d. B,C and D e. none of these

59. Using only the data presented under 'sanitation facilities' columns, it can be concluded that rural population in India, as a percentage of its total population is approximately
a. 76 b. 70 c. 73
d. Cannot be determined e. None of these

60. Again, using only the data presented under 'Sanitation facilities' columns, sequence China, Indonesia and Philippines in ascending order of rural population as a percentage of their respective total population. The correct order is
a. Philippines, Indonesia, China b. Indonesia, China, Philippines
c. Indonesia, Philippines, China d. China, Indonesia, Philippines
e. cannot be determined

61. India is not on the coverage frontier because:
A. It is lower than Bangladesh in terms of coverage of drinking water facilities.
B. It is lower than Sri-Lanka in terms of coverage of sanitation facilities.
C. It is lower than Pakistan in terms of coverage of sanitation facilities.
D. It is dominated by Indonesia.
a. A and B b. A and C c. D
d. None of these. e. cannot be determined

Direction for question 62–65: Go through the data set given below and solve the questions based on it.

The figure below represents states sales and net profit in Rs. crore of IVP ltd. For five years from 1994-95 to 1998-99. During this period the sales increased from Rs.100 crore to Rs.680 crore. Correspondingly, the net profit increased from Rs.2.5 crore to Rs.12 crore. Net profit is defined as the excess of sales over total costs.

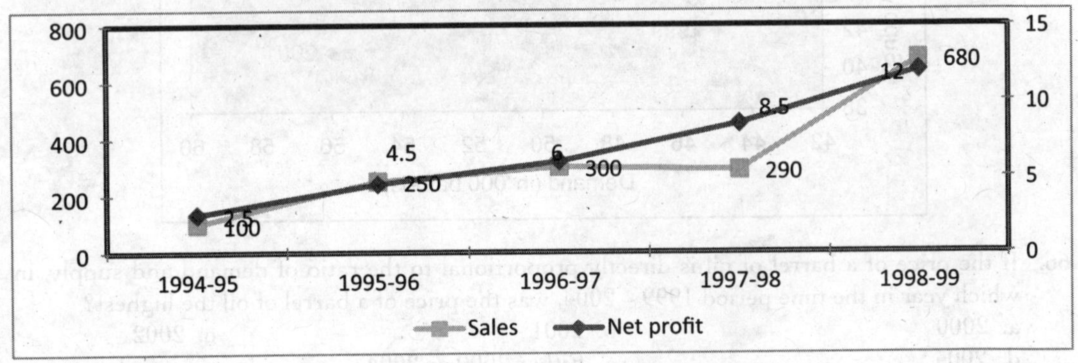

62. The highest percentage of growth in sales, relative to the previous year occurred in
a. 1995-96 b. 1996-97 c. 1997-98
d. 1998-99 e. Either 1997-98 or 1994-95

63. The highest percentage growth in net profit, relative to the previous year, was achieved in
a. 1998-99 b. 1997-98 c. 1996-97
d. 1995-96 e. Either 1998-99 or 1994-95

64. Defining the profitability as the ratio of net profit to sales, IVP Ltd., recorded the highest profitability in
a. 1998-99
b. 1997-98
c. 1994-95
d. 1996-97
e. Either 1998-99 or 1994-95

65. With profitability as defined in question 19, it can be concluded that:
a. Profitability is non-decreasing during the five years from 1994-95 to 1998-99.
b. Profitability is non-decreasing during the five years from 1994-95 to 1998-99.
c. Profitability remained constant during the five years from 1994-95 to 1998-99
d. None of above.
e. cannot be determined

Directions for questions 66 to 69: Go through the data set given below and solve the questions based on it.

The following graph captures the demand and supply situation of barrels of oil in the country Utopia over the years 1999 - 2004.

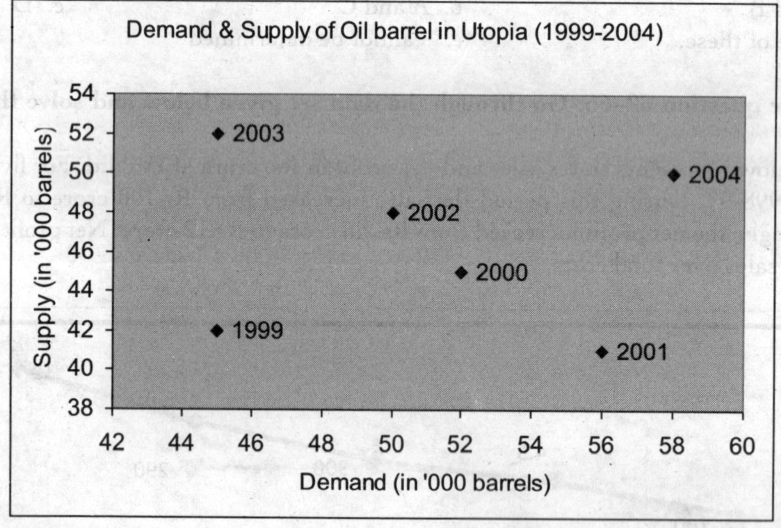

66. If the price of a barrel of oil is directly proportional to the ratio of demand and supply, in which year in the time period 1999 – 2004, was the price of a barrel of oil the highest?
a. 2000
b. 2001
c. 2002
d. 2004
e. Either 2000 or 2004

67. In how many years did both demand and supply show a similar trend i.e. either both increased or both decreased?
a. 1
b. 2
c. 3
d. 4
e. Cannot be determined

68. If Utopia had an inventory of 20,000 barrels of oil at the start of 1999, in which year was the deficit of oil the highest? Deficit is defined as demand minus available quantity and available quantity is supply of year added to the inventory. In a year where availability is less than

the demand, the demand goes unsatisfied in that year and is not carried forward. Excess availability over demand goes into inventory.

a. 2004 b. 2003 c. 2002
d. 2001 e. Either 2000 or 2004

69. If the data of demand and supply were to be drawn as line graphs on the same graph with the year along the X axis and the demand and supply along the Y axis, at how many points would the two lines intersect?

a. 0 b. 1 c. 2
d. 3 e. Cannot be determined

70. Of the 200 candidates who were interviewed for a position at a call center, 100 had a two-wheeler, 70 had a credit card and 140 had a mobile phone. 40 of them had both, a two-wheeler and a credit card, 30 had both, a credit card and a mobile phone and 60 had both, a two wheeler and mobile phone and 10 had all three. How many candidates had none of the three?

a. 0 b. 20 c. 10 d. 18 e. 25

71. A tank is fitted with 8 pipes, some of them that fill the tank and others that are waste pipe meant to empty the tank. Each of the pipes that fill the tank can fill it in 8 hours, while each of those that empty the tank can empty it in 6 hours. If all the pipes are kept open when the tank is full, it will take exactly 6 hours for the tank to empty. How many of these are fill pipes?

a. 2 b. 4 c. 6 d. 5 e. 1

72. A girl bought a bunch of flowers at the rate of 14 for Rs.180 and sold all of those at the rate of 16 for Rs.220. In this transaction, she gained Rs.50. How many flowers did the bunch contain?

a. 48 b. 52 c. 56 d. 50 e) 56

73. I started climbing up the hill at 6 a.m. and reached the top of the temple at 6 p.m. Next day I started coming down at 6 a.m. and reached the foothill at 6 p.m. I walked on the same road. The road is so short that only one person can walk on it. Although I varied my pace on my way, I never stopped on my way. Then which of the following must be true?

a. My average speed downhill was greater than that of uphill
b. At noon, I was at the same spot on both the days.
c. There must be a point where I reached at the same time on both the days.
d. There cannot be a spot where I reached at the same time on both the days.
e. cannot be determined

74. There are two containers: the first contains 500 ml of alcohol, while the second contains 500 ml of water. Three cups of alcohol from the first container is taken out and is mixed well in the second container. Then three cups of this mixture is taken out and is mixed in the first container. Let A denote the proportion of water in the first container and B denote the proportion of alcohol in the second container. Then

a. A > B b. A < B c. A = B d. Cannot be determined
e. None of these

75. A father left a will of Rs. 35 lakhs between his two daughters aged 8.5 and 16 such that they may get equal amounts when each of them reach the age of 21 years. The original amount of

Rs. 35 lakhs has been instructed to be invested at 10% p.a. simple interest. How much did the elder daughter get at the time of the will?

a. Rs. 17.5 lakhs b. Rs. 21 lakhs c. Rs. 15 lakhs
d. Rs. 20 lakh e. Rs. 22.5 lakhs

76. If the letters of the word CHASM are rearranged to form 5 letter words such that none of the word repeat and the results arranged in ascending order as in a dictionary what is the rank of the word CHASM?

a. 20 b. 30 c. 36 d. 42 e. None of these

77. Three friends Alice, Bond and Charlie divide $1105 amongst them in such a way that if $10, $20 and $15 are removed from the sums that Alice, Bond and Charlie received respectively, then the share of the sums that they got will be in the ratio of 11 : 18 : 24. How much did Charlie receive?

a. $ 495 b. $ 510 c. $ 480 d. $ 375 e. $ 300

78. Of the 200 candidates who were interviewed for a position at a call center, 100 had a two-wheeler, 70 had a credit card and 140 had a mobile phone. 40 of them had both, a two-wheeler and a credit card, 30 had both, a credit card and a mobile phone and 60 had both, a two wheeler and mobile phone and 10 had all three. How many candidates had none of the three?

a. 0 b. 20 c. 10 d. 18 e. 22

79. How often between 11 O'clock and 12 O'clock (both inclusive) are the hands of the clock together at an integral number value?

a. 55 b. 56 c. 4 d. 5 e. 40

80. In a game of 200m race, A can win B by 50 m and B can win C by 8 m. In the same race, A can win C by:

a. 52m b. 58m c. 56m d. 54m e. 60m

Section 3: General and Banking Awareness

81. What is the initial capital amount to start Small Finance Banks?

a. 100 crore b. 200 crore c. 500 crore d. 1000 crore e. None of these

82. The promoters of Small Finance Banks should have ________ experience in banking and finance?

a. 8 years b. 11 years c. 7 years d. 10 years e. None of these

83. If a promoter setting up a small finance bank desires to set up a Payments Bank, the firm should set up both types of banks under a ________ structure

a. NBFC b. NOFHC c. LAB d. MFI e. None of these

84. What is the initial stake of promoters in the paid-up equity capital of Small Finance Banks?

a. 25% b. 30% c. 45% d. 50% e. 40%

85. How much percentage of the net credits of Small Finance Banks should be in priority sector lending?

a. 25% b. 30% c. 45% d. 50% e. 75%

86. The small finance bank shall be registered as a _________company under the Companies Act, 2013.
a. Private Limited
b. Unlimited
c. Public limited
d. Limited Liability Partnership
e. None of these

87. The small finance bank cannot be a _______ for another bank.
a. Agent
b. Promoter
c. Business Correspondent (BC)
d. Ombudsman
e. None of these

88. In Payment Banks, the stake of the promoter should be 40% minimum for _____ years
a. 3 years
b. 4 years
c. 5 years
d. 2 years
e. 6 years

89. In Payment Banks, the voting right of any shareholder is capped at 10%, which can be raised to ____by Reserve Bank of India.
a. 26%
b. 30%
c. 45%
d. 50%
e. 75%

90. The minimum capital requirement Payment Banks is Rs._______
a. 100 crore
b. 50 crore
c. 500 crore
d. 1000 crore
e. None of these

91. ________ is a standard format of Bank Identifier Codes (BIC) for banks to identify banks and financial institutions globally.
a. RTGS
b. IFSC
c. NEFT
d. SWIFT
e. None of these

92. How many characters are there in SWIFT code?
a. 8
b. 11
c. 7
d. Both (B) and (C)
e. Both (A) and (B)

93. Development expenditure of the Central government does not include
a. defence expenditure
b. expenditure on economic services
c. expenditure on social and community services
d. grant to states
e. None of these

94. In the last one decade, which one among the following sectors has attracted the highest foreign direct investment inflows into India?
a. Chemicals other than fertilizers
b. Services sector
c. Food processing
d. Telecommunication
e. Defence

95. In pursuance with the recommendations of Narsimhan Committee, the RBI has framed new guidelines
a. to govern entry of new private sector banks to make the banking sector more competitive
b. to reduce the freedom given to banks to rationalize their existing branch network
c. to setup more foreign exchange banks
d. to lend more easily for industrial development
e. None of these

96. The last three characters in the SWIFT code denotes ________
a. Bank Code
b. Country Code
c. Branch Code
d. location Code
e. None of these

97. The Head Quarters of Society for Worldwide Interbank Financial Telecommunication (SWIFT) is located in _______
a. Bern, Switzerland
b. La Hulpe, Belgium
c. Geneva, Switzerland
d. New York, USA
e. Vienna Austria

98. SENSEX is associated with ______
a. BSE b. NSE c. CSE d. ISE e. PSE

99. India was __________ Nation to join Society for Worldwide Interbank Financial Telecommunication (SWIFT) Network
a. 78th b. 74th c. 76th d. 75th e. None of these

100. A non banking entity to function as BBPOUs, it should have a net worth of at least Rs. ________ as per the last audited balance sheet and the same has to be maintained at all times.
a. 100 crore b. 50 crore c. 500 crore d. 1000 crore e. None of these

101. Which of the following is merged with SEBI?
a. CRISIL b. NABARD c. FMC d. CIBIL e. SHCIL

102. Which of the following is the first demutualized electronic exchange in the country?
a. BSE b. NSE c. CSE d. ISE e. PSE

103. Which of the following is responsible for e-stamping system around India?
a. CRISIL b. NABARD c. FMC d. CIBIL e. SHCIL

104. Which of the following is/are the domestic share holder(s) of NSE?
a. LIC & SBI b. IFCI Limited c. IDFC Limited
d. Stock Holding Corporation of India Limited. e. All of these

105. Which was the first exchange in the country to provide a modern, fully automated screen-based electronic trading system?
a. BSE b. NSE c. CSE d. ISE e. PSE

106. The Chairman of SEBI is nominated by?
a. Union Finance Ministry b. RBI
c. Government of India d. All of these e. None of these

107. Which of the following is Asia's first and the world's fastest stock exchange?
a. BSE b. NSE c. CSE d. ISE e. PSE

108. SEBI has ________ functions rolled into one body.
a. Three b. Four c. Two d. Five e. More than five

109. Stock Holding Corporation of India Ltd (SHCIL) was established in 1986 as a ______ company
a. Private Limited b. Unlimited c. Public limited
d. Limited Liability Partnership e. None of these

110. Which of the following is the country's first and one of the largest security custodians to financial institutions?
a. CRISIL b. NABARD c. FMC d. CIBIL e. SHCIL

111. Where was the India International Science Festival (IISF) 2016 organized?
a. Pune b. New Delhi c. Hyderabad d. Ahmedabad e. None of these.

112. Which state Chief Minister inaugurated the insurance claim distribution programme on December 10, 2016, worth 4 thousand 416 crore rupees to 20 lakh 46 thousand farmers of the state under the Prime Ministers Crop Insurance Scheme?

a. Haryana b. Rajasthan c. Gujarat
d. Madhya Pradesh e. none of these

113. What is the maximum limit of free accident insurance cover that Indian Railways will provide to passengers who buy railway tickets online, in a bid to promote the cashless transaction post demonetization?
a. Rs. 10 Lakh b. Rs. 7.5 Lakh c. Rs. 15 Lakh d. Rs. 9 Lakh e. None of these

114. Name the committee constituted by the Internet and Mobile Association of India (IAMAI) to fight against online piracy.
a. Uday Sodhi Committee b. Salil Kapoor Committee
c. Ajit Mohan Committee d. Ratan Watal Committee e. None of these

115. Which state on December 11, 2016 flagged off the first fortnightly special train for children?
a. Himachal Pradesh b. Jammu & Kashmir
c. Madhya Pradesh d. Uttarakhand e. None of these

116. The world's longest rail tunnel, Gotthard Base Tunnel (GBT) is built in which country?
a. Japan b. France c. Switzerland d. China e. None of these

117. Which State Government has tied up with Tata Trusts to acquire digital platforms to ensure Aadhaar-enabled public distribution system (PDS)at fair price in the state?
a. Haryana b. Bihar c. Maharashtra d. Uttar Pradesh e. None of these

118. Who has been appointed as the new Prime minister of Italy on December 11, 2016?
a. Paolo Gentiloni b. Matteo Renzi
c. Sergio Mattarella d. Romano Prodi e. None of these

119. Which sport has been granted provisional recognition by the International Olympic Committee on December 6, 2016?
a. Chess b. Cheerleading c. Cricket d. Squash e. Kabbadi

120. Name the campaign launched by the President Pranab Mukherjee on December 11, 2016, to end child labour, child slavery and violence against children.
a. '100 Million for 100 Million' b. Fight Against Child Labour
c. One in a Million d. Stop Child Labour e. None of these

Section 4: ENGLISH LANGUAGE

(121–130). Read the following passage carefully and answer the questions given below it. Certain words have been printed in bold to help you locate them while answering the questions.

The United Nations was set up 70 years ago to save future generations from the **scourge** of war. While it has arguably succeeded in preventing another great war, its track record on peace and security has not always been **stellar**.

Assessments on the vitality, durability and success of diplomacy in any year — including 2015 — are best carried out away from high-decibel levels and **cantankerous** TV anchors. Preferably, assessments are best when undertaken by those who are not themselves camp followers and cheerleaders. Diplomacy is a fine art when well-practised and fashioned by the mature; not by those seeking the thrill of tomorrow's headlines. Subjectivity will, by definition, find its way into any human endeavour. The seasoned practitioner is trained to guard against premature excitement, euphoria and hubris.

How does 2015 stand out as a year of success amongst all others? The successes that stand out: The adoption of the 2030 Sustainable Development Agenda, the conference of parties (COP 21) climate change agreement and the US-Iran nuclear deal, which passed despite stiff domestic and Israeli opposition. This bore fruit in 2016, as epitomised by the recent prisoner exchange that took place over the weekend.

A closer look at some of these successes indicates that 2015 has reinforced the need for multilateralism. The 2030 agenda, for example, unlike the Millennium Development Goals of 2000, reflect a bottom-up negotiation process by the entire UN membership. Their impact could well prove to be transformational, even as issues relating to their financing and implementation need to be resolved. Equally, decisions taken by the COP 21 in Paris represent a decisive victory against the irresponsible, particularly the climate **sceptics.** The UN Secretary General, Ban Ki-moon, stated after COP 21: "For the first time, every country in the world has pledged to curb their emissions, strengthen resilience and act internationally and domestically to address climate change." But, here again, follow-up action to ensure that global warming can be limited to meet the ambitious targets will need to be demonstrated.

At the multilateral level, 2015 also marked the 15th anniversary of Resolution 1325 on women, peace and security. Resolution 2242, passed in September 2015, affirms the essential role of women in conflict prevention, peacemaking, and peace-building. Along with the establishment of UN Women in 2010, this has firmly entrenched the centrality of women's empowerment and gender equality in the international discourse, a big plus for diplomacy in 2015.

Among the major bilateral diplomatic successes of the year was the decision for the normalisation of relations between the US and Cuba. The apology by Japan and the offer of $8 million to Korean "comfort women" during World War II were widely welcomed as an initiative designed to deal with a troublesome past.

2015 has hopefully also driven home to the main stakeholders the fact that the major threats to international peace and security are best handled collectively. These are beyond the capability of any one of them. A lot went wrong in 2015 precisely because this principle was not always upheld: The continued **stalemate** on Syria with devastating humanitarian consequences, the inability to deal with the Islamic State (IS) adequately, the situation in Yemen, where there has been more physical destruction in five months than in Syria in five years. The roadmap for collective action against the IS produced by the UN Security Council provides just that glimmer of hope. If the Turks can overcome their desire to first go after the Kurds, and the Americans and Russians come to genuinely believe that the IS constitutes a bigger threat than Bashar al-Assad, cooperation may result in some hope for Syria. For this, the Saudis and their followers also need to play ball.

121. According to the passage, what Went wrong in 2015?
   a. Physical destruction in Yemen. b. IS constituted a bigger threat in 2015.
   c. The inability to deal with the Islamic State (IS) adequately.
   d. All of above e. None of these

122. Find the incorrect statement on the basis of the given passage?
   a. The United Nations was set up 70 years.
   b. Resolution 2242, affirms the essential role of women in conflict prevention, peacemaking, and peace-building.
   c. Physical destruction in Yemen five months than in Syria in five years.
   d. Either 1 or 2 e. None of these

123. According to the author, what world has pledged for the first time?
   a. Adoption of the 2030 Sustainable Development Agenda.
   b. The US-Iran nuclear deal.
   c. To curb their emissions, strengthen resilience and act internationally and domestically to address climate change.
   d. Affirms the essential role of women in conflict prevention, peacemaking, and peace-building.
   e. None of these

124. According to the Author, What were widely welcome initiative in 2015?
   a. As issues relating to their financing and implementation has been resolved among many countries.
   b. Americans and Russians come to genuinely believe that the IS constitutes a bigger threat than Bashar al-Assad.
   c. Apology by Japan and the offer of $8 million to Korean "comfort women".
   d. Major bilateral diplomatic success between US and Cuba.
   e. None of these

125. Which of the following is 'true' in the context of the passage?
   a. Resolution 2242, passed in December 2015.
   b. UN Women Established in 2009.
   c. 2015 has strengthened the need for multilateralism.
   d. All of Above   e. None of these

Directions (126–128): Choose the word that is most nearly the SAME in meaning as the word given in bold as used in the passage.

126. Sceptics
   a. Fraud   b. Establish   c. Doubt   d. Crucial   e. Forsake

127. Scourge
   a. Praise   b. Pity   c. Vulnerable   d. Threat   e. Pleasure

128. Stellar
   a. Dearth   b. Distinct   c. Dissipate   d. major   e. Common

Directions (129–130): Select the word which is most nearly the OPPOSITE in meaning of the word as used in the passage.

129. Stalemate
   a. Dead-end   b. Blocked   c. Progress   d. Impasse   e. Pause

130. Cantankerous
   a. Good-natured   b. Amiable   c. Ill-natured   d. Peevish   e. Cranky

(131–140). In the following passage there are blanks each of which has been numbered. These numbers are printed below the passage and against each five words have been suggested. One of which fits the blank appropriately. Find out the appropriate word in each case.

God intentions alone are not enough to secure the public interest. For governments, the (1) in which it is protected is equally vital. The Delhi High Court verdict quashing all notifications banning the manufacture and sale of 344 Fixed Dose Combination (FDC) drugs is a lesson in how not to administer a regulatory law. The ban on combination drugs that have little (2) value was undoubtedly done for bona fide reasons. However, the government could not (3) the court that the ban was valid despite statutory bodies such as the Drug Testing Advisory Board (DTAB) and the Drugs Consultative Committee (DCC) not being involved in the process. There is little doubt that a number of combination drugs should be (4) off the shelf. The government believes, as do many health activists, that some combinations are unsafe and/or promote antibiotic resistance, while others lack particular therapeutic value, justification or advantage. Justice Sahai has correctly (5) from going into the merits of the ban, and has chosen to subject to scrutiny the process by which the decision was arrived at. While concluding that the ban was invalid because the power under the Drugs and Cosmetics Act was (6) without consulting the DTAB and DCC, he has found that the government went about the process in a (7) manner.

Initially it was noted that in the case of FDC drugs for which manufacturing licences were granted by State licensing authorities between September 1988 and October 2012, the process was done without any approval from the Drugs Controller. When they applied (8) to the Centre, on being asked to do so, their applications were not considered by the Drugs Controller; instead, the Centre formed 10 committees. When these (9) failed to consider all the applications, another one, the ABC Committee, was formed. However, this panel went into the question whether these drugs posed a risk to consumers or lacked therapeutic value and (10) .

131. a. legerdemain
b. manner
c. individual
d. similar
e. lingered

132. a. injurious
b. untherapeutic
c. therapeutic
d. damaging
e. harmful

133. a. avoid
b. back out
c. desist
d. convince
e. pass up

134. a. apprehend
b. procure
c. assume
d. snag
e. taken

135. a. refrained
b. countenance
c. persuade
d. petition
e. entreat

136. a. obsolescence
b. exercised
c. desuetude
d. discontinuance
e. inept

137. a. haphazard
b. intentional
c. careful
d. designed
e. methodical

138. a. versed
b. afresh
c. debilitated
d. grizzled
e. senile

139. a. diagnostic
b. diacritic
c. idiosyncratic
d. panels
e. alone

140. a. protest
b. impugn
c. criticize
d. justification
e. assail

(141–145). Rearrange the following sentences in the proper sequence to form a meaningful paragraph then answer the following questions.

1. It is about a very deep understanding of the human mechanics – not only of the physical dimension but of all aspects of a human being.
2. It is a profound form of evolving a human being.
3. Another thing is to raise awareness that it is important that it is done precisely and correctly.
4. A lot of things are being planned for the International Day of Yoga.
5. Above all, we want to make the world understand that yoga is not an exercise system.
6. One thing is, we are looking at large-scale yoga programs in multiple locations.

141. Which of the following sentence should be the FIRST after rearrangement?
a. 2 b. 3 c. 4 d. 5 e. 6

142. Which of the following sentence should be the FORTH after rearrangement?
a. 2 b. 5 c. 1 d. 3 e. 6

143. Which of the following sentence should be the THREE after rearrangement?
a. 2 b. 3 c. 1 d. 5 e. 6

144. Which of the following sentence should be the TWO after rearrangement?
a. 2 b. 3 c. 1 d. 4 e. 6

145. Which of the following sentence should be the FIFTH after rearrangement?
a. 2 b. 3 c. 1 d. 5 e. 6

(146–150). Read each part of the sentence to find out if there is any error in it. The error, if any, will be in one part of the sentence. The number of that part is an answer. If there is no error mark your answer as (e)

146. 1)/Denmark introduced a surcharge few 2)/ years ago on foods that contain over 3)/ 2.3 per cent saturated fat, drawing 4)/criticism about excessive bureaucracy. 5) No error
a. 1 b. 2 c. 3 d. 4 e. No Error

147. 1)/ Robotics has already made significant inroads 2)/ in electronics assembly, with sewing trades, traditionally 3)/ many countries' first entry point to 4)/ the global trading system, likely to come next. 5)/ No Error
a. 1 b. 2 c. 3 d. 4 e. No error

148. 1)/ A project that daringly set out to bring 2)/to life iconic paintings — many created in just one 3)/day — have proved to be a staggeringly laborious 4)/ cinematic effort taking years to realize.5) No error
a. 1 b. 2 c. 3 d. 4 e. No Error

149. 1)/ As this trend continues, the imperative 2)/ to build supply chains based on the location of relatively 3)/ immobile and cost-effective labor will wane, 4)/ with production moving closer to the final market. 5)/ No error
a. 1 b. 2 c. 3 d. 4 e. No error

150. 1)/Chief Minister will leave for 2)/ New Delhi on Friday evening to attend the 3)/ Inter-State Council meeting convened by 4)/ Prime Minister the previous day.5)/ No error
a. 1 b. 2 c. 3 d. 4 e. No Error

(151–155): Each passage is followed by questions based on its content. After reading passage, choose the best answer to each question. Answer all questions following a passage on the basis of what is stated or implied in that passage.

151. Even though love as a constitutional right has never been expressly_______in Indian jurisprudence, this isn't as_______a notion as one might think.
a. articulated, far-fetched b. tacit, real c. vocal, seen
d. clear, Introduce e. Straight, been

152. We like to salve our needlessly guilty conscience by__________a religious significance to these sculptures, but few people are__________by this mock spiritual argument.
a. agree, understand b. renege, perceive
c. discredit, interpret d. ascribing, deceived
e. accord, understood

153. We organised feeding centres for the_________, fodder stalls for cattle, and transported drinking water over long_________.
a. secure, warmth b. rich, sympathy,
c. prosperous, friendliness d. destitute, distances e. secued, area

154. The NPAs eat into profits and that is why banks hide them. In fact, banks further lend to corporates and help them__________ their past loans.
a. Service b. Scheme c. Ramification d. Peerless e. Repay

155. It is almost certain that what could be an important_________of a radically different framework to deliver public________in India will soon get legislative backing.
a. factor, uncover
b. fundamental, disinter
c. element, services
d. hint, dig out
e. thing, expose

ANSWER GRID

1. c	2. d	3. a	4. e	5. b	6. c	7. e	8. b	9. c	10. d
11. e	12. c	13. d	14. c	15. b	16. d	17. b	18. a	19. d	20. d
21. b	22. a	23. c	24. e	25. a	26. e	27. d	28. b	29. a	30. b
31. c	32. d	33. c	34. d	35. b	36. a	37. d	38. e	39. c	40. a
41. b	42. b	43. a	44. a	45. b	46. d	47. b	48. a	49. b	50. b
51. b	52. a	53. c	54. a	55. c	56. c	57. c	58. b	59. c	60. a
61. d	62. a	63. d	64. b	65. d	66. b	67. a	68. d	69. c	70. c
71. b	72. c	73. c	74. c	75. b	76. e	77. a	78. c	79. d	80. c
81. a	82. d	83. b	84. e	85. e	86. c	87. c	88. c	89. a	90. a
91. d	92. e	93. a	94. d	95. a	96. c	97. b	98. a	99. b	100. a
101. c	102. b	103. e	104. e	105. b	106. c	107. a	108. a	109. c	110. e
111. b	112. d	113. a	114. c	115. b	116. c	117. d	118. a	119. b	120. a
121. d	122. e	123. c	124. c	125. c	126. c	127. d	128. d	129. c	130. a
131. b	132. c	133. d	134. e	135. a	136. b	137. a	138. b	139. d	140. d
141. c	142. b	143. b	144. e	145. a	146. a	147. e	148. c	149. e	150. d
151. a	152. d	153. d	154. a	155. c					

EXPLANATION
REASONING ABILITY

(1–5)

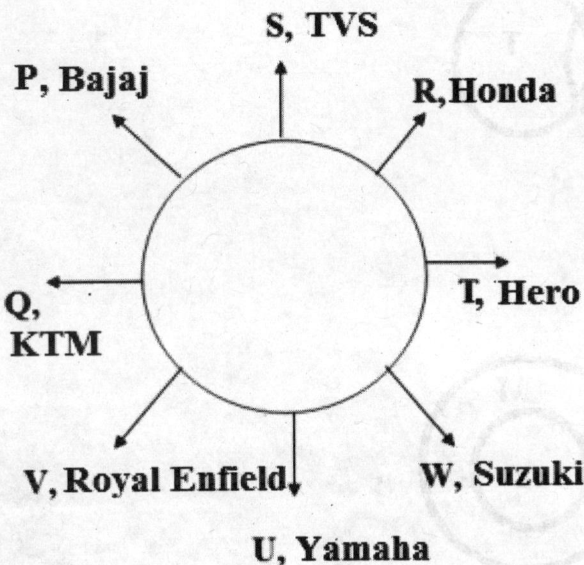

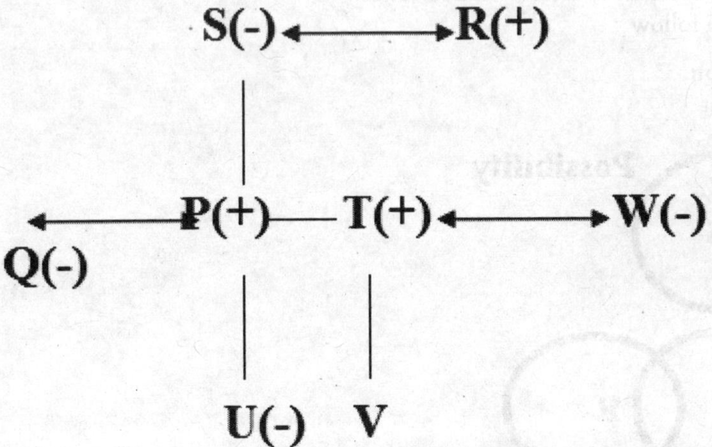

6. Some + Some => No conclusion=>I does not follow.
All R are S => Some S are R=> II follows
Some + All = Some = Some = Some+some = No conclusion => III does not follow.

All + Some = No conclusion => IV does not follow.

Basic Diagram:

7.

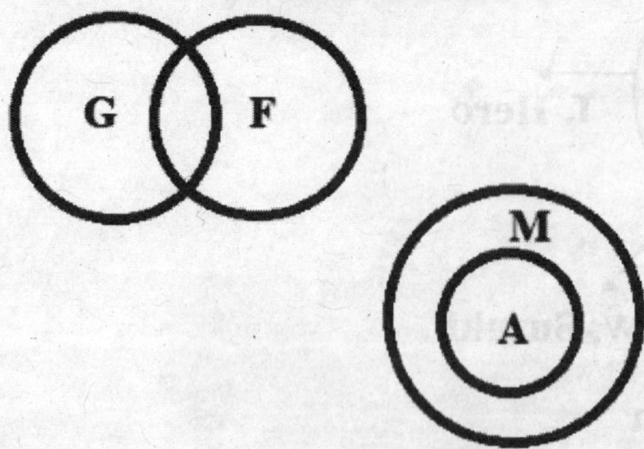

All+no =no => I not follow
some +no => some not =>but reverses=> ii not follow
Possibility exist => iii follow

8. No +No = No conclusion.
No=> possibility exist

Conc-2 **Possibility**

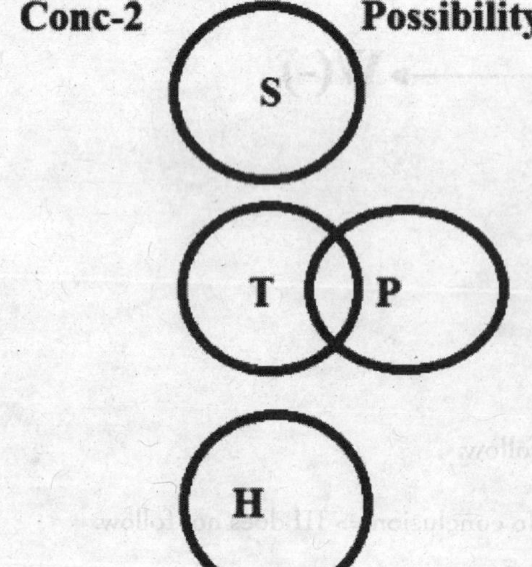

9. All+all = all => I follow
All+no = no => IV follows.
No+No=No conclusion=>II and III do not follow.

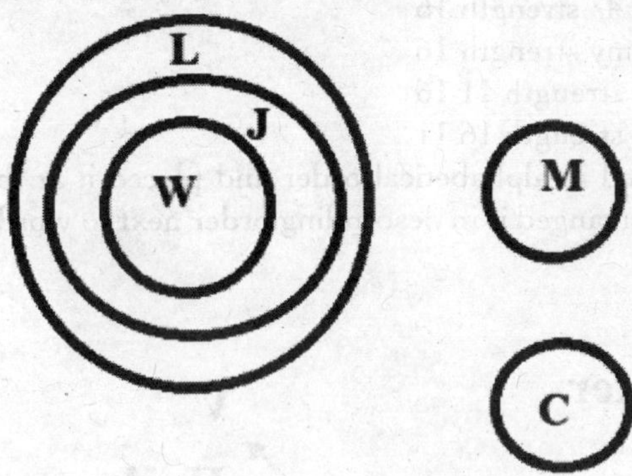

10. All+no =no => I follow
Some+all =some => II follow
Some box are Pen. & No box is pen => either or case

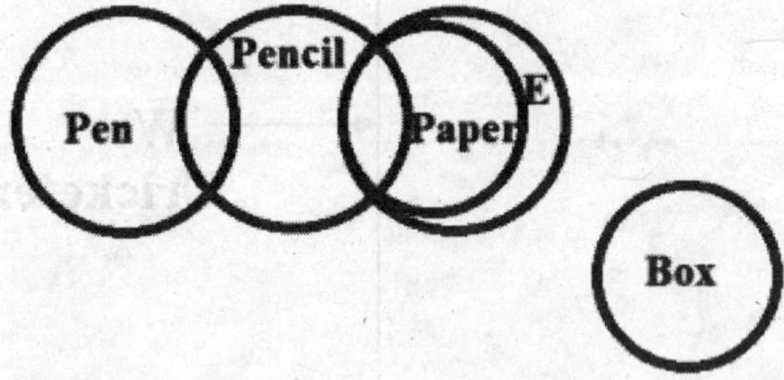

(11–15)

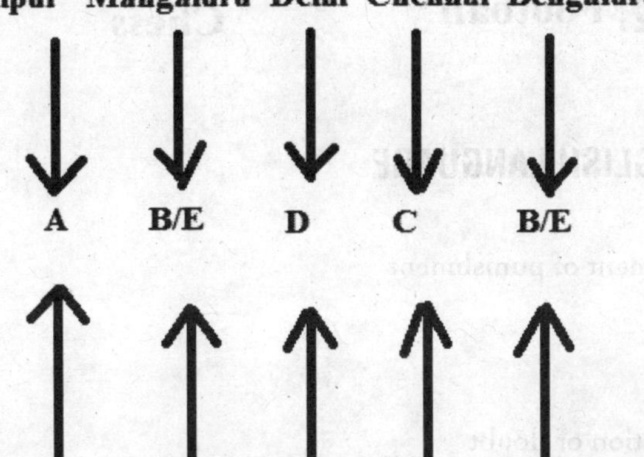

(16–20).

STEP 1 : all and best 11 25 my 47 81 equal 49 strength 16
STEP 2 : all and 81 49 best 11 25 my 47 equal strength 16
STEP 3 : all and 81 49 best equal 11 25 my 47 strength 16
STEP 4 : all and 81 49 best equal 47 25 11 my strength 16
STEP 5 : all and 81 49 best equal 47 25 my strength 11 16
STEP 6 : all and 81 49 best equal 47 25 my strength 16 11

Rule : In step 1 two words picked arranged in alphabetical order and placed it at the left corner and in step 2 , two numbers picked and arranged it in descending order next to words and so on.

(21–25).

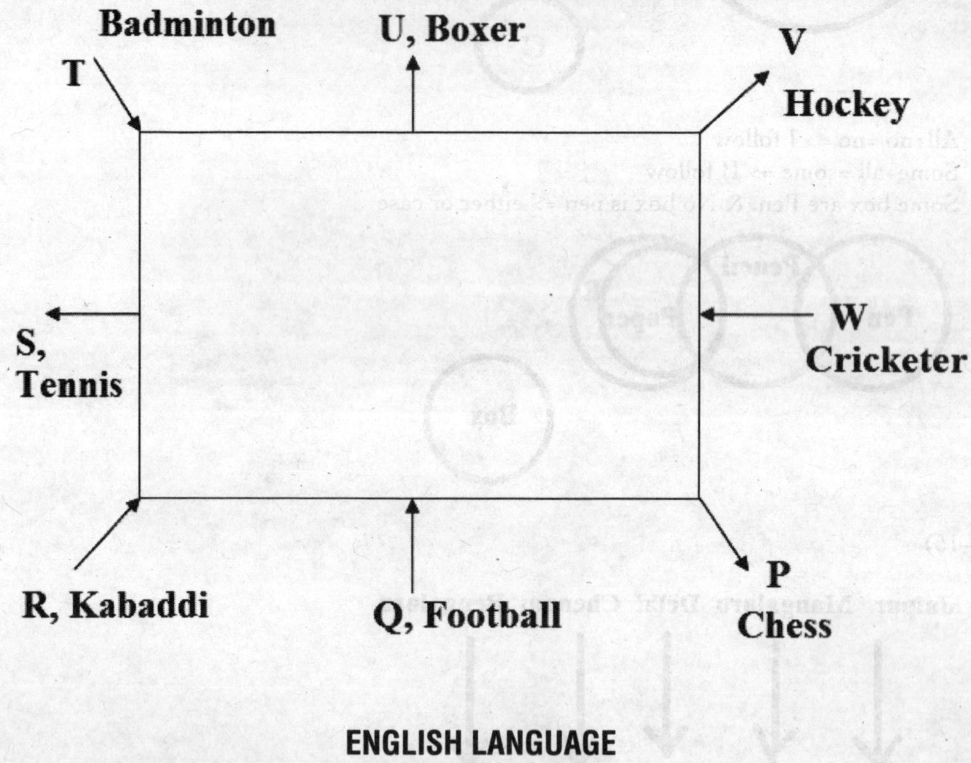

ENGLISH LANGUAGE

126. Scourge – a whio used as an instrument of punishment

127. Sreller – relating to stars

128. Cantankerous – bad tempered

129. Sceptics – a person inclined to question or doubt

130. Stalemate – a position counting as draw

146. replace "few" with "a few"
Few – when the amount is small and unsatisfactory

A Few – when the amount is small but still satisfactory

147. No error
148. it should be "has" instead of "have"
Here subject is one project so it should be has (singular H.V).
149. No error
150. it should be "the next day" instead of "the previous day". Because first part of sentence is in future tense so meeting should be held on the next day.

Solution to 46 to 50:

46. The least occurs in case of 7.56% GS 2014 which is more than 5 years. Hence answer is – all the years. Hence answer is option (4) None of these.
47. For 4 stocks, the desired yield is more than cut off yield. Hence option (2) is the answer.
48. Following stocks are having their cut-off price more than Rs. 100:

Name of Stock	Cut off price
7.56% GS 2014	103.47
7.94% GS 2021	102.5
7.56% GS 2014	106.75
8.24% GS 2027	107.82

None of these stocks have their cut-off yield more than its desired yield. Hence option (1) is the answer.

49. To obtain a minimum desired yield of 8%, Mr. Robert has to take 8.24% GS, as for remaining all the stocks, minimum desired yield is 8%. (One cannot have above 8% yield by mixing two stocks with less than 7% stock. It means that one stock has to be higher than 8 % and other has to be less than 8%).
He can mix 8.24% GS with any one of the remaining 6 stocks to obtain minimum 8% desired yield.
Hence option (2) is the answer.

50.

Rank 1	6.05% GS 2019	95.05
Rank 2	7.50% GS 2034	97.35
Rank 3	6.05% GS 2019	99.38
Rank 4	7.94% GS 2021	102.5
Rank 5	7.56% GS 2014	103.47
Rank 6	7.56% GS 2014	106.75
Rank 7	8.24% GS 2027	107.82

Hence option (2) is the answer.

Solution to 51 – 53:

One of the women spent 2517 – 1378 = 1139, she is Chellama. This is the only possibility as we add Rs. 1378 even to the least amount Rs. 1193, we will not be able to satisfy all the conditions given simultaneously.

So, the table obtained is:

A	C	D	H	S
2234	1139	1193	1340	2517

Solution to 54 – 56:

Let us make a table of the information given:

	Idli	Vada
Ignesh	6	6
Sandeep	1	0
Mukesh	4	2
Daljit	5	1
Bimal	8	4

Solution to 57 – 61:

57. Bangladesh > Philippines (97>86) for drinking water. And Philippines > any other countries for sanitation facilities. Thus, these two countries are on the coverage frontier for two facilities.

58. Statement A> Statement B only if statement A has higher percentage in total coverage for both drinking water and sanitation facilities taken independently and not as a total of the two facilities.

    Thus, only statement B and statement D are true
    India> China (81 > 67 and 29 > 24)
    India>Nepal (81 > 63 and 29 > 18)
    Also china > Nepal (67 > 63 and 24 > 18)

59. Let the urban population be x and rural population be y.

    From the sanitation column, we have 0.7x + 0.14y = 0.29(x+y), OR, 0.41x = 0.15y

    Therefore $x = \frac{15y}{41}$

    Therefore percentage of rural population $= \frac{y}{x+y} \times 100 = \frac{y}{\frac{15y}{41}+y} \times 100 = \frac{41}{56} \times 100 = 73.2\%$

60. In the same way as the previous questions, we can find percentage of rural population for Philippines, Indonesia and China.

P	50%
I	66.66%
C	79.8%

    Thus, Philippines < Indonesia < China.

61. India is not on coverage frontier because
    a. It is below Bangladesh and Philippines for drinking water.
    b. For sanitation facilities it is below Philippines *inter alia.*

SBI PO Mains MOCK Test Paper 12

Structure of this MOCK Test

S.No.	Name of section	No. of Questions	Total marks	Allotted Time
1	Reasoning and Computer Aptitude	45	60	60 minutes
2	Data Analysis and Interpretation	35	60	45 minutes
3	General/ Economy/ Banking Awareness	40	40	35 minutes
4	English Language	35	40	40 minutes
Total		155	200	3 hours

- There is 1/4th Negative marking for every wrong answer.
- If a question is left blank, i.e. no answer is marked by the candidate, there will be no penalty for that question

Section 1: Reasoning and Computer Aptitude

Direction for questions 1- 5: Read the passage given below and solve the questions based on it.
Five cricket coaches B, D, J, L and W were being judged for the award of best coach of the year. The selection committee ranked them on five different parameters viz. Empathy, Vision, Focus, Creativity, and Intuitions. The five coaches were given points on these five parameters. The best coach gets 5 points and the worst coach gets 1 point. There are no ties. The coach with highest total gets the award of best coach. B gets the award by scoring 24 points. W gets 5 points in Creativity and 3 points in Intuition. J got same score in four of the given five parameters. Their final standings were in alphabetical order of their names.

1. What is the overall score of J?
   a. 12 b. 13 c. 14 d. 11 e. Indeterminable

2. What is the rank of D in Creativity?
   a. 1st b. 2nd c. 5th d. 2nd e. Indeterminable

3. If L scored his highest points in empathy then what is the score of D in Vision?
   a. 1 b. 2 c. 3 d. 4 e. 5

4. For how many of the coaches given above, is it possible to determine the exact points obtained in different parameters?
a. 2 b. 3 c. 4 d. 5 e. 1

5. If L gets a score of 2 in each of the – Empathy, Vision and Focus – parameters, then what is the rank of D in intuition?
a. Rank 2nd b. Rank 4th c. Rank 3rd d. Rank 5th e. Rank 1st

6. Four of the following five are alike in a certain way and so form a group. Which of the one that does not belong to that group?
a. 18 b. 24 c. 36 d. 34 e. 26

7. If green means yellow, yellow means white, white means red, red means violet, violet means black, then which of the following means the colour of the human blood?
a. Red b. Black c. Green d. White e. None of these

8. How many such pairs of letters are there in the word GLIMPSE each of which has as many letters between them in the word as in the English alphabet?
a. None b. One c. Two
d. Three e. More than three

9. EARN is related to RANE and BOND is related to NODB in the same way as TEAR is related to?
a. AEART b. ATRE c. ARET d. REAT e. None of these

10. If '×' means add to, '/' means multiplied by, '+' means subtracted from and '–'means divided by then 24+36-12×8/4=?
a. 36 b. 53 c. 5 d. -20 e. None of these

11. How many such digits are there in the number 5831649 each of which is as far away from the beginning of the number as when the digits are rearranged in ascending order?
a. None b. One c. Two
d. Three e. More than three

12. Four of the following five are alike in a certain way and so form a group. Which is the one that does not belong to the group?
a. Coconut b. Lotus c. Lily d. Rose e. Marigold

(13–15) Directions

- 'P x Q' means 'P is brother of Q'
- 'P – Q ' means ' P is sister of Q'
- 'P + Q ' means ' P is father of Q'
- 'P / Q' means 'P is mother of Q'

13. Which of the following represents 'M is nephew of N'?
a. N – K + M b. N X K / M c. N / K X M
d. N – K / M X T e. None of these

14. How is T related to D in the following expression: H + T / R – D?
a. Nephew b. Niece
c. Nephew or Niece d. Data Inadequate e. None of these

15. Which of the following represents F is daughter of W?
    a. W / R + F b. W X R X F c. W + R X F – T d. W + R – F + T e. None of these

Direction for questions 16–20: In each of these questions below are given four statements followed by four conclusions. Read all the conclusions and then decide which of the given conclusions logically follows from the given statements disregarding commonly known facts.

16. **Statements**
    Some bags are trunks
    All trunks are bags
    Some shirts are books
    All books are shops
    Conclusions
    1. Some shops are bags
    2. Some books are bags
    3. Some shops are shirts
    4. Some shirts are bags
    a. Only 1 and 2 follows b. Only 1 and 3 follows
    c. Only 3 and 4 follows d. Only 2 and 4 follows e. None of these

17. **Statements**
    All pens are chairs
    All flowers are chairs
    All chairs are trucks
    All trees are trucks
    Conclusion
    1. Some trucks are pens
    2. Some trucks are chairs
    3. Some trees are pens
    4. Some trees are chairs
    a. Only 1 and 3 follows b. Only 1 and 2 follows
    c. Only 3 and 4 follows d. Only 2 and 4 follows e. None of these

18. **Statements**
    All desks are pillars
    Some pillars are towns
    All towns are benches
    Some benches are cars
    Conclusions
    1. Some cars are towns
    2. Some benches are desks
    3. Some benches are pillars
    4. Some cars are pillars
    a. None follows b. Only 1 follows c. Only 2 follows
    d. Only 3 follows e. Only 4 follows

19. **Statements**
All stations are house
No house is garden
Some gardens are rivers
All rivers are ponds
Conclusions
1. Some ponds are garden
2. Some ponds are stations
3. Some ponds are houses
4. No pond is station
a. Only 1 follows
b. Only either 2 or 4 follows
c. Only 1 and 2 follows
d. Only 1 and 4 follows
e. None of these

20. **Statements**
Some towers are lanes
Some lanes are roads
Some roads are rivers
Some rivers are jungles
Conclusions :
1. Some jungles are road
2. Some roads are lane
3. Some jungles are towers
4. No jungle is road
a. Only 1 follows
b. Only 2 follows
c. Only either 1 or 4 follows
d. Only 4 follows
e. Only either 1 or 4 and 2 follows

Direction for questions 21- 25: Read the passage given below and solve the questions based on it.

Five universities – A, B, C, L and K - participated in the last year inter-university athlete event. Each of the universities was represented by three members. According to the rules, the race-track maker gets wild card entry making the total number of athletes participating in the race equal to 16. The rank obtained by the individual will be the points obtained. And similarly the points obtained by an individual university will be equal to the sum of the ranks of the member athletes of the team. Lower the points, better the team and the best team wins the trophy.

The five universities tied for the trophy, their sum being equal, however no two athletes tied for the same position. In order to determine the order in which the universities will hold the trophy (they agreed to hold it for 73 days each), they multiplied the athletes positions together in each university. The university with the smallest product – K- will hold the trophy first and so on the university with the largest product – A – will hold the cup last. Unfortunately, universities B and C were still tied and had to be separated by a toss of coin.

It was also found that the no two athletes of a university finish at the consecutive positions. Had the race-track maker did not come in between two athletes of university B, university B would have achieved this feat of two athletes being at consecutive positions.

21. Which of the following is the position of the race- track maker?
a. 6 b. 11 c. either 6 or 11
d. cannot be determined e. None of these

22. What is the product of the university A?
a. 360 b. 455 c. 450 d. 128 e. None of these

23. What is the smallest point obtained by an individual of university L?
a. 1 b. 2 c. 3 d. 4 e. 5

24. What is the product of the ranks obtained by all the athletes of university K?
a. 120 b. 150 c. 128 d. 144 e. 360

25. Which of the following is not a rank obtained by the athletes of university C?
a. 15 b. 6 c. 4 d. 2 e. 3

Direction for questions (26–30): Each of these questions consists of a question and two statements numbered 1 and 2. You have to decide whether the data provided in the statements are sufficient to answer the question. Read both the statements and give the answer-

a. if the data in statement 1 alone is sufficient to answer the question, while the data in statement 2 alone is not sufficient to answer the question.
b. if the data in statement 2 alone is sufficient to answer the question, while the data in statement 1 alone is not sufficient to answer the question.
c. if the data either in statement 1 alone or in statement 2 alone is sufficient to answer the questions.
d. if the data in both the statements 1 and 2 together are not sufficient to answer the question.
e. if the data in both the statements 1 and 2 together are necessary to answer the question.

26. How is M related to F?
Statements:
1. F is sister of N who is mother of R.
2. M has two brothers of which one is R.

27. On which in March was Pravin's father's birthday?
Statements:
1. Pravin correctly remembers that his father's birthday is after 14th but before 19th March.
2. Pravin's sister correctly remembers that their father's birthday is after 17th but before 21st March.

28. Among M, N, T, R and D each having different age who is the youngest?
Statements:
1. N is younger than only D among them.
2. T is older than R and younger than M.

29. Village D is in which direction of village H ?
Statements:
1. Village H is to the South of village A which is to the South-East of village D.
2.. Village M is to the East of the village D and to the North-East of village H.

30. How is 'Food' written in a code language?
Statements:
1. 'Always eat good food' is written as 'ha na pa ta' in that code language.
2. 'Enjoy eating good food' is written as 'ni ha ja pa' in that code language.

31. How many bits is equal to 1 nibble?
a. 8 bits b. 4 bits c. 16 bits d. 6 bits e. None of these

32. The 16 bit Microprocessor means that it has
a. 16 address lines b. 16 buses
c. 16 data lines d. 16 routes e. None of these

33. What is ISO9362 related to in context to banking technology?
a. RTGS Transfer b. NEFT Transfer
c. SWIFT Transfers d. All of them e. None of these

34. Which of the following codes need 7 bits to represent a character?
a. ASCII b. BCD c. EBCDIC d. GRAY e. None of these

35. What is the full form of NEFT?
a. National Electronic Funds Transfer
b. Natural Electronic Funds Transfer
c. National Electronic Fast Transfer
d. Natural Electronic Fast Transfer
e. None of these

36. If I want to use Spelling and Grammar check in MS Word, which button shall I press on the keyboard?
a. F2 b. F3 c. F6 d. F7 e. F8

37. What is the full form of PSTN?
a. Public Switched Telephone Network
b. Public Switched Telecommunication Network
c. Public Service Telephone Network
d. Public Services Telecommunication Network
e. None of these

38. DSL is an example of a ________ connection
a. Slow b. Network c. Wireless d. Broad band e. None of these

39. Which of the following refers to a small, single-site network?
a. LAN b. DSL c. RAM d. USB e. CPU

40. Which of the following protocol is used by Internet mail?
a. HTTP b. TCP/IP c. FTP d. UTP e. None of these

41. MACROS is used to
a. Store the test b. Create the text c. Break the text
d. All of the above e. None of these

42. Structured Query Language(SQL) is used in the following.
    a. Create Database
    b. Create and Modify Database
    c. Create, Modify and Query Database
    d. Cannot create database
    e. None of these

43. It is the way text appears on a page. It is
    a. Format b. Font c. Form Letter d. Form e. Typecast

44. Chief component of first generation computer was
    a. Transistor
    b. Vacuum Tubes and Valves
    c. Integrated Circuits
    d. Semiconductor
    e. None of these

45. Which of the following is a standard code used to exchange information among data processing and communication system?
    a. ANSI b. ACM c. ASCII d. APL e. OSI

Section 2: Data Analysis and Interpretation

Directions for questions 46 – 50: Go through the chart given below and solve the questions based on it.

A test was performed on various food items to check for protein content, fat content and Mineral content. Five food items viz, Butter, Apple, Dal, Chicken and Bournvita.

The chart shows the quantity of foods checked:

Food Item	Quantity Checked	Protein content	Fat Content	Mineral content
Butter	2 gm	10mg	1.0gm	75mg
Apple	1 gm	15mg	35mg	60mg
Dal	2 gm	100mg	15mg	90mg
Chicken	3 gm	75mg	1gm	150mg
Bournvita	1 gm	25mg	20mg	80mg
Veg Burger	2gm	5mg	1.1gm	15mg

NOTE: 1gm = 1000mg

Based on these results, the foods are classified into the following categories:

Healthy food	If percentage of proteins the highest and the percentage of fats is the least as compared to the other foods.
Junk food	If the percentage of fat is the highest and the percentage of protein is the least.
Not recommended	If the percentage of fats is more than the percentage of proteins and the mineral content is least as compared to the other foods

Answer the questions on the basis of the information given above.

46. What is the highest percentage of protein any of the given foods?
    a. 0.5% b. 5% c. 1% d. 10% e. 2%

47. Which food can be referred to as Healthy?
    a. Butter b. Apple c. Dal d. Chicken e. Veg Burger

48. Which food can be classified as junk from amongst the above mentioned foods?
    a. Veg burger b. Apple c. Dal d. Chicken e. Butter

49. Which food is not recommended as per the criteria defined above?
    a. Butter b. Apple c. Veg Burger d. Chicken e. Dal

50. In how many foods is the percentage of fat more than the percentage of protein?
    a. 1 b. 2 c. 3 d. 4 e. 0

Directions for questions 51 – 54: Go through the chart given below and solve the questions based on it.

Following grid presents the percentage composition of five verticals under different sectors.

Sector	Factories	Employment	Fixed Capital	Variable Cost	Value Added
Government	18	15	14	22	25
Central	8	6	5	7	10
State	4	6	4	8	3
Central/State	6	3	5	7	12
Public	12	8	6	19	8
Private	55	65	72	54	62
Joint	15	12	8	5	5
Total	100	100	100	100	100

51. If the total work force was 76million whereas the total value added was 225 million, then which of the following had the maximum value addition per worker?
    a. Central b. State c. Central/State d. Public e. Joint

52. Which of the following sectors has the maximum fixed capital invested per factory?
    a. Central b. State c. Central/State d. Public e. Joint

53. If the variable is proportional to the number of employees and the production per employee, then for which of the following is the production highest?
    a. Government b. Private c. Joint d. Public e. Central

54. If the government has a fixed capital of $200 million in the Iron& Steel industry, which corresponds to 20.012% of its total investment as fixed capital, then how much did the government invest(in Rs. million) in Maruti Udyog Ltd. which forms 25% of the investment in the joint sector?(1US $ = Rs.45)
    a. 6500 b. 2500 c. 143 d. 145 e. 2450

Direction for questions 55 – 59: Go through the table below and solve the questions based on it.

Following table gives the details pertaining to the company's employee appointment in three different wings at different levels and the salaries offered:

	Finance Wing			Marketing Wing			H R D Wing		
Details / Level of entry	Entry Level	Middle Level	Top Level	Entry Level	Middle Level	Top Level	Entry Level	Middle Level	Top Level
Average gross salary drawn per month (in Rs.)	5000	8000	18000	4000	7000	17000	5500	7500	15000
Minimum Work Ex required for a graduate (in years)	0	2	NA	0	3	5	0	2	NA
Minimum Work Ex required for a PG (in years)	0	1	2	0	0	2	0	0	2
Number of Grads. Employed	1000	100	NA	1000	70	1	40	1	NA
Number of PG employed	200	100	5	Nil	80	2	80	4	1

Grads. Stands for graduate. A graduate has completed exactly 15 years of education. PG stands for post graduation and a post graduate has completed exactly 17 years of education.

A person is not allowed to shift from one wing to another wing.

Net salary=Gross Salary – taxes and other benefits

NA is given when it is not eligible.

55. Ravi is a graduate and he joins in a wing at a particular level. What is the minimum time that Ravi will take to save Rs. 200000, if 15% of his salary is deducted for tax and other benefits and he spends 50% of his net salary?
    a. 34 months b. 44 months c. 56 months d. 52 months e. None of these

56. Ravi's friend Aftab, a post graduate joins at a middle management cadre. He joins that particular wing which will help him in saving maximum money in two years, given that 15% of his salary is deducted for taxation and other benefits and he spends 40% of his net income. Which wing he must have joined?
    a. Finance b. Marketing c. HRD
    d. None of these e. cannot be determined

57. Ravi's another friend Indrajeet is a fresh graduate. He is confused about his next career move that should he go for post graduation or to start working. He finally decides to calculate her total earnings in 5 years' time in both cases for all wings and make his decision on that basis. Which of the following would be the best course of action assuming he keeps getting promoted immediately after meeting the minimum criteria? (cost of Post graduate program is Rs. 250000 keeping all the other things constant.)

a. Do post graduation and join marketing wing
b. Do post graduation and join HRD wing
c. Do not do post graduation and join HRD wing
d. Do not do post graduation and join finance wing
e. None of these

58. To facilitate the promotion of employees in a particular wing from lower level (L_1) to next higher level (L_2), a mechanism has been devised. The whole of this mechanism has been developed by Mr. Thomas and hence it is named as Thomas profile co-efficient. Thomas profile co-efficient (TPC) for any wing at any level is calculated as follows:
TPC = No. of the Employees in L_2 / No. of employees in L_1
Lower the TPC, higher is the chances of getting promoted.
What is the ratio of highest TPC of post graduate to the highest TPC of a graduate?
a. 1:5 b. 5:1 c. 7:3 d. 25:7 e. none of these

59. Under a new policy to improve the profile of the company, it has been decided that no graduates will be recruited now and all graduates at entry level and middle level will be replaced with post graduates. Which wing has the best TPC at any level now(Use the definition of TPC from Q 58)?
a. Finance b. HRD c. Marketing
d. Finance or Marketing e. none of these

Direction for questions 60 – 63: Go through the chart given below and solve the questions based on it.

Following bar chart presents the export value of 4 fruits exported from India.

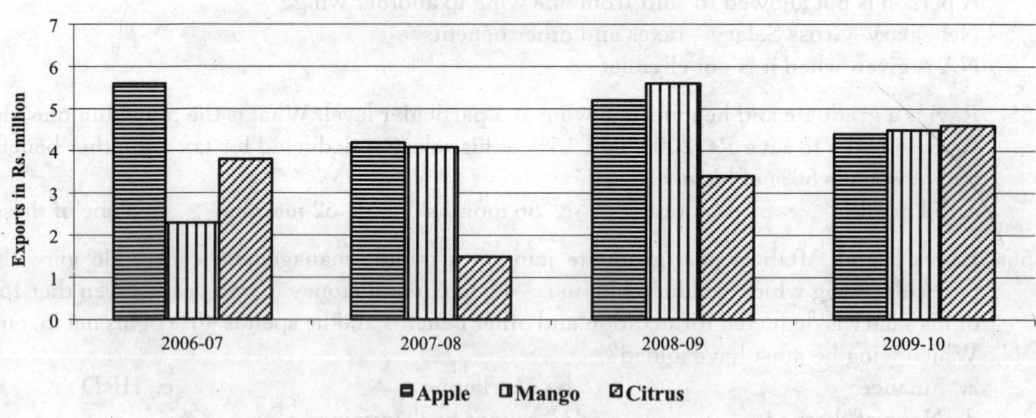

60. For how many years are the combined exports of mangoes and citrus greater than the exports of apples by at least 150%?
a. 0 b. 1 c. 2 d. 3

61. In how many years the average exports of all the three fruits in a given year is greater than the average yearly exports of all the fruits for all four years?
a. 11 b. 2 c. 3 d. 4

62. Combined Exports value of which fruit from India is the maximum in the given years?
a. Apple b. Mango c. Citrus d. cannotbe determined

63. From the given four years, which year the export value of the fruits given in bar chart is the maximum?
a. 2006-07 b. 2007-08 c. 2008-09 d. 2009-10

Direction for questions Q64 – Q66 – Answer the questions based on the statements given below.
There are two persons DiSiDo and DoSiDi. DiSiDo lies on Monday, Tuesday and Wednesday whereas DoSiDi lies on Thursday, Friday and Saturday. They both tell the truth on Sunday. You happen to meet them and they make following statements:
A: I will lie tomorrow.
B: I lied yesterday, and I will lie tomorrow.

64. Who is lying?
a. A b. B c. Both are lying d. cannot be determined

65. What is the day today?
a. Sunday b. Monday c. Wednesday d. cannot be determined

66. Who is DiSiDo?
a. A b. B
c. Either is possible d. cannot be determined

Direction for questions Q67 – Q69 – Answer the questions based on the statements given below.
A young girl Roopa leaves home with x flowers, goes to the bank of a nearby river. On the bank of the river, there are four places of worship, standing in a row. She dips all the x flowers into the river. The number of flowers doubles. Then she enters the first place of worship, offers y flowers to the deity. She dips the remaining flowers into the river, and again the number of flowers doubles. She goes to the second place of worship, offers y flowers to the deity. She dips the remaining flowers into the river, and again the number of flower doubles. She goes to the third place of worship, offers y flowers to the deity. She dips the remaining flowers into the river, and again the number of flowers doubles. She goes to the fourth place of worship, offers y flowers to the deity. Now she is left with no flowers in hand.

67. If Roopa leaves home with 30 flowers, the number of flowers she offers to each deity is
a. 30 b. 31 c. 32 d. 33

68. The minimum number of flowers that could be offered to each deity is
a. 0 b. 15 c. 16 d. Cannot be determined

69. The minimum number of flowers with which Roopa leaves home is
a. 16 b. 15 c. 0 d. Cannot be determined

70. A can work half as fast as B and C together. A and B together can work three times as fast as C. If all three of them complete a job in 15 days, how long would C take to complete the same work?
a. 45 days b. 54 days c. 60 days d. 65 days e. 75 days

71. One number is selected at random from first 25 natural numbers. What is the probability that it is a multiple of either 5 or 7?
a. 2/12 b. 8/25 c. 4/25 d. 1/8 e. None of these

72. A spherical metal ball of 6cm radius is melted and recast into three spherical balls. The radii of two of these balls are 3cm and 4cm. What is the radius of the third ball?
a. 4.5cm b. 5cm c. 6 cm d. 7 cm 5. 8 cm

73. Five tables and eight chairs cost Rs. 7,350. Three tables and five chairs cost Rs. 4,475. What is the price of one table?
a. Rs. 950 b. Rs. 325 c. Rs. 925 d. Rs. 350 e. Rs. 450

74. In the figure given, AB || CD and PQ is the transversal. Find the value of y (in degrees).

a. 60 b. 30 c. 45 d. 120 e. 75

75. Owner of book point does not get either profit or loss by selling 15 books for Rs. 225. How many books should he sell for the same amount to gain 25% profit?
a. 10 b. 11 c. 12 d. 13 e. 15

76. A reduction 20% in the price of the rice enables to get 6 kgs more of rice for Rs. 120. What is the initial price of rice (Rs./kg)?
a. 4 b. 5 c. 6 d. 10 e. None of these

77. Two boats, traveling at 5 and 10 kms per hour, head directly towards each other. They begin at a distance of 20 kms from each other. How far apart are they (in kms) one minute before they collide?
a. $\frac{1}{12}$ b. $\frac{1}{6}$ c. $\frac{1}{4}$ d. $\frac{1}{3}$ 5. $\frac{1}{2}$

78. If the price of an article rose by 25% every odd year and fell by 20% every even year, what would be the percentage change after 20 years?
a. 10% increase b. 25% increase c. No change d. 20% decrease e. 25% decrease

79. Three jars have their volumes in the ratio 3: 4: 5. They are full of mixtures of milk and water. The mixtures contain milk and water in the ratio of (4: 1), (3: 1) and (5: 2) respectively. The contents of all these three jars are poured into a fourth jar. The ratio of milk and water in the fourth jar is:
a. 4: 1 b. 151: 48 c. 157: 53 d. 5: 2 e. 2:7

80. Owing to heavy traffic on the route, a man finds that his speed is reduced by 25% today with respect to normal days. As a result, he reaches his office 20 minutes later than normal. How much time did he take today to reach the office?
a. 40 mins b. 45 mins c. 60 mins d. 75 mins e. 90 mins

Section 3: General and Banking Awareness

81. Which of the following rate signals the RBI's long term outlook on interest rate?
a. Repo Rate b. Reverse Repo Rate c. Bank rate
d. SLR e. CRR

82. To combat rising inflation, RBI has to do which of the following activities?
a. Increase Bank Rate b. Sell Govt Securities
c. increase reserve ratio d. All of the above e. None of these

83. Which of the following is a reason for deflation?
a. Surplus budgeting b. Growth in GDP
c. High Interest Rate d. All of the above e. None of these

84. Which of the following calculates National Income of India?
a. Planning Commission b. Finance Ministry
c. CSO d. RBI e. None of these

85. Which of the following publishes World Investment report?
a. IBRD b. IMF c. UNDP d. WTO e. None of these

86. Which is a type of crossing in a cheque?
a. Negotiable Crossing b. Special crossing c. Level Crossing
d. Precise Crossing e. Named Crossing

87. Long position in two call and put with the same strike price to expiration date is called
a. Spread b. Stock c. Straps d. Straddle e. None of these

88. Listing a company on the stock market requires that the company
a. Be a partnership firm b. Be proprietary firm
c. a limited liability company d. all of these e. None of these

89. In which of the following account are borrowings from the World Bank recorded in the balance of payments?
a. Capital Accounts b. Visible Goods
c. Current Account d. Revenue Account
e. Saving Account

90. Borrowing is included in which of the following account?
a. Current Account b. Saving Account
c. Capital Account d. Social Account e. None of these

91. Primary Deficit is defined as:
a. Fiscal Deficit-interest payments b. Fiscal deficit + interest payments
c. Fiscal Deficit-Revenue Expenditure
d. Fiscal Deficit-Capital Expenditure e. None of these

92. Sukanya Samriddhi account was launched on?
a. 21 Jan 2014 b. 21 Jan 2014 c. 22 Jan 2014 d. 22 Jan 2014 e. None of these

93. HRD Minister Launched a new IIT in?
a. Karnataka b. Kolkata
c. Himachal Pradesh d. Manipur e. None of these

94. First National Conference of Investigating Agencies was held in?
a. Mumbai b. New Delhi c. Hyderabad d. Kolkata e. None of these

95. World's Largest ' Aircraft Airlander 10' makes maiden Voyage in?
a. USA b. China c. Britain d. Australia e. None of these

96. Scientists Develop Mechanism to recycle which gas into Usable fuel?
a. Carbon Mono oxide b. Nitrogen
c. Helium d. Carbon di oxide e. None of these

97. Which country launched First Mobile Telecommunication Satellite on 6 August 2016?
a. USA b. Japan c. India d. China e. None of these

98. Urjit R Patel is appointed as __ Governor of Reserve Bank of India.
a. 23rd b. 24th c. 20th d. 22nd e. None of these

99. Author of book "India Rising: fresh hope, new fears" is?
a. Ravi Vellor b. Sanjeev Sanyal
c. Dinesh K Khara d. Ravindra Singh e. None of these

100. India's First Bio-CNG plant inaugurated in?
a. Jharkhand b. Madhya Pradesh c. Gujarat
d. Pune e. None of these

101. RBI announces interest subvention scheme for women self help group at _%?
a. 6.5% b. 7% c. 8% d. 7.5% e. None of these

102. UEFA Best player in Europe 2016 was won by?
a. Leonel Messi b. Luis Suarez
c. Cristiano Ronaldo d. Antino Greezman e. None of these

103. According to the Forbes List of most innovative companies which company among the following topped the list?
a. Tesla Motors b. Salesforce
c. Regeneron Pharmaceuticals d. Hindustan Unilever e. None of these

104. First SAARC Youth Parliamentarians Conference was held in?
a. India b. Iran c. Pakistan d. Bangladesh e. None of these

105. Elon Musk is not related with which of the following companies?
a. Tesla Motors b. Solarcity c. Paypal d. Zip2 e. None of these

106. India is on __ position in Wealthiest nations list?
a. 7th b. 10th c. 6th d. 8th e. None of these

107. Which Country won the Under-19 Cricket World Cup 2016?
a. India b. Australia c. England d. West Indies e. None of these

108. Jitu Rai is associated with which of the following?
a. Shooting b. Long Jump c. Badminton d. Archery e. None of these

109. PV Sindhu was awarded with which of the following awards?
a. Bharat Ratna b. Arjuna Award
c. Rajiv Gandhi Khel Ratna d. Dronacharya Award e. None of these

110. A country's economic development is dependent on?
a. Natural Resources
b. Capital Formation
c. Market size
d. All of these
e. None of these

111. From where did the Gross Happiness start?
a. Greece
b. Bhutan
c. Bangladesh
d. India
e. None of these

112. Which of the following is the regulator of money market?
a. Government of India
b. Reserve Bank of India
c. Insurance Regulatory Development Authority
d. Telecom Regulatory Authority of India
e. None of these

113. What is notice money?
a. It is an overnight loan in the money market
b. It is loan of above 1 day to 14 days in the money market
c. It is a loan of above 14 days to 364 days in the money market
d. It is a loan provided on certain terms and conditions by bank
e. None of these

114. Which of the following act defines a cheque?
a. Reserve Bank of India Act 1934
b. Negotiable Instrument Act 1881
c. Banking Regulation Act 1949
d. Companies Act 2013
e. Foreign Exchange Management Act 1999

115. Commercial Bill is a type of
a. Promissory Note
b. Cheque
c. Stamp
d. Bill of exchange
e. None of these

116. SEBI act 1992 empowers SEBI with _____ power
a. Constitutional Power
b. Non Statutory Power
c. Statutory power
d. None of these
e. All of these

117. An economy that does not export or import from other country, is said to be
a. Open Economy
b. Closed Economy
c. Mixed Economy
d. Socialist Economy
e. Capitalist Economy

118. In which of the following is the visible items recorded for a country?
a. Capital Account
b. The Balance of trade
c. Foreign Exchange
d. Reserve Bank of India
e. None of these

119. A bank Account held in foreign country by a domestic bank denominated In the currency of that country is called
a. Loro Account
b. Nostro Account
c. Vostro Account
d. Foreign Currency convertible account
e. Non resident ordinary account

120. Article 110 of the constitution of India is related to
a. Budget
b. Financial Bill
c. Money Bill
d. State Budget
e. None of these

Section 4: ENGLISH LANGUAGE

Directions for questions 121 – 130: Read the following passage carefully and answer the questions given below. Certain words are printed in bold to help you to locate them while answering some of the questions.

Frustration is an global cancer. It has spared no country. In some countries, frustration exists because these countries are populated by 'have-nots'. In other countries which are populated by 'haves'. Frustration is among them also because they do have as far as India is concerned its education system is breeding more and more frustration among both students and teachers. And yet no one seems to clear about what can be done to make it more meaningful. Many reforms have been discussed length but have come to nothing for one reason or another. The authorities are now peddling the idea of autonomous colleges as means of toning up the teaching standards. They argue that by allowing certain colleges to introduce their own courses, hold seminars and above all, to evolve their own methods of assessing students, students will get a far better deal. Indeed, they make out that such colleges will have free hand in nearly everything except granting degrees. In theory all this sounds, attractive enough. But there is little to show that the managements concerned are keen on such reforms. Even today, nothing prevents a college from inviting guest speakers on specialized or holding courses in English for term vernacular students, but not single one of those who are now clamouring for autonomy has bothered to do so. It is no secret that colleges which may be freed to an extent from university control are highest: In Mumbai for example, there is a big cultural gulf between city colleges and Jordon degree of autonomy, it will only heighten this disparity. The answer to the **vexed** problem of declining standards in higher education does not lie in encouraging the growth of model institutions, but in improving overall standards. This is of course easier said than done, since more and more young people are seeking degrees. The only solution, however unpalatable it may sound, is drastically to reduce the number of those who are admitted to colleges. Even though there is political pressure on many state governments to build new colleges and to reserve more seats for backward classes, it will be sheer **folly** to expand such facilities recklessly without giving any thought to the quality of the education imparted. If admissions are made for more selective, it will automatically reduce the number of entrants. This should apply particularly to new colleges, many of which are little more than degree factories. Only then can the authorities hope to bring down the teacher- student ratio to manageable proportions. Which is more, teacher should be given refresher courses every summer vacation to brush up their knowledge. Besides, if college managements increase the library budget it will help both staff and student a great deal. At the same time, however, it will be unfair to deny college education to thousands of young men and women unless employers stop insisting on degree even for clerical jobs. For a start, why can't the Government disqualify graduates from securing certain jobs say, class III and IV posts? Once the degrees are delinked from the jobs, at least in some important departments, it will make many young people think twice before joining college.

121. The author's chief concern seems to be-
    a. Frustration among students.
    b. Spread of college education
    c. Standard of education.
    d. Autonomy of colleges.
    e. Delinking of degrees.

122. The author's attitude is
    a. Cynical
    b. Optimistic
    c. Critical
    d. Conservative
    e. Constructive

123. What according to passage would be the result of granting autonomy to some colleges?
   a. The teacher student ratio will come down.
   b. Distance between city and suburban colleges will increase.
   c. collegeswill multiply. d. Some colleges will start selling degrees
   e. All of the above.

124. Which of the following is the most significant feature of the scheme of autonomous colleges according to the passage?
   a. They can introduce new courses. b. They can hold seminars.
   c. They can evolve their method of assessment.
   d. They can award degrees. e. They can make admissions without restrictions.

125. Which of the following does the author give precedence?
   a. Increasing library facilities.
   b. Holding refresher course for teachers.
   c. Abolishing reservation for backward classes.
   d. Stop opening of new colleges.
   e. Instituting entrance examinations.

126. Where has the author slipped while making suggestions?
   a. The teacher-student ratio be brought down.
   b. Improvement should be restricted to the selected institutions.
   c. College teachers need refresher courses.
   d. Political pressure should be withstood. e. None of these.

127. Frustration in the world is a result of which of the following?
   1. Large number of haves.
   2. Large number of 'have-not'.
   3. Cancerous cells.
   a. Only A b. Only B c. Only C d. A and B only e. None of these

128. Which of the following is the main difficulty according to the passage, in the way of improving standards?
   a. Paucity of library facilities.
   b. Paucity of Funds.
   c. Ever increasing number of young men wanting degrees.
   d. Grant of autonomy to colleges.
   e. Absence of Refresher courses.

129. Give one word related to the meaning of the word 'Vexed'?
   a. Annoyed b. Recurring c. Un-resolvable d. Complex e. Dangerous

130. Give one word opposite to the meaning of word 'folly'.
   a. Right b. Exact c. Mistake d. Action e. Wisdom

(131–140) In the following passages there are blanks each of which has been numbered, on of which fits the blank appropriately. Find out the appropriate word in each case.

The (11) age roared to life on a Friday in October 1957 (12) Russia's Old number seven rocket lobbed a thermometer, a sliver-zinc battery and a radio transmitter in a 23-in. polished aluminium ball from the (13) of Earth to a place

So high above the (14) it couldn't come all the way (15) again. The 184-lb ball was sputnik, mankind's first (16) Earth satellite. The (17) was pressurized with nitrogen circulated by a cooling fan. The thermometer changed the frequency of the two radio beacons. Attached to the outside of the satellite (18) two ten-ft radio antenna whips. For three weeks, as it twirled around the world every 96 minutes in a globe-grinding orbit 588 miles above our heads, sputnik beep-beeped its visionary (19) of a future above the ocean of (10).

131.
a. liberty b. horizon c. ignition d. space e. ancient

132.
a. while b. when c. until d. upto e. around

133.
a. exterior b. shell c. surface d. gorge e. plane

134.
a. ambience b. feasible c. meticulously d. impression e. atmosphere

135.
a. under b. downward c. meander d. down e. circuitous

136.
a. synthetic b. imitation c. artificial d. simulated e. genuine

137.
a. planet b. satellite c. spacecraft d. revolution e. stationary

138.
a. having b. boasted c. figured out d. were e. displayed

139.
a. material b. principle c. message d. vision e. theory

140.
a. air b. acid c. oxygen d. water e. salt

(141–145) Sentences given in each question, when properly sequenced, form a coherent paragraph. Each sentence is labelled with a letter. Choose the most logical order of the sentences from among the given choices to construct a coherent paragraph.

1. Settlement in 'real time' means the transaction is not subjected to any waiting period
2. It is a fund transfer mechanism.
3. Moreover as the money transfer takes place in the books of RBI. It is final and irrevocable.
4. The acronym RTGS stands for 'Real time Gross Settlement'
5. while 'Gross Settlement' means the transaction is settled without bunching it with any other transaction
6. The transfer of funds takes place on a real time and gross basis

141. Which of the following should be the Fifth statement?
a. 1 b. 4 c. 2 d. 5 e. 6

142. Which of the following should be the Second statement?
a. 2 b. 1 c. 3 d. 4 e. 5

143. Which of the following should be the First statement?
a. 1 b. 4 c. 3 d. 6 e. 2

144. Which of the following should be the third statement?
a. 1 b. 2 c. 3 d. 5 e. 6

145. Which of the following should be the last statement?
a. 6 b. 5 c. 4 d. 3 e. 1

(146–150) Read each sentence to find out whether there is any grammatical error in it. If there is no error choose option (e) as your answer.

146. Rakesh gave me(1)/two important information (2)/I had been waiting for(3)/the previous two months(4) / No error(5)

147. Wordsworth's poetry (1)/are characterized by his subtle description (2)/of the beauty and liveliness of nature (4)/ No error(5)

148. The brethrens(1)/of this locality are always(2)/at daggers drawn without any (3)/apparent reason(4)/ No error(5)

149. Pakistan's problem (1)/are also as(2)/ serious as(3)/that of India (4)/ No error(5)

150. The theory of relativity is (1)/so complicated (2)/as we cannot describe(3)/it in a few sentences(4)/ no error(5)

(151–155) Choose the correct phrase from the options below. If no correction is required then choose (e) as the answer.

151. **The series of our population** is changing significantly to drive organised retail growth.
a. Total of our population
b. too much of our population
c. little bit of our population
d. the demography of our population
e. No correction required

152. If the present trend continues the cost of a good personal computer system even **can be lowered from Rs 10,000 soon.**
a. Can be lowest up to Rs 10,000 soon
b. Can be as low as Rs 10,000 soon
c. could be lower to Rs 10,000 immediately
d. will be as lower as Rs 10,000 soon
e. no correction required

153. There was a total failure of the administration to **acted on time.**
a. act in time
b. acts on timely
c. act on time
d. acted within time
e. no correction required

154. More policemen **will be deployed** for the security of the foreign minister.
a. will have deploy
b. was to be liking to
c. Would like to
d. will have deployed
e. no correction required

155. He is in judicial custody **in connection to** a multi-core scan.
a) on connection at
b) in connection with
c) into connection around
d) around correction for
e) no correction required

ANSWER GRID

1. b	2. c	3. b	4. b	5. b	6. c	7. e	8. c	9. a	10. c
11. b	12. a	13. d	14. e	15. c	16. c	17. b	18. d	19. d	20. e
21. b	22. b	23. b	24. c	25. d	26. d	27. e	28. e	29. c	30. e
31. b	32. c	33. c	34. a	35. a	36. d	37. a	38. d	39. a	40. a
41. a	42. c	43. a	44. b	45. c	46. b	47. c	48. a	49. c	50. d
51. c	52. b	53. b	54. a	55. e	56. a	57. d	58. b	59. b	60. a
61. b	62. d	63. c	64. b	65. c	66. b	67. c	68. c	69. b	70. c
71. b	72. b	73. a	74. b	75. c	76. a	77. c	78. c	79. c	80. a
81. c	82. d	83. c	84. c	85. e	86. b	87. c	88. c	89. a	90. c
91. a	92.	93. a	94. b	95. c	96. d	97. d	98. b	99. a	100. d
101. b	102. c	103. a	104. c	105. e	106. a	107. d	108. a	109. c	110. d
111. b	112. b	113. b	114. b	115. d	116. c	117. b	118. b	119. b	120. c
121. c	122. e	123. b	124. c	125. d	126. d	127. d	128. c	129. d	130. e
131. d	132. b	133. c	134. e	135. d	136. c	137. b	138. d	139. c	140. a
141. e	142. a	143. b	144. a	145. d	146. b	147. b	148. a	149. d	150. e
151. d	152. b	153. c	154. e	155. b					

Solution to Questions 46–50:

46. % of protein is highest in protein = (100/1000) × (1/2) × 100 = 5%. **Ans(b)**

47. % of protein is maximum in dal and the % of fat is the least. Hence, is classified as 'Healthy'. **Ans (c)**

48. Clearly, Veg Burger has the highest percentage of fat and the least percentage of protein. Hence, butter is the junk food out of the above mentioned foods. **Ans (a)**

49. Butter, Apple, Veg Burger and Chicken. Hence, **Ans (d)**

Solution to Questions 51–54:

51. [c] Values added per worker for various sectors will be proportional to following ratios:

Central	10/6
State	3/6
Central/state	12/3
Public	8/8

52. [b] Fixed capital per factory will be proportional to the following ratios:

Central	5/8
State	4/4
Central/state	5/6
Public	6/12

53. [b] If the variables are proportional to the number of employees and the production per employee, then we can say that the variable cost is directly proportional to the production. Since the variable cost is maximum for private sector, it will also have the maximum production.

54. [a] If 20% of govt. fixed capital is equal to $200 million => Total govt. sector fixed capital = $ 1000 m which is equivalent to 14% of the total fixed capital. Now, 25% of Govt. investment in joint sector i.e. 25% of the 8% of the total=2% 0f total fixed capital will be given by: (1000x2) /14 = $ 143 million
Value in Rs. is given by: 143 × 45 = Rs.6450 million

Solution 55–59:

55. Minimum time will be if he earns maximum salary. This is possible if he works at the top level of Marketing Wing. He saves Rs.7225. Hence time taken to save Rs. 200000 is 28 months. Hence option [e] is the answer.

56. At the middle level, finance wing gives highest salaries. Hence he is bound to save most in this wing. Hence option [a] is the answer.

58. Highest TPC for a post-graduate is from entry level to middle level in finance wing (50%). Highest TPC for graduate is also from entry level to middle level in finance wing (10%). Hence ratio = 5:1. Hence option [b]is the answer.

59. Option b, from middle level to top level in HRD.

Solution 60–63:

60. Total combined exports of mango and citrus should be at least 2.5 times exports of apples. This is the case in none of the options.
Hence option (a) is the answer.

62. It is not given that only these fruits are exported from India in the given years. Hence cannot be determined.

Solution to Questions 67–69:

Place of worship	Number of flowers before offering	Number of flowers offered	Number of flowers left
1	(15/8)y	Y	(7/8)y
2	(7/4)y	Y	(3/4)y
3	(3/2)y	Y	y/2
4	y	Y	0

Number of flower before entering first place of worship is $\frac{15}{8}y$, hence, number of flowers before doubling = $\frac{15}{16}y$

This is equal to 30. Hence, y = 32

68. The minimum value of $\frac{15}{16}y$ so that is a whole number is 16. Therefore, 16 is the minimum number of flowers that can be offered. Hence option (c) is the answer.

69. For y to be 16, value of $\frac{15}{16}$y= 15.

Hence, the minimum number of flowers with which Roopa leaves home is 15. Hence option (b) is the answer.

SBI PO Mains MOCK Test Paper 13

Structure of this MOCK Test

S. No.	Name of section	No. of Questions	Total marks	Allotted Time
1	Reasoning and Computer Aptitude	45	60	60 minutes
2	Data Analysis and Interpretation	35	60	45 minutes
3	General/Economy/ Banking Awareness	40	40	35 minutes
4	English Language	35	40	40 minutes
Total		155	200	3 hours

- There is 1/4th Negative marking for every wrong answer.
- **If a question is left blank, i.e. no answer is marked by the candidate, there will be no penalty for that question**

Section 1: Reasoning and Computer Aptitude

Directions (1-5): Study the following information carefully and answer the following questions.

There are eight captains, namely P, Q, R, S, T, U, V and W, sitting around a circular table, facing the centre but not necessarily in the same order. Each of them is from a different cricket team, viz Australia, South Africa, Bangladesh, New Zealand, West Indies, Sri Lanka, India and Pakistan.

R and T are immediate neighbours of each other. Neither R nor T is an immediate neighbour of either Q or the captain of Sri Lanka. The captain of India sits second to the right of S, who is the captain neither of Sri Lanka nor of West Indies. U sits second to the right of the captain of Sri Lanka. The captain of West Indies is an immediate neighbour of the captain of Sri Lanka. Two people sit between the captain of West Indies and Q. V and the captain of New Zealand are immediate neighbours of each other. Q is not the captain of New Zealand. Only one person sits between R and the captain of Australia. W sits third to the left of the captain of Bangladesh. The captain of South Africa sits second to the left of the captain of Pakistan.

1. Which of the following sit exactly between Q and the captain of West Indies?
   a. P and the captain of India b. R and T c. W and P
   d. R and the captain of New Zealand e. V and U

2. Who among the following is the captain of Australia?
   a. R b. S c. T d. U e. V

3. Four of the following are alike in a certain way based on the given arrangement and thus form a group. Which is the one that does not belong to that group?
   a. W - captain of Sri Lanka
   b. Q - captain of Pakistan
   c. R - captain of Bangladesh
   d. V - captain of India
   e. S - captain of Australia

4. Who among the following sits second to the left of the captain of India?
   a. S b. Captain of Australia c. T d. Both a. and b.
   e. Captain of England

5. Which of the statement is/are correct?
   a. T is the captain of South Africa
   b. R is the captain of Bangladesh
   c. V is the captain of West Indies
   d. All a. b. and c.
   e. None of these

Directions (6-10): Study the following information carefully and answer the following questions.
A, N, M, R, J, V, S and D are eight friends sitting around a circular table. Two of them are not facing the centre. All of them like watches of different brands, viz Maxima, Puma, HMT, Titan, Fastrack, Rado, Quartz and Omega but not necessarily in the same order.

R and M are sitting third and second to the left of A respectively. R and S are neighbours of N, who likes Fastrack. The one who likes Titan sits on the immediate right of N. S is sitting third to the right of A and likes Maxima. D is third to the right of J and likes Quartz. A and D are not the neighbours of that person who likes Rado. V does not like HMT and Titan. The person who likes Omega is sitting opposite J.

6. The person who is sitting second to the left of A likes which of the following watches?
   a. Maxima b. Puma c. Rado d. Omega e. None of these

7. Who among the following likes Rado?
   a. N b. M c. R d. D e. None of these

8. What is the position of V with respect to A?
   a. Immediate left of A
   b. Second to the right of A
   c. Immediate right of A
   d. Cannot be determined
   e. None of these

9. If S is on the immediate right of N then by the same logic who among the following sits third to the right of N?
   a. M b. J c. D d. V e. None of these

10. How many persons sit between the one who likes Maxima and the one who likes HMT (count in clockwise direction starting from HMT)?
    a. 2 b. 0 c. 1 d. 3 e. None of these

Directions (11–15):- Go through the information given below and solve the questions based on it.
A word and number arrangement machine when given an input line of words and numbers rearrange them following a particular rule in each step. The following is an illustration of input and rearrangement.

Input: ***N 43 27 f j 38 g 62***
Step 1 : 62 N 43 27 f j 38 g
Step 2 : 62 f N 43 27 j 38 g
Step 3 : 62 f 43 N 27 j 38 g
Step 4 : 62 f 43 g N 27 j 38
Step 5 : 62 f 43 g 38 N 27 j
Step 6 : 62 f 43 g 38 j N 27
Step 7 : 62 f 43 g 38 j 27 N
According to the steps given answer the following questions:-

11. Input: w y 22 s 31 16 47 t
Which of the following steps will be last but one?
a. 4 b. 5 c. 6 d. 7 e. None of these

12. Input: c w 21 42 58 H B 78
How many steps will be required to complete the re-arrangement?
a. 4 b. 5 c. 6 d. 7 e. None of these

13. Step 4 of an input is : 94 b 75 c 19 39 h d
Which of the following is definitely the input?
a. h 94 b 75 c 19 39 d
b. c h 94 b 75 19 39 d
c. c h 94 75 b 19 39 d
d. None of these
e. Cannot be determined

14. Step 3 of an input is: 88 b 77 s H L 37 55
Which of the following will be step 6?
a. 88 b 77 H s L 37 55
b. 88 b 77 H 55 L 37 s
c. 88 b 77 H 55 L s 37
d. None of these
e. Cannot be determined

15. Input: g t A 1 91 88 43 s
Which of the following will be step 4?
a. 91 A 88 g 43 s t 11
b. 91 A 88 g 43 t 11 s
c. 91 A 88 g 43 s 11 t
d. 91 g t A 11 88 43 s
e. None of these

Directions (16–20):- In each of the questions, a question is followed by two statements, labelled (1) and (2). You have to decide whether the data given in the statements are sufficient for answering the question. Using the data given in the statements, mark your answer as:

Statement (1) ALONE is sufficient, but statement (2) alone is not sufficient to answer the question asked.

A. Statement (2) ALONE is sufficient, but statement (1) alone is not sufficient to answer the question asked.
B. BOTH statements (1) and (2) TOGETHER are sufficient to answer the question asked, but NEITHER statement ALONE is sufficient to answer the question asked.
C. EACH statement ALONE is sufficient to answer the question asked.
D. Statements (1) and (2) TOGETHER are NOT sufficient to answer the question asked, and additional data specific to the problem are needed.

16. If a salesman received a commission of 3% of the sales that he has booked in a month, what were the sales booked by the salesman in the month of November 2003?
    1. The sales booked by the salesman in the month of November 2003 minus salesman's commission was $245,000
    2. The selling price of the sales booked by the salesman in the month of November 2003 was 125 percent of the original purchase price of $225,000.

17. When Y is divided by 2, is the remainder 1?
    1. $(-1)^{(Y+2)} = -1$
    2. Y is prime

18. Is the two digit positive integer P a prime number?
    1. (P + 2) and (P - 2) are prime.
    2. (P - 4) and (P + 4) are prime.

19. If m, s are the average and standard deviation of integers a, b, c, and d, is s > 0?
    1. m > a
    2. a + b + c + d = 0

20. How is Bill related to Betty?
    1. Cindy, the wife of Bill's only brother Chris does not have any siblings.
    2. Betty is Cindy's brother in law's wife.

Directions(21-25): In these questions, relationship between different elements is shown in the statements. The statements are followed by two conclusions.

21. **Statements:**

$W \geq D < M < P$

$F = A > P > M$

Conclusions:

I. F > D

II. P < W

a. If only conclusion I is true.
b. If only conclusion II is true.
c. If either conclusion I or II is true.
d. If neither conclusion I nor II is true.
e. If both conclusions I and II are true.

22. **Statements:**

$H \geq P > F$

$F < A$

$S < B = A$

Conclusions:

I. H > B

II. P < S

a. If only conclusion I is true.
b. If only conclusion II is true.
c. If either conclusion I or II is true.
d. If neither conclusion I nor II is true.
e. If both conclusions I and II are true.

23. **Statements:**
B > T
Q < T
F = R < Q

Conclusions:
I. Q = F
II. T > F
a. If only conclusion I is true.
b. If only conclusion II is true.
c. If either conclusion I or II is true.
d. If neither conclusion I nor II is true.
e. If both conclusions I and II are true.

24. **Statements:**
S = R > Q
P < Q
R < K = B

Conclusions:
I. S≥P
II. R > P
a. If only conclusion I is true.
b. If only conclusion II is true.
c. If either conclusion I or II is true.
d. If neither conclusion I nor II is true.
e. If both conclusions I and II are true.

25. **Statements:**
S ≥ M < Y
Z > F > T
Y = Z < P

Conclusions:
I. S > F
II. Y > T
a. If only conclusion I is true.
b. If only conclusion II is true.
c. If either conclusion I or II is true.
d. If neither conclusion I nor II is true.
e. If both conclusions I and II are true.

Directions (Q.26 – 30): Study the following information carefully and answer the questions given below.
Eight friends Suchit, Sameer, Shivam, Shubham, Sneha, Swati, Somya and Shruti are sitting around a circular table. Three friends are facing outside the centre while five friends are facing towards the centre. Sameer sits third to the right of Swati. Shubham is not an immediate

neighbour of Shruti. Shivam sits third to the left of Shubham, who is second to the right of Suchit. Two friends are sitting between Shruti and Sneha and two are sitting between Swati and Sneha. Shivam is second to the left of Somya, who is facing the centre. Sameer is facing the centre. Sneha is not opposite Swati or Shivam. Shivam faces the centre whereas Shruti faces outside the centre.

26. Who sits fifth to the left of Shruti?
 a. Shivam b. Swati c. Sneha d. Suchit e. None of these

27. Which of the following statements is not true?
 a. Shruti is sitting third to the right of Shubham.
 b. Sneha is sitting opposite Suchit.
 c. Swati is sitting third to the left of Sneha.
 d. Somya is sitting between Shubham and Sneha.
 e. All are true

28. Who is sitting on the immediate right of Suchit?
 a. Sameer b. Somya c. Sneha d. Shruti e. None of these

29. Who is sitting opposite Somya?
 a. Sameer b. Sneha c. Shruti d. Shivam e. Shubham

30. Which group of three friends is facing outside the circle?
 a. Suchit, Shruti and Somya b. Sameer, Sneha and Shruti
 c. Suchit, Sneha and Swati d. Sneha, Suchit and Shruti
 e. None of these

31. Which of the following statements is/are true?
 a. Cache Memories are bigger than RAM
 b. Cache Memories are smaller than RAM
 c. ROM is faster than RAM
 d. Information in ROM can be written by users
 e. None of these.

32. Who built the first Mechanical Calculator?
 a. Joseph Marie Jacquard b. John Mauchly c. Blaise Pascal
 d. Howard Aiken e. None of these.

33. One million bytes of information are?
 a. 1 MB b. 1 GB c. 1 KB d. 1 TB e. None of above

34. SNMP full form is?
 a. Single Network Management Protocol
 b. Simple Network Mail Protocol
 c. Simple Network Management Protocol
 d. Simple Network Management Procedure
 e. None of these

35. SLIP stands for?
 a. Serial Line Internet Processing b. Serial Line Internet Protocol
 c. Serial Line Protocol d. Serial Line Internal Protocol
 e. None of above

36. Which of the following code used in present day computing was developed by IBM Corporation?
a. ASCII b. Hollerith Code c. Baudot Code
d. EBCDIC Code e. All of the above

37. What is a Pixel?
a. A computer program that draws picture
b. A picture stored in secondary memory
c. The smallest resolvable part of a picture
d. All of the above
e. None of the above

38. What kind of programming language is Java?
a. Object-oriented programming language
b. Relational programming language
c. Sixth-generation programming language
d. Database management programming language
e. None of the above

39. Which of the following is not one of the major data processing functions of a computer?
(i) gathering data
(ii) processing data into information
(iii) analyzing the data or information
a. only (i) b. (i) and (ii) c. All three
d. only (iii) e. None of these

40. When you save a Microsoft Access project, what file format do you use?
a. .adp b. .Xml c. .mbd d. All of these
e. None of the above

41. Who is said to be the first computer programmer?
a. Ada Lovelace b. Charles Babbage c. John Mauchly
d. Douglas Engelbart e. None of the above

42. An error in a computer program is called a ________.
a. crash b. power failure c. bug d. virus e. fatal error

43. Which of the following is not a binary number?
a. 10100 b. 10100 c. 20000 d. 11001 e. 01100

44. Different components on the motherboard of a PC unit are linked together by sets of parallel electrical conducting lines. What are these lines called?
a. Conductors b. Buses c. Connectors d. Consecutives
e. None of these

45. Which among the following options is a Window utility program that locates and eliminates unnecessary fragments and rearranges files and unused disk space to optimize operations?
a. Disk Cleaner b. Disk Cleanup
c. Disk Defragmenter d. Restore e. Disk Restorer

Section 2: Data Analysis and Interpretation

Direction for questions 46 to 49: Go through the data given below and solve the questions based on it.

Below given table gives the cost structure for packaged food products – Potato chips, Jam and Packaged Juice. All the data pertains to the 'N' grams packet of each of the three products. MRP = Maximum retail price = the price at which the retailer sells the article to the customer. All the questions pertain to this table only.

Cost structure for select packaged food products			
	Potato Chips	**Jam**	**Packaged Juice**
	INR	**INR**	**INR**
MRP	**10**	**50**	**68**
Retailer's Margin + discount	0.83	7.20	11.80
Distributor's Margin	0.44	2.18	3.50
Sales Tax	**0.94**	**5.37**	**8.20**
Excise Duty	**1.04**	**0.00**	**0.00**
Distribution	0.41	2.81	2.70
Returns	0.27	1.06	0.68
Manufacturing Cost	1.10	0.87	5.10
Packaging Cost	1.50	6.18	12.60
Raw Material Cost	1.25	9.52	5.80

46. For which of the following items, raw material cost as a percentage of MRP maximum?
    a. Potato chips b. Jam c. Packaged juice
    d. Potato chips and Jam e. None of these
47. A distributor sells 5 packets of potato chips, 12 packets of Jam and 8 packets of packaged juice (each of N grams each). What is his total margin for these items (INR)?
    a. 48.7 b. 56.36 c. 28.52 d. 38.24 e. 64.12
48. If there is no sales tax, then which of the following products price will come down over MRP by maximum percentage?
    a. Potato chips b. Jam c. Packaged juice
    d. Potato chips and Jam e. It will come down equal in all the three cases
49. What percentage of the MRP is the retailers' margin in case of packaged juice?
    a. 8.3% b. 7.2% c. 19.8% d. 16.2%
    e. Cannot be determined

Directions for Questions 50 to 55: Answer these questions based on the data provided in the table below:

Year	Production (in lacs)	Workers	Assets (Rs. Millions)	Sales (Rs Crores)
2005	12	80	200	16
2006	14	85	220	18
2007	13.5	90	220	21
2008	15	102	240	22
2009	17.5	120	250	25

Asset Utilization Factor (AUF) = Sales value/Assets
Worker productivity = Production in units/Number of workers
Assume that whatever is produced in a given year is sold in the same year.
All sales are of produced units only.

50. In which year is the worker productivity the highest?
a. 2005 b. 2007 c. 2008 d. 2006
e. cannot be determined

51. Which year has the highest AUF?
a. 2005 b. 2006 c. 20007 d. 2009
e. cannot be determined

52. In which year is the average selling price of a unit sold the highest?
a. 2005 b. 2008 c. 2007 d. 2009
e. cannot be determined

53. In which year is the average selling price of a unit sold the second lowest?
a. 2005 b. 2008 c. 2007 d. 2006 e. 2009

54. Worker Turnover is defined as the average sales (value) per worker in a given year. In which year is the worker turnover the highest?
a. 2007 b. 2006 c. 2008 d. 2005 e. 2009

55. The average cost of production in 2008 was Rs. 120/unit. What was the approximate profit percentage on a unit sold in the same year?
a. 17% b. 23% c. 31% d. 42% e. 47%

Directions for questions 56 to 60: Answer these questions based on the data provided in the table below:
The following table is the details of 5 companies who have taken corporate subscription of mobile phones for their employees. NO employee can have more than one connection. The details are on monthly basis.

Company	Mobile phone service provider	No. of employees covered	Rentals per employee (in Rs.)	Free calls per employee	Per call charge (in Rs.)	Per SMS charge (in Rs.)
A	BSNL	400	500	500	2.00	1.00
B	Reliance	700	0	250	2.50	0.75
C	Airtel	250	300	250	3.00	0
D	Aircel	400	400	500	2.50	0.50
E	Virgins	625	500	500	2.00	1.50

NOTE: Per call charges become effective only after free calls are exhausted.

56. Which company has made highest payment towards total bill of all the employees if, on an average, each employee has made 700 calls, no sms? (call charges = Rentals + charges after free calls)

a. A b. B c. D d. E e. C

57. If each employee sends a total of 1000 SMS per month, then what is the total annual SMS bill of company A and company B put together excluding the monthly rentals? (in Rs. Lakhs)

a. 212 b. 175 c. 111 d. 626 e. None of these

58. If another company F estimates that its 1000 employees will make 600 calls and send 200 SMS per month, then which mobile phone service provider should it opt for, such that its payout is least?

a. BSNL b. Reliance c. Aircel d. Virgins e. Airtel

59. What is the total bill for mobile phones of E if its employees send 200 SMS's each and make 500 phone calls each in a particular month?

a. Rs. 312500 b. Rs. 500000 c. Rs. 812500 d. 625000 e. None of these

60. If employees of both C and D send 100 SMS and make 600 calls each, then by what percentage has the revenue of Airtel exceeded that of Aircel from these 2 clients respectively?

a. 50% b. 80% c. 20% d. 17.75% e. None of these

Directions for questions 61 to 64: Answer these questions based on the data provided in the table below:

The following table gives the sales of various sections of three departmental stores which began operations in 2005. All values are in Rs. crores.

	2009	2008	2007	2006	2005
Shopper's Top:					
Men	12.5	11.5	9.8	12.5	13.5
Women	18.7	16.2	12.2	8.8	14.5
Others	25.2	21.7	25.6	16.2	21.2

	2009	2008	2007	2006	2005
Shopper's Top:					
Jivestyle:					
Men	15.4	18.5	17.2	18.5	21.5
Women	12.7	11.5	10.8	9.5	8.2
Others	21.5	22.7	21.5	18.5	16.5
Eastside:					
Men	9.5	11.2	8.6	5.4	4.3
Women	11.8	10.8	9.2	7.5	6.5
Others	7.5	6.5	6.8	7.2	6.5
Total	**134.8**	**130.6**	**121.7**	**104.1**	**112.7**

61. **For which year did sales increase the most, relative to the previous year for the Men's section of Jivestyle?**
    a. 2008 b. 2007 c. 2006 d. 2005 e. None of these

62. **The total sales of Men's sections of the three departmental stores lay between 30 and 40 percent of total turnover of the three stores, in the year/s…**
    a. 2009, 2008, 2006
    b. 2006 and 2005 only
    c. 2008, 2006, 2005
    d. 2001, 2000, 2006
    e. cannot be determined

63. **The highest percentage growth in sales of the three stores together, relative to previous year was achieved in…**
    a. 2005 b. 2008 c. 2006 d. 2007 e. None of these

64. **Which of the following statements is correct?**
    a. During 2006 to 2009, sales of Women's section of Shopper's Top declined steadily whereas that of 'others' sections steadily increased.
    b. The Women's section sales at Eastside have always been higher than average sales of the three sections of Eastside.
    c. 'Others' section has contributed to more than 50% of sales for shopper's Top for all the years.
    d. None of the above statements are true.
    e. cannot be determined

65. **Three Englishmen and three Frenchmen work for the same company. Each of them knows a secret not known to others. They need to exchange these secrets over person-to-person phone calls so that eventually each person knows all six secrets. None of the Frenchmen knows English, and only one Englishman knows French. What is the minimum number of phone calls needed for the above purpose?**
    a. 5 b. 10 c. 9 d. 15 e. None of these

Directions for questions 66 to 68: In each question, there are two statements: A and B, either of which can be true or false on the basis of the information given below.

A research agency collected the following data regarding the admission process of a reputed management school in India.

Year	Gender	Number bought application forms	Number appeared for written test	Number called for interviews	Number selected for the course
2002	Male	61205	59981	684	171
	Female	19236	15389	138	48
2003	Male	63298	60133	637	115
	Female	45292	40763	399	84

Choose a. if only A is true
Choose b. if only B is true
Choose c. if both A and B are true
Choose d. if neither A nor B is true
Choose e. if cannot be determined

66. **Statement A:** The success rate of moving from written test to interview stage for males was worse than for females in 2003.
Statement B: The success rate of moving from written test to interview test to interview stage for females was better in 2002 than in 2003.

67. **Statement A:** In 2002, the number of females selected for the course as a proportion of the number of females who bought application forms, was higher than the corresponding proportion for males.
Statement B: In 2002, among those called for interview, males had a greater success rate than females.

68. **Statement A:** The percentage of absentees in the written test among females decreased from 2002 to 2003.
Statement B: The percentage of absentees in the written test among males was larger than among females in 2003.

69. At Compound Interest, a sum of money amounts to x times the original sum in y years. Same sum amounts to 81 times the original sum in 4y years. What is the value of x?
a. 2 b. 3 c. 4 d. 5 e. None of these

70. Mayank, Mirza, Little and Jaspal bought a motorbike for $60. Mayank paid one-half of the sum of the amounts paid by the other boys. Mirza pad one-third of the sum of the amounts paid by the other boys. Little paid one-fourth of the sum of the amounts paid by the other boys. How much did Jaspal have to pay?
a. $15 b. $13 c. $17 d. $130 e. None of these

71. At a bookstore, 'MODERN BOOK STORE' is a flashed using neon lights. The words as individually flashed at the intervals of $2\frac{1}{2}$ s, $4\frac{1}{4}$ s and $5\frac{1}{8}$ s respectively, and each word is put off after a second. The least time after which the full name of the bookstore can be read again is
a. 49.5s b. 73.5s c. 1744.5s d. 855s e. None of these

72. If pqr = 1, the value of the expression $\frac{1}{1+p+q^{-1}} + \frac{1}{1+q+r^{-1}} + \frac{1}{1+r+q^{-1}}$ is equal to

a. p + q + r   b. $\frac{1}{p+q+r}$ c. 1   d. $p^{-1}+q^{-1}+r^{-1}$

73. It takes six technicians a total of 10 hr to build a new server from Direct Computer, with each working at the same rate. If six technicians start to build the server at 11 am, and one technician per hour is added beginning at 5 pm, at what time will the server be completed?

a. 6.40pm   b. 7pm   c. 7.20pm   d. 8pm   e. 8:20 pm

74. There are 10 positive real numbers $n_1 < n_2 < n_3 ... < n_{10}$. How many triplets of these numbers (n_1, n_2, n_3), (n_2, n_3, n_4), ... can be generated such that in each triplet the first number is always less than the second number, and the second number is always less than the third number?

a. 45   b. 90   c. 120   d. 180   e. 240

75. Three small pumps and a large pump are filling a tank. Each of the three small pump works at $\frac{2}{3}$ the rate of the large pump. If all four pumps work at the same time, they should fill the tank in what fraction of the time that it would have taken the large pump alone?

a. $\frac{4}{7}$ b. $\frac{1}{3}$ c. $\frac{2}{3}$ d. $\frac{3}{4}$

e. None of these

76. A survey on a sample of 30 new cars being sold at a local auto dealer was conducted to see which of the three popular options–air conditioning, radio and power windows were already installed. Following were the observation of the survey:
15 had air conditioning. 2 had air conditioning and power windows but no radios. 12 had radio. 6 had air conditioning and radio but no power windows. 11 had power windows. 4 had radio and power windows. 3 had all three options
What is the number of cars that had none of the options?

a. 9   b. 8   c. 6   d. 7   e. 2

77. Krishna owns several cows, some black and some white. He finds that 4 black cows and 3 white cows provide the same amount of milk in 5 days as 3 black cows and 5 white cows provide in 4 days. What is the ratio of milk provided by a black cow in a day to that by a white cow in a day?

a. 8:5   b. 5:8   c. 3:5   d. 5:3   e. 3:6

78. At the end of year 1998, shepherd bought nine dozen goats. Henceforth, every year he added p% of the goats at the beginning of the year and sold q% of the goats at the end of the year, where p > 0 and q > 0. If shepherd had nine dozen goats at the end of year 2002, after making the sales for that year, which of the following is true?

a. p =q   b. p < q   c. p > q   d. p = q/2   e. None of these

79. Left pan of a faulty balance weighs 100 gram more than its right pan. A shopkeeper keeps the weight measure in the left pan while buying goods but keeps it in the right pan while selling his goods. He uses only 1 kg. weight measure. If he sells his goods at cost price, what is his gain percentage?

a. $\frac{200}{11}$ %   b. $\frac{100}{11}$ %   c. $\frac{1000}{9}$ %   d. $\frac{200}{9}$ %   e. None of these

80. Average of five positive numbers is x. If each number is increased by 10%, then x:
a. increases by 10%
b. decreases by 10%
c. remains unchanged
d. decreases by 9.09%
e. cannot be determined

Section 3: General and Banking Awareness

81. The IMGC is the sole provider of mortgage guarantor for housing finance in India. The alphabet "I" in the abbreviation IMGC stands for________
a. India
b. Institute
c. Internal
d. Informative
e. International

82. The national agency mandated to control, analyse and disseminate Suspicious Transaction Reports (STR), Cash Transaction Reports and counterfeit currency reports to various investigative agencies of the country after receiving it from banks and other financial intermediaries is ________
a. RBI
b. Financial Intelligence Unit (FIU)
c. Intelligence Bureau (IB)
d. Central Bureau of Investigation (CBI)
e. Central Intelligence Unit (CIU)

83. According to RBI guidelines the term 'bulk deposit' is used for single rupee term deposit of ________
a. Rs. 1 crore and above
b. Rs. 25 lakh and above
c. Rs. 75 lakh and above
d. Rs. 50 lakh and above
e. Rs. 15 lakh and above

84. A collection of non-bank financial intermediaries that provide services similar to traditional commercial banks is known as ________
a. Off-shore Banking
b. Investment Banking System
c. Shadow Banking System
d. Conventional Banking
e. Merchant Banking System

85. According to Reserve Bank of India Regulations, "Universal Banks" are permitted to pick up stake in Payment Banks up to ________
a. 35%
b. 25%
c. 20%
d. 40%
e. 30%

86. The "Stand Up India" is aimed at promoting entrepreneurship among women and scheduled castes and tribes. The bank loans under the scheme shall be referenced to ________
a. SIDBI
b. NABARD
c. RBI
d. MUDRA
e. DRDA

87. An NBFC-MFI is defined as a non-deposit taking NBFC (other than a company licensed under Section 25 of the Indian Companies Act, 1956) with Minimum Net Owned Funds of ________
a. Rs. 5 crore
b. Rs. 4 crore
c. Rs. 3 crore
d. Rs. 2 crore
e. None of the Above

88. The Minimum Net Owned Fund for NBFC-MFIs registered in the North Eastern Region of the country is ________
a. Rs.5 crore b. Rs.4 crore c. Rs.3 crore d. Rs.2 crore
e. None of the Above

89. Which are defined as total assets other than cash and bank balances and money market instruments?
a. Net Assets b. Qualifying Assets c. Commercial Papers
d. Both a. and c. e. All of the Above

90. In SNRR Account, SNRR stands for ________
a. Statutory Non Resident Rupee b. Single Non Resident Rupee
c. Statutory Non Reflex Rupee d. Single Non Resident Rupee
e. Special Non Resident Rupee

91. ________ is an account maintained in foreign currency with an Authorised Dealer Bank.
a. Exchange Earner's Foreign Currency Account
b. Exchange Eligible Foreign Currency Account
c. Earners' Eligible Foreign Currency Account
d. Earners' Exchange Foreign Currency Account
e. Equity Exchange Foreign Currency Account

92. An EEFC account can be held only in the form of ________
a. Savings Bank Account b. Deposit Account
c. Current Account d. Both b. and c.
e. None of the Above

93. Who is/are eligible to open an EEFC Account?
a. Individuals b. Companies
c. Residents of India d. Both b. and c.
e. All of the Above

94. Which of the following percentage of foreign exchange earnings can be credited to the EEFC account?
a. 80% b. 90% c. 75% d. 95% e. 100%

95. What is the minimum maturity period for Rupee Denominated Bonds?
a. 2 years b. 3 years c. 4 years d. 5 years
e. None of the Above

96. Which of the following can issue Rupee denominated bonds?
a. Real Estate Investment Trusts (REITs)
b. Infrastructure Investment Trusts (InvITs)
c. Limited Liability Partnerships
d. Both a. and b.
e. None of the Above

97. What is the maximum amount that can be raised through issuance of Rupee denominated bonds under automatic route?
a. INR 50 billion b. INR 60 billion c. INR 55 billion d. INR 65 billion e. No limit

98. Under Liberalised Remittance Scheme, PAN card need not be insisted upon for remittance made towards permissible current account transactions up to ________
a. USD 25,000 b. USD 20,000 c. USD 15,000 d. USD 10,000
e. None of the Above

99. Which of the following account can be repatriable?
a. NRE Account b. NRO Account
c. FCNR b. Account d. Both a. and c.
e. All of the Above

100. Which of the following does not have savings account?
a. NRE Account b. NRO Account
c. FCNR b. Account d. Both a. and c. e. All of the Above

101. What are the services available under IMPS?
a. Funds Transfer and Remittances b. Merchant Payments c. NUUP
d. Both a. and c. e. All of the Above

102. What is the full form of NUUP?
a. National Unified USSD Protocol b. National United USSD Platform
c. National United USSD Protocol d. National Unified USP Platform
e. National Unified USSD Platform

103. Which of the following is a USSD based mobile banking service from NPCI that brings together all the Banks and Telecom Service Providers?.
a. WAP b. QSAM c. NUUP
d. Both a. and b. e. Both b. and c.

104. In NUUP, a customer can access banking services by just pressing ________ from his/her mobile phones.
a. *999# b. #*99# c. *99# d. 1*99#
e. None of the Above

105. What is the full form of QSAM?
a. Quality Service on Aadhaar Mapper
b. Query Sending on Aadhaar Mapping
c. Query Service on Aadhaar Mapper
d. Quality Service on Aadhaar Mapping
e. Query Sending on Aadhaar Mapper

106. ________ service helps user in knowing their Aadhaar Seeding status with their bank account.
a. WAP b. QSAM c. NUUP d. Both a. and b.
e. Both b. and c.

107. What is the lock-in duration of Tax Saving scheme ELSS (Equity Linked Savings Scheme)?
a. 3 years b. 4 years c. 5 years d. 10 years e. 15 years

108. How many digits are there in Mobile Money Identifier(MMID)?
a. 7 digits b. 9 digits c. 10 digits d. 11 digits
e. None of the Above

109. A customer can link how many accounts to the same mobile number?
a. Only One
b. Only Two
c. Only Three
d. More than One
e. None of the Above

110. An unbanked customer can initiate IMPS transaction using the services of _______.
a. PPI
b. PCI
c. PFI
d. PDI
e. None of the Above

111. When is the International Anti-Corruption Day observed?
a. December 7
b. December 9
c. December 10
d. December 6
e. None of these

112. On December 8, 2016, Union Finance Minister announced several incentive programmes to promote cashless economy. Which among the following statement is true regarding the incentive measures?
i. Consumers will get a discount of 0.50 % to make digital payment while buying petrol and.
ii. Online Railway ticket booking will attract free accident insurance cover of Rs. 10 lakh.
iii. Online purchase of new insurance policy of PSUs will deliver 10% discount on General Insurance and 8% discount on life Insurance policies
a. Only ii
b. Only i & ii
c. Only ii & iii
d. All correct
e. All wrong

113. Where was the India-UK Conference on Ease of Doing Business inaugurated which began on December 8, 2016 ?
a. Mumbai
b. Chandigarh
c. New Delhi
d. Pune
e. Kolkata

114. Which autonomous body on December 7, 2016 has directed to impose a ban on the use of newspapers for wrapping or packing of food item, as the newspaper ink can contaminate food items leading to serious health concerns?
a. World Health Organisation (WHO)
b. Department of Food and Public Distribution
c. Food Safety and Standards Authority of India (FSSAI)
d. Bureau of Indian Standards (BIS)
e. None of these

115. Which country has emerged top most in the Global Terrorism Index (GTI),2016, for being the worst country to be impacted by terrorism in 2015?
a. Pakistan
b. Iraq
c. Afghanistan
d. Syria
e. Bangladesh

116. Which has bagged a contract from Gujarat Cricket Association (GCA) to convert the Sardar Patel Cricket Stadium of Gujarat into world's biggest cricket stadium in terms of seating capacity?
a. Godrej Prop
b. Ansal Housing
c. DLF Limited
d. Larsen & Turbo (L&T)
e. None of these

117. How much amount will be spent by NABARD for deployment of Point of Sales (PoS) devices in one lakh Indian villages having a population of up to 10,000 to promote digital transaction in rural area.
a. Rs. 225 Crore
b. Rs. 120 Crore
c. Rs. 108 Crore
d. Rs. 95 Crore
e. Rs 100 Crore

118. Who has been appointed as the new director of National Gallery of Modern Art (NGMA) replacing Rajeev Lochan?
   a. Rajeev Lochan
   b. Sabeena Gadihoke
   c. Adwaita Gadanayak
   d. Ahmad Ngma
   e. None of these

119. Who has been appointed as Non-Executive Chairperson of Mumbai based IDFC Bank with effect from December 9, 2016 up to July 26, 2018?
   a. Rajiv Lall
   b. Anil Baijal
   c. Vinod Rai
   d. Veena Mankar
   e. None of these

120. Name the Android App launched by the Indian Army on December 6, 2016, dedicated to the Army Veterans & Veer Naris.
   a. Veer Outreach App
   b. Veterans Reachout App
   c. Veterans Outreach App
   d. Veterans Outroute App
   e. Veterans Outreach App

Section 4 : English Language

Directions (121-155): Read the following passage carefully and answer the questions given below it. Certain words have been printed in bold to help you locate them while answering some of the questions.

For years now, George W. Bush has told Americans that he would increase the number of troops in Iraq only if, the commanders on the ground asked him to do so. It was not a throw away live. Bush said it from the very first days of the war, when he and pentagon boss Donald Rumsfeld were criticized for going to war with too few troops. He said it right up until last summer, stressing at a news conference in Chicago that Iraq commander General George Casey will make the decisions as to how many troops we have there. Seasoned military people suspected that the line was a dodge that the civilians who ran the pentagon were testing their personal theory that war can be fought on the cheap and the brass simply knew better than to ask for more in any case the president repeated the mantra to dismiss any suggestion that the war was going badly. Who, after all, knew better than the generals on the ground? Now as the war nears the end of its fourth year and the number of Americans killed has surpassed 3,000 Bush has dropped the generals know best line sometime next week the president is expected to propose a surge in the number of 45 forces in Iraq for a period of up to two years. A senior official said reinforcements numbering about 20,000 troops and may be more could be in place within months; the surge would be achieved by extending the stay of some forces already in Iraq and accelerating the deployment of others.

The irony is that while the generals would have liked more troops in the past, they are cool to the idea of spending more now that's in past because the politicians and commanders had trouble agreeing on what the goal of a surge would further erode the readiness of the US's already stressed ground forces and even those who back a surge are under no illusions about what it would mean to the casualty rate. If you put more American troops on the front line said a white house official, you're going to have more casualties. Coming from Bush, a man known for bold strokes the surge is a strange half-measure-too large for the political climate at house too small to crush the insurgency in Iraq and surely three years too late Bush has waved off a bipartisan rescue mission out of pride stubbornness or ideology or same combination of the three, Rather than reversing course, as all the wise elders of the Iraq study group advised, the commander in chief is betting that more troops will lead the way to what one white house official calls "victory."

121. Bush and Rumsfeld had received brick bats for-
   a. waging a war against Iraq
   b. testing their personal theories
   c. their assertion in the news conference in Chicago
   d. turning down the demands of general George Casey
   e. None of these

122. George Bush gave an impression to his subjects that his army commanders were given the autonomy to decide-
   a. when to start or stop the war in Iraq
   b. the reasonable requirement of American troops to fight the war in Iraq
   c. how many troops should Iraq use to fight against the Americans
   d. the pentagon policies regarding war in Iraq
   e. None of these

123. From the content of the passage, which of the following can be definitely inferred?
   (A) The US troops in Iraq are happy with their victory
   (B) The troops already fighting the war in Iraq are sufficient enough to combat the situation effectively
   (C) The Generals who were earlier not in favour of increasing troops in Iraq are now insisting on surge.
   a. A and B only b. B and C only c. A and C only d. None e. All of three

124. Which of the following best describes Bush's persistent reaction to the observations that the Iraq war strategy was not effective due to inadequate American forces?
   a. Such strategies are better left to army commanders to decide on the ground.
   b. Civilians are the best assessors of such strategies
   c. War can be fought on the cheap
   d. The brass knew better of war but not of politics.
   e. None of these

125. The author of the passage appears to be-
   a. in favour of enhancement of American troops in Iraq
   b. critical about Bush's strategy of handling situation in Iraq
   c. an impartial assessor of the US strategy related to the situation in Iraq.
   d. an indifferent on lookers of what is happening in Iraq
   e. inclined to the idea of with drawl of American troops to save casualty.

126. Which of the following is the assessment of the commander-in-chief of US forced in Iraq on the present situation there?
   a. America's desired goal will be achieved if more troops are deployed in Iraq.
   b. Withdrawal of troops from Iraq is essential to raise the moral of US army.
   c. Further strengthening of the US army in Iraq will be suicidal as it means more destruction of US forces.
   d. Pentagon's civilians should not have been allowed to interfere with the army commanders' strategies.
   e. None of these

127. Which of the following strategies would achieve the desired increase in American forces in Iraq?
   (A) Continuation of stay of troops for a further period.

(B) Expeditious deployment of additional troops.
(C) Seeking additional input from politicians and commanders of neighboring friendly countries.

a. A and C only b. C only c. B only d. A and B only
e. None of these

128. Why do the army commanders disfavour enhancement of troops now?
(A) More force means more casualties.
(B) Difference of opinion between politicians and commanders about the aim of the troop enhancement
(C) Probable adverse psychological impact on ground forces.

a. Only A and B b. Only B and C c. All the three
d. Only A and C e. None of these

129. Which of the following made Bush change his thinking about the requirement of forces in Iraq?
(A) The unreasonably long period for which the war continued
(B) The large number of American soldiers killed in the war
(C) Demand from the army commanders

a. Only A and C b. Only A and B c. Only B and C
d. All three e. Only C

Directions (10-12): Which of the following is most OPPOSITE in meaning of the word given in bold as used in the passage?

130. Cool
a. Warm b. Enthusiastic c. Unwelcome
d. Intemperate e. Indifferent

131. Surge
a. Enhancement b. Trivializing c. Reduction
d. Strengthening e. Up gradation

132. Stubbornness
a. Uncertainty b. Weakness c. Acceptability
d. Infirmity e. Flexibility

Directions (133-135): Which of the following is most nearly the SAME in meaning as the word given in bold as used in passage?

133. Illusion
a. Reality b. Reflection c. Fantastic d. Delusion e. Deviation

134. Insurgency
a. Rebellion b. Ingredient c. Combat
d. Debacle e. Violation

135. Irony
a. Levelling b. Precaution c. Controversy
d. Mockery e. Perception

Directions (Q. 136-140): Pick out the most effective word from the given words to fill in the blanks to make the sentence meaningfully complete.

136. Vision is usually ....most effectively when many different..................are used.
   a. developed, manifestations
   b. adapted, organizations
   c. communicated, vehicles
   d. exhibited, forms
   e. described, thought

137. People who have been through difficult, painful and not very.................change efforts often end up............both pessimistic and angry conclusions.
   a. successful, drawing
   b. meaningful, projecting
   c. reliable, evolving
   d. strong, following
   e. challenging, lamenting

138. The human mind is never ....; it advances or it...............
   a. absolute, diminishes
   b. dynamic, stops
   c. perfect, disintegrates
   d. stationary, retrogrades
   e. happy, decomposes

139. If misery is the effect of ill-fortune, it ought to be pitied, if of .... to be..............
   a. virtue, criticized
   b. calamity, revered
   c. virtue, protected
   d. vice, revered
   e. virtue, revered

140. It would be impossible for us to continue living in this world if each of us..................exactly what fate had in ....for him.
   a. follow, plan
   b. appreciate, strategy
   c. design, anticipation
   d. visualize, hidden
   e. knew, store

141. It is the ....of selfishness for man, who fully ....in their own case the great advantages of good education, to deny these advantages to women.
   a. parody, demand
   b. height, appreciate
   c. height, assimilate
   d. degree, appreciate
   e. level, advance

142. The learner should be ....to take a small first step, one that will provide immediate success and ....the learning.
   a. encouraged, reinforce
   b. forced, organise
   c. directed, reorganize
   d. cautioned, reinforce
   e. encouraged, acknowledge

143. His death.................more tributes than have been paid at the ....of any other human in history.
   a. brought, passing
   b. directed, helm
   c. delivered, description
   d. invited, living
   e. acknowledged, perpetuate

144. Only with executive......................can the organization concentrate its energies on ....competitive advantage over time.
   a. position, embarking
   b. development, directing
   c. contingent, fabricating
   d. commitment, sustaining
   e. satisfaction, moulding

145. All the performances of human art, at which we look with praise or wonder, are………… of the restless…………of perseverance.
- **a. manifestations, pronouncement**
- **b. projections, component**
- **c. instances, force**
- **d. proofs, humanity**
- **e. visions, future**

Directions (Q.146-155): In the following passage there are blanks each of which has been numbered. These numbers are printed below the passage and against each, five words/phrases are suggested one of which fits the blank appropriately. Find out the appropriate word/phrase in each case:

The idea of the documentary was …1…by Samar in the year 2016 while he was …2… to his undergraduate course …3… the Western International University, New Delhi, India as a possible …4… for an annual inter university competition …5… SIFE (Students in Free Enterprise) …6… his institution rejected his …7… on account of non-feasibility. …8… then he is independently working on this documentary and has …9… interviewed famous personalities from all walks of …10…

	a.	b.	c.	d.	e.
146.	**accepted**	**conceived**	**borrowed**	**taken**	**swallowed**
147.	**attending**	**arriving**	**catching**	**noticing**	**presenting**
148.	**on**	**in**	**at**	**as**	**with**
149.	**exit**	**entry**	**retirement**	**allocation**	**suffocation**
150.	**for**	**from**	**if**	**form**	**into**
151.	**except**	**only**	**but**	**yet**	**so**
152.	**angle**	**proposal**	**motion**	**news**	**media**
153.	**Since**	**nearby**	**convenient**	**beside**	**outside**
154.	**presently**	**lastly**	**old**	**already**	**firstly**
155.	**light**	**live**	**alone**	**life**	**dark**

ANSWER KEY

1. c	2. b	3. d	4. d	5. d	6. d	7. e	8. c	9. d	10. a
11. b	12. c	13. e	14. c	15. b	16. d	17. a	18. d	19. a	20. c
21. a	22. d	23. b	24. b	25. b	26. e	27. e	28. e	29. c	30. d
31. b	32. c	33. a	34. c	35. c	36. d	37. c	38. a	39. e	40. a
41. a	42. c	43. c	44. b	45. c	46. b	47. b	48. c	49. e	50. d
51. d	52. c	53. a	54. a	55. b	56. b	57. c	58. c	59. b	60. c
61. a	62. c	63. d	64. b	65. c	66. d	67. b	68. a	69. b	70. b
71. b	72. c	73. d	74. c	75. b	76. d	77. b	78. c	79. d	80. a
81. a	82. b	83. a	84. c	85. e	86. a	87. a	88. d	89. a	90. e
91. a	92. c	93. e	94. e	95. b	96. d	97. a	98. a	99. d	100. c
101. e	102. e	103. c	104. c	105. c	106. b	107. a	108. a	109. d	110. a
111. b	112. c	113. c	114. c	115. b	116. d	117. b	118. c	119. d	120. c
121. e	122. b	123. d	124. a	125. b	126. a	127. d	128. b	129. b	130. a
131. c	132. e	133. d	134. a	135. d	136. d	137. a	138. d	139. e	140. e
141. b	142. a	143. a	144. d	145. c	146. b	147. a	148. c	149. b	150. a
151. c	152. b	153. a	154. d	155. d					

Solution and Explanations

(1-5)

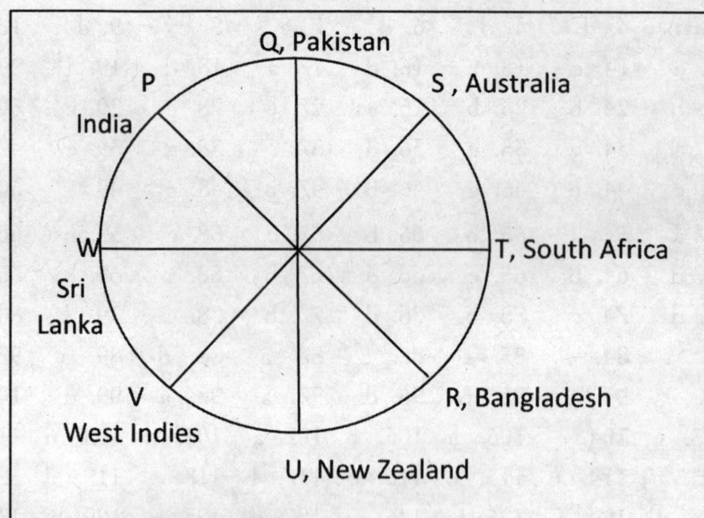

(6-10)

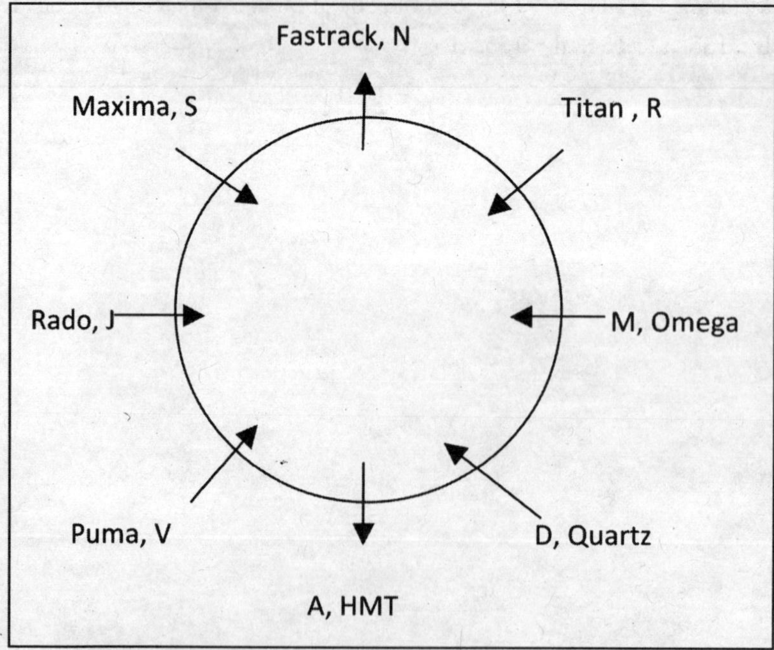

11. Input : w y 22 s 31 16 47 t
    Step 1 : 47 w y 22 s 31 16 t
    Step 2 : 47 s w y 22 31 16 t
    Step 3 : 47 s 31 w y 22 16 t
    Step 4 : 47 s 31 t w y 22 16

Step 5 : 47 s 31 t 22 w y 16
Step 6 : 47 s 31 t 22 w 16 y

12. Input : c w 21 42 58 H B 78
Step I : 78 c w 21 42 58 H B
Step II : 78 B c 58 w 21 42 H
Step III : 78 B 58 c w 21 42 H
Step IV : 78 B 58 c 42 w 21 H
Step V : 78 B 58 c 42 H w 21
Step VI : 78 B 58 c 42 H 21 w

14. Step III : 88 b 77 s H L 37 55
Step IV : 88 b 77 H s L 37 55
Step V : 88 b 77 H 55 s L 37
Step VI : 88 b 77 H 55 Ls 37
Step VII : 88 b 77 H 55 L 37 s

15. Input : g t A 11 91 88 43 s
Step I : 91 g t A 11 88 43 s
Step II : 91 A g t 11 88 43 s
Step III : 91 A 88 g t 11 43 s
Step IV : 91 A 88 g 43 t 11 s
Step V : 91 A 88 g 43 s t 11
Step VI : 91 A 88 g 43 s 11 t

16. **From statement (1)**, we know that the sales value after the salesman's commission. If his commission is 3% of the sales booked. Then the net sales value is 100 - 3 = 97% of the sales booked.
From statement (1), we know that 97% of sales booked = $245,000. So we can find out the sales booked.
Statement (1) alone is sufficient.
Hence, choice (A) or (D) is the answer.
From statement (2), we know that the original cost of the products is $225,000. We know the sales booked = 1.25 * 225,000.
Hence, statement (2) is also sufficient.
As each of the two statements is independently sufficient to answer the question, choice (D) is the correct answer.

17. **Let us evaluate statement 1.**
$(-1)^{(Y+2)} = -1.$
$(-1)^{\text{ODD NUMBER}} = -1$
Therefore, Y + 2 is an odd number.
Hence, Y has to be an odd number.
So, when Y is divided by 2, the remainder is 1.
Statement 1 is sufficient.
The answer is either choice (A) or choice (D).

Now let us evaluate the statement 2.
Now is prime
Y could be '2' which is an even number.

So, when Y is divided by 2, the remainder is '0'.
All other prime numbers are odd numbers.
So, when Y is divided by 2, the remainder is '1'.
We cannot conclude is Y is 2 or other prime numbers.
As we are not able to conclude if Y is an even number or an odd number with statement 2, it is not sufficient.
Hence, answer is choice (A).

18. **Statement (1):** P + 2 and P - 2 are prime.
One out of 3 consecutive odd integers, (P - 2), P, and (P + 2) will definitely be a multiple of '3'. If (P + 2) and (P - 2) are prime, then P has to be a multiple of '3', which is not prime. The only exception is if the 3 consecutive odd numbers are 3, 5 and 7. However, we are dealing with two digit positive integers.
SUFFICIENT.

Statement (2): P - 4 and P + 4 are Prime.
One out of 3 consecutive odd integers, (P - 4), P, and (P + 4) will definitely be a multiple of '3'. If (P + 4) and (P - 4) are prime, then P has to be a multiple of '3', which is not prime. The only exception is if the 3 consecutive odd numbers are 3, 7 and 11. However, we are dealing with two digit positive integers.
SUFFICIENT.
Hence, the correct answer is D.

19. **Statement 1: m > a**
If a = b = c = d, the average m will be the same as a.
Since m > a, all the elements in the set cannot be the same, and therefore, s > 0.
Statement 1 ALONE is sufficient.
Eliminate choices B, C and E. Choices narrow down to A and D

Statement 2: a + b + c + d = 0
Example: When a = b = c = d = 0, s = 0
Counter Example: When a = -4, b = 0, c = 0, and d = 4, s > 0
Statement 2 ALONE is NOT sufficient.
Eliminate choice D. Choice A is the answer.

20. **From statement 1,** we know that Cindy has no siblings and she is the wife of Bill's only brother Chris. However, this statement does not provide any information about Betty and is hence not sufficient to answer the question.
So, choice A and D are eliminated.
From statement 2, we know that Betty is Cindy's brother in law's wife. This statement establishes a relatión between Cindy and Betty. This does not answer the question of how Bill is related to either Cindy or Betty. Hence, statement 2 alone is not sufficient to answer the question. Hence, we can eliminate choice (B). Now, if we combine the two statements, we know that Bill and Cindy are related to each other through Chris, who is the only brother of Bill and that Cindy is Betty's brother in law's wife. Cindy does not have any siblings and hence her brother in law has to necessarily be her husband's sibling. As Chris is the only brother of Bill, Cindy's brother in law has to

be Bill and Betty is his wife. As we could answer the question by combining the information in the two statements, choice (C) is the correct answer.

21. F>M, M>D, hence F>D is true.

22. H>F< A=B so there is no direct relation between H and B. P>F<A>S, hence there is no direct relation between S and P.

23. As F<Q, hence F=Q is false. As T>Q>F, thus T>F is true.

24. S>Q>P, hence S is only greater than P not equal to. R>Q>P, thus R>P is true.

25. S≥ M<Y=Z>F, no direct relationship between S and F. Y=Z>F>T, thus Y>T is true.

130. Cool and warm are opposites.

131. Surge and reduction are opposites in meaning. Surge means sudden increase.

132. Stubbornness and Flexibility are opposites in meaning.

133. Illusion and delusion are synonyms in meaning.

134. Insurgency and Rebellion are synonyms in meaning.

135. Irony and Mockery are synonyms in meaning which means the expression of one's meaning by using language that normally signifies the opposite, typically for humorous or emphatic effect.

SBI PO Mains MOCK Test Paper 14

Structure of this MOCK Test

S. No.	Name of section	No. of Questions	Total marks	Allotted Time
1	Reasoning and Computer Aptitude	45	60	60 minutes
2	Data Analysis and Interpretation	35	60	45 minutes
3	General/ Economy/ Banking Awareness	40	40	35 minutes
4	English Language	35	40	40 minutes
Total		155	200	3 hours

- There is 1/4th Negative marking for every wrong answer.
- If a question is left blank, i.e. no answer is marked by the candidate, there will be no penalty for that question

Section 1: Reasoning and Computer Aptitude

1. Which of the following expression will be true if the expression given below
A < C ≤R=M≤≤R=M≤ R > B < N is definitely true?
1. P≥≥ N 2. M ≤≤ A 3. A < M 4. C ≤≤ B
a. 1 b. 2 c. 3 d. 4 e. None of these

2. Which of the following symbols should replace the question mark (?) in the given expression in order to make the expressions P > C as well as X > F definitely true?
X≥≥B = P ? D = F >L C ≥≥L
1. < 2. ≤≤ 3. > 4. Either < or =
a. 1 b. 2 c. 3 d. 4 e. None of these

3. Which of the following symbol should be placed in the blank spaces respectively (in the same order from left to right) in order to complete the given expression in such a manner that makes the expression R > E definitely true and B ≥≥E definitely false?
P _ R _ O _ B _ L _ E _ M
1. >,<,≥≥,≥≥,≥≥, < 2. >,=<,≥≥, ≥≥,< 3. >,>,≥≥, ≥≥,=,< 4. ≥≥, ≥≥,≥≥,>,≥≥,<
a. 1 b. 2 c. 3 d. 4 e. None of these

4. Which of the following expression will be true if the expression A = E ≤≤B < C ≤≤N = T is definitely true?

1. C≥≥ A 2. B < T 3. B ≤≤ T 4. E ≤≤N

a. 1 b. 2 c. 3 d. 4 e. None of these

5. Which of the following symbols should be placed in the blank spaces respectively (in the same order from left to right) in order to complete the given expression in such a manner that makes the expression U ≤≤T & O ≥≥M definitely false?

M _ O _ U _ N _ T

1. ≤≤, =, ≤≤, ≤≤ 2. ≤≤, =, =,≤≤ 3. ≤≤, =, ≤≤, < 4. ≤≤, >, ≤≤, =

a. 1 b. 2 c. 3 d. 4 e. None of these

Directions (Q.6–10) : Study the information and answer the following questions.

In certain code language, 'total flooring area with wood' is written as 'pa da te ro hi', 'marble cost in total' is written as 'co hi ni zo', 'Marble with tiles' is written as 'te zo ga', 'wood tiles cost much' is written as 'ga cha da ni', 'square area' is written as 'ro su'.

6. What is the code for 'flooring' in the given code language?

a. hi b. ro c. pa d. te e. None of these

7. Which of the following does 'ga' stands for?

a. cost b. much c. tiles d. wood e. None of these

8. Which of the following is the possible code for 'wood door in cost'?

a. su do ni co b. mo da ni zo c. su ga re mo
d. mo co da ni e. None of these

9. Which of the following is represented by the code 'da ni cha'?

a. wood cost much b. wood flooring area
c. much flooring area d. wood much total e. None of these

10. Which of the following is the code for 'Marble flooring area.'?

a. pa da ga b. zo ro pa c. su ra za
d. pa ro su e. None of these

Directions (11–15): Each of the questions below consists of a question and two statements numbered I and II given below it. You have to decide whether the data given in the statements are sufficient to answer the questions. Read both statements and give answer as option:

1) If the data in statement I alone are sufficient to answer the question, while the data in statement II alone are not sufficient to answer the question.
2) If the data in statement II alone are sufficient to answer the question, while the data in statement I alone are not sufficient to answer the question.
3) If data either in statement I alone or statement II alone are sufficient to answer the question.
4) If the data in statement I and II together are not sufficient to answer the question.
5) If the data in both statement I and II together are necessary to answer the question.

11. Among Arun, Farhan, Dolly, Era, Chintu and Babu, who the lightest than only the heaviest?

I. Babu is heavier than Arun and Era.

II. Farhan is heavier than Babu but lighter than Dolly, who is not the heaviest.

12. How is M related to N?
    I. N is the only daughter of Y, who is P's grandfather.
    II. P is sister of S, who is son of M.

13. Six persons M, N, O, P, R and S are sitting around a circular table facing centre. Who is sitting on the immediate left of M?
    I. N is sitting opposite O, and P is sitting opposite R.
    II. S is sitting on immediate left of N.

14. How many students are there in the class?
    I. Richa's rank is 19 from the bottom and she is 4 ranks above of Nilesh.
    II. Anuj's rank is 7th from the top and is 8 ranks above Tarun, Who is 30 from the bottom.

15. In which direction city A is with respect to city B?
    I. A is in south of X which is to the east of P.
    II. A is to the south- east of P. X is to the south-east of B.

Directions (Q. 16–20): Study the following information and answer the questions given below:
Eight politicians - Aakash, Bhuvan, Rayis, Digvijay, Ishwar, Firoj, Arind and Hitesh- are sitting around a circular table, facing the centre but not necessarily in the same order. Each of them win from a different assembly seats, viz. Laxmi Nagar, Sahadra, Chandni Chowk, Preet Vihar, Nirman Vihar, Tilak Nagar Lajpat Nagar and Dawarka. Aakash sits third to the right of the person who wins from Dawarka. The politician who wins from Chandni chowk and Lajpat Nagar are immediate neighbours. Only two politicians sit between the winner of Dawarka seat and Hitesh. Neither Aakash nor Hitesh won from Chandni Chownk and Lajpat Nagar Seats. The politicians who wins from Lajpat Nagar seat is not an immediate neighbour of the politician who wins from Dawarka seat. The winner of Laxmi Nagar seat sits second to the left of Ishwar. Ishwar is not an immediate neighbour of Hitesh. The winner of Laxmi Nagar seat is an immediate neighbour of both Nirman Vihar seats winner and Preet Vihar seats winner. The winner of Nirman Vihar seat sits third to the right of Bhuvan. Bhuvan do not win from Lajpat Nagar seat Rayis sits on the immediate right of the winner from Sahadra seat. Aakash do not win from Sahadra. Firoj is not an immediate neighbour of Aakash. Arvind is not an immediate neighbour of the winner from the Laxmi Nagar seat.

16. Four of the following five are alike in a certain way based on the given arrangement and thus form a group. Which is the one that does not belong to the group?
    a. Firoj- Sahadra
    b. Arvind - Tilak Nagar
    c. Bhuvan - Dawarka
    d. Aakash - Nirman Vihar
    e. None of these

17. Who among the following sits third to the left of Ishwar?
    a. Hitesh b. Aakash c. Digvijay d. Arvind e. None of these

18. Who among the following is the winner of Tilak Nagar seat?
    a. Aakash b. Rayis c. Hitesh d. Arvind e. None of these

19. Which seat does Bhuvan win from?
    a. Sahadra b. Laxmi Nagar c. Preet Vihar d. Chandni Chowk
    e. None of these

20. Who sits on the immediate left of politician who wins from Dawarka seat?
    a. Rayis b. Firoj c. Bhuvan d. Hitesh e. None of these

Direction for questions 21–25: Study the following information carefully to answer the given questions.

Eight persons – J, K, L, M, N, O, P and Q are sitting around a circular table facing the centre with equal distances between each other (but not necessarily in the same order). J, K, L, M, N, O, P and Q represents M. Ajay and his family members – Father, Mother, Sister, Brother, Wife, Daughter and Son. No two females or males are immediate Neighbours of each other.

M. Ajay's father sits second to the left of Ajay. Q is son of Ajay and sits third to the right of M. Ajay's Wife. K is married to L, who sits second to the right of Ajay's daughter. The daughter-in-law of K is J. Ajay and his wife sits adjacent to each other. M and N are not females but P is a female. Ajay's father sits adjacent to Ajay's daughter. O is the daughter of Ajay's Mother and sits on the immediate right of her brother. There are two members sitting between Ajay and his sister. K is the father of Ajay and sits second to the right of Q. N is not Ajay's brother.

21. In the given arrangement, how many people will sit between L and O?
    a. Two b. Three c. Four d. More than four e. One

22. Who amongst the following sits third to the right of J?
    a. M b. Q c. Other than those given as options d. N
    e. O

23. How is J related to L?
    a. Mother-in-law b. Son-in-law c. Sister-in-law
    d. Father-in-law e. Daughter-in-law

24. Four of the following five are alike in a certain way based upon their seating arrangement and so form a group. Which of the following does not belong to the group?
    a. QM b. MO c. MN d. PO e. NK

25. Who amongst the following is the son of N?
    a. Q b. P c. K d. J e. M

Direction Questions(26–28): Read the information given below and solve the questions based on it.

In a family there are two fathers, two mothers, one sister, one brother, two daughters, one mother-in-law, one daughter-in-law, two sisters-in-law, one son, one grandfather, one grandmother and one granddaughter.

26. How many married couples are there in the family?
    a. Three b. One c. Two d. Four e. None of these

27. How many female members in their family?
    a. Three b. Two c. Four d. One e. None of these

28. What is the maximum number of people in the family?
    a. 8 b. 7 c. 5 d. 6 e. None of these

Direction for questions 29–30: Go through the information given below and solve the questions based on it.

P × Q means P is father of Q

P + Q means P is wife of Q

P ÷ Q means P is daughter of Q

P – Q means P is son of Q

29. Which of the following relations are true based upon the relation given in the equation A – B × C + D – E?
a. E is mother-in-law of C
b. D is brother of A
c. E is wife of B
d. A is brother of C
e. None of these

30. What will come in the place of '?' to establish that M is the nephew of N in the expression M ? K ÷ L × N
a. +
b. ÷
c. ×
d. -
e. None of these

31. If a new device is attached to a computer, such as a printer or scanner, its _______ must be installed before the device can be used.
a. buffer
b. driver
c. Pager
d. Server
e. Maker

32. _________ is a self-replicating virus that does not alter files but resides in active memory and duplicates itself.
a. Time Bomb
b. Worm
c. Mellissa virus
d. Macro virus
e. Trojan

33. What is gutter margin?
a. Margin that is added to the left margin when printing
b. Margin that is added to the right margin when printing
c. Margin that is added to the binding side of page when printing
d. Margin that is added to the outside of the page when printing
e. None of the Above

34. ________ is a signalling method that handles a relatively wide range of frequencies.
a. Broadband
b. DLF
c. Dial-up
d. Both (A. and (C)
e. Wireless

35. A _______ is a computer connected to two networks.
a. link
b. server
c. gateway
d. bridge way
e. Client

36. A small amount of memory included in the processor for high speed access ID called _______
a. Register
b. Cache
c. RAM
d. ROM
e. Virtual

37. Which of the following terms is just the connection of networks that can be joined together?
a. Virtual Private Network
b. Internet
c. Intranet
d. Extranet
e. Public Network

38. An affordable technology that uses existing telephone lines to provide high-speed connections is called ________
a. ISDN
b. Microwave
c. Cable modem
d. DSL
e. ALU

39. The capacity of a communication channel is measured in _________
a. bandwidth
b. bit capacity
c. data rate
d. data flow
e. store data

40. ________ is the act of copying or downloading a program from a network and making multiple copies of it
a. Network Piracy
b. Plagiarism
c. Software Piracy
d. Hardware Piracy
e. None of the Above

41. A computer virus normally attaches itself to another computer program known as a ______
    a. Host Program
    b. Target Program
    c. Backdoor Program
    d. Trojan Horse
    e. None of the Above

42. Decreasing the amount of space required to store data and programs is accomplished by ______
    a. Crashing
    b. Disk Caching
    c. RAID
    d. File Compression
    e. Other than those given as options

43. When a file contains instructions that can be carried out by the computer, it is often called a(n) ______ file.
    a. information
    b. application
    c. executable
    d. data
    e. Other than those given as options

44. When you first turn on a computer, the CPU is preset to execute instructions stored in ______
    a. RAM
    b. Flash memory
    c. ALU
    d. ROM
    e. Other than those given as options

45. Documents converted to ______ can be published to the web.
    a. a doc file
    b. http
    c. machine language
    d. HTML
    e. Other than those given as options

Section 2: Data Analysis and Interpretation

Direction for questions 46–50: Go through the data set given below and solve the questions based on it.

The graph given below shows the number of seats won by the Congo party in the last six general elections between 1989 and 2004.

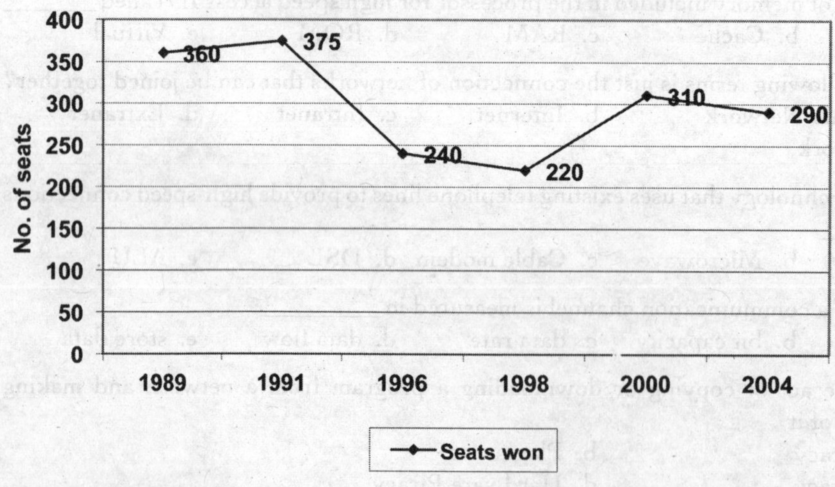

NOTE: The total seats in parliament are 450 for all the elections held between 1989 to 2004.

46. In how many elections did congo get a two-third majority?
a. 1 b. 2 c. 3 d. 4 e. 0

47. In how many elections did the party have to seek external support to form a government, assuming that the party sought external support whenever it did not win 60% of the seats in parliament?
a. 1 b. 2 c. 0 d. 3 e. 0

48. In which election did congo witness the maximum percentage change in the number of seats it won over the previous election?
a. 1991 b. 1996 c. 1998 d. 2000 e. 2004

49. In how many elections is the number of seats won by the congo less than the average number of seats won by the congress in these six elections?
a. 0 b. 1 c. 2 d. 3 e. 4

50. If 56% seats are required to form a government, by what percentage seats is the congo short in order to form a government in the elections?
a. 6.2% b. 7.11% c. 8.12% d. 6.76% e. 10.11

Direction for questions 51–55: Go through the data set given below and solve the questions based on it.

Answer the questions on the basis of the table given below.

DATE	Number of Jeans supplied by a wholesaler agent from 1st April 2016 to 15th April 2016.											
	Loot				Reebok				Levis			
	SIZE (S – small, M – medium, L – large, XL –extra large)											
	S	M	L	XL	S	M	L	XL	S	M	L	XL
1	30	50	70	40	20	40	80	30	40	60	30	20
2	20	40	50	30	40	0	90	50	60	20	80	30
3	30	40	60	50	80	50	70	20	40	50	20	0
4	50	60	0	60	90	60	40	0	30	40	50	40
5	30	60	30	50	60	50	30	30	50	60	90	30
6	40	30	90	40	40	20	30	90	80	40	20	20
7	0	60	70	20	30	30	50	20	40	50	30	30
8	60	80	20	40	50	20	40	60	40	70	30	50
9	40	30	60	60	70	30	60	30	70	30	60	40
10	30	50	70	20	90	50	0	40	20	80	60	20
11	20	0	80	40	20	80	60	80	0	40	50	40
12	50	50	30	50	0	90	20	50	40	30	50	20

DATE	Number of Jeans supplied by a wholesaler agent from 1st April 2016 to 15th April 2016.											
	Loot				Reebok				Levis			
	SIZE (S – small, M – medium, L – large, XL –extra large)											
	S	M	L	XL	S	M	L	XL	S	M	L	XL
13	50	70	40	70	50	70	70	60	40	30	70	40
14	40	50	0	60	40	30	40	50	30	90	40	30
15	70	40	50	40	30	50	30	40	60	50	80	40

51. The number of days on which at least 30 jeans were supplied is
a. 4 b. 5 c. 6 d. 7 e. 3

52. How many XL size T-shirts supplied during the tenure, were not of Reebok?
a. 1050 b. 1120 c. 1180 d. 1210

53. Whenever the supply of T-shirts, for a particular brand, of a particular size on two consecutive days is the same; it is considered as STAGNANT SUPPLY.
The number of times stagnant supply occurs during the above tenure is
a. 7 b. 8 c. 9 d. 10 e. 0

54. Which of the following can be defined as the most successful day for the whole sale agent? The most successful day is defined as the day on which maximum number of T-shirts were supplied by him.
a. 2nd April b. 5th April c. 8th April d. 13th April e. None of these

55. The difference between the most successful day and the least successful day is referred to as MAXIMUM VARIATION IN SUPPLY. What is the maximum variation in supply for the given tenure? (Least successful day is the opposite of the most successful day as defined in the previous question)
a. 90 b. 130 c. 170 d. 230 e. 210

Direction for questions 56–60: Go through the data set given below and solve the questions based on it.

Following graph shows the Total GDP of India from 2003-04 to 2007-08.

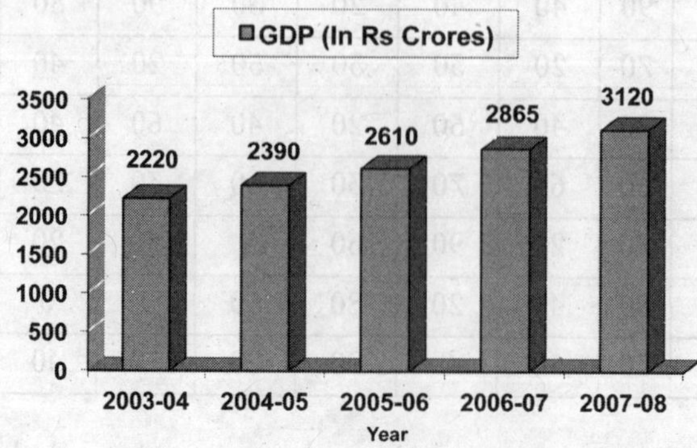

The following graph shows the contribution of service sector to the GDP from 2003-04 to 2007-08:

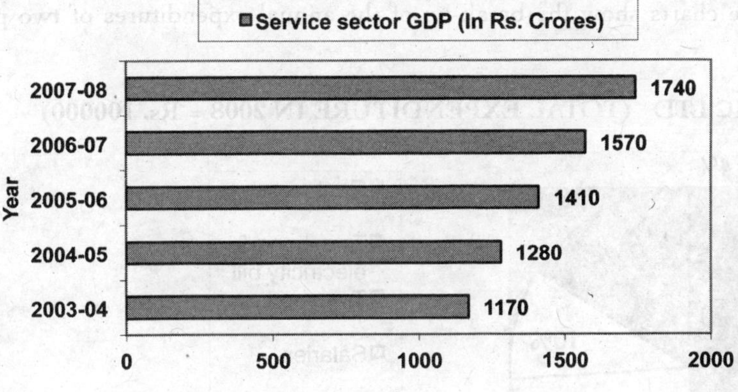

56. For how many years the percentage growth in GDP of the service sector is greater than the average percentage GDP growth of the service sector?
a. 1 b. 0 c. 2 d. 3 e. 4

57. Arrange the percentage growth in GDP of service sector in ascending order?
a. 2004-05, 2005-06, 2006-07, 2007-08
b. 2004-05, 2005-06, 2007-08, 2006-07
c. 2004-05, 2006-07, 2005-06, 2007-08
d. 2007-08, 2004-05, 2005-06, 2006-07
e. None of these

58. In which year the contribution of service sector to the overall GDP is maximum?
a. 2003-04 b. 2004-05 c. 2005-06 d. 2006-07
e. None of these

59. Arrange the percentage growth in GDP in descending order?
a. 2004-05, 2005-06, 2006-07, 2007-08
b. 2007-08, 2004-05, 2005-06, 2006-07
c. 2004-05, 2006-07, 2005-06, 2007-08
d. 2004-05, 2007-08, 2005-06, 2006-07
e. None of these

60. Which of the following is/are true?
(i) The contribution of Service sector to overall GDP is increasing for every year from 2003 to 2008.
(ii) Both overall GDP growth and services sector GDP growth falls in the last year from amongst the given years.
(iii) For two years the percentage overall GDP growth is less than the average percentage overall GDP growth.
a. Only (i) b. Only (ii) c. Only (iii) d. Both (i) & (ii)
e. All three

Direction for questions 61–65: Go through the data set given below and solve the questions based on it.

The following pie charts show the break-up of the annual expenditures of two private sector companies:

SYMBIOTIC LTD (TOTAL EXPENDITURE IN 2008 = Rs. 100000)

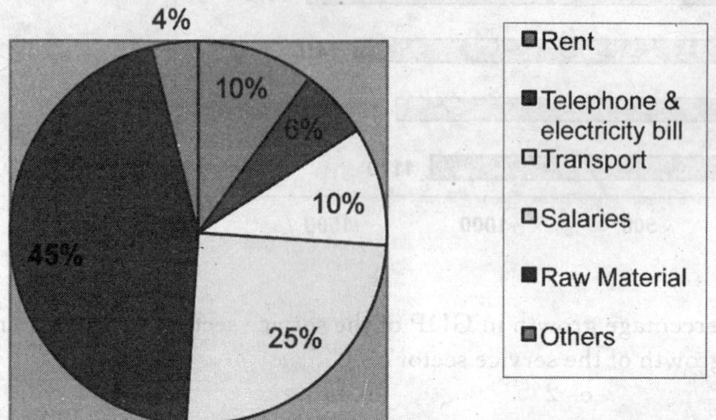

SABPAISA TECHNOLOGIES (TOTAL EXPENDITURE IN 2008 = Rs. 80000)

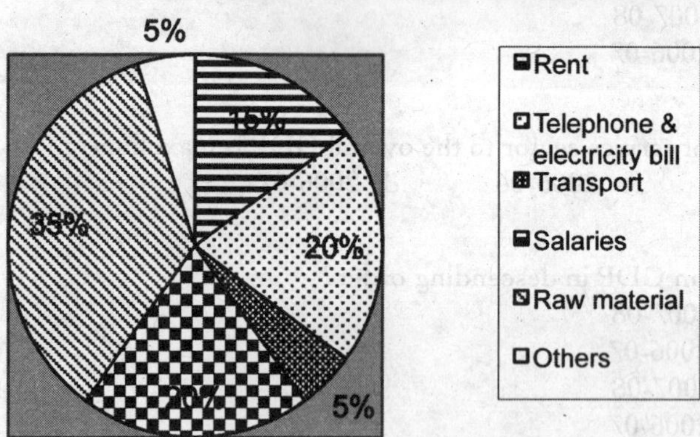

61. The amount spent on transport by SabPaisa technologies is what percentage of the amount spent by Symbiotic Ltd on transport?
    a. 30% b. 35% c. 40% d. 45% e. 50%

62. The expenditure on raw material for both companies taken together, is what fraction of the total expenditure in 2008?
    a. 0.2 b. 0.25 c. 0.3 d. 0.4 e. 0.65

63. Both Symbiotic Ltd and SabPaisa Technologies spend the same amount on which category?
    a. Rent b. Transport c. Salaries d. Others e. None of these

64. For which category the difference in expenditure is maximum?
    a. Telephone & Electricity Bill b. Transport c. Salaries
    d. Raw Material e. None of these

65. What is the difference in the amount spent by the two companies on telephone and Electricity bills?
   a. SabPaisa Technologies spends Rs. 6000 more on telephone and Electricity bills.
   b. SabPaisa Technologies spends Rs. 10000 more on telephone and Electricity bills.
   c. Symbiotic Ltd spends Rs. 4000 less on telephone and Electricity bills.
   d. Symbiotic Ltd spends Rs. 6000 less on telephone and Electricity bills.
   e. None of these

66. What is the value of $\frac{2^{2014}+2^{2012}}{2^{2014}-2^{2012}}$?
   a. -1 b. $\frac{5}{3}$ c. 2013 d. 2^{4024} e. 1

67. In a bag of marbles, $\frac{3}{5}$ of the marbles are blue and the rest are red. If the number of red marbles is doubled and the number of blue marbles stays the same, what fraction of the marbles will be red?
   a. $\frac{2}{5}$ b. $\frac{3}{7}$ c. $\frac{4}{7}$ d. $\frac{3}{5}$ e. 1/3

68. What is the product of all positive odd integers less than 10000?
   a. $\frac{10000!}{(5000)!^2}$ b. $\frac{10000!}{2^{5000}}$ c. $\frac{9999!}{2^{5000}}$ d. $\frac{10000!}{2^{5000}.5000!}$ e. None of these

69. It takes Mary 30 minutes to walk uphill 1 km from her home to school, but it takes her only 10 minutes to walk from school to her home along the same route. What is her average speed, in km/hr, for the round trip?
   a. 3 b. 3.125 c. 3.5 d. 4 e. 3.33

70. Suppose July of year N has five Mondays. Which of the following will definitely occur five times in the August of the same year?
   a. Monday b. Thursday c. Wednesday d. Tuesday e. Friday

71. What is the probability that a randomly drawn positive factor of 60 is less than 7?
   a. $\frac{1}{10}$ b. $\frac{1}{4}$ c. $\frac{1}{2}$ d. 2/3 e. None of these

72. What is the value of $(3x - 2)(4x + 1) - (3x - 2) 4x + 1$ when $x = 4$?
   a. 0 b. 1 c. 10 d. 11 e. 21

73. Sum of the squares of marbles the three children have is 600 and the sum of products taken two at a time of marbles is 150. Then what is the sum of all the three numbers?
   a. 30 b. 35 c. 40 d. 45 e. 60

74. Samar sets his watch to the correct time at noon. At the actual time of 1:00 PM, he notices that his watch reads 12:57 and 36 seconds. Assuming that his watch loses time at a constant rate, what will be the actual time when his watch first reads 10:00 PM?
   a. 10:22 PM and 24 seconds b. 10:25 PM c. 10:25:24 PM
   d. 11:25:21 e. None of these

75. A grocer makes a display of cans in which the top row has one can and each lower row has two more cans than the row above it. If the display contains 100 cans, how many rows does it contain?
   a. 8 b. 9 c. 10 d. 11 e. 12

76. Josh and Mike live 13 km apart. Yesterday, Josh started to ride his bicycle toward Mike's house. A little later Mike started to ride his bicycle toward Josh's house. When they met, Josh had ridden for twice the length of time as Mike and at four-fifths of Mike's rate. How many km had Mike ridden when they met?

a. 4 b. 8 c. 6 d. 5 e. 3

77. If $x < 0$, then which of the following must be positive?

a. $-x^{-1}$ b. $-x^2$ c. -2^x d. $\sqrt[3]{x}$ e. None of these

78. Sum of the products of the ten numbers $\pm1, \pm2, \pm3, \pm4, \pm5$ taking two at a time is

a. 165 b. –55 c. 55 d. 0 e. None of these

79. Ram runs 7/4 times as fast as Sham. If Ram gives Sham a start of 300m, how far must the winning post be if both Ram and Sham have to end the race at the same time?

a. 700m b. 1400m c. 350m d. 210m e. 300m

80. Radha can do 3/4th of a work in 12 days. After working for 8 days Mira joins her and both works together for three days after which Radha leaves. If Mira takes 12 more days to complete the work then how many days Mira will take alone to do it?

a. 16 b. 12 c. 48 d. 24 e. 32

Section 3: General Awareness

81. What does the Economic Survey 2015-16 describe as "The Chakravyuha Challenge of the Indian Economy"?

a. High fiscal deficit and current account deficit
b. Various cycle of poverty, health and development
c. Double fiscal repression
d. Exit problems for companies in India
e. None of these

82. Which of the following statement are true?

1. To stop the depreciation of rupee the RBI should purchase dollars from the market.
2. To stop the appreciation of rupee the RBI should sell dollars to the market.

a. 1 only b. 2 only c. Both 1 and 2 d. Either 1 or 2
e. None of the above

83. International Monetary Fund (IMF) has included China's Yuan into its elite reserve currency basket. What implications can it have on the International reserve asset system?

1. Nations will now prefer holding more Yuan in their Forex Reserves.
2. Yuan will now be used for calculation of the value of a SDR.

Which of the above statement is/are correct?

a. 1 only b. 2 only c. Both 1 and 2 d. Either 1 or 2
e. None of the above

84. In the states of India, the State Financial Corporations have given assistance mainly to develop ___________

a. medium and small scale industries b. small-scale industries
c. medium-scale industries d. irrigation projects e. none of the above

85. Which of the following is not viewed as a national debt?
a. Provident Fund b. National saving Certificate
c. Long-term Government Bonds d. Life Insurance Policies
e. None of the above

86. Who among the following has been appointed as the Chairman of India's Oscar Jury by Mumbai–based Film Federation of India?
a. Anupam Kher b. Amol Palekar c. Jaya Bachhan
d. Amitabh Bachchan e. None of these

87. Who is the author of the new book "Knowledge Innovation Strategy"?
a. Amish Tripathi b. Durjoy Datta c. Ravinder Singh
d. Parag Kulkarni e. None of these

88. A recent Joint Military Exercise Mitra Shakti 2016 was conducted between India and ___?
a. Sri Lanka b. Bangladesh c. Myanmar d. Nepal e. Israel

89. What was India's rank according to the World Bank latest "Doing Business" report?
a. 135 b. 120 c. 130 d. 131 e. None of these

90. Who won the women's WTA Finals title held in October 2016?
a. Angelique Kerber b. Serena Williams
c. Dominika Cibulkova d. Maria Sharapova e. None of these

91. The European Union signed the Comprehensive Economic and Trade Agreement (CETA) in 2016 with which country?
a. Iran b. Canada c. Belgium d. India e. Russia

92. The World Bank pledged a $2-Billion aid to which country to tackle climate change?
a. South Korea b. Nigeria c. Bangladesh d. Sri Lanka e. None of these

93. Mr. A. Guterres has been appointed as the new UN Secretary-General. He was the former Prime Minister of Which country?
a. Sweden b. Argentina c. Portugal d. Columbia e. None of these

94. There has been a persistent deficit budget year after year. Which action/s of the government of the following can be taken by the government to reduce the deficit?
1. Reducing revenue expenditure
2. Introducing new welfare schemes
3. Rationalizing subsidies
4. Reducing Import Duty
a. 1 only b. 2 and 3 only c. 1 and 3 only
d. 1,2,3 and 4 e. None of the above

95. The establishment of 'Payment Banks' is being allowed in India to promote financial inclusion. Which of the following statement/s is /are correct in this context?
1. Mobile telephone companies and supermarket chains that are owned and controlled by residents are eligible to be promoters of Payment Banks.
2. Payment Banks can issue both credit cards and debit cards.
3. Payment Banks cannot undertake lending activities.
a. 1 and 2 only b. 1 and 3 only c. 2 only
d. 1,2 and 3 e. None of these

96. Which of the following is true?
    a. Surplus funds with banks can be invested in pass through certificates
    b. This will be indirect expansion of credit portfolio
    c. Both A and B
    d. None of the above
    e. Either A or B

97. The process of credit Derivative involves?
    a. The Protection Seller guarantees payment of principal and interest or both of the Asset owned by the Protection Buyer in case of credit default
    b. The Protection Buyer pays a premium to the Protection Seller
    c. Both A and B
    d. None of the above
    e. Either A or B

98. Which one of the following statements is incorrect?
    a. Advances against gold ornaments are exempt from NPA norms
    b. Classification of NPA should be done borrower wise and not facility wise
    c. An NPA need not go through the various stages of classification
    d. The existence of security should be ignored if the value is less than 10 per cent of the outstanding in the borrowable account
    e. None of the above

99. Which one of the following statements is 'false'?
    a. The provision on standard assets can be included as Tier-II Capital
    b. Statutory reserves kept by foreign banks in India are eligible for inclusion under Tier-I Capital
    c. Nationalised banks can raise 51 per cent of their capital funds from the public
    d. For foreign banks in India, foreign currency loans granted to India parties are not eligible for inclusion in capital funds
    e. None of the above

100. Specially Developed Economic Zones (SEZs) in India where some of the economic laws and restrictions of the land are relaxed with the purpose of giving incentives to investors are commonly known as?
    a. Preferential Zones
    b. Economic Corridors
    c. Industrial Parks
    d. Special Economic Zones
    e. None of the above

101. When it comes to money market instruments, which among the following is not true?
    a. Treasury bills
    b. Term money
    c. Certificate of deposits
    d. Corporate securities
    e. Commercial paper

102. Which among the following is not under the control of central banking authority?
    a. Monetary control
    b. Management of government debts
    c. Lender of last resort to banks
    d. Banker to government
    e. Equity market and debt market supervision and control

103. The capital markets regulatory authority has supervision over:
a. Stock exchanges b. Foreign institutional investors
c. Equity and debt raisers d. Mutual funds e. All the above

104. Cash reserve ratio is the ________deposit to be held by banks with Reserve Bank of India
a. Voluntary b. Mandatory c. Optional
d. As decided by the chairman and managing director
e. None of the above

105. Urban cooperative banks are controlled by________and ____________
a. State government-RBI b. NABARD – RBI c. SEBI – RBI
d. Central government – NABARD e. NABARD – state governments

106. Leasing, hire purchase and bill discounting are the domain of________
a. Non banking companies b. Mutual funds
c. Commercial banks d. Development banks
e. None of the above

107. New and re-issuable currency notes are stored in ____________maintained by the banks as agents of Reserve Bank of India
a. Currency chests b. Treasuries c. Branches
d. Service units e. Godowns

108. To control inflationary situation in the economy, RBI can increase one or more of these monetary tools:
a. CRR-SLR-BANK Rate b. SLR-CRR-BASE Rate
c. CRR-SLR-REPO Rate d. CRR-SLR-REVERSE REPO Rate
e. CRR-SLR-BENCHMARKING PLR

109. When it comes to retail deposit products, which among the following is irrelevant?
a. Recurring deposit accounts b. Term deposit accounts
c. No frills accounts for common man d. Depository services
e. Senior citizen deposit accounts

110. Safe deposit locker – a product offered in the Indian retail banking segment under:
a. Retail loan products b. Retail deposit products c. Retail services
d. Retail facilities e. Retail comforts

111. According to the information available it has been the experience of banks in the country in recent years under retail lending that the following loans had the least level of impairment (defaults)
a. Home loan portfolio b. consumer loan portfolio
c. vehicle loan portfolio d. personal loan portfolio
e. none of the above

112. When it comes to the term called as "OTCEI", what do you mean by "E"?
a. Exchange b. Environment c. Environment d. Entitlement e. Enlistment

113. ____________ refers to a market where securities are traded after being initially offered to the public in the primary market and/or listed on the stock exchange.
a. Security market b. secondary market c. stock market
d. Bond market e. debenture market

114. "C" in the term called as FMCG stands for?
a. Customer b. consumer c. creditor d. country
e. none of the above

115. Which among the following are participants in call/notice money market?
a. Banks b. primary dealers
c. development finance institutions d. insurance companies e. all the above

116. ______ maintain a register of share and debenture holders and process share and debenture allocation, when issues are subscribed.
a. Mutual funds b. depositories c. registrars
d. brokers e. stock exchanges

117. Non banking finance companies are licensed and supervised by the______and it prescribes that no NBFC can operate without a valid license from the central banking authority
a. State governments b. finance ministry
c. central banking authority d. RBI e. both (c) and (d) as above

118. The Reserve Bank of India was constituted under the Reserve Bank of India act, ______and started functioning with effect from 1st April______
a. 1934-1935 b. 1935-1934 c. 1944-1945
d. 1936-1937 e. none of the above

119. The overall money supply in the economy is controlled by the central bank through:
a. Money supply b. volume of bank credit
c. cost of bank credit d. all the above
e. none of the above

120. Reserve Bank of India is the central banking authority in our country and according to you which is the central banking authority in United Kingdom?
a. Bank of London b. Bank of England c. Federal Reserve Bank
d. Bank of UK e. none of the above

Section 4: ENGLISH LANGUAGE

(121–130). Read the following passage carefully and answer the questions given below it. Certain words have been printed in bold to help you locate them while answering the questions.

India's Intended Nationally Determined Contribution has been widely hailed as a significant next step for not only meeting the country's domestic development goals but its international commitments to **combating** climate crises as well. Submitted to the UN for the period 2021 to 2030, it promises to reduce the emissions intensity of its GDP by 33 to 35 per cent by 2030, from its 2005 level. This is half of what China has declared (60-65 per cent) and a few notches higher than the target set by the US (26-28 per cent).

Why has India, which is low in terms of its cumulative global emissions and per capita emission in comparison to both China and the US, set such high targets? Is it an exercise in global climate diplomacy or an **astute** move to **garner** global funds for technology transfer and capacity building support to achieve the targets? For it to deliver on the promised commitments, the country would need no less than $2.5 trillion over the next decade or so.

At 2.44 tonnes per capita, India may be at the bottom of the current list of leading emitters, but the promised emission targets will bequeath it with per capita emission of 8.98 tonnes in 2030, far below the projected per capita emissions of 12 tonnes by China and the US, but some three times more than the present. No wonder these targets by the top polluters — including India — aren't significant enough to deal with the climate crisis, as they are more than what is required in order to limit global temperature rise by 2°C.

In reality, there has been a need to cut emissions to the tune of 70 per cent below the 2010 levels by 2050, if the world is to be on the path to restrict the increase in temperature. However, the emissions sum-game played by the leading emitters has polarised the global climate negotiations. By entering into an agreement whereby China would match its emissions with that of the US in 2030, carbon space has been conveniently appropriated. This leaves a lot to speculate about the role of corporations in the deal.

No wonder, to satisfy their energy demands in the face of **lopsided** economic growth, the developing countries have promised emission targets that seem carbon-friendly on paper but not on the ground. India's intention to achieve 40 per cent cumulative electric power installed capacity from renewable sources alongside creating an additional carbon dioxide sink of 2.5-3 billion tonnes through additional tree cover by 2030, can be read in that light. It will only fuel per capita emission some three times by 2030.

With India considering both hydro and nuclear power to be environmentally **benign**, good intentions may get lost in smoke. Since coal continues to find favour as the dominant source of energy followed by hydro and nuclear power, the proposed green energy alternatives will hardly get the desired push.

Thermal power contribution to India's installed capacity is unlikely to change from the present 60 per cent; energy contribution from hydro power is projected to double and nuclear power some six times from the present installed capacities. This can only trigger three times more per capita emissions.

Globally, coal-based power provides 40 per cent electricity, and China emits one-third of the global carbon dioxide on account of its coal consumption. India is the second largest coal consumer after China, which is responsible for 1.5 tonnes of carbon dioxide emissions per person per year. The question is whether clean coal technologies will deliver on the promise to cut down on carbon dioxide emissions. Even if it does, the destruction of forests and habitats will release carbon dioxide.

With INDC focused predominantly on emissions reduction, social and environmental issues get pushed to the periphery. That thermal, hydro and nuclear projects cause environmental destruction, deforestation and large-scale displacement doesn't get counted in the emissions scenario. The premise of 'coal-cess' and 'compensatory a forestation' offer a trade-off: first sacrifice environmental concerns for development projects, and then invest funds thus generated in creating carbon sinks.

121. According to the passage, which of the following counties are top polluters?

a. China and UK b. China and India c. China and US
d. India and US e. None of these

122. Find the incorrect statement on the basis of the given passage?

1) The developing countries have promised for carbon-friendly.
2) India's intention to achieve 40 per cent cumulative electric power installed capacity from renewable sources.

3) At 2.44 tonnes per capita, India may be at the bottom of the current list of leading emitters.

a. Only A b. Only B c. Only C d. All A, B or C e. None of these

123. According to the author, what will hardly get the desired push?

a. Carbon dioxide emissions
b. Green energy alternatives
c. Emission targets of countries
d. Environmental concerns for development projects
e. None of these

124. What is the central theme of the passage?

a. Climate changes and its effects
b. Causes of Global worming
c. Climate crisis
d. Climate changes
e. None of these

125. Which of the following is 'true' in the context of the passage?

a. The thermal, hydro and nuclear projects cause environmental destruction and deforestation
b. China emits one-fourth of the global carbon dioxide on account of its coal consumption
c. India is the third largest coal consumer after China
d. All of Above
e. None of these

Directions (126–128): Choose the word that is most nearly the SAME in meaning as the word given in bold as used in the passage.

126. Astute

a. Morose b. Brutish c. Smart d. Cheeky e. Churlish

127. Combating

a. Accurate b. Fight c. Genuine d. Amiable e. Absolute

128. Benign

a. Aggressive b. Strict c. Irritate d. Kind e. Confused

Directions (129–130): Select the word which is most nearly the OPPOSITE in meaning of the word as used in the passage.

129. Lopsided

a. Comparable b. Coordinate c. Commensurate d. Straight e. One sided

130. Garner

a. Dissipate b. Freebie c. Gratis d. Collect e. Gratuitous

(131–135). Rearrange the following sentences in the proper sequence to form a meaningful paragraph then answer the following questions.

1. Assuming the same incidence of black money held as cash will come into the banking system to be replaced, government has an opportunity to utilise the resultant trail to boost its tax collections.
2. The size of the parallel economy can be brought down.
3. Demonetisation will affect about 86% of total currency in circulation, amounting to Rs. 14.6 trillion.

4. According to a World Bank estimate the parallel economy makes up about one-fourth of the total.
5. It is not merely a one-time gain as a trail can bring hitherto unaccounted economic activity into the system.

131. Which of the following sentences should be the FIRST after rearrangement?
a. 1 b. 2 c. 4 d. 5 e. 3

132. Which of the following sentences should be the THIRD after rearrangement?
a. 1 b. 5 c. 4 d. 2 e. 3

133. Which of the following sentences should be the FIFTH after rearrangement?
a. 2 b. 4 c. 1 d. 5 e. 3

134. Which of the following sentences should be the FOURTH after rearrangement?
a. 3 b. 1 c. 4 d. 2 e. 5

135. Which of the following sentences should be the SECOND after rearrangement?
a. 1 b. 2 c. 3 d. 4 e. 5

(136–145). Read each part of the sentence to find out if there is any error in it. The error, if any, will be in one part of the sentence. The number of that part is an answer. If there is no error mark your answer as (e)

136. 1)/Denmark introduced a surcharge few 2)/ years ago on foods that contain over 3)/ 2.3 per cent saturated fat, drawing 4)/criticism about excessive bureaucracy. 5) No error
a. 1 b. 2 c. 3 d. 4 e. No Error

137. a)/Robotics has already made significant inroads b)/ in electronics assembly, with sewing trades, traditionally c)/many countries' first entry point to d)/the global trading system, likely to come next. e)/No Error
a. 1 b. 2 c. 3 d. 4 e. No error

138. a)/A project that daringly set out to bring b)/to life iconic paintings — many created in just one c)/day — have proved to be a staggeringly laborious d)/cinematic effort taking years to realize. e. No error
a. 1 b. 2 c. 3 d. 4 e. No Error

139. a)/ As this trend continues, the imperative b)/ to build supply chains based on the location of relatively c)/ immobile and cost-effective labour will wane, d)/ with production moving closer to the final market. e)/ No error
a. 1 b. 2 c. 3 d. 4 e. No error

140. a)/Chief Minister will leave for b)/New Delhi on Friday evening to attend the c)/Inter-State Council meeting convened by d)/Prime Minister the previous day. e)/ No error
a. 1 b. 2 c. 3 d. 4 e. No Error

(141–150). In the following passage there are blanks each of which has been numbered. These numbers are printed below the passage and against each five words have been suggested. One of which fits the blank appropriately. Find out the appropriate word in each case.

India still remains a non-signatory to 1951 United Nations Refugee (141) and the 1967 Protocol, which help define the legal obligation of states to protect refugees. Yet the legal situation of refugees remains (142), a situation (143) to international standards. We simply do not have a national asylum policy.

It remains the duty of a state, especially one with a democratic (144) like India's, to keep its doors open for people in (145). Any refugee, whose grant of asylum has been approved, should be given a formal recognition of his/her asylum status along with an identity document and a travel document. They should be able to apply for residence permits, and be able to choose their place of residence across India. Their documents must also (146) them to seek employment in the private sector. Primary education, a powerful enabler, should be offered on no-charge basis in government schools, while primary healthcare services available to Indian citizens should be offered as well.

Policy instruments available to the government are (147) for an upgrade. Refugees have been accorded constitutional protection by the judiciary (National Human Rights Commission vs State of Arunachal Pradesh, 1996). In addition, the Supreme Court has held that the right to equality (Article 14) and right to life and personal liberty (Article 21) extend to refugees. The Foreigners Act(1946) and the Registration of Foreigners Act (1939) currently (148) the entry and exit of all refugees, treating them as foreigners without due consideration of their special circumstances. India remains the only significant democracy without legislation specifically for refugees. A well-(149) asylum law would establish a formal refuge (150) process with suitable exclusions (war criminals, serious offenders, etc.) kept.

141. a. Convention b. strangeness c. nuttiness d. quaintness e. weirdness
142. a. apparent b. peculiarity c. oddness d. nebulous e. definite
143. a. immorality b. block c. hinder d. anomalous e. conforming
144. a. ethos b. prevent c. inhibit d. standard e. corruption
145. a. regular b. usual c. distress d. health e. normal
146. a. comfort b. happiness c. disallow d. enable e. stop
147. a. pleasure b. halt c. agree d. ripe e. oppose
148. a. comply b. yield c. obey d. govern e. surrender
149. a. adjusted b. provided c. defined d. managed e. organised
150. a. granting b. allegation c. arraignment d. attribution e. beef

(151–155). Fill in the blanks

151. Noting that "an issue like this has arisen never before", the Supreme Court on Monday decided to hear arguments for _______ to a Constitution Bench a plea challenging the restriction on women aged between 10 and 50 years to enter the _________ Sabarimala temple in Kerala.
   a. causing, obscure
   b. blocking, noted
   c. referring, famed
   d. accusing, famous
   e. alluding, unknown

152. The water level in the Godavari _________near the danger mark at Bhadrachalam town with all its tributaries in spate in the upper reaches of the river posing flood threat to around 19 villages comprising several riverside _________in Bhadrachalam division.
a. hovered, habitations
b. slumped, holes
c. descended, domiciles
d. followed, dwellings
e. lifted, cavities

153. Tense moments _______at the Government Observation Home for Boys in Kelly on Monday afternoon after over 35 _____escaped from the home reportedly following a clash between two groups of boys.
a. failed, tenants
b. prevailed, inmates
c. collapsed, residents
d. busted, occupants
e. triumphed, outpatients

154. The Barrage started receiving heavy _______from Monday evening and irrigation officials announced the first warning around 7 p.m. and said the second warning could be expected tonight if the water level crossed 11.75 ft. at the_______.
a. outflows, cannonade
b. effluences, storm
c. confluents, twaddle
d. floods, vacate
e. inflows, barrage

155. By using computer ________and data collected by the NASA's Cassini and Huygens mission, researchers have revealed that under Titan-like cold environmental conditions, polyamine is ________and can absorb the sun's energy and become a possible catalyst for life.
a. models, flexible
b. modals, tractable
c. inferiors, malleable
d. forms, brittle
e. patterns, inflexible

ANSWER KEY

1. c	2. c	3. d	4. b	5. c	6. c	7. c	8. d	9. a	10. b
11. d	12. d	13. d	14. b	15. b	16. c	17. c	18. a	19. d	20. c
21. b	22. b	23. e	24. b	25. a	26. c	27. c	28. d	29. d	30. d
31. b	32. b	33. c	34. a	35. d	36. b	37. b	38. d	39. a	40. c
41. d	42. d	43. c	44. d	45. d	46. c	47. b	48. d	49. d	50. b
51. a	52. b	53. d	54. b	55. b	56. d	57. b	58. a	59. d	60. d
61. c	62. d	63. d	64. d	65. b	66. b	67. c	68. d	69. a	70. b
71. c	72. d	73. a	74. c	75. c	76. a	77. a	78. b	79. a	80. c
81. d	82. d	83. c	84. a	85. b	86. b	87. d	88. a	89. c	90. c
91. b	92. c	93. c	94. c	95. b	96. c	97. c	98. a	99. c	100. c
101. d	102. e	103. e	104. b	105. b	106. a	107. a	108. a	109. d	110. c
111. a	112. a	113. b	114. b	115. e	116. c	117. c	118. a	119. d	120. b
121. c	122. d	123. b	124. c	125. a	126. c	127. b	128. d	129. d	130. a
131. e	132. a	133. a	134. e	135. d	136. a	137. e	138. c	139. e	140. d
141. a	142. d	143. d	144. a	145. c	146. d	147. d	148. d	149. c	150. a
151. c	152. a	153. b	154. e	155. a					

Solution and Explanations:

1. A < C ≤≤R = M ≤≤P > B < N We can't compare P and N and C and B. Hence option 1 & 4 do not follow. But A ≤≤M or M ≥≥A is not true. Hence option 2 does not follow. Now, A < M; a is true. Hence option 3 is true

2. We put '>' in place question mark (?) in the given expression. We have x ≥≥B = P > D = F > C ≥≥L Thus, P > C and X> F are definitely true.

3. Check the option one by one
1) P > R < O≥≥B ≥≥L ≥≥E < M
This leads to B ≥E. Hence, does not follow.
2) P > R = O < B ≥≥L≥≥E < M
This leads to B ≥E . Hence, does not follow.
3) P > R > O ≥≥B ≤≤L = E < M
Thus R and E can't be compared. Hence does not follow.
4) P ≥≥R ≥≥O ≥≥B > L ≥≥E M
Thus, R > E is definitely true. B > E.

4. Given expression: A = E≤≤B < C ≤≤N = T
Thus C < A, Hence C ≤≤A is not true.
Now, B < T holds true. Hence, option b. is true. But B ≤≤T is not. Hence, option 3 is not true.
Now, again E < N. Hence, option 4 is not true.

5. Option 1) M ≤≤O = U ≤≤N ≤≤T
So, U ≤T and O ≤≤M is true.
option 2) M ≤≤O = U = N ≤≤T
So, O ≤≤M and U ≤≤T is true
Option 3) M < O = U ≤≤N < T
So, M ≤≤O is true. It means O < M
Again T > U is True, U≤≤is not True
Option 4) M ≤≤O > U ≤≤N = T
So, M < O or O

6–10:
Total flooring area with wood - pa da te ro hi .... (i)
Marble cost in total - co he ni zo .... (ii)
Marble with tiles - te zo ga .... (iii)
Wood tiles cost much - ga cha da ni .... (iv)
square area - ro su .... (v)
We get the following:
From I, II : Total - hi
From I and III - with - te
From I and IV - wood - da
From I and V - arca - ro
From II and III - Marble - zo
From III - tiles - ga
From II and IV - Cost - ni

From IV - much - cha
From V - square - S 4
From II - in - Co
From I - Flooring – Pa

11. From I: Babu > Arun > Era
From II: Dolly > Farhan > Babu and Dolly is not heaviest.
From I and II together:
Chintu > Dolly > Farhan > Babu > Arun and Era, Chintu must be the heaviest. So, Dolly will be the only one lighter than heaviest. Thus, both I and II are necessary.

12. Nothing is said about N so we can't find relationship between M & N. So, II alone is not sufficient From I and II together: M is husband of N. Thus, both I and II are necessary.

13. **From I and II together-**

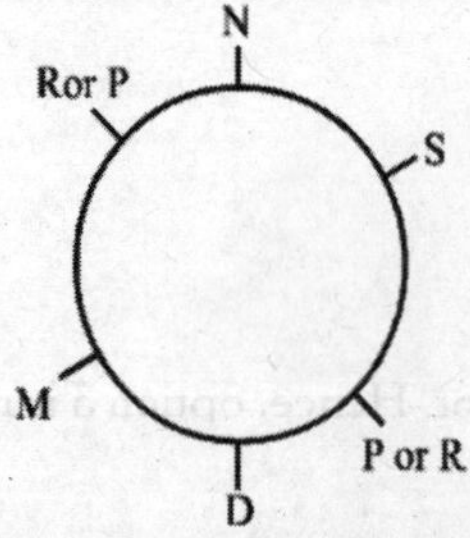

either R or P is on the left of M. So, we can't be sure
Thus, I and II are not sufficient.

14. From I : Since Nilesh rank not specified, we can't determine total no. of students.
From II: Anuj is seventh from top & 8 ranks above Tarun. That means there are 7 students between them. Tarun's rank from the bottom is 30.
So, No. of students= (8 + 7 + 30 – 1)= 44
Hence, only II is sufficient.

(16–20). Following is the arrangement:

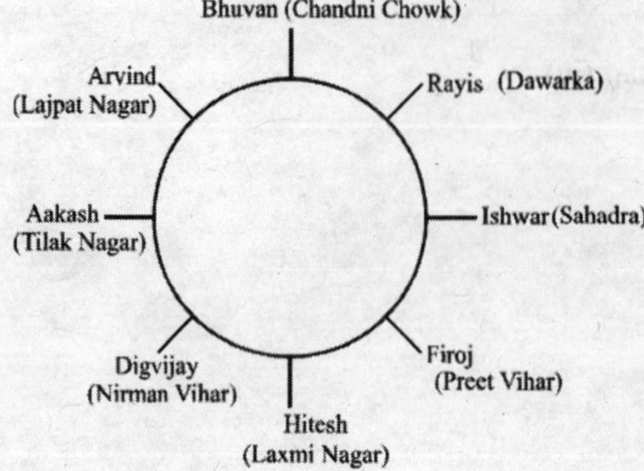

(21–25). Following is the arrangement:

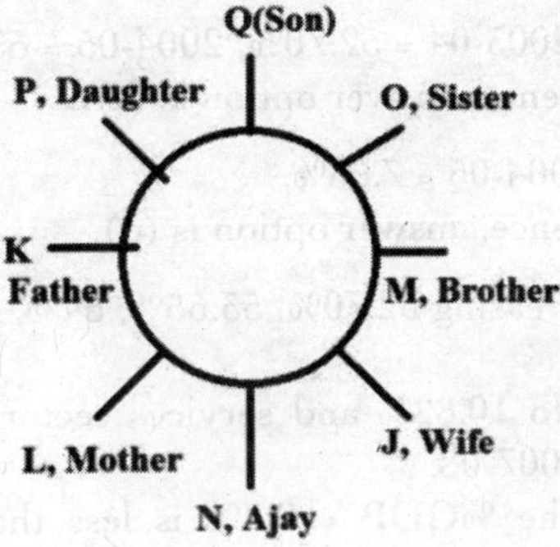

Solution to 46–50:

46. 2/3 of 450 = 300 seats. In 1989, 1991 and 200 the congo has managed two-third majority. Hence, answer option is (c).

47. To form a government, the number of seats required => 60% of 450 = 270. In 1996, 1998 the party sought external support. Hence, answer option is (b).

48. For the election in the year 2000, (310 - 220)/220 × 100 = 40.9%, which is maximum. Hence, answer option is (d).

49. Average number of seats won => 1785 / 6 = 298. In 1996, 1998 and 2004 the number of seats won by congo is less than the average number of seats. Hence, answer option is (d).

50. 56% of 450 = 252. Number of seats won in 1998 = 220. Hence, number of seats short => 252 – 220 = 32. Required percentage = (32/450) × 100 = 7.11%. Hence, answer option is (b).

Solution to 51–55:

51. The days on which at least 30 jeans were sold => 5th, 9th, 13th and 15th. Hence, answer option is (a).

52. Number of XL T-shirts of LOOT => 670 while number of XL T-shirts of Levis => 450. Hence, 670 + 450 = 1120. Hence answer option is (b).

53. By counting, stagnant supply occurs 10 times from 1st April to 15th April. Hence answer option is (d).

54. On 13th April, the total number of T-shirts supplied by the agent = 660, which is maximum on any day during the given tenure. Hence answer option is (b).

55. The most successful day is 13th April with 660 T-shirts supplied and the least successful day if 7th April with 430 T-shits supplied. Hence answer option is (b).

Solution to 56–60:

56. Average percentage GDP growth of the services sector = (7.66 + 9.2 + 9.77 + 8.9) / 4 = 8.88%. Hence, answer option is (d)

57. The percentage growth in GDP for various years => 2004-05 = 9.4%, 2005-06 => 10.15%, 2006-07 => 11.34%, 2007-08 => 10.82%. Hence, answer option is (b).

58. The contribution of service sector to overall GDP => 2003-04 = 52.70%, 2004-05 = 53.55%, 2005 – 06 = 54%, 2006 – 07 = 54.8, 2007-08 = 55.8% Hence, answer option is (a).

59. The percentage growth in GDP for various years => 2004-05 = 7.66%, 2005-06 = 9.2%, 2006-07 = 9.77%, 2007-08 = 8.9%. Hence, answer option is (d).

60. (i) True as contribution of service sector to GDP is increasing 52.70%, 53.55%, 54%, 54.8%, 55.8%.
   (ii) True as overall GDP growth falls from 11.34% to 10.82% and services sector GDP growth falls from 9.77% to 8.9% from 2006-07 to 2007-08.
   (iii) False because only for one year i.e., 2004-05 the %GDP = 9.4% is less than the average GDP of 10.42%. Hence, answer option is (d).

Solution to 61–65:

61. Amount spent by SabPaisa technologies on transport = 5% of Rs. 80000 = Rs. 4000
Amount spent by Symbiotic Ltd on transport = 10% of Rs. 100000 = Rs. 10000
Hence, (4000 × 100) / 10000 = 40%. Hence, answer option is (c).

62. (45+35) / 200 = 0.4. Hence, answer option is (d).

63. Others for both the companies = Rs. 4000. Hence, answer option is (d).

64. For the category, raw material the difference is maximum = 45000 – 28000 = Rs. 17000. Hence, answer option is (d).

65. Symbiotic technologies spends 6% of Rs. 100000 = Rs. 6000 on telephone and Electricity bills while SabPaisa Technologies spends 20% of Rs. 80000 = Rs. 16000 on telephone and Electricity bills. Hence, answer option is (b).

126. Astute- able to understand a situation quickly

127. Combating- to fight for something

128. Benign- gentle and kind

129. Lopsided- with one side lower or smaller than other

130. Garner- to collect or gather

136. Replace “few” with “a few”
Few – when the amount is small and unsatisfactory
A Few – when the amount is small but still satisfactory

137. no error

138. it should be “has” instead of “have”
Here subject is one project so it should be has (singular H.V).

139. No error

140. it should be “the next day” instead of “the previous day”. Because first part of sentence is in future tense so meeting should be held on the next day.

SBI PO Mains MOCK Test Paper 15

Structure of this MOCK Test

S.No.	Name of section	No. of Questions	Total marks	Allotted Time
1	Reasoning and Computer Aptitude	45	60	60 minutes
2	Data Analysis and Interpretation	35	60	45 minutes
3	General/ Economy/ Banking Awareness	40	40	35 minutes
4	English Language	35	40	40 minutes
Total		155	200	3 hours

- There is 1/4th Negative marking for every wrong answer.
- If a question is left blank, i.e. no answer is marked by the candidate, there will be no penalty for that question

Section 1: Reasoning and Computer Aptitude

Direction for questions 1 to 5: Read the information given below and solve the questions based on it.

A, B, C, D, E, F, G and H are sitting around a circle facing the center. B is third to the left of H. C is fourth to the left of A, who is not an immediate neighbor of F or B. E is not an immediate neighbor of B. G is second to the right of D.

1. Who is the immediate left of B?

   a. D b. G c. D or G
   d. Data inadequate e. None of these

2. Who is to the immediate left of H?

   a. A b. E c. F
   d. Data inadequate e. None of these

3. Which of the following pairs represents the immediate neighbors of F?

   a. CH b. ED c. HD
   d. CE e. None of these

4. In which of the following pairs is the first person sitting to the immediate right of the second person?
   a. BG b. GA c. AH
   d. HE e. CF

5. Who is third to the left of E?
   a. A b. C c. G
   d. Data inadequate e. None of these

Directions for questions 6 to 8: answer the question on basis of the given information.

There are five friends- Amit, Binay, Chetan, Dheeru and Emran – who live in different cities among – Delhi, Mumbai, Kolkata, pune and Bangalore, in no particular order. Age of two friends among the five is the same. It is also known that:

(i) Both Amit and Chetan are older than the friend who lives in Bangalore.
(ii) The friend who lives in Mumbai is the oldest and the one who lives in Kolkata is the youngest among the five friends
(iii) Binay is older than Chetan
(iv) Chetan is younger than the among the five friends
(v) Dheeru is not the youngest among the five friends
(vi) Sum of the ages of Emran and Binay is the same as the ages of Chetan and Amit.

6. Who among the five friend is the oldest?
   a. Dheeru b. Binay c. Amit
   d. Chetan e. None of these

7. How many friends are younger than the one who lives in Pune?
   a. 1 b. 2 c. 3
   d. 4 e. None of these

8. Who among the five friends lives in Delhi?
   a. Amit b. Chetan c. Binay
   d. Dheeru e. None of these

Directions for questions 9 to 11: Answer the question on basis of the given information.

Each of the six people – Ram, Mohan, Jatin, Vijay, Kripal and Santosh – has a different surname among- Singh, Vats, Rehman, Joshi,Kohli and Tyagi, not necessarily in the same order. These Six people are standing in a row such that each of them is facing East. It is also known that:

(i) There are exactly two people standing between Kirpal and Ram.
(ii) Tyagi is the only person standing between Jatin and Rehman.
(iii) Singh is standing to the right of joshi.
(iv) Ram is standing to the right of Vijay who is standing to the immediate left of Vats
(v) Kirpa's surname is neither joshi nor Rehman.
(vi) Mohan is standing to the immediate left of Santosh, who is standing at one the ends of the row.

9. What is the surname of Kirpal?
   a. Kohli b. Tyagi c. Singh
   d. Vats e. None of these

10. How many people are standing between Ram and Santosh?
a. 0 b. 1 c. 2
d. More than 2 e. None of these

11. What is the surname of the person who is standing to immediate right of Ram?
a. Rehman b. Joshi c. Vats
d. Kohli e. None of these

Directions for questions 12 to 15: answer the question on basis of the given information.
Pallavi, Qureshi, Ramesh, Suruchi, Teena and Urvashi are sitting in two parallel rows facing each other, three in each. Teena is not at the end of any row. Suruchi is second to the left of Urvashi. Ramesh the neighbor of Teena , is sitting diagonally opposite to Suruchi, Qurashi is neighbor of Urvashi.

12. Who from the following are sitting diagonally opposite to each other?
a. Urvashi, Ramesh b. Suruchi, Pallavi c. Pallavi, Ramesh
d. Pallavi, Urvashi e. None of these

13. Who is facing Qurashi?
a. Pallavi b. Ramesh c. Teena
d. Data inadequate e. None of these

14. Who of the following are in the same row?
a. Teena, Suruchi b. Pallavi, Teena
c. Ramesh, Qurashi d. Pallavi, Qurashi e. None of these

15. Who of the following are in one row
a. Uravashi, Qurashi, Ramesh b. Urvashi, Teena, Ramesh
c. Urvashi, Qurashi, Pallavi d. Data inadequate
e. None of these

Directions: (16 to 20) – below is given a passage followed by several possible inferences which can be drawn from the facts stated in passage. Examine contextual inferences and decide the degree of its truth and falsity.
Mark Answer a) if the inference is definitely true.
Mark Answer b) if the inference is probably true.
Mark Answer c) if the data is inadequate.
Mark Answer d) if the inference is probably false.
Mark Answer e) if the inference is definitely false.
The pace of recruitment has unmistakably picked up in the last few months. After two abysmal quarters the business sentiment has turned positive. A flurry of hiring activity has been observed across the manufacturing sector and the IT and ITES sector catering to telecom and legal process outsourcing. The advent of new players and an aggressive expansion of telecom giants has seen a bullish outlook for the industry with a promise of exponential growth. But is the worst over for business across the spectrum? Firms are going back to the drawing board and dusting off their plans to see if there is scope for at least incremental hiring in specific domains where they want to build expertise. Besides that, there are few signs to show that there is a board –based revival in the market.

1. Many companies in the manufacturing sector have decided to reduce their fresh intake of employees next year.
2. Persons with legal qualifications and expertise will earn more in the future.

3. Most companies across sectors have decided to increase their manpower requirement manifold.
4. The telecom sector has experienced negative growth in the past few years.
5. Companies in various sectors have projected higher business growth in the near future.

Directions: (21 to 25): in each question below is given a group of letters followed by four combinations of digits/symbols numbered 1,2,3 and 4. Find out which combination represents the group of letters.

T	A	G	R	S	D	N	E	V	U	X	P
@	4	9	#	%	3	©	5	1	β	7	6

Conditions

i) **if the first letter is a constant and the last letter is a vowel, only the first letter may be coded and no code may be given to the last letter.**

ii) **if both first and last letters are vowel, then both are to be coded as $.**

iii) **if the first letter is a vowel and the last letter is a consonant, the codes are to be interchanged.**

21. NERSPU
    a. @5#%6@
    b. @5#56©
    c. ©5#%6
    d. ©5#%6 β
    e. None of these

22. UXPTGN
    a. ©76@9β
    b. $76@9©
    c. β76@9©
    d. β76@9β
    e. None of these

23. DESGRT
    a. 35%9#
    b. 35%9#@
    c. @5%9#3
    d. 359%#@
    e. None of these

24. XNTPGA
    a. 7©@694
    b. 7©©964
    c. 4©©69
    d. 7©@69
    e. None of these

25. ESVNTU
    a. $%1©@$
    b. 5%1©@ β

c. $%1©@6
d. $%1© β 5
e. None of these

Direction for questions 26 to 28: Read the information given below and solve the questions based on it.

Four sisters Suruchi, Tara, Uma and Vibha are playing a game such that the loser doubles the money of each of the other players from her share. They played four games and each sister lost one game in alphabetical order. At the end of fourth game, each sister had Rs. 32. In each of the rounds, only one players lost the match.

26. How many rupees did Suruchi start with?
a. Rs. 60
b. Rs. 34
c. Rs. 66
d. Rs. 28
e. Rs. 41

27. Who started with the lowest amount?
a. Suruchi
b. Tara
c. Uma
d. Vibha
e. cannot be determined

28. What was the amount with Uma at the end of the second round?
a. 36
b. 72
c. 16
d. 32
e. None of these

Direction for questions 29–30: Read the information given below and answer the questions that follow:

There are five friends – Babu, Om, Qadir, Munu and Ani – each having some marbles with them. Following is given the sum of the marbles with them taken three at a time, making sure no group of three friends is repeated - 212, 214, 219, 216, 215, 217, 222, 217, 221, and 219.

It is also known that:

Ani is having more marbles than Om but less than Munu.
Babu is having the lowest number of marbles.
Average number of marbles with Qadir and Munu is equal to the number of marbles with Ani.
Maximum number of marbles with any of the friends can be 100, however it is not known if anyone of them actually possessed 100 marbles or not?

29. How many marbles are there with Qadir?
a. 70
b. 72
c. 74
d. 62
e. None of these

30. What is the average of number of marbles with all of them?
a. 73.2
b. 72.4
c. 71.3
d. 70.5
e. 69.8

31. Antivirus is a/an
a. Application software
b. System software
c. Network software
d. Utility software
e. None of these

32. SMTP, FTP and DSN are applications of the________?
a. Physical layer
b. Network layer
c. Transport layer
d. Application layer
e. None of these

33. An internet address is __________- bits in length.
a. 4
b. 8
c. 16
d. 32
e. 64

34. MACROS is used to __________
a. Break the page
b. Create the page
c. Store the page
d. All of these
e. None of these

35. Computer collect data, it means they allow user to ________ data.
a. Present
b. Transmit
c. Output
d. Input
e. Store

36. The _________ of a system includes the programs or instructions.
a. Software
b. Peripheral
c. Information
d. Hardware
e. None of these

37. COBOL is widely used in_____________?
a. Commercial
b. Scientific
c. Space
d. Mathematics
e. None of these

38. The item cut is temporarily store in _______?
a. Clipboard
b. Dashboard
c. Diskette
d. Hard disk
e. CD

39. A collection of program that controls how your computer system runs and processes information is called ?
a. O S
b. Computer
c. Office
d. Loader
e. Compiler

40. Microsoft office is
a. Shareware
b. Public domain software
c. Open–source software
d. An application suit
e. None of these

41. Alerts mostly appear in __________?
a. Check box
b. Combo box
c. Dialog box
d. Window
e. None of these

42. An error is also called____?
a. Bug
b. Debug
c. Cursor
d. Icon
e. None of these

43. The software component of an expert system that draws conclusions is __
a. User interface
b. Database
c. Inference engine
d. I/O controller
e. None of these

44. Linux is a _______ operating system.
a. Open source
b. Microsoft
c. Windows
d. Mac
e. Freeware

45. How many bits is equal to 1 nibble?
a. 4
b. 8
c. 16
d. 32
e. 64

Section 2: Data Analysis and Interpretation

Direction for questions 46 – 50: Refer to the table given below and answer the questions that follow.

Given below are the forecasts of world and Asian energy demand for the years 1991, 2001 and 2011. The demand is given in million barrels per day, crude oil equivalent.

	1991		2001		2011	
	World	Asia	World	Asia	world	Asia
Petrol	50.0	4.0	70.0	10.0	80.0	15.0
Naphtha	30.0	0.5	40.0	2.5	50.0	5.0
Solid Fuels	50.0	4.0	60.0	5.0	75.0	10.0
Nuclear Fuel	10.0	0.5	20.0	1.0	25.0	1.3
Hydro Energy	10.0	1.0	10.0	1.5	20.0	2.0
Total	150.0	10.0	200.0	20.0	250.0	33.3

46. What can be inferred from the given table?
    a. Percentage increase in the number of Petrol using vehicles/agents have increased in Asia than the world in the decade 1991-2001.
    b. Exploration of Naphtha is low in Asia and is less than the exploration of Naphtha in the world throughout the period.
    c. Both (1) and (2)
    d. Neither (1) nor (2)
    e. Not enough data to conclude.

47. Over 1991-2011, which two fuels meet more than 60% of the total energy demand of both the world and Asia?
    a. Petrol and Naphtha b. Petrol and Solid fuels
    c. Naphtha and Solid fuels d. Petrol only
    e. None of these

48. Which fuel's proportion in the total energy demand increases over the decade 1991-2001 and decreases over the decade 2001-2011 for both the world and Asia?
    a. Petrol b. Naphtha c. Solid fuels
    d. Nuclear Fuel e. None of these

49. Which is the fuel whose proportion in the total energy demand will decrease continuously over the period 1991-2011, in Asia?
    a. Naphtha b. Solids fuels c. Nuclear Fuel
    d. Hydro Energy e. None of these

50. Which is the fuel whose proportions to the total energy demand of the world will remain constant over the period 1991-2011 but whose proportion will increase in the total energy demand in Asia?
    a. Naphtha b. Solids fuels c. Nuclear Fuel
    d. Hydro Energy e. None of these

Direction for questions 51 – 54: Refer to the table given below and answer the questions that follow.

Following table gives some incomplete information on the marks obtained by four persons Amit, Binit, Charu & Dilip in four different subjects.

	Physics	Chemistry	Maths	English	Total
Amit	80	70	-	80	-
Binit	60	-	60	-	-
Charu	-	-	60	-	220
Dilip	90	-	70	60	-

Additional Information:

(i) Amit's average marks was 72.5, in all the four subjects.

(ii) The average marks in Physics for all four persons was 67.5.

(iii) Binit's Average marks for all four subjects was 1.5 times Charu's marks in physics.

(iv) Binit & Dilip scored the same marks in English. The average English marks were the same as the average Physics marks.

(v) The total marks in Chemistry was 10 less than the total marks in physics for all four persons.

51. Who scored the lowest total?
    a. Amit
    b. Binit
    c. Charu
    d. Dilip
    e. either Amit or Binit

52. The average marks for all four persons (for all the four subjects) is (approx.)
    a. 65.625
    b. 81.225
    c. 99.5
    d. 105.6
    e. 62.5

53. Who is the highest scorer in chemistry?
    a. Amit
    b. Binit
    c. Charu
    d. Dilip
    e. Either Binit or Charu

54. Who is the lowest scorer in physics?
    a. Amit
    b. Binit
    c. Charu
    d. Dilip
    e. Either Binit or Charu

Direction for questions 55 to 57: Go through the data given below and solve the questions based on it.

Following bar chart gives the distribution of green land in the following countries.
Total green land area = 13,754 sq km.

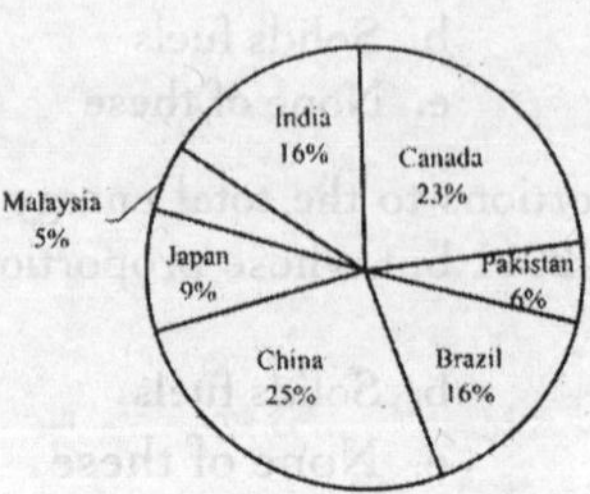

Some of these green lands are protected and remaining are unprotected. Following bar chart gives that distribution.

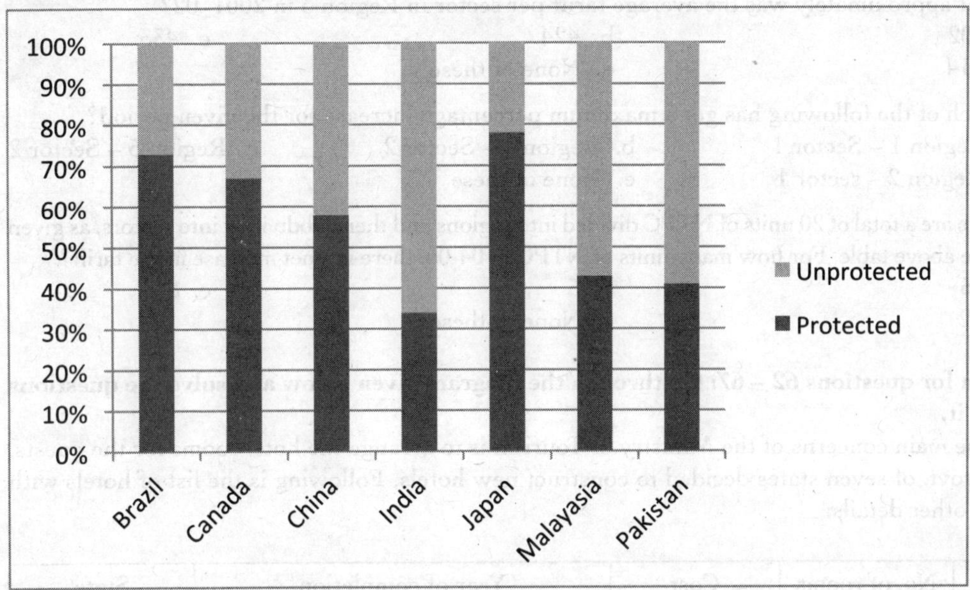

55. What is the difference of protected and unprotected Greenland (approx. sq km)?
a. 3015 b. 2382 c. 2845
d. 2654 e. 1243

56. Which country has the maximum protected greenland?
a. China b. Japan c. Brazil
d. Canada e. India

57. Protected green land of India is what percentage of the protected green land of Pakistan?
a. 48% b. 65% c. 160%
d. 220% e. 12%

Direction for questions 58 – 61: Go through the table given below and solve the questions based on it.

The following table gives the tariff (in paisa per kilo–watt–hour) levied by the NTPC in 2004–05, in the four sectors and the regions within them. The table also gives the percentage change in the tariff as compared to 2001–02.

	Region 1		Region 2		Region 3		Region 4		Region 5	
Sector 1	425	+15	472	+5	420	–4	415	+8	440	+10
Sector 2	430	+12	468	+8	448	+7	423	–3	427	+11
Sector 3	428	+8	478	–4	432	+6	441	+10	439	+8
Sector 4	434	–5	470	+15	456	+10	451	+12	446	–12

58. If the amount of power consumed by the various Regions in Sector 1 is the same, then, as compared to 2001–02, the net tariff in 2004–05…

a. Increased by 9.5% b. Decrease by 1.5% c. Decrease by 13.3%
d. Decreases by 2.5% e. None of these

59. What approximately was the average tariff per sector in Region 3 in 2001–02?
a. 402 b. 424 c. 433
d. 414 e. None of these

60. Which of the following has got a maximum percentage increase for the given period?
a. Region 1 – Sector 1 b. Region 1 – Sector 2 c. Region 5 – Sector 2
d. Region 2 – sector 1 e. None of these

61. There are a total of 20 units of NTPC divided into regions and then subdivided into sectors, as given in the above table. For how many units of NTPC in 04-05, there is a net increase in the tariff?
a. 15 b. 5 c. 8
d. 12 e. None of these

Direction for questions 62 – 67: Go through the diagram given below and solve the questions based on it.

One of the main concerns of the Ministry of Tourism is to arrange the hotel rooms for the guests. For this govt. of seven states decided to construct new hotels. Following is the list of hotels with state and other details:

Hotel	No. of rooms	Cost (Rs. crore)	Year of completion (on 31st December)	State
A Hotel	600	275	2008	DELHI
B hotel	320	210	2009	Haryana
C hotel	250	250	2009	Rajasthan
D Hotel	400	430	2008	Punjab
E Hotel	520	310	2010	HP
F Hotel	450	400	2008	MP
G hotel	500	250	2010	J and K

62. What is the cost of hotels completed in 2008 as a percentage of cost of hotels to be completed in all the three years?
a. 39% b. 52% c. 47%
d. 58% e. 40%

63. What is the average number of rooms that would be built per crore of rupees over the whole period?
a. 1. 25 b. 1.72 c. 0.69
d. 1.43 e. 0.46

64. Assume that all the projects are delayed and rooms can be completed only in 2010. It is also given that the cost increases at a simple interest rate of 10% per annum, what is the average cost per room for all projects in year 2010 (Approx)?
a. Rs.0.62crore b. Rs.0.69crore c. Rs.0.78crore
d. Rs. 0.84 crore e. R.s 1.42 crores

65. What would be the value of all the investments, in 2007, if the interest rate is 10% compounded annually?
a. Rs. 1800 crore
b. Rs. 2125 crore
c. Rs. 1670
d. Rs. 2445 crore
e. Rs. 1250 crores

66. For which of the following states, cost per room built is maximum?
a. MP
b. Delhi
c. Punjab
d. Haryana
e. None of these

67. For which of the following states, cost per room built is 2nd lowest?
a. MP
b. Haryana
c. J and K
d. Delhi
e. None of these

Direction for questions 68 – 71: Go through the diagram given below and solve the questions based on it.

dueNorth Inc. arranges a training program for its employees from the Finance, Marketing and HRD departments. Each participant is awarded a grade at the end of the training program. It is also known that the total number of HRD employees participating in the training is equal to the number of marketing employees getting an Average grade.

Your boss has given you the incomplete chart to be completed.

Dept. / Grade	Excellent	Good	Average	Total
Finance Dept		9	0	
Marketing Dept	0			38
H R D Dept			8	
Total	22	27		95

68. The number of marketing employees getting a Good grade is:
a. 0
b. 7
c. 3
d. 6
e. 2

69. The maximum number of excellent grades is obtained by:
a. Marketing Dept.
b. Finance Dept.
c. HRD Dept.
d. Both (a) & (b)
e. both (a) and (c)

70. The number of Good grades received by HRD is:
a. 18
b. 28
c. 38
d. 24
e. None of these

71. The number of Finance employees getting excellent grade form what percentage of the total number of employees participating (approx)?
a. 5%
b. 15%
c. 10%
d. 13%
e. 22%

72. Which of the following discount options is better for a customer:
i. successive discounts of 20%, 30% and then pay a service tax of 10%.
ii. successive discounts of 30%, 20% and then pay a service tax of 10%.
iii. Pay service tax of 10% first, then successive discounts of 20% and 30%.
a. i or ii
b. iii
c. either of these three
d. i and iii OR ii and iii
e. ii or iii

73. What is the sum of the greatest number of five digits which when divided by 4, 6, 10 and 15 leaves the same remainder 3 in each case?
a. 33 b. 36 c. 39
d. 42 e. 54

74. Forty percent of the employees of a certain company are men, and 75% of the men earn more than Rs. 25,000 per year. If 45% of the company's employees earn more than Rs. 25,000 per year, what fraction of the women employed by the company earn less than or equal to Rs. 25,000 per year?
a. $\frac{2}{1}$ b. $\frac{1}{4}$ c. $\frac{1}{3}$
d. $\frac{3}{4}$ e. $\frac{1}{3}$

75. There are fifty successive percentage discounts given in a series of 2%, 4%, 6%, 8%...............and so on. What is the net discount?
a. 98% b. 2550% c. 100%
d. 2006% e. None of these

76. Neo is going to NDLS from PNBE by his car at a speed of 40 kmph. While coming back, he returns with a speed of x kmph. What should be the value of x so that his average speed during the whole journey is 80 kmph?
a. 160kmph b. 40 kmph c. 120 kmph
d. 240 kmph e. It is not possible

77. Kunal, Saurav and Gopi assemble for a dutch party. Kunal brings 3 guavas while Saurav brings 5. Since Gopi did not have any guavas, he contributed Rs. 8. How many rupees should Kunal and Saurav respectively get, assuming each of the three consumes an equal portion of the guavas?
a. 1, 6 b. 2, 5 c. 5, 7
d. 1,7 e. None of these

78. On the eve of the foundation day party of *due North inc.*, ratio of males to females was 5 : 3. However when 10 males left the party, this ratio got changed to 1:1. How many people were there originally at the party?
a. 48 b. 32 c. 64
d. 40 e. 56

79. Two candles of the same length are lighted at 12 noon. The first is consumed in 6 hours and the second in 4 hours. Assuming that each candle burns at a constant rate, in how many hours after being lighted was the first candle twice the length of the second?
a. 3 PM b. 2 PM c. 1:30 PM
d. 2:30 PM e. 3:30 PM

80. Satish used 6L of oil paint to paint a map of India of 6 m high. How many litres of paint would Santosh need for painting a proportionally scaled map of height 18 m?
a. 54 b. 18 c. 30
d. Cannot be determined

Section 3: General and Banking Awareness

81. Which of the following is not included in the core sectors of Indian economy?
a. Transport b. Coal c. Steel
d. Cement e. Electricity

82. As per the report published by the International Monetary Fund (IMF), the developing economies across the world are holding a massive stockpile of foreign exchange reserves. Which of the following is/are the resultant consequences of this type of stockpiling by various nations?
(A) A trade imbalance is generated between the developing and emerging economies and the rich countries. It is not healthy sign.
(B) Many economists are of the opinion that these imbalances created the underpinning of the current global economics crisis.
(C) This stockpiling is responsible not only for problems in trade balance but has also created a problem of money laundering.
a. Only A b. Only B c. Only C
d. Only A and B e. All A, B and C

83. Government of India has set up a special group to devise a long-term pricing formula so that it can cope up with the prevailing global volatility in the prices of which of the following commodities?
a. Sugar b. Paddy c. crude oil & petroleum
d. gold e. pulse

84. As we all know, India has a three-tier structure of tax administration. There are taxes levied by Central Government , State Government and local Government . Which of the following taxes is levied by the Local Government Bodies?
a. Value –Added Tax b. Stamp Duty c. Service tax
d. Land Revenue e. Tax on water supply and drainage etc

85. Which of the following is one of the most successful programs under Bharat Nirman?
a. Pradhan Mantri Gram Sadak Yojana b. Watershed Development scheme
c. Grameen Vidyutikaran Yojana d. Indra Awas Yojana
e. None of there

86. What is/are the major roles of "Banking Ombudsman"?
(A) Banking Ombudsman is a quasi-judicial authority having powers to summon the banks and the customers both in case of dispute.
(B) The banking ombudsmen are appointed by the President of India and are retired judges of the High or Supreme Courts.
(C) The decisions/judgments given by the Banking Ombudsman cannot be taken to any court of justice as their decisions are last in case of bank- related problems/ disputes.
a. Only A b. Only B c. Only C
d. All A, B and C e. None of these

87. The Reliance Power is working on four hydropower projects in Arunachal Pradesh which are "Run –of-River" type of projects. What is a main characteristic of R-O-R projects?

a. These projects are developed only in hilly areas. They can't be developed on plains.
b. In these projects, there is no need of storing the water in dams, which is very costly.
c. In ROR projects, the only requirement is to make a big reservoir and turn the flow of the direction in which we need it.
d. ROR projects are three-to-four times costlier as compared to old patterned dam type of projects.
e. None of these

88. India inducted Airborne Warning and control System platforms in its air force. These sophisticated machines are supplied by which of the country?
a. Australia b. Germany c. Israel d. France e. Russia

89. Which of the following pairs of countries are the signatories of a gas pipeline deal christened as peace pipeline?
a. Iran-Iraq b. Iraq-UAE c. Kuwait-Iran
d. Pakistan-Iran e. Pakistan-India

90. PM Modi announced demonetization of higher value currency on 8th November. After that, RBI issued directives to deposit/exchange the Rs. 500 and Rs. 1000 notes. Which of the following directives was NOT announced on 8th November 2016 regarding Rs. 500 and Rs. 1000 notes?
a. Exchange upto Rs. 4000 per day per person
b. ATMs were to be closed on 9th November 2016.
c. ATM withdrawal upto Rs. 2000 per day per card.
d. Withdrawal limit from bank branches was Rs. 24,000 per account per week.
e. Post offices could be used to exchange these notes.

91. Which state has 'Mahila Court' in every district?
a. Tamil Nadu b. Andhra Pradesh c. Karnataka
d. Delhi e. kerala

92. Who amongst the following is the author of the book *"Faith and Compassion"*?
a. Arun Gandhi b. Kuldeep Nayyar
c. Amit Chaudhury d. Navin Chawala e. None of these

93. We hear a term "Carbon Foot Print" these days very frequently. What does it indicate?
(A) The amount of carbon dioxide released in the atmosphere every day by an electronics gadget/ organization or even by an individual.
(B) The quantity of Co_2 released when one ton of air is recycled by an air conditioner during every hour of its functioning.
(C) The quantity of all greenhouse gases put together required to maintain the temperature of the environment at a fixed level of 30° c at nodal points in a country.
a. Only A b. Only B c. Only C
d. All A, B and C e. None of these

94. Which of the following books has NOT been written by Doaris Lessing?
a. The Golden Notebook b. Memories of a Survivor
c. The City of Joy d. The Summer Before the Dark
e. The Fifth Child

95. Which country won the Kabaddi World Cup 2016?
a. India b. Iran c. Pakistan d. Bangladesh e. None of these

96. Who won the men's singles title in the 2016 Rogers Cup?
a. Kei Nishikori
b. Novak Djokovic
c. Rafel Nadal
d. Andy Murray
e. None of these

97. Name the Train that was flagged off by Railway Minister Suresh Prabhu Between Agartala and Delhi .
a. Tripura Sundari Express
b. Sunder Tripura Express
c. Agartala-Delhi Express
d. Tripura Express
e. None of these

98. Name the state has decided to recruit transgender persons as jail warders as per the directive of the Supreme Court.
a. Odisha b. Bihar c. Kerala d. Goa e. None of these

99. CRPF recently decided to appoint which of the following sportspersons as its commandant and Brand Ambassador?
a. Jeetu Rai
b. P V Sindhu
c. Sakshi Malik
d. Deepa Karmakar
e. None of these

100. The West Bengal State Assembly recently passed a resolution to change the name of the state. What would be the state called in English?
a. Bengal b. Bangal c. Bangla d. Bang e. None of these

101. Which facility was launched by Union Government in August 2016 that allows people to sign documents digitally from remote places?
a. Legal Desk
b. eSign Desk
c. Aadhaar Desk
d. e-KYC Desk
e. None of these

102. Who has been elected as the 39th Prime Minister of Nepal?
a. Ram Baran Yadav
b. Khadga Prasad Oli
c. Pushpa Kamal Dahal
d. Manish Koierala
e. None of these

103. Which of the following become the first state of India to approve sewage and waste water policy?
a. Bihar
b. Maharashtra
c. Rajasthan
d. Jharkhand
e. UP

104. Which country won first time Gold in Olympic Women's Rugby championship in Rio de Janeiro?
a. Australia
b. New Zealand
c. Canada
d. Britain
e. None of these

105. The Mental Health care Bill 2013, that was passed in Rajya Sabha Seeks to repeal the Mental Health Act of the year?
a. 1976
b. 1956
c. 1987
d. 1996
e. 2001

106. Who was appointed as the Chief Executive officer (CEO) of the CSS Corp in August 2016?
a. TG Ramesh
b. Manish Tandon
c. Rajesh Krishnamurthy
d. Vishal Sikka
e. None of these

107. Recently, Ministry of Civil Aviation gave green signal for expansion of which airport?
a. Agartala b. Ranchi c. Lucknow
d. Guwahati e. None of these

108. Which country has shown its intention to revive Comprehensive Economic Cooperation and Partnership Agreement (CECPA) with India recently?
a. Sri Lanka b. Pakistan c. Mauritius
d. Singapore e. Thailand

109. Who authored the book *Life In Diplomacy?*
a. Natwar Singh b. M K Rasgotra c. Shashi Tharoor
d. Karan Singh e. Rahul Gandhi

110. Which country topped the 9th edition Global Innovation Index (GII) 2016 that was released recently?
a. USA b. Finland c. Germany
d. Switzerland e. Canada

111. What is the final Summer Olympics 2016 tally of India?
a. Gold – 1, Silver – 1, Bronze – 1 b. Gold – 0, Silver – 1, Bronze - 2
c. Gold –0, Silver – 2, Bronze - 2 d. Gold – 0, Silver – 2, Bronze - 1
e. Gold – 0, Silver – 1, Bronze - 1

112. Which of the following cities was hosted the 2016 Kabaddi World Cup?
a. Ahmedabad b. Pune c. Mumbai
d. Bangalore e. Jaipur

113. Name the two states that signed MoU to build three barrages for water utilization of Godavari River and its tributaries.
a. Telangana and Goa b. Telangana and Andhra Pradesh
c. Telangana and Maharashtra d. Maharashtra and Goa
e. None of these

114. Which country launched the KN-11 ballistic missile from a submarine in Sea of Japan?
a. Japan b. North Korea c. China
d. South Korea e. None of these

115. Union Cabinet approved revised Double Taxation Avoid Agreement (DTAA) for avoidance of double taxation and prevention of fiscal evasion with respect to taxes on income with a nation. Name the nation.
a. Finland b. France c. Fiji
d. Cyprus e. South Africa

116. Union Cabinet enhanced the compensation to victims of terror and left extremism from three lakh rupees to:
a. Four lakh b. Five lakh c. Six lakh
d. Eight lakh e. Ten lakh

117. Which South Indian City inaugurated the first Children's Court in August 2016?
a. Vijayawada b. Hyderabad c. Bangalore
d. Chennai e. Cochin

118. How many breeds of livestock and poultry was recently registered with the national Bureau of animal Genetic Resources?
a. Three b. Two c. Seven
d. Nine e. Ten

119. As per RBI's direction, what will be the percent at which the women self-help groups (SHGs) in rural areas will be granted loans by all banks?
a. 5 Percent b. 6 Percent c. 7 Percent
d. 7.5 Percent e. 8 Percent

120. Which Indian city will host the Pravasi Bhartiya Divas in 2017?
a. Bengaluru b. Hyderabad c. Delhi
d. Jaipur e. Ahmadabad

Section 4: English Language

Direction for questions 121–135: Read the passage and solve the questions based on it.

The education sector in India is in ferment, hit by a storm long waiting to happen. The butterfly that flapped its wings was the much-reiterated statement in a much –published report that hardly a fourth of graduating engineers, and an even smaller percentage of other graduates, was of employable quality for IT-BPO jobs. This ***triggered a cyclone*** when similar views were echoed by other sectors and led to widespread debate. Increased industry-academia initiated as immediate measures to bridge skill deficits. These, however, did not work as some felt that these are but band –aid solutions instead, radical systemic reform is necessary.

Yet, there will be serious challenges to overdue reforms in the education system. In India –as in many countries education system is treated as a holy cow; sadly, the administrative system that oversees it has also deceived. Today, unfortunately, there is no protest against selling drinking water or paying to be cured of illness, or for having to buy food when one is poor and starving; nor is there an outcry that in all these cases there are commercial companies operating on a profit making basis. Why, then is there an instinctively in the realm of education? Is portable water, health or food less basic a need, less important a right, then higher education?

While there are strong arguments for free or subsidized higher education, ***we are not writing on a blank page***. Some individuals and businessman had entered this sector long back and found devious ways of making money, through the law stipulates that educational institutes must be 'not-for-profit' trusts or societies. Yet there is opposition to the entry of 'for-profit'corporate, which would be more transparent and accountable. As a result, desperately needed investment in promoting the wider reach of quality education has been stagnated at a time when financial figures indicated that the allocation of funds for the purpose is but a fourth of the need.

Well–run corporate organizations, within an appropriate regulatory framework, would be far better than the so called trusts which-barring some noteworthy exceptions-are a blot on education. However, it is not necessarily a question of choosing one over the other; different organizational forms can coexist, as they do in the health sector. A regulatory frame work which creates completion, in tandem with a rating system, would automatically ensure the quality and relevance of education. As in sectors like telecom, and package goods, organizations will quickly expand. Easy Loan/scholarship arrangements would ensure affordability and access.

The only real structural reform in higher education was the creation of the institutes for technology and management. They were also given autonomy and freedom beyond that of the universities. However, in the last few years, determined efforts have been under way to curb their autonomy. These institutes, however, need freedom to decide on recruitment, salaries and admissions, so as to compete globally. However such institutes will be few. Therefore, we need a regulatory framework that will enable and encourage States and the Centre, genuine philanthropists and also corporate to set up quality educational institutions. The regulatory system needs only to ensure transparency, accountability, competition and widely-available independent assessments or ratings. It is time for radical thinking, bold experimentation and new structures; it is time for the government to bite the bullet.

121. Why, according to the author, did the indicatives such as increased industry-academia and finishing schools did not help to bridge the skill deficit?
   (A) These steps were only superficial remedies and the problem could be answered only by reforming the entire education system.
   (B) These initiative operated on a profit-making basis rather than aiming at any serious systemic reforms
   (C) The allocation of funds to such indicatives was only one-fourth of the need.
   a. Only A b. Only B c. Only B and C
   d. Only A and B e. None of these

122. Which of the following suggestions have been made by the author to improve the state of education in India?
   (A) Allowing the corporate organizations to enter the education sector
   (B) Easy availability of loans and scholarships for making education more affordable
   (C) A rating system for all the organizations to ensure quality
   a. Only A b. Only A and B c. Only A and C
   d. All A , B and C e. None of these

123. According to the author, what ***'triggered a cyclone'*** which saw similar views on the state of education being echoed across other sectors as well?
   a. The campaign for allowing corporate in the education sector on a 'for –Profit' basis
   b. The supports for the increase in the industry-academia interaction
   c. The report mentioning that only a small percentage of graduates were employable in software industry
   d. The report supporting the idea of making education completely 'for-profit' in order to improve upon the standers
   e. None of these

124. What does the author mean by the phrase ***'we are not writing on blank page'*** in the context of the passage?
   a. Corporate would never enter education if they are force to function on a non-profit-making basis.
   b. The commercialization of education has already started in India.
   c. Education has been reduced to a profit-making sector by some corporate organizations.
   d. Government will not allow corporate to enter educations as India can't afford to have costly education.
   e. None of these

125. According to author, which of the following was the only step taken in order to reform higher education?

a. Allowing organizations to enter the education sector on a 'for-profit' basis
b. Creation of autonomous institutes for management and technology which were not under university control
c. Setting up the regulatory framework for all the existing universities.
d. Making the availability of educational loans and scholarships easier
e. None of these

126. Which argument does the author put forward when he compares the education sector with sectors catering to health, potable water etc?
a. Education should also be provided free of cost to all as health services and water.
b. Taking an example from these sectors, there should be a protest against the commercialization of education as well.
c. Allowing corporate entry in education would result in rampant corruption as in the sectors of health, potable water etc.
d. As in these sectors, commercial organizations should also be allowed to enter the education sector
e. None of these

127. What is the author's main objective in writing the passage?
a. To suggest the ways to improve quality of education in India
b. To highlight the corruption present in the education sector
c. To compare the education sector with other sector
d. To suggest some temporary solutions to the problems in education
e. None of these

128. Which suggestion does the author make in order to make the institute of higher learning for technology and management capable of competing globally?
a. To limit their autonomy to acceptable limits and give partial controls to the government
b. To allow corporate organizations to take over in order to provide more funds
c. To increase the allocation of funds to such institutes
d. All of these
e. None of these

129. Which of the following is not true in the context of the given passage?
a. According to the law, education institutes should not be run for profit.
b. There has been no protest against the selling of drinking water and paying for health services.
c. Only either corporate organizations or government-controlled organizations can exist in the education sector.
d. The introduction of 'for-profit' corporate in the education sector has been facing a lot of criticism
e. All are true

Directions (130–132): Choose the word which is most similar in meaning to the word printed in bold as used in the passage

130. DEVIOUS

a. Dishonest	b. Different	c. Severe
d. Various	e. Trivial	

131. MEASURES
   a. Amount b. Quantity c. Steps d. Capacity e. Length

132. BRIDGE
   a. Connect b. Eliminate c. Unite d. Link e. Fuse

Directions (133–135): Choose the word/phrase which is most opposite in meaning to the word printed in bold as used in the passage.

133. PROMOTING
   a. Demoting b. Delaying c. Postponing d. Broadening e. Hampering

134. NOTEWORTHY
   a. Unnoticed b. Insignificant c. Indefinite d. Remarkable e. Obsolete

135. TRANSPARENT
   a. Reputed b. Opaque c. Defective d. Corrupt e. Thick

Directions for questions 136–145: Read each sentence to find out whether there is any grammatical error in it. The error, if any will be in one part of the sentence, and the number of that part will be the answer. If there is no error, mark e as the answer. (Ignore errors of punctuation, in any.)

136. The merchant counted (a) / the number of pearls (b) / to make sure that (c) / none of them were missing (d). No error (e)

137. When deep sea diving (a) / one should always take care (b) / that oxygen cylinder is (c) / tied to the back tightly (d). No error (e)

138. As the salary (a) / did not match (b)/ his expectations, he did not (c) / accept the job (d). No error (e)

139. The reason behind his success (a)/ in the recent past (b)/ is due to hard-work (c) / and presence of mind (d). No error (e)

140. No sooner did the students (a) / seen the principal approach (b) / then they ran (c) / from the playground (d). No error (e)

141. My elder sister and I am (a)/ interested in painting (b)/ and therefore have joined (c)/ the coaching classes (d). No error.

142. Only after a lot a persuasion, (a) / the illiterate villager allowed(b) / himself's girl child (c)/ to study in the school (d) . No error (e)

Direction for questions 143–145: Answer these questions independently.

143. In the 1950's sixty percent of treated cancer patients lived at least five years after detection of the disease. Now, sixty percent live at least seven years after detection. This fact demonstrates that, because of improved methods of treatment, cancer patients now live longer after they contract the disease than cancer patients did in the 1950's.

   The conclusion of the argument above depends on which of the following assumptions?
   a. In the 1950's only sixty percent of cancer patients received treatment, whereas now a substantially higher percentage does.

b. Free medical treatment is more likely to be available now to people who have no health insurance than it was in the 1950's.
c. Detection of cancer does now take place, on average, significantly earlier in the progression of the disease than it did in the 1950's.
d. Physicians now usually predict a longer life for cancer patients after detection of the disease than did physicians in the 1950's.
e. None of these

144. The large amounts of carbon dioxide now being released into the atmosphere by the burning of fossil fuels will not, in fact, result in a greenhouse effect – an increase in average global temperatures. Since plants use carbon dioxide in larger quantities if the supply is increased, they are able to grow larger and multiply more vigorously, and atmospheric carbon dioxide concentrations will eventually become stable.

Which of the following, if true, would most seriously weaken the conclusion that a greenhouse effect will not result from the current release of large amounts of carbon dioxide into the atmosphere?
a. The expected rise in average global temperatures has not yet been observed.
b. Ocean waters absorb carbon dioxide at a greater rate when the atmospheric concentration of carbon dioxide is higher.
c. Since the beginning of the Industrial Revolution, increased atmospheric concentrations of carbon dioxide have resulted in improved agricultural productivity.
d. When plants decay, they produce methane, another gas that can have a marked greenhouse effect.
e. None of these

145. The number of people 85 or older in the United States started increasing dramatically during the last ten years. The good health care that these people enjoyed in the United States during their vulnerable childhood years is primarily responsible for this trend.

Which of the following, if true, most seriously weakens the explanation above?
a. Seventy-five percent of the people in the United States who are 85 or older are the children of people who themselves lived less than 65 years.
b. The people in the United States who are now 85 represent an age group that was smaller in numbers at birth than the immediately preceding and succeeding age groups.
c. Thirty-five percent of the people in the United States who are 85 or older require some form of twenty-four-hour nursing care.
d. Many of the people in the United States who are 85 or older immigrated to the United States when they were 20 years old or older.
e. None of these

Instructions: For each of the word given below, a contextual usage has been provided. Pick the word, from the given alternatives that is most inappropriate.

146. Headway – The talks between the authorities and the hijackers made no <u>headway</u> even as the crisis entered its tenth day.
a. Progress b. mistake c. breakthrough d. advance e. None of these

147. Obsequious – Being <u>obsequious</u> will not help you in career in long run.
a. Servile b. Sycophantic c. Observant
d. Stubborn e. None of these

148. Percolate – Too little uncovered soil will not allow sufficient amount of rain water to <u>percolate</u> down.

a. Filter b. Permeate c. Egress
d. Trickle e. None of these

149. Wry – Very few people seem to enjoy her <u>wry</u> humor.

a. Distorted b. Contorted c. Interesting
d. Twisted e. None of these

Instructions: Choose the order of the sentences marked A,B,C,D and E to form a logical paragraph.

150. A. Some of the people of New York – Children, dependent wives – would ordinarily have held no formal jobs.

B. when the Unemployment rate ran to around a quarter of the workforce in 1932, about 11.5 million Americans had no work.

C. To put this in some perspective, we might imagine that nearly the entire population of New Work, then the most populous state, had no jobs: that from the easternmost tip of Long Island to the shores of lake Erie, from the Canadian border to Pennsylvania, nobody had work.

D. But this perspective does not give quite the right picture

E. And the 11.5 million out of work represented only the workers who had no paycheck.

a. CDAEB b. ABCDE c. BCDAE
d. EDCBA e. None of these

151. A. The sense of innocence, together with vulnerability, from crucial elements in what may be called the 'process of terror' – the process by which violence generates political effects.

B. And in politics, as distinct from courts of law, subjectivity and feeling are supreme.

C. This provides a key to what I shall call 'pure' terrorism.

D. Targets may not be in an objective sense innocent, but they must be in practical terms defenseless ('soft').

E. The essence of terrorism is the use of violence by the armed against the unarmed.

a. EDCBA b. ABCDE c. BCDAE
d. BACDE e. None of these

Instructions: In each of the following questions, a sentence has to been written in four different ways. Choose grammatically correct.

152. a. The Greek poetry of Homer was at first transmitted orally, stored in the memory, as were the Vedas, the Sanskrit hymns of the ancient Hindus, which were unwritten for centuries.

b. The Greek poetry of Homer was at first transmitted orally, stored in the memory, as were the Vedas, the Sanskrit hymns of the ancient Hindus which were unwritten for centuries.

c. The Greek poetry of Homer was first transmitted orally, stored in the memory, as were the Vedas, the Sanskrit hymns of the ancient Hindus, that were unwritten for centuries.

d. The Greek poetry of Homer was at first transmitted orally, stored in the memory, as were the Vedas, the Sanskrit hymns of the ancient Hindus, that were unwritten for centuries.

e. None of these

153. a. Even as this goes to press, number of lives lost to the Asian tsunami and its aftermath appears literally countless.

b. Even as this goes to press, the number of lives lost to the Asian tsunami and its aftermath appears literally countless.

c. Even as this goes to press, the number of lives lost to the Asian tsunami and it's aftermath appears literally countless.

d. Even as this goes to press, the number of lives lost to the Asian tsunami and its aftermath appears literally countless.

e. None of these

Instructions: Choose the appropriate opinion for the blanks.

154. The economy of Iran is in a ______________. People's discontent with the government's policies is __________________.

a. chaos, shimmering
b. mess, shriveling
c. quagmire, riveting
d. shambles, simmering
e. None of these

155. ______________________ the general had been told by the field staff that continuing warfare would be __________________ to his soldiers, he insisted on deploying more battle tanks.

a. Because…. Instrumental
b. Although… Detrimental
c. Although… formidable
d. Because… immediate
e. None of these

ANSWER KEY

1. a	2. b	3. d	4. e	5. c	6. b	7. c	8. b	9. a	10. b
11. a	12. d	13. c	14. b	15. e	16. e	17. a	18. d	19. c	20. b
21. c	22. a	23. b	24. d	25. a	26. c	27. d	28. b	29. b	30. b
31. d	32. d	33. d	34. c	35. e	36. a	37. a	38. a	39. a	40. d
41. c	42. a	43. c	44. a	45. a	46. e	47. b	48. a	49. d	50. d
51. c	52. a	53. d	54. c	55. b	56. d	57. d	58. e	59. e	60. a
61. a	62. b	63. d	64. c	65. a	66. c	67. c	68. a	69. c	70. a
71. c	72. c	73. b	74. d	75. c	76. e	77. d	78. d	79. a	80. a
81. a	82. d	83. c	84. e	85. a	86. a	87. b	88. c	89. d	90. d
91. b	92. d	93. a	94. c	95. a	96. b	97. a	98. a	99. b	100. a
101. b	102. c	103. c	104. a	105. c	106. b	107. a	108. c	109. b	110. d
111. e	112. a	113. c	114. b	115. d	116. b	117. b	118. d	119. c	120. a
121. a	122. d	123. c	124. b	125. b	126. d	127. a	128. e	129. c	130. a
131. c	132. b	133. e	134. b	135. d	136. d	137. a	138. e	139. a	140. a
141. a	142. c	143. c	144. d	145. d	146. b	147. d	148. c	149. c	150. c
151. d	152. a	153. b	154. b	155. d					

Solutions and Explanations:

1 – 5:

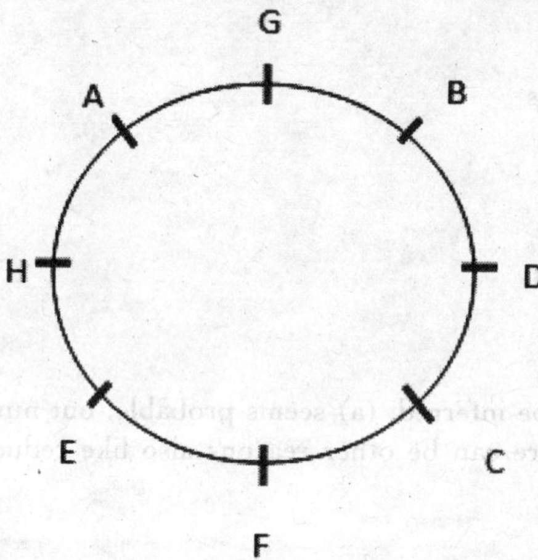

Solution to 6–8:

Increasing order of age (Left to Right)				
Kolkata	Bangalore	Delhi	Pune	Mumbai
Emran	Dheeru	Chetan	Amit	Binay

Solution to 9 – 11:

Left to Right						
Name	Kirpal	Vijay	Jatin	Ram	Mohan	Santosh
Surname	Kohli	Joshi	Vats	Tyagi	Rehman	Singh

Solution to 12 to 15:

Following is the arrangement:

16. e - On the contrary, "a flurry of hiring activity has been observed across the manufacturing sector".
17. a - the passage says, "a flurry of hiring activity has been observed across… the IT and ITES sector catering to ………legal process outsourcing".
18. d - there are still reservations galore

19. c – "a bullish outlook" doesn't necessarily mean negative growth in the past; it may also imply positive but slow growth.

20. b – Seems so from the positive tone of the passage.

21. c – condition (i) applies

22. a - condition (iii) applies

23. b - no condition applies

24. d - condition (i) applies

25. a - condition (ii) applies.

Solution to 46–50:

46. (e) Obviously cannot be inferred. (a) seems probable, but number of vehicles/agents need not be increasing. There can be other reasons also like reduction in the efficiency of the vehicle etc.

47. (b)

		1991		2001		2011	
		World	Asia	World	Asia	World	Asia
Total energy		150	10	200	20	250	33.3
Naphtha	Value	30	0.5	40	2.5	50	5
	Proportion	20%	5%	20%	12.50%	20%	15.01
Solid fuels	Value	50	4	60	5	75	10
	Proportion	33.30%	40%	30%	25%	30%	30.03
Petrol	Value	50	4	70	10	80	15
	Proportion	33.30%	40%	35%	50%	32%	45.04

Hence, solid fuels and Petrol combined constitute more than 60 percent of total energy in both the world and Asia for the given period.

48. (a)
It can be seen from the table that Petrol is the fuel whose proportion in the total energy demand increases during 1991-2001 and decreases during 2001-2011 for both the world and Asia.

49. (d)
For the answer choices given and for Asia we can take make the following table.

		1991	2001	2011
	Total energy	10	20	33
Naphtha	Value	0.5	2.5	5
	Proportion	5%	12.50%	15.15%
Solid fuels	Value	4	5	10
	Proportion	40%	25%	30.30%

Nuclear Fuel	Value	0.5	1	1.3
	Proportion	5%	5%	3.90%
Hydro Energy	Value	1	1.5	2
	Proportion	10%	7.50%	6.06%

Hence, we can see that the proportion of Hydro Energy goes on decreasing over the period.

50. (d)

For answer choices given and for the worlds, we can make the following table.

		1991	2001	2011
	Total energy	150	200	250
Naphtha	Value	30	40	50
	Proportion	20%	20%	20%
Solid Fuels	Value	50	60	75
	Proportion	33%	30%	30%
Nuclear Fuel	Value	10	20	25
	Proportion	6.66%	10%	10%
Hydro Energy	Value	10	10	20
	Proportion	6.66%	5%	8%

Hence, we can see that the proportion of Naphtha remains constant over the given period.

Solution to 51– 54:

From the given information the following table can be prepared:

	Physics	Chemistry	Maths	English	Total
Amit	80	70	60	80	290
Binit	60	60	60	60	240
Charu	40	50	60	70	220
Dilip	90	80	70	60	300

Now all the questions can be answered.

Solution to 55–57:

Let us 1st decide that what should be the order of attempting questions:

In my perception, 56 should be attempted 55st, then 57 and then 55 at the end. Rather you may choose to not attempt 55 as it will take atleast 3-4 minutes to calculate.

What all is required to solve which question:

55. Pure Calculation
56. Observation

57. Interpretation and Calculation technique

How to solve:

56. Let us 1st have a look at all the options (we are not looking at 5th option as it is unlikely to be answer).

1. China 2.Japan 3. Brazil 4.Canada

Japan seems to be very unlikely, as its percentage share of Greenland is 9% only. Out of remaining three options, China and Canada are having very close shares at 25% and 23% but percentage of protected land in Canada is far higher than China (Canada = 67%, China = 58%), so quantity of protected land in Canada will be higher than that of China.

Next we have to compare Canada's protected greenland and Brazil's protected Greenland. Look at the following data:

Country	%age	Protected
Canada	23%	67%
Brazil	16%	73%

Obviously 23% of 67% of X is larger than 16% of 73% of X. It can be calculated following ways:

1st way

For Canada

67% = 2/3 (approx.), so 67% of 23% = approx 2/3 of 23% = 46%/3 = 15.33%

For Brazil

16% = 1/6 (approx.), so 16% of 73% = approx 1/6 of 73% = 73%/6 = 12% approx.

Hence Canada's protected Greenland is maximum.

Hence option 4 is the answer.

Authors' Note: Please keep in your mind that all the calculations that you are seeing above should be done through mental calculation.

Now we would look at 57:

57. Let us look at the data pertaining to India and Pakistan:

Country	%age	Protected
India	16%	34%
Pakistan	6%	41%

Question is asking for:

Protected green land of India is what percentage of the protected green land of Pakistan?

Protected Greenland of India = 16% of 34% of X

Protected Greenland of Pakistan = 6% of 41% of X

We have to just calculate ratio or percentage value, hence don't need to calculate this of total Greenland, hence we can take it X or any value.

$$\text{Answer} = \frac{0.16 \times 0.34}{0.06 \times 0.41} \times 100$$

Now before you actually calculate the final answer, look at the options. Our actually answer is clearly more than 200%, and there is just one option having a value more than 200%. Hence option 4 is the answer.

Now we would look at 55:

55. Ideally, in an examination condition, one should not attempt this question.

Following calculation solves and answers this question:

Country	%age	Protected	Unprotected	Protected Area	Unprotected Area
India	0.16	0.34	0.66	748.2176	1452.4224
Canada	0.23	0.67	0.33	2119.4914	1043.9286
Pakistan	0.06	0.41	0.59	338.3484	486.8916
Brazil	0.16	0.73	0.27	1606.4672	594.1728
China	0.25	0.58	0.42	1994.33	1444.17
Japan	0.09	0.78	0.22	965.5308	272.3292
Malaysia	0.05	0.43	0.57	295.711	391.989
			Total	8068.0964	5685.9036

Difference of protected area and unprotected area = 2382

Hence option 2 is the answer.

Solution to Questions 68–72:

Following is the grid:

Dept. / Grade	Excellent	Good	Average	Total
Finance Dept	10	9	0	19
Marketing Dept	0	0	38	38
H R D Dept	12	18	8	38
Total	22	27	46	95

Now all the questions can be answered.

121. a) Read the last sentence of the first paragraph

122. d) Read the fourth paragraph.

123. c) Read the second and third sentences of the first paragraph closely

124. b) Clear from the succeeding sentence in the third paragraph

125. b) Read the first two sentences of the fifth paragraph.

126. d) Citing these examples, the author concludes: "Why, then , is there an instinctively adverse reaction to the formal entry of 'for-profit' institutes in the realm of education?"

127. a) Focus on the first and last sentence of the passage and things would fall in place.

128. e) To allow them "Freedom to decide on recruitment, salaries and admissions"

129. c) Read the second sentence of the fourth paragraph.

136. d) Replace were with was.

137. a) Use "when diving into deep sea"

138. e)

139. a) Delete "the reason behind"

140. a) Use "had."

141. a) Use "are."

142. c) Substitute his

143. An assumption is the missing link in the argument. The argument talks about increased life of cancer patients after the detection of disease compared to that in the 1950's and leads to the conclusion that improved methods of methods of treatment are behind the change. The argument assumes that the stage at which cancer is detected is earlier now in light of the advances in medical science. Hence option (c) is the answer. Option (a) talks about percentage of patients getting treatment, and it does not talk about the longer period of being alive after detection. Option (b) is not related to the passage given. Option (d) talks only about prediction and hence not relevant.

144. The argument contends that larger concentration of CO_2 in the atmosphere will not result in greenhouse effect as it will be compensated by faster growth of plants. If we can suggest something that something will cancel out the positive effect of plants on the green house gases, the argument will be weakened. D gives a reason, production of methane, a greenhouse gas by decaying plants that would cancel out the benefits of higher absorption by plants. Hence option (d) is the answer.

145. The argument attributes greater longevity of 85+ year old in the US to good healthcare facilities available to them during their growing up, childhood years. As we have to weaken the argument, if these people immigrated to US after the age of 20, which way above the formative years of vulnerable childhood, we can rule out the possibility of them availing the medical facilities. The other three choices do not touch the issue of healthcare facilities available to them during the formative years, so eliminated. Hence option (d) is the answer.

146. b – 'Headway' means 'Progress' , ' breakthrough' or 'advance' , so the inappropriate word is 'mistake' .

147. d – 'Obsequious' refer to a person who listens to others and follows others. 'Servile', 'Sycophant' and 'observant' also means the same so the most inappropriate word is 'stubborn' which is the opposite of 'Obsequious'.

148. c – 'Percolate' means to reach the lower levels slowly and steadily so synonyms with 'filter', 'permeate' and 'trickle'. Hence, most inappropriate word is 'egress' meaning exit

149. c – 'Wry' refers to dry humor which everybody cannot understand or appreciate and at times, it pains the other person' so the most inappropriate word is 'interesting'.

150. c – BC is a mandatory pair as 'this' in C refers to the Unemployment rate mentioned in B. D follows C because 'this perspective' in D refers to the perspective discussed in C. So, BCD should come together. D gives the perspective a twist and subsequent statements A and E talk about a contrary approach. Hence, the correct answer is option (c).

151. d – Statement B should precede statement A as 'subjectivity and feeling' in B refers to 'the sense of innocence', together with vulnerability in A. So B and A are linked. Also, B should be the opening sentence since it doesn't fit into sequence with any other sentence in the jumble. Hence, option (d) is correct.

152. a – 'at first' is the correct expression. The Greek poetry of homer was is the correct expression according to the subject verb agreement rule. 'which' is correct in this case. Hence, (a).

153. b – There must be a definite article 'the' before 'number'. It's is a contraction of it is so correct, 'literally countless' is correct. Hence, (b).